WELFARE AND WORK INCENTIVES

Welfare and Work Incentives

A North European Perspective

Edited by

A. B. Atkinson
and
Gunnar Viby Mogensen

CLARENDON PRESS · OXFORD
1993

Oxford University Press, Walton Street, Oxford OX2 6DP
Oxford New York Toronto
Delhi Bombay Calcutta Madras Karachi
Kuala Lumpur Singapore Hong Kong Tokyo
Nairobi Dar es Salaam Cape Town
Melbourne Auckland Madrid
and associated companies in
Berlin Ibadan

Oxford is a trade mark of Oxford University Press

Published in the United States
by Oxford University Press Inc., New York

British Library Cataloguing in Publication Data
Data available

Library of Congress Cataloging in Publication Data
Data available
0–19–828860–3

Typeset by Pentacor PLC, High Wycombe, Bucks.

Printed in Great Britain
on acid-free paper by
Biddles Ltd., Guildford and Kings Lynn

PREFACE

The welfare states of Northern Europe have tax and transfer levels well above the average for the industrialized world. It is not therefore surprising that the possible disincentive effects of these taxes and transfers, on labour supply and other decisions, play a large role in the debate about the future of the welfare state in these countries—an issue which is likely to be one of the most important of the 1990s. What *is* surprising is that the debate in Europe has been so little influenced by empirical evidence about the extent to which work incentives have in fact been affected. Public discussion seems little informed by scientific research.

Such a discrepancy between public debate and available economic and social research is exactly the kind of issue that was identified as a high priority area by the Danish Rockwool Foundation when it decided in 1987 to establish an independent unit for social science research in the Central Bureau of Statistics in Copenhagen. Between 1993 and 1995 an empirical project on 'Welfare and Incentives in Denmark' will be carried out by the Unit, based on new empirical data. As a prelude to this study, we were asked to establish an overview of the existing economic and econometric knowledge in Denmark and three neighbouring countries: Germany, Sweden, and the United Kingdom.

Several leading experts agreed to help with the overview. Professor Klaus Zimmermann of the University of Munich agreed to write the chapter on Germany (both West and East); Professor Peder J. Pedersen of the University of Aarhus contributed to the chapter on Denmark; Professor Anders Klevmarken and Björn Gustafsson of the University of Gothenburg wrote the chapter on Sweden; and Professor Richard Blundell of University College London and the Institute for Fiscal Studies agreed to write the first of two chapters on the United Kingdom (the second is by Tony Atkinson). We are very grateful to them all for the time they have devoted to the project and for their flexibility in meeting tight deadlines.

All of these authors have been active in empirical labour-supply research in their own countries, but our aim has been to produce a volume which is useful to readers from outside the country in question and which allows conclusions to be drawn from the similarities—and the differences—across countries. After initial bilateral discussions, based on short outlines from us, we held a two-day meeting at the Schæffergaarden Conference Centre in Copenhagen in November 1992, at which preliminary country papers were discussed. Following this meeting, a draft was made of the contents for the introductory chapters, and the structure of the book finalized. The full country papers were discussed at the second meeting at Schæffergaarden in April 1993, and revised in the light of this discussion, which also identified the final conclusions. It should be added that these meetings were not only instructive but also very enjoyable.

In preparing the final version, we have tried to make the contents accessible to more than just technical experts. No doubt some professional jargon has slipped through, but we hope that much of the text will be readable by a broader audience. We hope that the book will contribute to a closer relation between public debate and economic facts in this important field for decisions about future policy in the welfare states of Europe.

We would like to thank warmly all those who have made possible the production of this book. Our gratitude goes first to the present and the former chairmen of the Board of the Rockwool Foundation, Tom and Claus Kahler, as well as its Managing Director, Bent Løber, for the opportunity to work on this project and their helpful assistance all the way through. Our thanks go also to those at the Research Unit in Copenhagen—Bent Jensen, Claus Larsen, and Hanne Lykke—who have done all the hard work of assembling the final manuscript and seen it through production. In Cambridge, Tony Atkinson would like to thank Nacirah Lutton, Gerry Redmond, and Holly Sutherland. In Munich, Klaus Zimmermann would like to thank Stefan Hochgürtel, Anja Koch, Lucie Merkle, and Martin Mühleisen for able research assistance, and for valuable comments on various drafts, and Helmut Kaiser, Gebhard Kirchgässner, and Peter Kugler for helpful discussions. In Gothenburg, Anders Klevmarken and Björn Gustafsson would like to thank Lennart Flood for comments on the manuscript and Mats Johansson for research assistance. In Aarhus, Peder J. Pedersen would like to thank Nina Smith. In Cambridge, Richard Blundell would like to thank Costas Meghir, Alan Duncan, and colleagues at IFS. Richard Blundell would also like to thank the ESRC Centre for help in background research.

A. B. Atkinson
Cambridge University

Gunnar Viby Mogensen
Rockwool Foundation Research Unit
Copenhagen

CONTENTS

THE AUTHORS

A. B. Atkinson is Professor of Political Economy at the University of Cambridge and Fellow of Churchill College. His research is associated with the Microsimulation Unit in the Department of Applied Economics.

He has worked in the fields of microeconomic policy and income distribution, with particular reference to taxation and social security. He has been particularly concerned with the measurement of inequality and poverty. He has written *The Economics of Inequality*, *Lectures on Public Economics* (with J. E. Stiglitz), *Poverty and Social Security* (Wheatsheaf), and *Economic Transformation in Eastern Europe and the Distribution of Income* (with J. Micklewright).

He is Past President of the International Economic Association, and has served as President of the Econometric Society and the European Economic Association. He is a Fellow of the British Academy and was a founding member of the Academia Europea. He is editor of the *Journal of Public Economics*. He has been a member of the Royal Commission on the Distribution on Income and Wealth, served as a specialist adviser to House of Commons Select Committees, and is a member of the Pensions Law Review Committee.

Richard Blundell is Professor of Economics at University College London and Research Director of the Institute for Fiscal Studies, where he directs the research programme of the ESRC Research Centre for the Microeconomic Analysis of Fiscal Policy.

He has worked on microeconometrics, public economics, labour economics, and consumer behaviour. He has been particularly concerned with the development of statistical techniques for the measurement of behavioural responses using microdata sources. He has published a number of technical papers dealing with simultaneity and selection in such models which have appeared in *Econometrica, Review of Economic Studies*, and other international journals. He has also written a number of policy-oriented papers using such techniques, which have been published in journals such as *Journal of Econometrics, Journal of Public Economics, American Economic Review*. He has edited a volume of readings on *Unemployment, Search and Labour Supply* (with Ian Walker) and one on *The Measurement of Household Welfare* (with Ian Preston and Ian Walker).

In 1990 he was made editor of the *Journal of Econometrics* and was elected Fellow of the Econometric Society. He was visiting Professor of Economics at MIT during 1993. He recently gave an invited address at the

6th World Meeting of the Econometric Society entitled 'Evaluating Structural Microeconometric Models of Labour Supply', and was Econometrics Chairman of the 1992 European Meeting of the Econometric Society.

Björn A. Gustafsson is Associate Professor of Economics and Senior Lecturer in Social Work at Göteborg University. He received his Ph.D. in economics in 1979 at the same university. Previously he was a senior lecturer in public economics at University College at Örebro.

Gustafsson has been commissioned for special reports by the expert group on Public Finance at the Swedish Ministry of Finance on income transfers between the public sector and household, on social assistance and economic well-being, and on marginal effects and poverty traps. He has written a report on distributional consequences of the public sector for the Swedish Medium-Term Plan. For the Swedish Study of Power and Democracy in Sweden he has analysed changes in the distribution of well-being in Sweden.

Gustafsson's research covers empirical studies on social assistance, poverty, the distribution of economic well-being and the welfare state, immigrants, and the economics of child care. He has been involved in various comparative studies as well as in projects in developing countries. He has published in journals such as *European Economic Review, Labour, Review of Income and Wealth, Scandinavian Journal of Economics*, and *Journal of African Economics*.

N. Anders Klevmarken is Professor of Econometrics at the Swedish Research Council for the Humanities and Social Sciences and the Department of Economics, Göteborg University, Sweden. He received his Ph.D. in statistics from the University of Stockholm in 1972 and was at the same time appointed docent in statistics. In 1983 he became docent in economics at the University of Göteborg. Among his previous positions were Professor of Statistics at the University of Göteborg, head of the division for evaluation and research at the National Swedish Insurance Board, senior research associate at the Industrial Institute for Economic and Social Research (IUI), and associate Research Professor of Empirical Econometrics at the Swedish Council for Social Science Research. He has taught at the Stockholm School of Economics and at the University of Stockholm. He has also been a visiting professor at the University of Michigan and at the University of Georgia.

Klevmarken is a member of the Swedish Council for Social Research, the Tore Browaldh Scientific Foundation, the scientific council of Statistics Sweden, and of the standing committee for the consumer price index of Sweden. In 1992 he was the President of the European Society for Population Economics.

Klevmarken's research covers topics in labour economics, in particular studies of pay setting and the structure of earnings and has been published in four monographs and, for example, in the *Journal of Political Economy, Annales de l'INSEE*, and the *Scandinavian Journal of Economics*; and his work on demand analysis and index theory has been published in two monographs and in the *Journal of Econometrics* and *Econometrica*. His interests also include market and non-market time-use, the causes of differences in fertility, and distributional issues, as well as microeconometrics. He is currently directing the HUS panel study of Swedish households which is part of the European Science Foundation Network on Household Panel Studies.

Peder J. Pedersen is Professor of Economics at the University of Aarhus. He was previously Assistant Professor at the Copenhagen School of Business, Associate Professor at the University of Aarhus, and Professor of Economics at the Aarhus School of Business. From 1985 to 1991 he was a member of the Danish Council of Economic Advisers. He is a member of government commissions on social policy, unemployment insurance, and the reconstruction of the economy of the Faroe Islands. The social-policy commission has produced a number of analyses of the factors behind, and the trend in, transfer incomes in recent years, based mainly on longitudinal panel data. The other part of the work in the commission has been the preparation of far-reaching proposals for the reform of Danish social policy.

His research and teaching are in the areas of labour economics and macroeconomics. He has edited a book on unemployment, and has contributed to Danish and international journals and books. A main activity in recent years has been participation in the implementation of a longitudinal database based on registers and covering 5% of the adult Danish population in the years 1976–90. A great number of papers and contributions to journals and books have been produced using this database. He has also participated in a joint Nordic labour market project, the results of which are due to be published in late 1993.

Gunnar Viby Mogensen is an economist, and Director of the independent Rockwool Foundation Research Unit at the Danish Central Bureau of Statistics (Danmarks Statistik) in Copenhagen. He is a part-time Associate Professor at the Economic Institute of the University of Copenhagen, in the field of economic and social history.

He has been involved with research in labour market and welfare problems, up to 1987 as a Programme Director at the Danish National Institute of Social Research. His special interest in recent years has been related to attempts to establish measures for the size and structure of the untaxed economy in Denmark. His published work on this subject include United Nations *Guidebook to Statistics on the Hidden Economy* and two chapters in *Time and Consumption*, which he also edited. His most recent publication is *Unemployment and Flexibility on the Danish Labour Market.*

He was a member of the National Social Science Research Board from 1977 to 1981, and has been a member of the Scientific Advisory Committee for the Rockwool Foundation since 1991. He was a member of the government commission on taxes in 1992.

Klaus F. Zimmermann is Professor of Economics, Director of the Seminar for Labour and Population Economics, and Director of the Archive of Applied Economics at the University of Munich; he is also Co-director of the human resources programme of the Centre for Economic Policy Research (CEPR) in London.

He has written widely on labour, population, industrial organization, consumer economics, and applied econometrics, and is editor of *Economic Theory of Optimal Population*, *Demographic Change and Economic Development* (with A. Wenig), *Migration and Economic Development*, and *Labour Markets in an Ageing Europe* (with Paul Johnson).

Previously he taught at the University of Mannheim, and was a Visiting Professor at the University of Pennsylvania, Philadelphia, University of Dortmund, and the Humboldt University, Berlin. He has also been a Research Fellow at the Centre for Operations Research and Econometrics, Université Catholique de Louvain, and at the Science Centre Berlin. He is President-Elect of the European Society of Population Economics (ESPE), managing editor of the *Journal of Population Economics*, and associate editor of *Recherches Économiques de Louvain*, *Labour Economics*, the *Journal of Applied Econometrics*, and the *European Economic Review*. He is also a member of the Council of the Ifo-Institute for Economic Research, Munich.

LIST OF FIGURES

LIST OF TABLES

1
Introduction

A. B. ATKINSON

1.1. CONTENT AND STRUCTURE OF THE BOOK

Central to the debate about the reform of the welfare state in Europe is the effect of welfare benefits, and the taxes necessary to finance them, on the working of the economy. People hold strong views about the possible disincentive effects of taxes and transfers. These views are highly influential in decisions about future policy-decisions which will have major implications for a generation or more, and which are of concern to us all. Yet these views about the disincentive effects of benefits and taxes are too often based on a superficial analysis of economic behaviour. Too often these views are unsupported by reference to empirical evidence as to how work incentives have in fact been affected.

The aim of this book is to review the evidence regarding work incentives and their implications for the welfare state. Have high income taxes been a disincentive to work? Has the existence of unemployment benefit caused people to delay return to work? Do disability benefits cause people to withdraw prematurely from the labour force? What are the effects of child benefits or parental-leave programmes or transfer programmes for single parents? In seeking answers to these questions, it is natural to compare the experience of different countries. Have taxes had similar effects in Sweden and Germany? Have some countries devised transfers systems which have less impact on labour supply? Are the same issues of concern in different countries? One of the main features of the present book is that it aims to set side by side evidence about work incentives in four different countries: Sweden, the UK, Germany, and Denmark.

The book is therefore largely about the *European* experience with the welfare state. Although these countries are not chosen to be representative of Europe as a whole, and a study of countries such as France or Italy might well lead to different conclusions, we believe that valuable lessons can be drawn from those examined here. Not only are these European welfare states distinctly different from welfare provisions in, say, the USA, Canada, Australia, or Japan, but there are reasons to expect their impact on work incentives to be different. Much of the empirical evidence about incentives derives from the USA and, while we feel that this has added very considerably to our understanding of the methodological issues, there is no reason to suppose that empirical findings will carry over unchanged to a European context. As is emphasized in this book, an important role is played by the institutional features of tax and transfer systems on the one hand and of the labour market on the other. These institutions differ greatly across continents and, indeed, across countries, which is our reason for considering a range of countries.

The four countries chosen for study here are both similar and dissimilar. They are all drawn from Northern Europe and, if it were not for the sea, would be contiguous. Over the period studied their economies shared a number of common features, and all had sizeable welfare states. At the same time there are important differences, including the fact that Sweden is not a member of the European Community. The differences are particularly relevant to the welfare state. The demographic situation of the four countries is different, leading, for example, to some countries being more concerned than others about the ageing of the population. Family structures are different, as are patterns of child care. The role of trade unions in the payment of transfers is different, as is the extent of employer-provided benefits.

As far as the welfare state itself is concerned, the countries illustrate some of the significant choices which can be made. Germany has a classical contributory social-insurance system, providing earnings-related benefits, which reached maturity while other countries were still developing their social-security provisions. The UK took over much from Bismarck, but has maintained a largely flat-rate benefit structure, with the major social-insurance benefits being the same cash amount for all, rather than earnings-related. In the UK there has also been substantial reliance on means-tested benefits. In contrast to the contributory social insurance of these countries, 'social benefits in the Nordic countries are granted according to uniform principles, which means that they are less dependent on the person having participated in working life' (Nordic Social-Statistical Committee, 1993: 10). Moreover, in both Denmark and Sweden, unlike the other two countries, unemployment insurance is voluntary. On the other hand, there are differences between Denmark and Sweden. Denmark has relied heavily on tax finance for welfare benefits. In the case of unemployment, Sweden has given prominence to active labour-market policy. In the field of family policy, Sweden has generous benefits for parental leave on the birth of children and in the event of their being ill. All countries differ in the extent and form of their cash family allowances, and in the interaction with income-tax allowances.

This study seeks to compare the experience of these different countries with their different tax and transfer provisions. Economists have not traditionally made great use of the comparative approach, certainly less so than other social scientists. There are indeed reasons to be cautious in drawing inferences from observed differences across countries. The fact that Sweden and Denmark tend to have higher ratios of taxation to GNP than Germany and the UK does not necessarily mean that we can make deductions about the disincentive effect of taxation from observations of differing hours of work in the two groups of countries. The fact that the labour-force participation rate of married women is much lower in West Germany, and, to a lesser extent, in the UK, than in the Scandinavian countries cannot necessarily be attributed to the size of the welfare state: differences in hours of work or labour-force participation might be expected in any case, as a result of differences in historical, cultural, legal, and institutional factors. The international comparison does not control for such 'country effects'. Moreover, the differences in taxation may themselves be influenced by such country effects, so that we are not observing a natural experiment.

Does this mean that international comparisons are without value? Two responses at least may be given. First, those employing the comparative method in other disciplines would argue that they are careful to consider the whole range of influences, and not just to concentrate on one statistical observation in isolation. The detailed case studies presented here try to provide a more rounded view of work incentives. A second response is to concentrate on *changes over time*. The fact that taxes have been cut in country A, but not in country B, may allow conclusions to be drawn from the relative movements in their labour supply. To the extent that country effects are constant over time, they are controlled for in this calculation; and the fact that we are comparing countries A and B means that we are also controlling for any change over time that was to be expected in any case. Of course, this approach is not without difficulties. Matching two countries may not adequately control for other changes: for example, where the business cycles are not in synchronization, or where labour supply in one country has a secular trend. Changes over time may be small in relation to other influences; by taking first differences we may be increasing the ratio of noise to signal. On the other hand, the aim of the case-study approach is to provide qualitative as well as quantitative information, and this may give greater confidence to the conclusions that can be drawn.

The main focus of the book is on *empirical* evidence. The central issue is, in the final analysis, an empirical one, since it is the *magnitude* of any adverse effects which will ultimately determine the appropriate policy stance with regard to the scale of the welfare state. The mere existence of a discouragement to work is not in itself a sufficient argument against taxes or transfers; disincentives become a matter for concern when they are sufficiently large to call into question the balance of advantage and disadvantage. In the USA, Okun, in his book *Equality and Efficiency* (1975), used the analogy of the 'leaky bucket'. The transfer of income may involve costs, either through disincentives or administrative expenses, and these 'leaks' from the bucket have to be balanced against the social benefits from the redistribution of income. If the bucket leaks only a moderate amount, this may be quite acceptable. The question is not just whether the welfare state affects economic behaviour, but also how large any effect is.

The sphere of economic behaviour on which we concentrate is that of work incentives. There can be little doubt that taxes and transfers affect other decisions, such as those concerned with savings and portfolio choices, and that these in turn affect economic performance (as discussed briefly below). It is, however, the work decision that has received most attention, and on which there is most empirical evidence. There are therefore reasons for concentrating primarily on this aspect. In the same way, we do not consider the impact of the welfare state on private transfers. The existence of pensions may have reduced the extent to which the elderly are supported by their children. Young people may now live independently, drawing state benefits, rather than at the expense of their parents. These are potentially important, but are not easily investigated. Finally, the population with which we are concerned is that of working age. We do not in general consider whether people continue to work after the minimum statutory retirement age (or normal retirement age).

Empirical evidence receives most attention in what follows, but theoretical analysis is an essential complement. Evidence can only be interpreted within the context of a theoretical model. The purpose of Chapter 2 is to review the theory of labour supply, starting from a simple textbook model, and to describe the conclusions which may be reached with regard to the impact of taxes and transfers. It attempts to provide a framework for the subsequent chapters, although here—as in other fields of economics—the match between theory and evidence is less than 100%. The theoretical models ignore important features of empirical reality; the empirical studies are limited as to the dimensions of labour supply which they can cover and the extent to which they can take full account of the functioning of the labour market.

The main part of the book is concerned with the welfare state and its finance in the four countries. Chapter 3 deals with Sweden, Chapters 4 and 5 with the UK, Chapter 6 with Germany, and Chapter 7 with Denmark. The chapters have been written independently, after discussion of a common plan, and have been revised following group discussion.

Each country part deals with both taxes and transfers (in the case of the UK, Chapter 4 is primarily concerned with taxes and Chapter 5 with transfers). Each chapter gives background material on the tax and social-security systems and the most significant changes in recent decades. It then reviews the evidence about work incentives. Different aspects have received different emphasis in each of the countries, and the findings have been presented in different ways. For these reasons it is not possible to produce a simple tabulation of comparable findings. Instead, the final chapter (Chapter 8) summarizes in a more qualitative way the main conclusions that can be drawn.

The remainder of this first chapter sets the scene, by summarizing the main issues and by providing a brief introduction to the labour market and economic performance of each country, with the US as a point of reference.

1.2. THE OBJECTIVES OF THE WELFARE STATE

The term 'welfare state' is at best imprecise, and its use in a comparative study is particularly treacherous, given the differences in practice and coverage in different countries. In broad terms, most people will agree that it covers state-provided transfers in cash and kind, and state spending on health care and education, but, as such, it excludes many aspects of government policy which contribute to similar objectives, such as the construction of low-cost housing or subsidies on food or the provision of retraining. Indeed, many other forms of spending may be said to contribute to general 'welfare'. If attention is focused on *state expenditure*, then we are neglecting those programmes which take the form of tax remissions: transfers to families with children, for instance, may be made via tax allowances rather than cash benefits. Welfare objectives may be achieved by requiring employers to provide benefits, possibly with the inducement of fiscal concessions: sick pay may be statutorily provided by employers rather than the state. Employers may be required to provide paid time off for maternity; their provision of pensions may be regulated by government agencies.

The imprecision in definition has implications both for the analysis and for the comparison across countries. In this study we are primarily concerned with income maintenance, and do not in general discuss health care nor education. There are, however, obvious points of overlap, such as the provision of financial support for students, the relation between retraining programmes and unemployment benefit, and the separation of sickness benefit from the refunding of health costs. Because of the differences across countries in the policies pursued, the dividing line cannot be followed neatly in all cases.

The ambiguity as to what we mean by the welfare state is in part a reflection of the fact that it is perceived as meeting a variety of objectives. Historically, the major objective of cash transfers was (*a*) the alleviation of poverty, and this remains an important function, accompanied today by concern that poverty relief should be provided in a form which ensures the dignity of recipients. A closely related but different objective is that of (*b*) avoiding social exclusion. The European Community has attached particular importance to combating social exclusion, and it is one of the objectives incorporated in the Maastricht Social Policy Accord. Exclusion is concerned both with the capacity for individuals to exercise their social rights and with their integration within society, the latter having particular relevance to active labour-market policies.

In more recent times, the redistributive objective of the welfare state has become broader, not being limited to the ensuring of a guaranteed minimum income, but seeking through the combined effect of taxes and transfers to secure (*c*) a fair distribution of income. In some countries, less weight has been placed on this objective, but in Scandinavia there has been 'strong support for the idea that redistribution policy should narrow income differentials more generally' (Sandmo 1991: 215–16). Redistribution may not just be between rich and poor. There may be concern for gender equality or for the balance between different regions (such as the position of East and West Germany, discussed in Chapter 6).

Redistribution may take place in terms of lifetime incomes, as with a state pension scheme which pays flat-rate pensions out of earnings-related contributions. But it may also involve redistribution between different stages of the life-cycle. A fourth major objective of the welfare state is (*d*) to smooth out income over the individual life-cycle. Such a concern was evident in Rowntree's early account in Britain of the 'five alternating periods of want and comparative plenty' (1901). The periods of want were those of childhood, when the people themselves had children, and old age. These have become of greater significance today with increased life expectancy and with greater incidence of marital breakdown (albeit a reduction in widowhood). The smoothing out of income over the life-cycle is an aspect of the more general objective of the welfare state of (*e*) providing individual security. Apart from providing for expected contingencies such as old age, this involves the protection of accustomed living standards in the face of events such as sickness, disability, or unemployment.

Any particular welfare-state programme may serve several of these objectives. Unemployment insurance may provide individual security; it may narrow income differentials; and it may be effective in the reduction of poverty. Retirement pensions may be redistributive both over the life-cycle and between rich and poor; they may be important in preventing poverty among the elderly. Parental leave may provide for a particular stage of the life-cycle but may also contribute to reducing gender inequality.

By the same token, the degree of success of different transfer programmes can only be assessed by reference to these diverse objectives. It is a mistake to concentrate on one to the exclusion of others. There is, for example, much discussion of the 'inefficient targeting' of social-security benefits, in the sense that benefits are not confined to the poor. Such a statement, however, takes no account of the other functions of the welfare state. To reject earnings-related unemployment benefit on the ground that it is not targeted on the poor is to ignore the function of this programme in providing individual security.

The primary concern of this book is with the costs of the welfare state—that is to say, the negative side of the balance sheet. It is therefore important to stress at the outset the positive functions of the welfare state. Reference was made earlier to the social benefits from redistribution, and there have been a number of studies designed to cast light on the success of the welfare state in meeting its objectives. These studies have tended to concentrate on certain objectives, notably the alleviation of poverty and the redistribution of income, and they have faced a number of difficulties, particularly that of establishing the counterfactual position as to what would have happened in the absence of the welfare state.

One approach to assessing the anti-poverty effectiveness of the welfare state is to compare the poverty rate with that calculated by subtracting transfer payments from the income of each household. The results of such a study, using data from the Luxembourg Income Study (LIS), are shown in the upper part of Table 1.1 for three of the countries studied here (Denmark is not included in LIS) and for the USA. A family is defined as being in 'poverty' for this purpose if it has income calculated per equivalent adult which is below 50% of the median. In all cases the pre-transfer poverty rates are substantial, whereas in the three European countries the post-transfer poverty rates are very much lower. The poverty rate is reduced by at least two-thirds. In contrast, in the USA the reduction is less, although none the less sizeable.

The overall redistribution of income may be similarly evaluated. In the UK, studies of the impact of the government budget on household incomes show that the largest change in recorded inequality is that associated with cash transfers. In 1990, for example, the Gini coefficient for the distribution of household equivalent income was 52% if cash transfers were not included in the calculation, but was reduced to 38% with cash transfers (Central Statistical Office, 1993). (The Gini coefficient

TABLE 1.1. Poverty rates and Income Distribution Before and After Transfers and Taxation

	Sweden 1981	UK 1979	West Germany 1981	USA 1979
Poverty rate (below 50% median)				
Before transfer	41.0	27.9	28.3	27.3
After transfer	5.0	8.8	6.0	16.9
Reduction (%)	87.8	68.5	78.8	38.1
Income distribution (Gini coefficient %)				
Before transfer	41.7	39.3	40.7	42.5
After transfer	24.1	29.3	28.0	36.9
After tax and transfer	19.7	26.4	25.2	31.7

Notes: 1. The poverty figures refer to family equivalent income, applying a scale of 1 to the first individual, 0.5 to subsequent individuals, up to a maximum of 3.0; the income distribution figures apply a scale of 0.7 for subsequent *adults*.
2. The W. German data are affected by a relatively large number of zero and negative incomes in the sample.

Sources: Poverty rates: Smeeding *et al.* (1990: table 3.5); income distribution: Mitchell (1990: table 6).

is a measure of income inequality, with higher values indicating greater inequality. Twice the Gini coefficient is equal to the expected absolute difference in incomes, as a percentage of the average, of any two people drawn at random from the population—see Atkinson 1983: 53). This substantial difference attributed to cash transfers may be contrasted with the impact of direct taxation, which is only associated with a reduction in the Gini coefficient from 38% to 36% (same source).

Similar calculations based on the LIS data for four countries are shown in the lower part of Table 1.1. In Sweden the Gini coefficient after transfers is more than 17 percentage points lower than that for pre-transfer income. The difference in West Germany is more than 12 points; in the UK it is 10 points; but in the USA it is less than 6 points. Turning to the impact of taxation, we see that in the USA the difference after tax and transfer, compared with after transfer, is not much smaller than that for transfers. But in Europe, the fall in the Gini coefficient in moving from after transfer to after tax and transfer income is relatively much smaller. These results suggest that there is a difference between the two sides of the Atlantic: transfers are more important in redistribution in Europe, and that taxation is, relatively, more important in the USA.

These calculations can, however, only be taken as an accurate measure of the effectiveness of the welfare state in reducing poverty and income inequality *if* the existence of transfers has no impact on other sources of income, whereas this is precisely the issue which needs to be addressed. A vigorously argued criticism of the welfare state is that it has served at least in part to create the problem which it purports to solve. It is claimed that the existence of benefits has led people to alter their behaviour in order to qualify. The existence of pensions means that people retire earlier, and that they save less for their old age; disability insurance has allowed those below retirement age to withdraw from the labour force; unemployment insurance allows people to delay their return to work; social-security benefits have allowed families to pass responsibility to the state. If the transfers have led to reduced labour income, to reduced savings, or to reduced family transfers, the poverty rate in the absence of transfers would be lower than that shown in the first row of Table 1.1.

In order to assess the redistributive success of the welfare state, we need, therefore, to examine the impact of taxes and transfers on other sources of income. The issue of incentives is important not just in its own right but also in evaluating redistribution. At the same time, the position from which we start is that there is a large arithmetic impact of cash transfers, and a rather more modest effect of progressive taxation, so that any adverse behavioural responses would have to be correspondingly large to outweigh completely the social benefits from redistribution.

1.3. THE ECONOMIC IMPLICATIONS OF THE WELFARE STATE

The most obvious economic impact of the welfare state is in terms of its budgetary cost. The growth in public expenditure on the welfare state from 1960 up to the beginning of the 1980s in the four countries studied here and the USA is shown in Fig. 1.1. (In the case of Denmark, the available figures only cover the period 1970–9.) The 'welfare state' is defined in this figure to include all public spending on cash transfers and on health care and education. As noted earlier, there is a degree of arbitrariness to any definition. In the UK, for example, the figures exclude occupational pensions, provided by employers, even though these form an integral part of statutory provision for retirement (an employer can 'contract out' of the state earnings-related pension scheme if the occupational scheme provides comparable cover). In countries such as West Germany which provide fiscal concessions to families with children, the extent of support for children is understated by these figures, which only take account of cash family allowances. The statistics can therefore only be taken as broadly indicative.

Over the two decades, welfare-state spending in Sweden rose from 15% of GDP to 33%. This is the most dramatic increase, but the Danish figures move more or less in line over the 1970s. In the UK, welfare-state

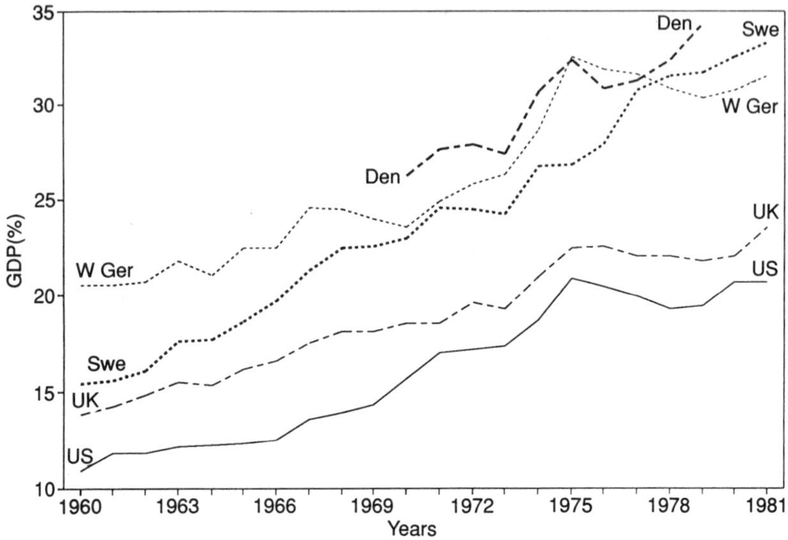

FIG 1.1. Welfare-State Spending as a Percentage of GDP
Source: OECD (1985: annexe C).

expenditure grew from 14% to 24% and in the USA it grew from 11% to 21%. A rather smaller growth is recorded in West Germany, but spending in 1960 was already above 20%. Whereas one tends today to associate large welfare states with Scandinavia, in the 1960s it was in fact West Germany that was 'in the lead'; the Scandinavian countries have in this sense been catching up with the already mature German welfare state.

The growth in welfare state spending reflected a number of factors. The most discussed is the increase in pension expenditure. In Sweden, public-pension expenditure rose from 4.4% of GDP in 1960 to 10.9% in 1980; in Denmark, it rose from 4.6% to 9.1% (OECD 1988: table 7, p. 33). Rather smaller increases were recorded in West Germany, already at a higher level in 1960 (from 9.7% to 12.1%) and in the UK (from 4.0% to 6.3%). These increases are attributable to demographic changes, the maturing of pension schemes, the expansion of coverage, and the increased generosity of programmes.

The picture as far as cash transfers are concerned (i.e. excluding spending on health care and education) is brought up to date in Fig. 1.2. In 1960, cash transfers represented around 7–8% of GDP in Denmark, Sweden, and the UK; they were 5% in the USA; whereas in West Germany they were 12% (other high-transfer countries at the time were France, Belgium, and the Netherlands). Between 1960 and 1980, transfers more than doubled as a percentage of GDP in Denmark and

Sweden, so that they had caught up West Germany, where the rise was less than 5 percentage points. Increases in the UK and the USA were of a similar absolute magnitude to (and hence proportionately larger than) that in West Germany. Over the 1980s as a whole there was little increase in the UK and the USA, but the proportion went up by some 2 percentage points in Denmark and Sweden.

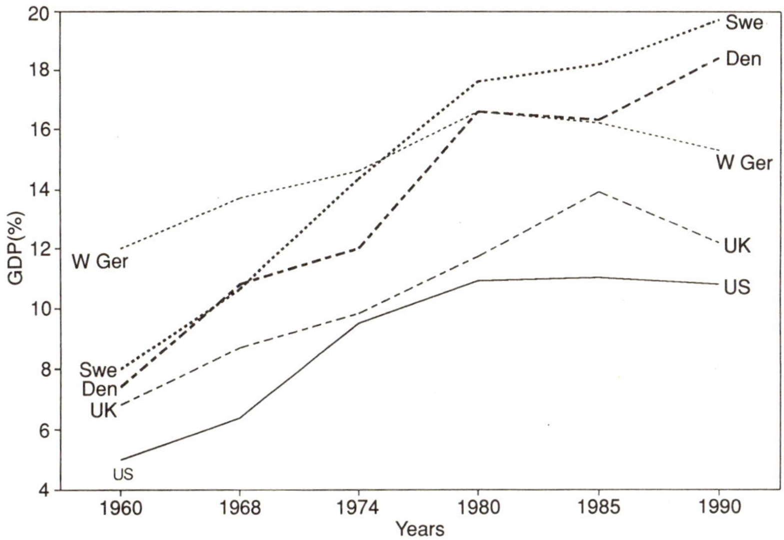

FIG 1.2. Social-Security Transfers as a Percentage of GDP
Note: Latest data for USA are for 1989.
Source: OECD (1992*a*: table 6.3, p. 67).

The growth in welfare-state spending was a major factor in the increase in government spending overall. Fig. 1.3 shows the ratio of social-security transfers to total current government spending (final consumption plus social security), providing an indication of the role played by social security in the general debate about rising tax burdens. Social security increased sharply as a proportion in the USA from 1960 to 1974, bringing it more or less into line with the UK, Sweden, and Denmark. They in turn have tended to converge with West Germany, with social-security spending accounting for about 40% of the total current spending (which does not include interest payments).

The funding of the social-security budget is evidently a major item. The sources of funding not only differ across countries but also have changed noticeably over time. Table 1.2 shows the ILO analysis of the sources of funding for social security and national health services. In the

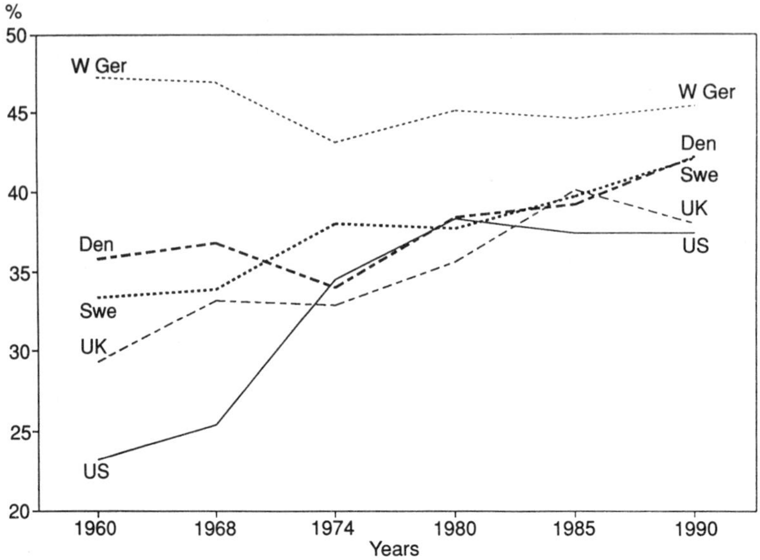

FIG 1.3. Social-Security Transfers as a Percentage of Government Current Spending

Note: Current spending is that of government final consumption, plus social-security transfers.

Source: OECD (1992*a*: tables 6.2, 6.3. pp. 66–7).

USA, in 1985, about a quarter of the finance came from contributions by insured persons, and one-third each from employers and government (the remainder financed by interest on accumulated funds). In the UK, with the greater importance of health spending, the balance is more in the direction of the state, which provides around half the finance, with the shares of employers and insured being reduced to about one-quarter and one-fifth respectively. In Sweden, too, the state financed in 1985 about one-half, but the balance was financed by employers and income from capital, contributions by the insured being virtually abolished after 1970. There has been a major shift in the source of finance. The same is true of contributions by the insured in Denmark, but employer contributions provide less than 10%, and the state finances around 90% of the budget.

Economic Impact on Output and Growth

The issue of financing has been addressed in a variety of ways in the four countries studied here, but it does not follow that the economic impact of the welfare state has been different. Both employer and employee contributions, for example, lead to a 'wedge' between the cost to the

TABLE 1.2. Sources of Finance for Social Security and National Health Services (% of Total)

	Insured persons	Employers	State/public authorities
Denmark			
1959/60	14.9	10.6	74.0
1964/5	16.0	11.4	72.3
1969/70	14.1	8.9	75.8
1974/5	1.1	5.6	91.9
1980	1.8	5.9	90.2
1985	3.1	7.8	86.1
Sweden			
1960	20.5	11.0	66.9
1965	14.0	26.4	55.9
1970	11.4	27.6	54.6
1975	0.8	35.6	56.3
1980	1.0	45.9	45.3
1985	1.3	36.4	52.2
West Germany			
1960	25.9	44.4	26.5
1965	26.0	40.3	30.8
1970	28.9	42.3	25.9
1975	28.2	39.6	28.5
1980	34.0	34.2	28.9
1985	36.3	34.7	26.4
UK			
1959/60	20.0	17.9	58.7
1964/5	21.7	24.9	49.5
1969/70	19.7	25.1	52.8
1974/5	18.8	27.3	51.4
1980	15.6	26.2	55.0
1985	18.3	23.5	55.5
USA			
1959/60	21.8	34.9	38.8
1964/5	22.3	35.9	36.9
1969/70	24.3	33.4	36.9
1974/5	22.7	34.1	37.8
1980	23.4	40.4	29.8
1985	24.7	34.4	30.4

Notes: 1. The columns do not necessarily add to 100%, since certain sources of finance (income from capital and other receipts) are not included.

Sources: ILO (1985: table 6; 1992: table 8).

employer of taking on a worker and the net amount that the worker receives. It could well be that the labelling of contributions as paid by employers or employees has no effect on the final outcome in terms of net incomes and prices. Employee contributions and income tax are typically both deducted at the same stage from gross pay and, again, their economic impact may be similar. On the other hand, employees may not react in the same way to social security contributions as to income taxes, so that the choice of financing does in fact make a difference.

In order to explore these questions, we need to consider the microeconomics of the labour market, including the supply and demand for labour and the setting of wages. We need to go beyond the labour market to consider the determination of prices by firms, and the full general equilibrium of the economy. The same applies when we ask about the economic impact of the transfer side of the account. The level and structure of benefits may be expected to influence the decisions of households and firms. Much of this book is concerned with such microeconomics of taxes and transfers.

Such microeconomic analysis is, however, complex, and it is tempting to seek to cut through the detail of schemes and individual behaviour and to focus on the macro-, rather than micro-, picture. It is macro-, rather than micro-, considerations which lead to analysis of relative levels of national income per head or to rates of growth. In the present context, can we not learn from simple observations of the size of the welfare state in relation to such macroeconomic indicators of performance? Attempts have been made, for example, to relate the rate of growth of national income to the relative size of public spending, like the assertions in Sweden that the large size of the welfare state has been responsible for Sweden growing at a slower rate than the OECD average—with the inference being drawn that cuts in the welfare state would lead to higher growth.

Drawing conclusions from such aggregate indicators is, however, difficult. Suppose that we found a negative correlation between the size of the welfare state and the rate of growth of national income. Such a correlation says nothing about causality. It could be that countries which grew rapidly—for example, on account of discovering offshore oil—were able to afford higher social-security benefits, so that the causal mechanism operates in the opposite direction. Both the size of the welfare state and the rate of growth could reflect a third (unobserved) variable which influenced them both, so that cuts in the welfare state would not bring about the desired improvement in economic performance. Nor could we conclude anything from the absence of a correlation. A diagram relating growth and the size of the welfare state for different countries may reveal simply a random scatter of points, but this may be because we have not controlled sufficiently for other influences—like the oil discoveries just instanced. The case would rest 'not proven'.

In order to establish any causal mechanism, we have to be confident that we understand the underlying mechanisms. What determines the rate of growth or the level of income per head? Although economists cannot claim to have a satisfactory explanation, the theory of production and growth does provide a framework within which the discussion can be organized. It identifies the principal ingredients. On this approach, aggregate output depends on the availability and utilization of factors of production, usually taken to be labour, capital, and natural resources, and on the available technology. Output per head of the population may be increased by increasing the total volume of labour (what is meant by this is discussed further in Chapter 2) or by increasing its productivity, including investment in human capital (education and training). Growth may be enhanced by capital investment, adding to or improving the equipment with which the labour works. Output may grow as a result of the discovery of new natural resources or the better utilization of existing resources. Growth may result from the invention of new technologies or from the diffusion of best-practice techniques, which may go together with new investment.

From this analysis of the sources of growth, we can identify routes by which welfare-state spending may influence the level of output or its rate of growth. The existence of state pensions may, for example, reduce the savings available to finance capital accumulation; the taxes necessary to pay for welfare spending may discourage investment or risky activities such as innovation. Not all these effects need be negative. The assurance of a basic state pension may encourage people that they can provide for an independent old age, and hence lead them to *increase* their savings; the existence of a safety net may allow people to take the risk of becoming self-employed.

In this book we concentrate on the impact of the welfare state on labour and associated questions of human-capital formation. We are concerned with one of the factors which determine production. The reader may object that this is only part of the story, and we accept that this is the case. Examination in depth does, however, necessitate a limitation of the field covered. It is also the case that other causal links have been less fully investigated.

The Labour Market

The economic framework just outlined may seem a little removed from the current economic issues that dominate the newspaper headlines. It may, for example, quite reasonably strike the reader as ridiculous to express concern about the volume of labour supplied when Europe is facing high rates of unemployment. Unemployment rates are shown for the period 1972–91 in Fig. 1.4. (The rates in four countries are those standardized by the OECD to conform as far as possible with internationally agreed definitions, but no standardized rate is given for Denmark.) Throughout the 1980s the highest recorded rates were those in the UK and Denmark (not necessarily comparable), with the USA and West Germany in the middle, and the lowest rates in Sweden. Over the period as a whole the trend was upward in West Germany, Denmark, and the UK, but not in the USA and Sweden, although unemployment in the latter has risen since 1991. It should be noted that the rates recorded are those for 'open' unemployment, excluding those on government programmes, which have been particularly important in Sweden.

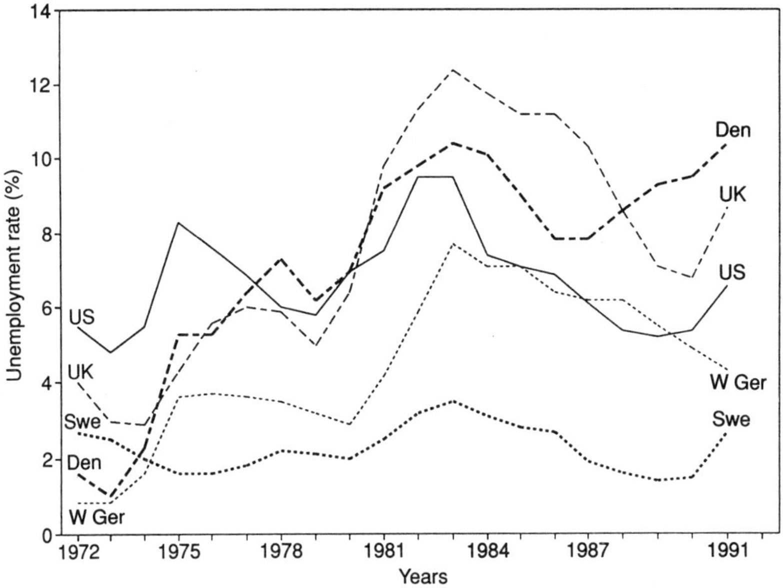

FIG 1.4. Unemployment Rate
Note: Standardized unemployment rates used for all countries except Denmark.
Source: OECD (1992*b*: tables R18, R19).

This background of high unemployment does indeed mean that it is difficult to make any simple statement about the consequences of changes in labour supply, induced by the welfare state, for economic performance. There appears to be considerable scope for expansion of labour demand before the supply limitations come into play. One has here to distinguish between shorter-term macroeconomic management and longer-term considerations. The incentive debate may be interpreted as concerned with the impact of the welfare state on the medium-term and long-term potential of the economy. The use which is made of this potential depends on government choices in the management of the economy, subject to external and other constraints.

On the side of labour supply, the main features have been the rise in participation of women and the fall in participation of men. Considering first the latter, we may express the male labour force as a percentage of the male population aged 15–64 (inclusive). This proportion could exceed 100% where people are at work outside these ages, and in 1960 it was close to this figure in Denmark, Sweden, and the UK (OECD 1992*a*: table 2.7, p. 39). It was at that time 94% in West Germany and 91% in the USA. By 1990, labour-force participation had fallen to 90% in Denmark and below this figure for the other countries, being only 81% in West Germany. In all countries there has been a decline in male participation, reflecting later entry into the labour force, earlier retirement, and withdrawal at prime ages.

The female labour force in 1960, again expressed as a percentage of the female population aged 15–64, was close to 50% in Sweden and West Germany, and around 45% in the other countries (OECD 1992*a*: table 2.8, p. 39). Over the next thirty years participation grew, but at different rates in the different countries. The proportion in West Germany increased little—to 57%—which in 1990 was the lowest figure for the five countries. Next in 1990 came the UK (65%) and the USA (68%), with much higher figures in Denmark (78%) and Sweden (81%).

Taken together, these changes in participation, together with the demographic factors, mean that the total labour force as a percentage of total population (of all ages) in West Germany was virtually the same (at 48%) in 1990 as in 1960, and increased slightly in Sweden (from 49% to 54%) and the UK (from 47% to 50%). In the USA, it increased from 40% to 50%, and in Denmark from 46% to 57% (OECD 1992*a*: table 2.2, p. 36). These are big differences. It is, however, interesting to note that the growth of real GDP per capita over the three decades was relatively similar, indicating that there were differences in the rate of productivity growth. The average growth rate in 1960–90 was 2.0% per capita in the USA, 2.1% in the UK, 2.4% in Sweden, 2.5% in Denmark, and 2.6% in West Germany (OECD 1992*a*: table 3.2, p. 48). Moreover, there were differences *within* the period, as brought out by Fig. 1.5, which shows the growth experience of the five countries in more detail. Growth was fastest in the Scandinavian countries in the 1960s and in West Germany in the 1970s. All countries grew more slowly in the 1980s than they had done in the 1960s and early 1970s.

Economic performance is judged not just in terms of unemployment and growth but also by other indicators. Fig. 1.6 shows the rates of inflation, measured by the consumer price indices, in the five countries from 1960 to 1990. Over the period as a whole, the average rate of

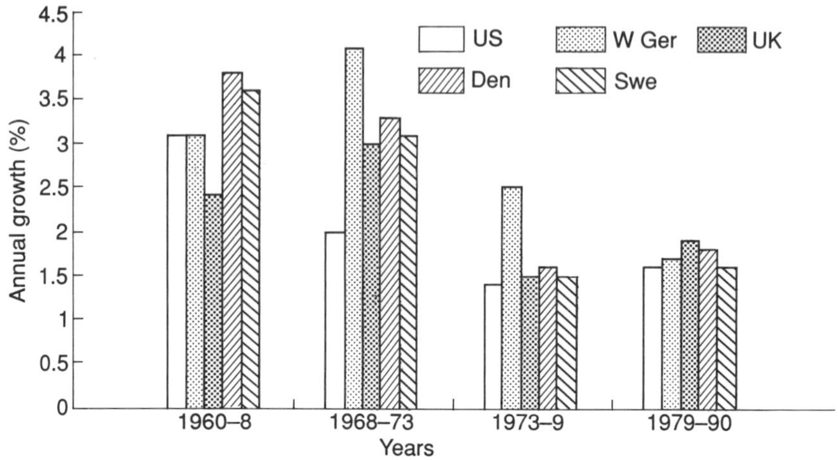

FIG 1.5. Annual Growth of Real GDP Per Capita
Source: OECD (1992*a*: table 3.2, p. 48).

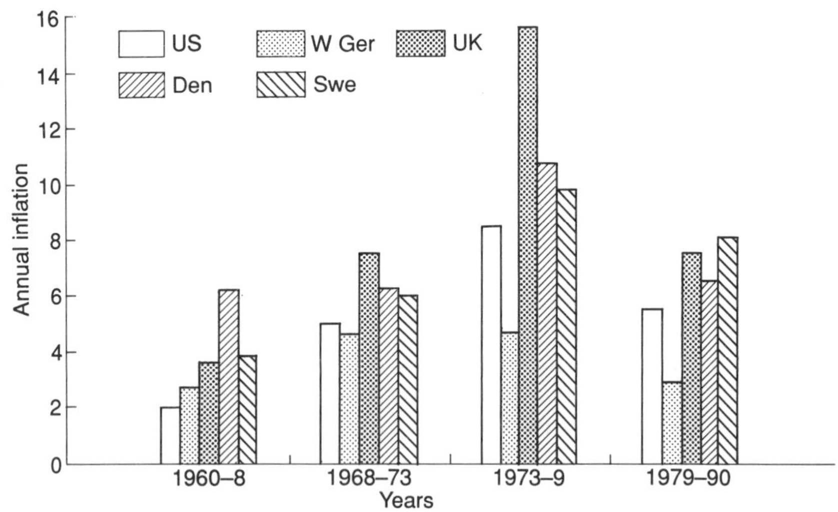

FIG 1.6. Annual Rate of Inflation
Source: OECD (1992*a*: table 8.11, p. 87).

inflation has been 3.5% in West Germany, 5% in the USA, and 7–8% in Denmark, Sweden, and the UK. Inflation in Sweden and the UK, only 1% higher than in West Germany in the 1960s, rose to more than double the West German rate in the 1970s, and the difference became even more marked in the 1980s.

To some extent, as in the case of Sweden, the higher rate of inflation went together with lower unemployment, but in other countries the performance was poor on both counts. Applying the journalistic practice of adding the unemployment and inflation rates, to obtain a 'misery index', we find that over the decade 1980–90 West Germany scores best, with the lowest total of 9.6%, followed by Sweden with 10.5%, the USA with 12.5%, Denmark with 14.6%, and the UK at the bottom with 16.7% (OECD 1992*a*: tables 2.15, 8.11). Whether anything can be read into such scores is open to debate.

What is not open to debate is the fact that economics in recent years has directed much effort to the attempt to create coherent theories for this interplay between incentives and labour-supply. We will now turn to some of the most important of these attempts.

2
Work Incentives

A. B. ATKINSON

2.1. INTRODUCTION

The aim of this chapter is to provide a conceptual framework for the analysis of labour supply, setting the scene for the empirical studies which follow. As in many branches of economics, there is a considerable gap between theoretical models and empirical evidence. The theoretical models tend to be highly simplified and to ignore important features of empirical reality. The empirical studies tend to focus on those aspects of labour supply that are readily quantified. There may be only a limited match between the theoretical constructs and the empirical observations. The purpose of this chapter is to help bridge the gap, or at least allow the reader to relate the one to the other.

Work decisions are affected by many considerations. Amongst the most important of these are non-economic. People work because their jobs are fulfilling in their own right, providing social esteem and a sense of social integration. Being in work provides a structure to people's daily lives. The cost of unemployment is much more than the loss of earnings. For the early retired, replacement of their earnings by a pension may be inadequate compensation for the non-economic benefits of working. People may work harder out of loyalty to their employer or workmates. They may feel a sense of identification with their firm. Conversely, people may give up their jobs or drop out of the labour market for non-economic reasons. There may be no financial reward sufficient to compensate for working in conditions that are considered to be damaging to health or to the environment. Freedom from work discipline may be valued above the money gain from working.

In what follows, it is mainly—but not exclusively—the *economic* incentives to work that are considered. This is not because we believe them to be more important, but because it is these aspects that are directly affected by taxes and transfers. If the growth of the welfare state has called into question the incentive to work, it is through the impact on the financial returns to working and on the benefits received when not in work.

Just as there are many motives for working, so too there are many dimensions to the work decision. When people allege that high taxes or high benefits discourage work, they may have in mind quite different aspects. The standard textbook model of the labour supply-decision (Section 2.2) is of a person choosing his or her hours of work. Taxes and transfers may indeed cause people to work shorter hours or not to accept overtime or not to take a second job. But they may also cause people to put in less effort, or not to seek promotion. People may be less willing to take responsibility. More generally, annual hours may be reduced by workers taking longer holidays; they may be reduced by the fact that people spend longer between jobs. Lifetime hours may be reduced by people entering the labour force later or by retiring earlier. And, in an increasingly integrated world economy, workers may migrate to a neighbouring country.

These manifold dimensions, considered in Sections 2.2 and 2.3, mean that we should look at a range of variables when seeking to measure the disincentive effect of taxes and benefits. It is not sufficient simply to investigate hours of work. The different dimensions of labour supply may also have different implications. Whereas longer spells of unemployment between jobs may quite rightly be regarded as social waste, reduced labour supply in the form of earlier retirement may be considered to have compensating advantages. Not all withdrawal from the labour force is economically damaging: people who continue in education, for example, may be acquiring valuable human capital.

The standard textbook discussion of the individual labour-supply decisions may also be criticized for ignoring important institutional features of the labour market. The worker is assumed to make choices freely in the absence of collective bargaining between unions and employers. The employment contract is assumed to be a simple spot market, workers making a current decision in response to a current job offer, with no implications on either side beyond today. There is no consideration of work careers, let alone 'lifetime jobs'. There are no pension considerations to be taken into account. The unemployed worker is assumed to be able to reject job offers without any fear of infringing the unemployment compensation regulations. The tax structure may be quite complex, with different rate brackets, exemption levels, etc., to say nothing of the poverty trap which may be generated by the withdrawal of income-related benefits.

In Section 2.4. a number of institutional features are described, including collective bargaining, the informal (or shadow) economy, tax and benefit schedules, and benefit entitlement. Such institutional features are of particular importance in a comparative study such as the present one, since the countries clearly differ in their institutions. While such differences may not necessarily change the thrust of the theoretical analysis, they certainly influence the interpretation of the empirical evidence.

What form does the empirical evidence take? As will be clear from the chapters that follow, there are many different types of evidence, each with advantages and disadvantages. The different types are reviewed in Section 2.5, which summarizes the main methods which have been employed. In the past twenty-five years there has been a great deal of empirical research on work incentives. Much of this research relates to the United States, and in this chapter—as opposed to the rest of the book—the United States experience receives especial attention.

One important reason for considering the theoretical framework is that it allows us to place the determination of labour supply within the wider economic context. In considering individual decisions, we have to bear in mind that this is only one side of the labour market. The choices open to the individual are constrained by those made available by the employer (and vice versa). The individual worker may indeed have no choice at all, in that he or she is unable to secure any employment. Put another way, if we observe wages and hours of work in the labour market, these are the result of the interaction of supply and demand. Changes in hours of work may reflect changes on either side, so that reduced hours per week may be the result of developments on the employer side (e.g. on account of technological progress) as well as on the side of workers.

The theory of individual labour supply has been criticized for being *partial partial* analysis. The first 'partial' refers to the neglect of the employer side of the market, just discussed. The second 'partial' refers to the fact that analysis of a single market, such as the labour market, is only part of the general equilibrium of the economy. Changes in the labour market spill over into the rest of the economy. Increases in wages have implications for product prices, and for the pattern of demand. The demand for labour is a derived demand, in that it depends on the demand for the goods and services produced. Macroeconomic models have equations for wage-formation and employment which form part of a whole system determining the evolution of the economy. In concentrating on the labour market, as we do here, these wider linkages need to be borne in mind.

A second important reason for considering the theoretical framework is that it raises questions that may not at first be evident. The possibility that taxes and transfers may discourage work is widely regarded as a matter for concern. But what is the reason for this concern? Economic analysis suggests two distinct answers. The first is that the existence of taxes and transfers *distorts* the choices that people would otherwise make. The existence of retirement pensions has, it is argued, induced people to retire earlier than they otherwise would choose: 'I would like to have carried on working but it simply was not worth my while.' In this case, the cost of the welfare state is measured by the leakage from the bucket in making the transfer; in the terms defined below, it is the 'substitution effect' of the tax or benefit.

A second reason for concern about the effect of the welfare state on incentives is that we attach a value to work as such. In this case, it is the *total* effect, not just the distortion, that matters (it is, in the terminology of Section 2.2, both income and substitution effects). This is a different criterion, and raises the further question as to why we should be so concerned. Why should we seek to raise the level of work? Why are people not making the correct decision when balancing work and leisure? One answer to this question is that these decisions are made in a context which is already distorted, notably by the need to finance government expenditure. Inducing people into the paid labour force widens the tax base; reducing unemployment has a beneficial impact on the government deficit. On the other hand, some might argue, for instance on environmental grounds, that people should work less, not more. In such a case, taxes and transfers which discouraged work would be desirable. These are, of course, matters of judgement, on which each person has to form their own view, but the theoretical framework may be of value in thinking them through.

2.2. WHAT IS LABOUR SUPPLY?

The standard textbook model is grossly oversimplified, but it serves as a useful point of departure, not least because it can be reinterpreted to cover a variety of situations.

The Standard Textbook Model

The standard textbook model of the individual labour-supply decision sees a person as choosing hours of work on the basis of an *income/leisure* trade-off. There is a choice between the additional utility derived from a further hour of leisure against the additional utility from the disposable income which would be earned by devoting that hour to paid work.

It is central to this model that the individual *has* a choice. In reality, it may be that there are no jobs available, the person being unemployed and hence forced involuntarily to consume leisure. For the present, we assume that the person has a choice of jobs; initially, indeed, we assume that the possibilities open to the individual worker include working anywhere between 0 and T hours, at a fixed hourly wage rate, denoted by

w. These possibilities are shown by the budget constraint MA in Fig. 2.1, where the person is assumed to have income from other sources (such as savings) equal to M.

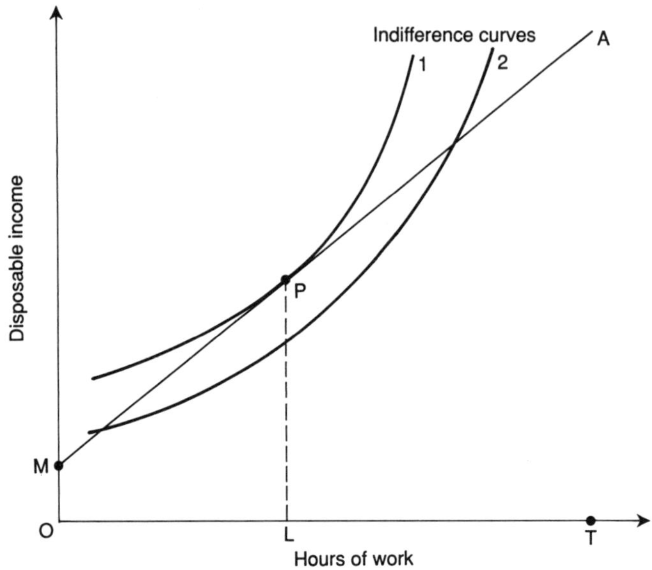

FIG 2.1. Income/Leisure Trade-Off

The underlying behavioural assumption is that the person has preferences between leisure and consumption (here equated with disposable income). In graphical terms, these preferences may be represented by indifference curves, two of which are shown in Fig. 2.1, with the person seeking to attain the highest indifference curve (so that the curve labelled 1 is preferred to that labelled 2). The indifference curves slope upward to the right, since work is assumed to generate disutility, and hence to require compensation in terms of extra disposable income in order for the person to be equally well off (to be indifferent).

These preferences determine the labour-supply choice. Faced with the budget constraint MA, the highest indifference curve that the person can attain is that labelled 1, so that the predicted choice is shown by the point P, where the person works L hours. This generates gross income of $(wL + M)$, which in the absence of taxes and social-ssecurity benefits is the same as the disposable income. The choice made by the person is a function of the parameters describing their economic opportunities, here w and M. As w and M change, so too will L. A convenient way of representing these changes are in terms of *elasticities*. The elasticity of labour supply with respect to the wage, for instance, is the percentage change in L resulting from a 1 percentage point change in w. Where the elasticity is, for example, equal to 0.5, this means that a 10% rise in wages induces a 5% rise in hours of work.

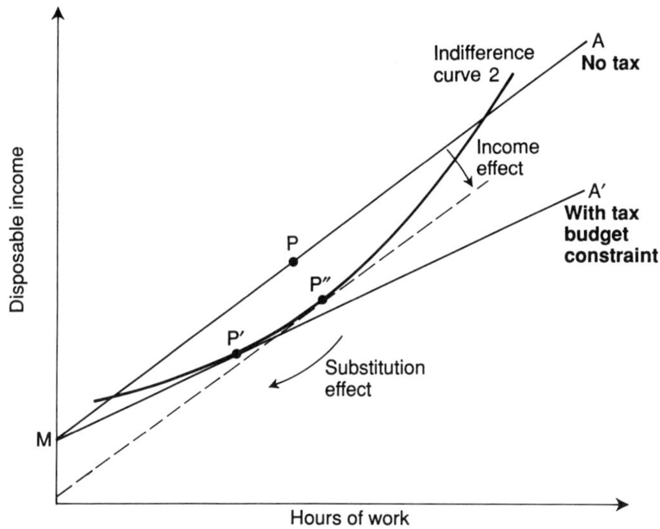

FIG 2.2. Effect of Proportional Tax on Earned Income

Suspending for the moment our disbelief at the assumptions which are required for this model to apply, we may use the textbook model to examine the effect of a tax on wage income. Suppose that there is a social-security tax of t on all earnings (but not on other sources of income). This reduces the person's disposable income to

$$w\,(1-t)\,L + M \tag{2.1}$$

where L may now have changed as a result of the tax. Geometrically, the budget line still starts at M (see Fig. 2.2), but now has slope $w(1-t)$ in place of w. It becomes MA′. The impact is to shift the labour-supply choice to point P′ on indifference curve 2. This shift may be seen as the combination of two effects:

the *income effect* (shift from P to P″), according to which the person is worse-off, being on a lower indifference curve,

and

the *substitution effect*, which involves a movement round the indifference curve from P″ to P′, since the slope of the budget line is now only w(1 − t), rather than t.

The second of these effects is clearly negative, leading to a reduction in hours worked. The first effect, on the other hand, is usually expected to be positive, in that the person is less well off and therefore less able to afford leisure. The overall impact is therefore ambiguous, depending on the relative strength of the income and substitution effects. The tax may cause people to work less, as shown in Fig. 2.2, or it may have the reverse effect, with P′ to the right of P. Put another way, the elasticity of labour supply may be negative rather than positive (since the introduction of the tax is just like a fall in the wage rate).

The possibility that taxation may *encourage* rather than discourage work effort comes as a surprise to many lay commentators, but it is quite intuitive and corresponds to what many people report: for example, according to one respondent to a British interview study, taxation is 'a two-edged sword. High deductions make you want to work more overtime to make up what you lose [*income effect*]—but if you get to a certain amount it's not worth working for [*substitution effect*]' (quoted by Brown and Levin, 1974: 845). (Passages in square brackets added.) It is the combination of two effects that makes for problems in interpreting the evidence, since we need to distinguish the two effects.

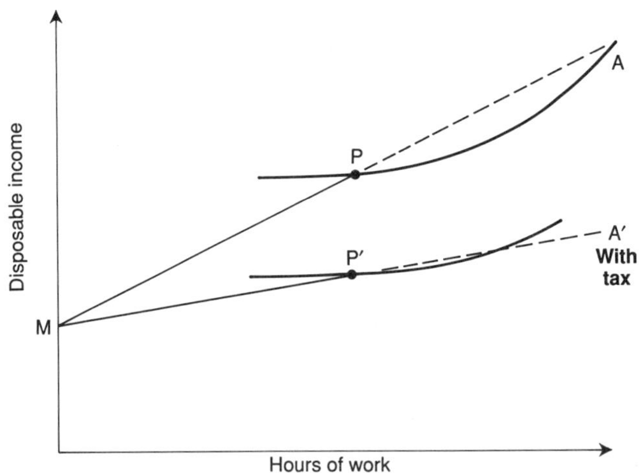

FIG 2.3. Effect of Introducing Exemption

The need to distinguish the income and substitution effects becomes evident when we consider a tax system that departs from being simply proportional. Suppose that the government introduces into the social-security tax an exemption of an initial tranche of earnings. The effect—see Fig. 2.3—is to shift the budget line upward, so that it only departs from the 'No Tax' line after a certain level of earnings is reached. It becomes MB″A″, and is therefore non-linear, with a kink at B″. Below B″ the marginal return in terms of extra net income from working an extra hour is w; above B″ the marginal return is $w(1-t)$. The effect of this non-linearity is taken up below; for the present we assume that the person chooses a point on the dashed part above B″. The effect of the exemption is then the same as an addition to M (equal in value to t times the exemption), and we have a pure income effect. Where a rise in income means that the person chooses to consume more leisure, the adjustment is as indicated by the arrow. This example shows why, in order to predict the consequences of the introduction of the exemption, we need to be able to separate the income and substitution effects.

Different Dimensions of Labour Supply

The story in terms of hours of work encompasses decisions about standard hours per week, about overtime hours (assuming that no premium is paid for overtime), and about days per week, which may be varied contractually via part-time work or *de facto* through absenteeism or unpaid leave. The move from P to P′ in Fig. 2.2 may be achieved via working seven rather than eight hours per day, or by switching to part-time work. The story may be further elaborated to take account of adjustments through weeks of holiday, and it is interesting in this respect that a number of countries, including the United States, tend to measure labour supply in annual hours, rather than weekly hours as is common in Britain.

The main variations in annual hours are not the result of holidays but are attributable to periods out of the labour force (non-participation) or unemployment. The latter represents a constraint on the choices open to people: they are rationed in their hours of work. As shown in Fig. 2.4, the worker can only choose from the solid part of the budget line, not the dashed part. In such a situation, the choice of point P may be inferior to points on the dashed part: the constraint is binding. Where it is binding, the imposition of a tax, moving the budget line to MA', may leave the choice of hours unaffected. With the tax the person would still, as shown in Fig. 2.4, like to work longer hours.

The participation decision may be treated by reinterpreting the textbook account to apply to discrete rather than continuous decisions. Take the decision whether or not to retire from employment. The person then has a discrete choice (see Fig. 2.5) between the point R, with disposable income equal to M plus the pension, and continuing to work

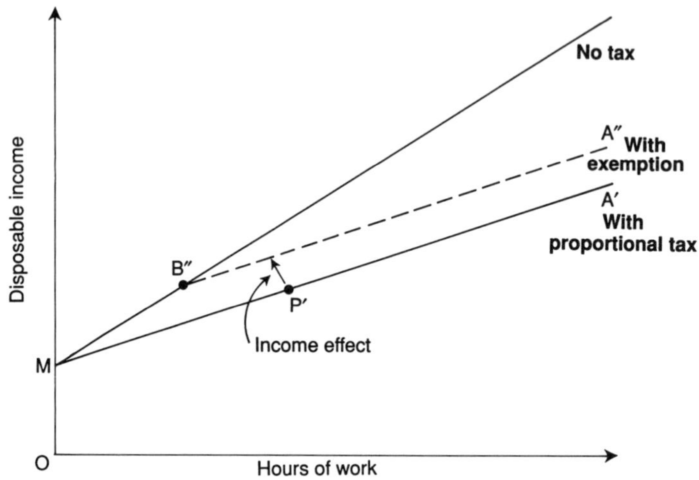

FIG 2.4. Effect of Limit on Hours of Work Available (Rationing)

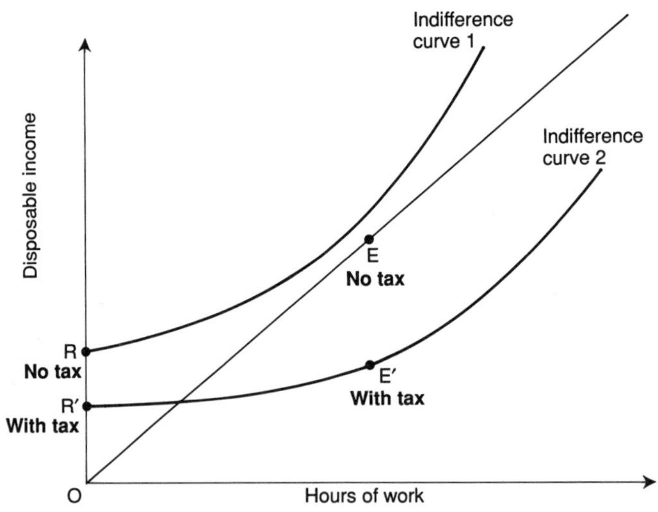

FIG 2.5. Analysing a Discrete Choice: Work/Not Work

with a fixed number of hours, a choice denoted by E. The choice depends on whether the indifference curve through R passes above or below that through E. As shown in Fig. 2.5, the person chooses to retire. Suppose now that an income tax is introduced, so that the choices become R′ and E′. As drawn, the person now chooses not to retire. As before, there are income and substitution effects. A tax on both earnings and pension makes the person worse off, but also gives rise to a substitution effect against continuing employment. As drawn in Fig. 2.5, the income effect dominates and the tax causes the person not to retire, but the reverse could be true. The person might choose E over R but prefer R′ to E′.

The discrete choice could be reinterpreted as that of a married woman considering whether or not to take up paid work, in which case R represents the family income derived from other earners. Or it could be the decision of a young person as to whether to continue in education, with R representing the income from scholarships, etc., or to enter the labour force. It could be the decision of an unemployed person deciding whether or not to return to work, with R representing unemployment benefit.

Such a reinterpretation allows us to see that the contraposition of income and substitution effects applies more widely than just the simple hours-of-work model. It also allows us to make predictions about parameters other than just the tax rate. A reduction in the retirement pension, for instance, lowers the point R without affecting E (unless the tax rate is cut at the same time). It is clear that this would make people less likely to retire. (As stressed at the beginning of this chapter, there are, of course, many other considerations apart from the financial ones which enter such decisions.) A cut in the tax rate levied on husbands would have the effect of reducing both R and E by the same amount for a married woman, and hence have a pure income effect on her decision, making it less likely that she participated in the labour market.

We can, moreover, take account of the fact that people can vary their labour supply by varying their intensity of work, or how hard they work when they are actually at their place of employment. In some cases this may be directly remunerated: for example, where there is piece-work or payment by results. Where people are paid according to how much they produce, the actual hours may not be the key variable as much as the output. We can then relabel the horizontal axis in Fig. 2.1 as 'output', and apply the same analysis. The effect of taxation may be that people take it easier, producing less in a given number of hours, but this would only be the case where the substitution effect dominated the income effect.

Finally, we can apply the analysis to emigration. If the horizontal axis measures the disutility, not from work, but from living abroad, then the decision may be treated as that between a better-paying job abroad (E in Fig. 2.5) and a less well-paid job at home (R). A tax which affected earnings in both countries, such as a European Community-wide income tax, would have both income and substitution effects, and hence be ambiguous in its impact. A tax which affected only income at home would encourage emigration. This, again, is an example of a decision where non-economic considerations are likely to be of much greater importance than the purely financial ones.

2.3. RICHER MODELS OF LABOUR SUPPLY

The extension of the standard model to other dimensions of labour supply illustrates the versatility of the simple framework, but it also highlights important features which are missing. What people do when they are retired cannot be simply described as the consumption of 'leisure'. Many retired people regard themselves as hard at work; it is just that they are not being paid a cash income. The same may apply to married women. We need to consider unpaid work inside or outside the home. Account needs to be taken of work that is paid but which is outside the formal economy and not subject to taxation. The example of married women's participation draws attention to the fact that the decision-making unit is often not the individual but the family or household. We need to consider the collective decision-making process. A number of the decisions are essentially dynamic, and cannot be treated simply at a point in time. This applies to the retirement decision, which is likely to be irreversible, and to the decision about education. A richer treatment of these aspects is the subject of this section, which gives four examples of ways in which the standard model has been developed in recent research.

Unpaid Work and Household Production

The time not spent on paid work may well be spent on similar activities in the unpaid sector. A person may turn down the opportunity of overtime in order to work as a volunteer in a youth club. A person may take early retirement in order to act as an unpaid secretary of the lifeboat association. These—obviously emotive—examples point to the fact that unpaid activities may generate benefits to others. This in turn may affect the policy conclusions drawn. In the discussion of the reasons why we are concerned about work effort, it was noted that we may want to encourage or discourage work *per se*. If unpaid work gives rise to positive externalities to others, then society may want to tilt the playing field in this direction. A tax on paid work may in this context be socially desirable.

Unpaid work affects the analysis even where it takes place solely within the household and benefits only household members. This work activity within the household is recognized explicitly in models of *household production*. On this view, goods purchased in the market are not the final objects of consumption, but are rather inputs into the household production process. A household production 'activity', say 'having dinner', involves goods and time. The cost of this activity is the sum of the goods inputs and the cost of time. There may be an activity of pure leisure, involving time but no goods, but in general activities require both time and goods. The trade-off faced is therefore not a simple one between net income and leisure, but between working more and having more goods for consumption versus working less and having more time as an input to consumption activity. The harried executive (Linder 1970) may be unable to find the time to spend his salary.

The underlying consumer decision is that regarding the level of activities consumed. Since the price of consumption activities depends on the net wage rate (via the cost of the time input), the effect of a tax on earnings may be different from that in the traditional model. By reducing the opportunity cost of time, it makes cheaper activities which are relatively time-intensive. It might be thought that the consequences for labour supply would be different from those in the earlier model, and Becker (1965) suggested that the substitution effect could be reversed. In the fixed-coefficient activity model (requiring goods and time in fixed proportions), this cannot, however, happen (Atkinson and Stern 1979), and the substitution effect has the same properties as in the textbook model. The textbook model is enriched by considerations of household production, but certain underlying principles continue to apply.

The household production model provides a framework within which a number of household decisions may be examined explicitly. Several of these involve joint decisions of household members, to which we now turn.

Family Decision-Making

The treatment of labour supply on an individual basis assumes in effect that the decisions are made independently. They are only interrelated to the extent that the earnings of the husband enter the 'other income' of the wife and vice versa. Even then the interrelations may be quite complex. Where a couple are taxed as a unit, with, for example, the tax being twice that payable by a single person with their total income divided by 2, the marginal tax rate faced by one partner depends on the income of the other. Where unemployment benefit is based on a family means test, the family income being brought up to some guaranteed level, there may be little incentive for the partner of an unemployed person to continue in paid work.

At the opposite extreme from the individualist model is that of *joint family decision-making*. The family is seen as behaving like a single individual, with preferences defined over the labour supplies and consumptions of the different members, and facing a budget constraint which combines all sources of income. In this case, changes in the tax and benefit treatment of one member of the household are predicted to have both income and substitution effects on the labour supply of other members. Without specifying further the nature of preferences, however, it is difficult to make predictions as to the likely impact. Suppose, for example, that the value of time spent at home goes up if the spouse is also at home, so that their leisure is highly complementary; this means that a disincentive to work faced by one partner may reduce the labour supplied by the other. On the other hand, if their time is substitutable in household production, then more time spent at home by one partner may reduce the marginal value of the contribution of the other, leading them to spend more time in paid work.

This 'glued-together' model of the family has been contrasted with models which recognize the individual interests of members and the possibility of conflict. These may involve bargaining, with marriage partners having as a position of last resort the possibility of withdrawing from the relationship. They may involve sharing rules, where rules of thumb govern the division of income and the balance between personal and shared consumption. No clearly preferred model of this kind has emerged, but these considerations are likely to widen the range of possible reactions to taxes and transfers.

Life-Cycle Decisions

The standard model of labour supply is timeless. Decisions are made only for one period and there are no repercussions for the future. At the opposite extreme is the *life-cycle model* of consumer behaviour, which sees the individual as maximizing a lifetime utility function defined over consumption and leisure in all periods of the lifetime and subject to a lifetime budget constraint. Where the person is assumed to be able to borrow or lend freely at a specified rate of interest, r, the budget constraint requires that the present discounted value (at discount rate r) of consumption, and any transfers to others (including bequests), should equal the present value of wage income plus any transfers received.

In such a model, labour-supply decisions become more complex. The trade-off with net income depends on the whole lifetime consumption plan; there is an interdependence between decisions at all dates. Current decisions depend on the present value of all expected future earnings, and on the rate of interest. The individual draws up a lifetime labour-supply plan. A tax on income may have different effects at different points of the individual life-cycle. Moreover, the person must base decisions on the *expected* future values of taxes and benefits (as well, of course, as expectations regarding wages and prices). The expectation that taxes and contribution rates for social security are going to rise in the future may induce people to work harder now (even leaving aside the income effect).

Such a complex model may seem like an unrealistic representation of human behaviour. Some kind of adaptive learning model may be more appropriate. People may experiment with different kinds of job, finding, for example, that doing overtime conflicts too much with family life, or, alternatively, becoming accustomed to a standard of living which can only be maintained by working additionally at weekends.

The life-cycle story does, however, seem to capture some important elements. Provision for retirement is an example where individual plans, however incoherent, have an essential lifetime dimension. People use the working lifetime, particularly the periods when they do not have dependent children, to build up assets in state or private pensions, or in savings more generally, on which they can draw in retirement. The decision as to the date of retirement may be seen as balancing the costs of continuing to work against the gain in higher consumption over a shorter retirement period. Where the decision to retire is irreversible, there may be an option value attached to continued employment, in that it keeps open the option. In this case, a significant role may be played by expectations with regard to future taxes and transfers.

The life-cycle perspective applies particularly to decisions regarding investment in human capital, and this is an area of considerable policy interest. Suppose that a person reaching the minimum school-leaving age can choose between two jobs, one of which can be entered at once at a wage W_1, assumed for simplicity to be constant, and the other of which involves a period of training, say five years, during which the person has no earnings. The second job must presumably offer a higher level of earnings, W_2 (again assumed constant), to compensate for the training period, so that we have $W_2 > W_1$. According to the human capital theory, for people to be indifferent it must be the case that the present discounted value (at interest rate r) of earnings over the whole working lifetime (taken to be 45 years) is the same in the two jobs:

$$\sum_{1}^{45} W_1/(1+r)^i = \sum_{6}^{45} W_2/(1+r)^i \tag{2.2}$$

It has been argued that the income tax discriminates against such human capital investment. T. W. Schultz said of the US tax system that 'our tax laws everywhere discriminate against human capital' (quoted in Rosen, 1980: 173). But a proportional tax on earnings reduces the two sides of equation (2.2) by the same proportion; it would neither discourage or encourage training. Nor would it be affected by a progressive tax with a constant tax rate and a tax credit (giving the value of the tax allowance to everyone). Such a tax (which is progressive, in the sense that the average tax rate rises with income) would not affect the choice, since it would only involve adding the value of the tax exemption to both sides (in addition to reducing both sides of equation (2.2) by the same proportion).

It is to the extent that the marginal rates of tax are graduated, being higher on W_2, that the return to training is reduced and investment in human capital discouraged. Of course this is an oversimplified representation. For example, the introduction of costs such as university fees which are not tax-deductible may mean that taxation tilts the balance against training. But the essential point is that human capital investment largely takes the form of foregone earnings, so that if these earnings would have been taxed, the cost of the investment is reduced as well as the benefits.

Effort and Work Discipline

The earlier discussion of work effort was concerned with the situation where it was rewarded directly via piece-rate; we should also consider situations where effort is rewarded indirectly, or, conversely, where lack of effort is penalized by dismissal. This links with the recent literature on *efficiency wage* theories, which have received considerable attention in labour economics and macroeconomics.

The most popular efficiency-wage story assumes that there are jobs in which people 'shirk' if their work performance is not monitored. Monitoring is not 100%, so that people face a probability of less than 100% of being caught shirking. If they are caught, then they are fired and have to rely on unemployment benefit, b, for which they are assumed to be eligible (an assumption questioned below). In these circumstances, employers have to pay a wage premium to make sure that workers put in the necessary effort and do not shirk. If the cost of effort is denoted by e, and the probability of being caught is p, then the necessary wage for risk-neutral workers is such that the net benefit to putting in effort is equal to the expected net benefit when shirking:

$$w - e = w(1-p) + bp \qquad (2.3)$$

There is a gamble with a probability $(1-p)$ of winning, which means that one gets w with no effort, and a probability p of losing and getting b. From this we can deduce that the wage has to be set by the employer as

$$w = e/p + b \qquad (2.4)$$

What happens if a tax is imposed on the wage income (but not on b)? If w were unchanged, this would reduce the left-hand side of equation (2.4) and the worker would not feel that it paid to put in the effort. The only way in which he can be induced to do so is if the wage rises so that the after-tax wage remains equal to $e/p + b$. On the other hand, the after-tax wage changes with the level of unemployment benefit. It should, however, be noted that this ignores the institutional fact that unemployment benefit is typically refused, or denied for an initial period, where a person has entered unemployment as a result of 'industrial misconduct'.

What the efficiency-wage model does—in contrast to the earlier analysis—is to bring in the other side of the labour market. We have moved from a 'partial partial' model, focused purely on the supply side, to one which is 'partial' in that it looks only at the labour market, but which does introduce employer reactions. In the efficiency-wage model described above, in effect the supply of labour is perfectly elastic at a specified after-tax wage ($e/p + b$) and the tax is fully shifted. This is an extreme case, but we need to bear in mind that the effect of the tax may show up in wage changes as well as labour-supply changes. This may indeed happen in the textbook model. Where the labour-supply curve is shifted by the introduction of taxes and transfers, the new equilibrium may involve changes in both hours of work and the wage rate.

The efficiency-wage model serves also to remind us that there may be less than full employment, and that unemployment may not be eliminated by wage flexibility. The total labour demanded at the wage rate determined by equation (2.4) may not equal that supplied, but employers will not find it profitable to employ people at a lower wage, since they know that it will not induce effort. Workers who would prefer to work at the going wage rather than be unemployed on benefit may find that jobs are rationed.

2.4. INSTITUTIONAL FEATURES OF THE LABOUR MARKET

The discussion of the labour-supply decision so far has tended to take place in an institutional vacuum, and one of the welcome advances of recent years has been an increased recognition of the importance of institutional features. In this respect, there has been a rapprochement between mainstream labour economics and the more institutional school of labour economics.

Collective Bargaining

The most obvious conjunction of labour supply with institutional features is in the field of collective bargaining. The decisions that we are seeking to understand cannot be seen as made purely at the level of the individual family. In many occupations there is a standard working week, and this standard working week is determined by collective agreements negotiated between unions and management. The same may apply to the number of days of annual holiday. In such circumstances, an individual cannot unilaterally decide to work a 60-hour standard week, nor typically to take 13 weeks' vacation. The extent of collective agreements, and the role of unions, do of course vary considerably across countries, as is illustrated by those studied in this volume.

The existence of such collectively negotiated dimensions does not mean that taxes and transfers have no effect, but it does mean that the decisions to be studied are not just individual ones but also those reached via collective negotiations. If taxes cause individual members to want to work shorter hours, this may lead them to put pressure on their union executive, but it depends on a majority being affected in the same way. If people do not like the decision made by the union, they may be able to take another job, but the scope for this is limited, and in some countries standard working weeks are negotiated at the national level by the social partners.

Many collective agreements cover not just standard hours but also overtime premium rates. This is an aspect of the individual budget constraint not yet taken into account. Just like the tax exemption in Fig. 2.3, this generates a *non-linearity* in the budget constraint: the marginal return in terms of extra net income from working an extra hour is no longer the same at all hours. But in contrast to the situation of the tax exemption, the marginal return now rises as we move to a higher level of hours. Working above the standard hours gives a higher return on account of the overtime premium—see Fig. 2.6. The budget constraint is now *non-convex*, in that the person may be able to choose points P_1 and P_2 but not the average of these two points. In such a situation, it is possible that an indifference curve touches two distinct segments of the budget constraint, as is drawn in Fig. 2.6, where the person is indifferent between P_1 and P_2.

The same diagram may be used to illustrate another source of non-convexity: the existence of fixed costs of working. Suppose that there are travel-to-work costs, or clothing costs, or union subscriptions, which have to be paid at a fixed amount whenever the person works. This means that the net income when not working (point C in Fig. 2.6.) is at a higher point on the vertical axis than the starting point of the in-work budget constraint. As drawn, the person is indifferent between not working and working P_1 (or P_2) hours. From this, it is clear that small changes in the fixed costs may induce a discrete change in labour supply. There may be discontinuities in the labour-supply response. A lump-sum social-security tax paid by all employees, for example, may lower the schedule relative

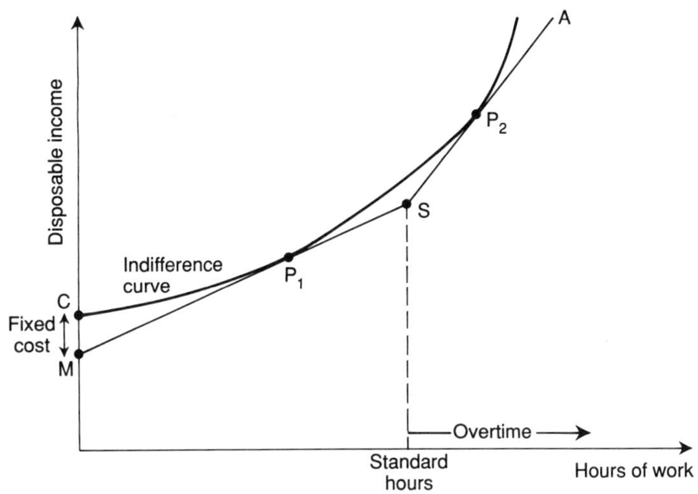

FIG 2.6. Overtime Premium and Fixed Costs of Work

to C and cause people to withdraw totally from the labour force. They do not gradually reduce their hours to zero: before the tax the person was working P_1 hours, after the tax the person has left the labour force entirely.

Collective decision-making has been interpreted in terms of union bargaining, but it may operate at a less formal level. Decisions may be influenced by the social norms of the workplace. People may base their decisions about early retirement on factory attitudes towards older workers. For instance, there may be a feeling that in times of recession older workers should take early retirement to make room for those with family responsibilities. Where there is payment by results, people who deviate a lot from the average may be subject to peer group pressure. This applies especially to those who want to work harder, since their output may be used by the employer when it comes to fixing the rate. Again we may be in a position where it is average rather than individual preferences which are important when assessing reaction to taxes and benefits.

Formal and Informal (Shadow) Economy

The household production model saw people as working in either the unpaid household economy or the market economy. Within the latter we may also distinguish the formal from the informal or shadow economy. It is frequently alleged that taxation causes people to switch their activity out of the formal economy, governed by employment regulations and subject to income tax and social-security contributions. Where the activity involves a service to households, the informal sector also evades value-added tax. If the rate of valued-added tax is v, and the income tax rate t, then this means that, rather than having to earn £$(1 + v)/(1 - t)$ in order to purchase £1 of services, the customer only has to earn £1. The cost via the informal sector is the same as that if the person carried out the service themselves, but with an income tax rate of 40% and a value-added tax of 20%, the cost via the formal sector is double. This gap between the cost to the purchaser and the net receipt by the supplier is often referred to as the 'tax wedge'.

The considerations which influence the decision whether or not to operate in the informal sector have been extensively discussed in the literature on tax evasion (see Cowell 1990 for a survey). There is a risk of being caught, which has to be set in the balance with the higher expected cash income. As far as the income tax is concerned, the effect depends on the way in which penalties are calculated. It is conceivable that an increase in the tax rate increases the risk and hence reduces the extent of evasion (as well as a possible income effect in reducing the willingness to take risks).

In the case of social-security contributions, a further factor enters the picture. Contributions are not a pure tax but also provide entitlement to subsequent benefits. The cost of working in the informal economy may be the loss of rights to unemployment or sickness insurance benefits and, in the longer term, to a retirement pension. While in some cases social assistance may provide for those who do not satisfy the contribution conditions for social insurance, the benefits may be at a lower level and may be subject to a test of means. Social insurance may therefore be a powerful mechanism for encouraging participation in the formal economy.

Non-linearity of the Tax and Benefit Schedule

One area where considerable progress has been made in the past two decades has been in the treatment of tax and benefit schedules. Earlier reference was made to the implications of non-linearities and non-convexities in the budget constraint, and these arise particularly on account of the fact that the marginal tax rates vary with income.

The typical graduated income-tax schedule involves a series of brackets where the marginal rate of tax is higher in successive brackets. This generates a budget constraint like ABCDE drawn in Fig. 2.7. As a

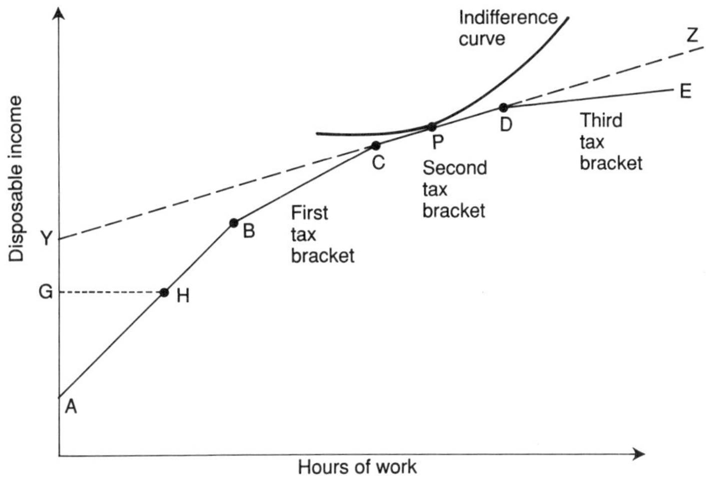

FIG 2.7. Non-Linear Budget Constraints

consequence, the marginal return to working depends on the number of hours worked. It is possible to carry out the same analysis as before. For example, the point P chosen in Fig. 2.7 may be seen as the choice made by a person faced with the linear budget constraint YZ (marked with a dashed line): i.e. with a marginal tax rate corresponding to that bracket and with a 'virtual' lump-sum income Y in place of A. The difficulty is that this virtual income, and the marginal tax rate, depend on the choice made by the individual. They cannot be treated as parametric to the problem. A person with a taste for hard work will be observed to have high earnings and a high marginal tax rate. He or she will be found on segment DE, but we cannot draw any direct inferences from a comparison with a person who enjoys fishing and is found on segment BC with a low marginal tax rate.

The typical income-tax schedule generates a non-linear but *convex* budget constraint. The payment of income-tested benefits, on the other hand, may lead to non-convexities. The withdrawal of benefits as earnings rise mean that marginal tax rates may be higher at low earnings than further up the scale. This is exhibited in Fig. 2.7 in the extreme form of a minimum-income guarantee. The dotted line GH shows that a person is guaranteed this minimum income, and that over this range all earnings are implicitly taxed at a rate of 100%. There is then the possibility of discontinuities in the labour-supply function, in that we would not expect to observe people choosing points in the interval GH (or, indeed, on HB close to H). In these situations, the labour-supply decision has to compare different discrete points, and any empirical model has to allow for this complexity of the individual budget constraint.

2.5. SOURCES OF EVIDENCE ABOUT WORK INCENTIVES

To an outsider, the simplest approach to the empirical investigation of labour supply may appear to be to ask the subjects themselves. However, this kind of evidence is regarded with considerable suspicion by economists: As it has been put by McCloskey:

> One can get an audience of economists to laugh out loud by proposing ironically to send out a questionnaire on some disputed point. Economists are so impressed by the confusions that might possibly result from questionnaires that they have turned away from them entirely, and prefer the confusions resulting from external observation. . . . But self-testimony is not useless. (McCloskey 1986: 514)

In the first part of this section, we consider some of the ways in which hypothetical questions can indeed be useful in casting light on how people perceive their own motives. Here, as elsewhere in the section, illustrative examples are drawn from different countries, particularly but not exclusively the USA. From there, we go on to studies based on observed behaviour, considering both artificial experiments and natural experiments generated by variation across time, states, or in cross-sections.

Hypothetical questions

This approach involves a kind of market research, insofar as people are asked about their decisions about labour supply, how they make them, and—the distinctive feature of this approach—how their decisions would be altered if the tax rates were different. In practice, the studies have been conducted with considerably more care than most market research.

A good—if dated—example is provided by the study made by Holland (1969), who interviewed intensively 125 business executives in the United States in 1965–6. In the majority of these interviews, he discussed the response of the executive to the replacement of the income tax by a hypothetical lump-sum tax. The findings showed that 15% would put in more effort on their primary job and that 26% would devote more effort to 'little ventures and consulting'. Against this, 24% would bring forward retirement. On the other hand, the most striking feature was the high percentage reporting 'no effect': for example 80% reported this with respect to effort on their primary job.

In the same way, the study by Brown and Levin (1974) of weekly-paid workers in the United Kingdom found that 74% reported that taxation had no effect on their decision whether to work overtime. The large proportion recording no effect may be attributable to these people having no option to work more. Brown and Levin did a second calculation, omitting those who appeared to be constrained. They also omitted those whose answers were felt to be implausible for one reason or another: for example, those who said that taxation had caused them to work more overtime but who had also said that they had chosen their present job because it had no overtime. The number reporting no effect was still as high as 69%.

In order for this evidence to be informative, there are several prerequisites. First, the respondents have to understand the question. Taxation is a complex area which most people find highly confusing. Clarity is particularly difficult to achieve if one is seeking to separate the income and substitution effects. Secondly, people have to be able to assess their own motives and articulate their response. Reactions to taxation may be instinctive, rather than calculated—an issue which was widely debated in the case of firms in the literature on 'full-cost' pricing and whether businessmen maximize profits. Thirdly, the respondents, even if they know the answer, will not necessarily tell the truth. The respondent may condition his answer by 'what he believes the questioner expects him to answer, by what he considers it will be in his own best interests that the questioner should be led to believe' (Williams 1966).

For all these reasons, the hypothetical questionnaire method has to be applied with care; and we are going to need other sources as well, particularly in order to *quantify* the increase or decrease in labour supply. At the same time, it should not be dismissed out of hand, since all other sources of evidence are subject to major limitations.

Experimental Evidence

The remaining sources of evidence treat the subjects essentially as dumb animals, from whom we can learn by observing their actual behaviour, but no recourse is had to any *explanation*.

The natural-science parallel suggests that the obvious way to generate such evidence is by means of an experiment where people are confronted with different economic environments. There has been considerable recent interest in experimental economics, but most of this research has involved 'artificial' experiments, in the sense that the decision-making of subjects is limited to the laboratory and not part of their everyday life. Rather different are the experiments which have presented participants with a changed tax and benefit schedule and observed how they varied their real-world labour-supply and other decisions. Nearly all these experiments have been in the United States, where the interest in proposals for a negative income tax (NIT) led the government to finance several large-scale experiments. Under a NIT those people whose income is below the tax threshold would receive a supplement to their income related to the extent of the short fall, being reduced to 0 as income reaches the tax treshold. This means that those with the low income would be receiving NIT supplement rather than paying income tax.

In contrast to the effects of income taxation in general, in the case of a negative income tax, the *direction* of the effect can be predicted: both income and the substitution effects operate in the direction of reduced labour supply. The question is, however, by how much? One major reason why the idea of experimentation was supported by the Office of Economic Opportunity is that they hoped to measure the strength of the disincentive effect. How much would the NIT reduce labour supply? They wanted also to show that a NIT could be made to work: it was a 'demonstration project'. Probably the best-known experiment is that in New Jersey (see e.g. Pechman and Timpane 1975), carried out in 1968–72, on which attention is concentrated here. In addition, there were experiments in Gary, Indiana, Denver, Colorado, Seattle, and the Rural Income Maintenance Experiment, as well as one in Canada in Manitoba.

The New Jersey experiment took 1,374 families, of whom 650 were controls, that is, families who were studied in the same way but for whom the tax parameters were not changed. The experimental families were assigned to one of eight different negative income tax plans, with guaranteed incomes ranging from 50% to 125% of the poverty line and marginal tax rates at which the benefits were withdrawn ranging from 30% to 70%. The New Jersey experiment collected a large volume of data, and the full findings cannot be presented here. In order to see the broad type of result, and the problems which arise in its interpretation, we simply show in Table 2.1 the average weekly hours of work for white families for the control and the experimental group (averaged over all the plans).

TABLE 2.1. Results of New Jersey Negative Income Tax Experiment

	Weekly hours of husbands (wives)	
	Control	Experimental
Before experiment	34.8 (2.7)	34.1 (3.8)
During experiment	34.4 (4.5)	31.8 (3.9)

Source: Hall (1975: 122).

There are several ways of estimating the effect of the NIT. The most obvious thing to do is to compare the situation for the experimental group before and after the change. This suggests that there was a reduction of

2.3 hours as a result of the NIT, which would be a modest reduction (less than 10%). On the other hand, the changes may have been due to other changes at the same time. The economic environment was not held constant, and we have to take account of the business cycle and other influences. What is more, it is possible that the very act of studying people may have led them to modify their behaviour. The implicit assumption in the calculation described above is that the behaviour of the experimental group would have been unchanged if it were not for the NIT.

This is a good reason for employing the controls. They are also being studied, and they are subject to the same changes in the economic climate. A second estimate of the experimental effect is, therefore, to ignore the pre-experiment evidence and take simply the difference between the hours of the controls and those of the experimental group. This gives in fact a similar figure—a reduction of 2.6 hours. On the other hand, this method is based on the assumption that the control group is exactly matched; it assumes that there are no other sources of difference. Since the groups were chosen randomly, they should in theory have the same composition: for example, family size, or age, or other variables likely to affect hours of work. But in practice they may turn out to be different, particularly with relatively small sample numbers, and some evidence for suspecting that this is the case is provided by the fact that before the experiment the control group worked on average 0.7 hours more a week.

It would therefore be better to avoid the risk that they may not be exactly matched and take a third estimate, which is the *difference* in the change of hours. Given that the experimental group worked 0.7 hours less before the experiment, this means subtracting this amount from the 2.6 difference found during the experiment, giving an effect of a 1.9 hour reduction. Or, put the other way, the experiment group showed a decline which was 1.9 hours greater than the decline for the control group.

This was indeed the broad conclusion from the experiments: there was a noticeable but not massive reduction in work effort. At the same time, the effects for the wives were rather different. The results for the wives of the white males included in the New Jersey experiment are shown in Table 2.1 in brackets. Here there is clear evidence that there was an upward trend over time in the hours worked by the control group; and a simple 'before' and 'after' comparison for the experimental group would be misleading. The estimate of the NIT effect based on the difference in the change is $(3.9-3.8)-(4.5-2.7)=-1.7$ hours. These numbers are similar in absolute magnitude to those for men, but as a proportionate change it is evidently quite important.

Our concern here is less with the substantive findings, interesting though these are, than with the experimental approach. What are we to make of this evidence? It clearly represents a major addition to our knowledge, but we have to bear in mind that there are certain respects in which an experiment of this kind cannot capture the full effect of a NIT if it were actually introduced.

The first is that an experiment is of limited duration and known to be such by the participants. They may therefore react to it in a different manner than if it were expected to be permanent. Some of the adjustments in which we are interested involve quite major changes in life-style, like seeking a new job, or retiring, or moving to a different part of the country. On this basis, we should expect the effect recorded in the experiment to be less than if there were a permanent NIT. On the other hand, an experiment may be seen as a 'limited-period offer', in which leisure is temporarily subsidized; and people may take advantage of this offer, as is supposed in models of intertemporal substitution of labour. This would lead the effect to be greater than if the NIT were permanent.

The second problem is that the experiment only applies to a sample of people. This means that the collective responses described in the previous section may not show up in the experiment. Where the effect operates via changes in the standard working week, then this may require trade union negotiators to take it on board; and they are unlikely to be influenced by the fact that a small percentage of their members are in an experiment—which in any case is temporary. This adds further force to the suggestion that the experiment may *understate* the effect.

While the NIT experiments have added greatly to understanding of labour supply in the USA, therefore, their findings do have to be qualified. And there is no necessary reason to expect the results to apply equally in a European context.

Natural 'Experiment' I: Variation over Time and States

The limited scope for carrying out experiments like those with the NIT means that we have mainly to rely on 'natural experiments' generated for us in the real world, such as those that arise when governments decide to change tax rates or benefit schemes, or when different governments set different tax rates. Such 'natural' experiments may have certain advantages: for example, they tend to affect the population as a whole, so that we avoid the second problem with the NIT experiments described above. There is, however, a basic question as to the extent to which natural experiments are indeed 'experiments'. This arises with all four of the different types summarized here.

The evidence cited in early discussions of labour supply was typically observation at different dates of aggregate labour supply: for example, average hours of the whole labour force. This *time-series* evidence may show the effect of changes over time in tax rates. In broad terms, over time, taxes have risen and average hours of work have fallen. This information may be plotted as a labour-supply curve. Suppose that we plot (see Fig. 2.8) the average hours against the average net-of-tax wage rate, expressed in real terms, and denoted by $w(1-t)$, where t is the tax rate and w the gross wage rate. Typically, taken over a long run of years, this suggests that the labour-supply curve is backward-bending (the income effect is larger than the substitution effect), since hours have fallen as real wage rates have risen (the rise in t is less than the rise in w). If a fall in $(1-t)$, via increased taxation, has the same effect as a fall in w, which is the maintained hypothesis of the theoretical model, then such a set of time-series observations would imply that taxes have encouraged labour supply.

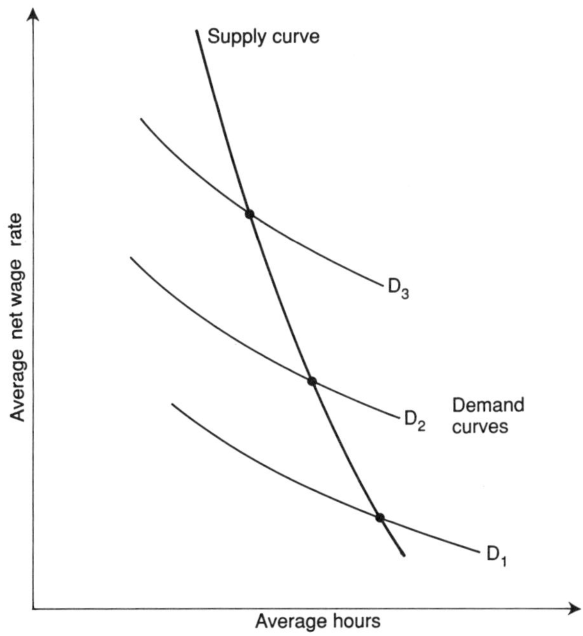

FIG 2.8. Aggregate Labour Market, with Shifting Demand Curve

However, we have to consider just what experiment this could be said to represent. How can these observations be interpreted? The first key assumption is that the points observed lie on the supply curve, an assumption which may be far from plausible in periods of high unemployment, when it may be more reasonable to regard workers as rationed on the labour market. This means that we should confine attention to years in which the labour market may reasonably be supposed close to equilibrium. The second key assumption is that the labour-supply curve is stable over time. All the observed points are assumed to belong to a single supply curve, as is shown in Fig. 2.8. Implicitly it is being assumed that the points are being generated by shifts in the demand curve (from D_1 to D_2, etc.); and it is by this assumption that we identify the supply curve.

There are, however, typically good reasons to imagine that the supply curve has shifted over time. Unless we can account adequately for these shifts, then we cannot be said to be observing a natural experiment and there is need for caution in interpreting such time-series evidence. It is quite possible that at any point the supply curve slopes upward, and that we are simply observing points on the demand curve.

The problem with time-series evidence is that we are not holding other things equal. The same applies to a second type of aggregate data, which relate to differences across countries or across states within a country. We may observe that low-tax countries tend to work longer hours than high-tax countries, but there is no reason to suppose that the points lie on the same supply curve. There are country-specific features which have to be taken into account.

This problem may be less serious if we consider cross-state or other variation across local-government districts in the same country. People living in Massachusetts may have the same labour-supply curve as those living in New York State. But the variation in tax rates may also be relatively small, and if they are large then there may be a problem that people migrate in response to the fiscal differences, so that they are not the same people.

Natural 'Experiment' II: Cross-Section Data

Suppose instead that we look at the behaviour of individuals who are living in the same country and at the same time. Such *cross-section* data have been widely employed in recent econometric studies of labour supply, and are usually derived from sample surveys of families, where information is recorded on the labour supply, wages, social-security benefits, and other variables.

Cross-section data can be used, on the one hand, to measure a number of dimensions of labour-supply, such as hours, participation, early retirement, and, on the other, to calculate the budget constraint which the family faces. The latter poses a number of problems, to the solution of which considerable ingenuity has been devoted. A major example is the fact that we do not observe the potential wage of non-participants (or the potential social-security benefit out of work of participants). In seeking to estimate, for example, the potential retirement pension of those currently still at work from the observed pensions of those who are retired, we have to allow for the fact that both groups are selected samples. It is possible, for example, that those retiring at 55 will appear identical, as far as the survey information is concerned, with those continuing to work but will in fact be covered by a more generous pension plan.

From such data, it may be possible to estimate the relation between labour supply and the parameters of the budget constraint. The probability of early retirement may be related to the level of pension or other benefits. Hours of work may be related to the parameters of the tax system, an approach which in the United States has led to the general conclusion that the labour supply of men of normal working age is not very responsive. Stiglitz summarizes the US evidence as showing that 'male labour supply is relatively unresponsive' (1988: 470). He quotes the estimate of Hausman (1981) that the effect of the US federal income tax in 1988 was to reduce the labour supply of the average married man in the US by some 6.5%. On the other hand, the response of married women was estimated to be larger, Stiglitz quoting a reduction due to the US income tax of 25%. It should be noted that these refer to the total effect on labour supply; Hausman estimated a relatively large substitution effect (being offset by the income effect), with consequently large estimates of the distortion of decisions, although there is less consensus about this finding.

There are, however, difficulties in drawing conclusions from cross-section studies. First of all, there is the same question as with time-series evidence—are we observing the choices made by people, or the constraints with which they are faced? Some evidence is provided by those studies which ask about the options open to individual workers. In the USA, the Michigan Panel Study of Income Dynamics asked whether there was more work available, so that the respondent could have worked more if he had wanted to, and, if not, whether he had wanted to work more. The proportion answering yes, indicating that they were constrained, ranged from 13% to 20% over the period 1967–74 (Ham 1982: table I). Respondents to the Swedish survey of Household Market and Non-market Activities asked whether the employer would allow the respondent to work more or fewer hours, and whether the respondent would like to do so. The results for 1984 are summarized in Table 2.2. They indicate that adjustments in hours on the primary job were not possible for about two-thirds of respondents, and that about 10% would like to have varied their hours.

The second question regarding cross-section evidence is precisely what experiment is being performed. The experiment is not in the tax system, since everyone faces the same tax and benefit system. Leaving aside random factors in administration, people receive different benefits and face different tax rates on account of some difference in their circumstances. The difficulty is that these differences in their circumstances cannot always be controlled. A person has a higher entitlement to a pension on account of his or her past employment record, and this career difference may in turn be related to unobserved personal characteristics which affect the retirement decision. A person paying a higher marginal income tax rate has by definition a higher taxable income, and the source of this higher income may be related to unobserved characteristics: for example, a workaholic may have accumulated more savings since he did not have time to spend his income.

The problems of controlling may be reduced by focusing on subsamples of the population. The US estimates of Hausman (1981), referred to above, exclude the self-employed, people aged under 25 or over 55, farmers, single women without children, and the disabled. These exclusions reduce the degree of heterogeneity, but by the same token mean that the results cannot be extrapolated to the whole population. The reactions of the self-employed, for instance, are likely to be rather different from that of employees. Both need to be taken into account when considering the overall impact of changes in taxation.

Another solution may be to combine cross-section and time-series in a *pooled cross-section*, or, where the same people are studied in several years, in *panel* (longitudinal) data. Suppose that we observe a sample before and after a tax increase. Will this not give us a measure of the impact of the tax rise, by examining for each person the difference in his or her hours of work? In this way, one is holding constant the other characteristics which may affect the labour supply. Workaholics will work more than others both before and after. However, while this deals with fixed characteristics, it is still open to the problem that there may be other changes at the same time. Suppose that taxes are raised as part of a national emergency, and that the government exhorts people to work harder—as during the war. There may be a shift in the labour-supply curve, so that people work more hours at any given wage rate, which more than offsets the movement down the labour-supply curve. There is the same problem as discussed in relation to experimental evidence, which was why we needed to have a control group. However, in this case we do not have a control group.

2.6. CONCLUSIONS

The purpose of this chapter has been to introduce the theoretical analysis of labour-supply decisions. It has drawn attention to the many dimensions

TABLE 2.2. Work Options and Preferences in Swedish Household Market and Non-market Activities Survey, 1984

	%		
	Yes	No	Uncertain
Would your employer permit you, on a permanent basis, to work *more* hours for pay at your primary job if you wanted to do so?	32	61	7
If you were able to do so, would you like to work more hours at the same hourly wage in order to earn more money?	11	88	1
Would your employer permit you, on a permanent basis, to work *fewer* hours per week at your primary job if you wanted to do so?	24	69	7
Would you like to work fewer hours at the same hourly wage, even if that would mean earning less overall?	12	85	3

Note: weighted sample numbers.
Source: N. A. Klevmarken (1990), 79–81.

of labour supply and the importance of institutional features of the labour market. From this it should be clear that—even before we encounter the details of the tax and transfer systems of different countries—the relationship between policy and incentives is one of some complexity. It is not possible to make simple statements as to what may be predicted on theoretical grounds.

One aim of the theoretical analysis is to provide a framework within which the empirical evidence may be interpreted. The last section described some of the main forms of empirical evidence and identified their strengths and weaknesses. This preview may have been discouraging in that, as pointed out by C.V. Brown, 'there are *no* studies of labour supply that are not open to serious objection on at least one important ground' (1983: 167). But the objections are not always the same, and to the extent that different studies reveal a consistent picture we may be able to draw some conclusions. As it has been put by Feldstein (1982: 830), we can learn from

> the children's fable about the five blind men who examined an elephant. The important lesson in that story is not the fact that each blind man came away with a partial and 'incorrect' piece of evidence. The lesson is rather that an intelligent maharajah who studied the findings of these five men could probably piece together a good judgemental picture of an elephant.

3

Taxes and Transfers in Sweden: Incentive Effects on Labour Supply

BJÖRN GUSTAFSSON AND N. ANDERS KLEVMARKEN

3.1. INTRODUCTION

The Public Debate

During the 1960s and 1970s the Swedish public sector grew rapidly. The growth rate was higher than the average in the OECD countries, and Sweden now has one of the largest public sectors in the Western world. As a result, it is also well known for its high taxes. In the post-war period Swedish welfare policy has been general in character and also based on the principle of giving compensation for income losses rather than just a minimum amount. There are means-tested programmes but they have not been dominant.

The size of the public sector and the high Swedish tax pressure have generated a debate about disincentives and distortions. In the 1980s, reforming the income tax system was of great political concern. In the debate preceding political decision-making, economists played a role. Matthiesen (1973) introduced the concept of 'marginal effect' or composite marginal tax rate when he showed the interplay between income taxes and housing benefits, and demonstrated how inflation increased the taxes because the tax scales were defined in nominal terms. Much public attention was given to Myrdal (1978), when he in his dramatic way claimed that the income tax system had turned Swedes into a population of cheaters. He pointed out that much ingenuity was used to find deductions and loopholes, which made the effective progressivity of the income tax system smaller than suggested by the tax scales.

The tax (and transfer) system was criticized for giving disincentives to work or incentives to work in the wrong activities. According to Stuart (1981), Sweden at the end of the 1970s was on the downward-sloping part of the 'Laffer Curve'. Hansson (1984) found that the marginal cost of public funds spent on transfer payments depended very much on revenue source. The cost of raising funds by progressive taxation was reported to be very high. In line with these ideas, a major tax reform was implemented in 1991.

Under the pressure of increasing (future) costs for the public pay-as-you-go pension system, and for the work injury and general sickness insurances, reforms of these transfer systems have also been debated. As in many other countries, changes in coverage and compensation rates have been suggested. A few decisions have recently been taken, and more are expected in the next few years.

Another major issue is a concern about efficiency in the production of public services, the most important being health care, child care, schooling, and services to the elderly. The Swedish public sector has three levels. At the central level most transfers are paid, but relatively few services are produced. The regional level is mainly responsible for health services. About 300 municipalities make up the local level, producing services such as child care, primary and secondary education, and social services. It has been argued that the social-engineering policy which has favoured production of services within the public sector leaves little room for competition, and thus insufficient incentives for a public producer to be efficient.

These and additional arguments converge towards the general claim that the welfare state slows down economic growth. Defenders of the current welfare state have emphasized the policy goals to reduce inequality both across the life-cycle and between households, and to reduce uncertainty about the future in the prospect of unemployment, sickness, work injury, etc. The *general* welfare system has also been defended on the ground that a system which covers a major share of or the entire population will receive much stronger support than a system which only covers a small share, i.e. 'the poor'.

A major issue of controversy is whether there are any effects on economic growth at all (see W. Korpi 1992). In evaluating the incentive effects of transfers and income taxes, one might be more likely to find major effects in an economy when there is a large public involvement than in one with a small public sector. Sweden should for this reason be an interesting case, in particular in comparison to other countries.

Cross-country studies in which growth rates have been related to the size of the public sector have not been able to show any correlation. For example, Olson (1990) compared government expenditures and GDP growth in 1951–87 for 17 OECD countries, and found no clear association. The same conclusion emerged when he analysed a much broader set of 121 countries for the period 1960–85. However, as discussed in Chapter 1, a simple bivariate analysis obviously does not say very much about the existence or nonexistence of disincentive effects and distortion from the welfare state.

The public sector has been increased with the good intention of increasing the health and welfare of the people. To the extent this has been successful, one could argue that the result should have been an increased ability to work and a positive contribution to growth. Publicly provided health care, child care, and education are obvious examples. Another is the active Swedish labour market policy, which has promoted structural changes. There are thus reasons to expect positive as well as negative incentives from the public sector.

The current debate about negative incentives can be seen in the light of the increasing external pressure on the Swedish economy at the end of the 1980s and a perceived slowdown in productivity increase during the 1980s. The issue is thus not whether the welfare state decreases economic growth but whether we have gone too far in providing welfare services to the people through the public sector. Although some would advocate a dismantling of the welfare system with its public involvement, such a policy would probably gain little support from the Swedish people.

The question asked in the popular debate about whether the welfare state slows down growth is thus not sharp and specific enough to become the subject of scientific inquiry. One has to look more closely into the detailed structure of the tax system and various benefit programmes in order to analyse the corresponding behavioural effects. Although this approach is probably the only feasible one, one could easily get lost in all the details and find it difficult to draw any general conclusions. In particular, it might become difficult to evaluate the importance of feedback effects through the macroeconomic system. In this chapter we will nevertheless follow this approach, first describing the Swedish tax and transfer systems and their evolution in the past few decades and then discussing the evidence we have found concerning their effects on labour supply. Our analysis is thus limited to the incentive effects of taxes and transfers on labour supply, while the broader issue of how these systems, through other channels and through public involvement in general, affect economic performance is not discussed further. A brief description of the macroeconomic context and a few trends in the labour market might, however, serve as a useful background.

The Macroeconomic Context

Until recently, unemployment rates were lower in Sweden than in most other OECD countries, while inflation was relatively high. The low unemployment figures must primarily be seen as the result of a policy priority given to low unemployment over low inflation, and partly achieved by Swedish labour market policy. Pushed by strong labour unions, it has a heavy emphasis on active measures. Expenditures for compensating the unemployed have traditionally been small relative to the expenditures for the active labour market policy.

Sweden, being a small, open economy, was like other countries exposed to oil price shocks in the early 1970s and at the beginning of the

1980s. The policy response during the 1970s was to keep unemployment down. As economic recovery came more slowly than expected by most policy-makers, a large and fast-growing public budget deficit changed the policy agenda at the end of the 1970s. In 1982 the Swedish krona was devalued and the economy recovered thereafter. The 1980s was a period of high economic activity, which came to an end because the international economy weakened but also as a result of internal problems such as a severe financial crisis.

The macroeconomic situation at the beginning of the 1990s parallels the one experienced at the end of the 1970s and beginning of the 1980s when it comes to public-sector deficit and changes in the exchange rate. Once again the public deficit is rising fast, and the value of the Swedish krona decreased by about 20% in autumn 1992. However, there are also differences compared to the earlier situation. Recently Sweden has applied for membership of the European Community, and many policy measures must be understood in this context. Macroeconomic priorities have changed drastically. Now the most important goal is to keep the inflation rate from becoming higher than that for the EC. This has been achieved, but at a cost of rising unemployment. At the time of writing, unemployment in Sweden is higher than ever experienced before by the present active generation.

Trends in Labour Force Participation and Hours Worked

As in other OECD countries, the Swedish population is ageing. The expected life-span of a female is 80.2 years and for a male 74.4 years. The average family size is small, only about two persons. The role of the family has decreased. It is common for people to live together without being formally married. The frequency of separations have increased, and many children will grow up in a family which does not include both biological parents. Over the decades several immigration waves have reached Sweden, and nowadays about 10% of the population is foreign-born. Immigration policy and the conditions under which immigrants live in Sweden have emerged as a much debated issue.

The labour force participation rate for females have risen in many developed countries but particularly so in Sweden. Fig. 3.1 shows an increase in participation rates from about 60% in 1970 to more than 80% at the end of the 1980s. Among the explanations, in addition to an increase in the average level of female schooling and an increased demand for female labour from the public sector, are public policies aiming at a greater gender equality. For instance, joint-income taxation was changed to separate taxation, and the supply of public child care at heavily subsidized prices has increased rapidly.

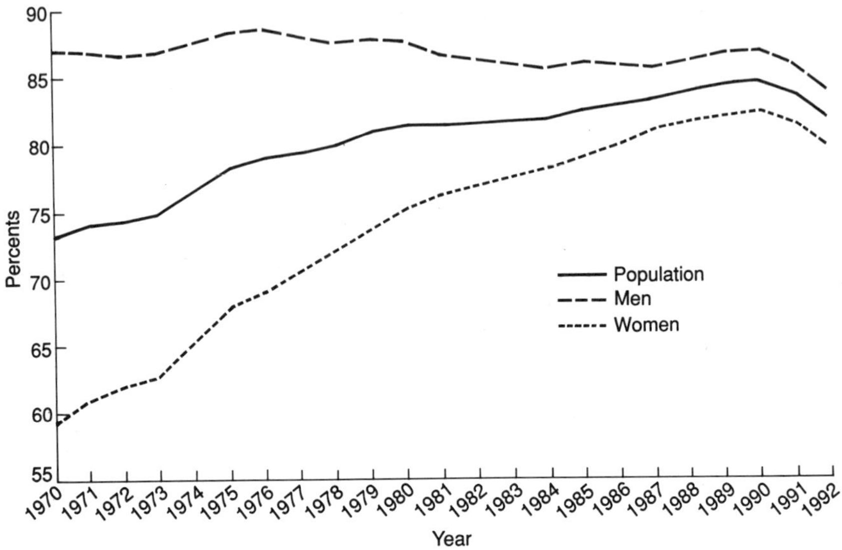

FIG 3.1. Labour Force Participation Rates, 1970–1992, by Gender
Source: Labour Force Surveys, Statistics Sweden.

During the 1970s and 1980s the participation rates for males declined somewhat, making the gender gap in participation rates relatively small. In the first few years of the 1990s the labour force participation rate for both genders have declined. Although the participation rates are similar, the work behaviour of males and females are quite different. Females on average work fewer hours than males, as part-time employment is common among Swedish women. Women in the labour force more than men stay at home from work to care for children or because children are sick. A time-use study (Flood and Klevmarken 1990) compared female market work in Sweden with that in a few other countries, and found that Swedish women did *not* on average work more hours in the market than, for instance, women in the United States. The explanation is that women in the US labour force more frequently work full-time and have fewer opportunities to be absent from work. Females are frequently found in other occupations and in other sectors of the labour market than men. For example, a disproportionately large proportion of Swedish women are employed in the public sector. On average, Swedish wives thus contribute considerably less to family income than their husbands. But their contribution is nevertheless much larger than in many other countries. For instance, according to the tables for the 1980s in Chapter 6,

Swedish wives contributed about one-third of family income (after tax), while this proportion was only just above 10% in Germany.

Many of the changes we have observed in the participation rates have taken place in the age ranges when people normally enter or leave the labour force. This can be seen in Figs. 3.2 and 3.3, showing data for males and females respectively. In the age bracket 16–19 there is a trend toward decreased participation for both sexes. This is probably caused by larger proportions of the new cohorts entering secondary education. However, the same is not true for higher education. Labour force participation among females aged 20–4 increased in the 1970s. At the end of the period there is for both sexes a profound decrease in participation rates for the two youngest groups. The likely explanation is that labour market programmes targeted at young persons have brought them out of the labour market.

The participation rates for the two oldest age classes have developed quite differently for males and females. Among males there are decreases. For those 60–4 years old, the participation rate decreased from 80% in 1970 to about 60% at the end of the period. Among females participation rates trended upwards, which might be interpreted as a cohort effect.

Finally, we look at average hours of work for persons at work. Fig. 3.4 shows that the difference between males and females is fairly stable. Generally, average hours of work decreased in the 1970s but increased again during the 1980s. Thus there is no large difference in average hours of work between the beginning of the 1990s and the beginning of the 1970s. The stylized time-series facts for Sweden are thus that increased transfers and taxes have co-occurred with somewhat decreasing participation rates for males, strongly increasing participation rates for females, and, seen over the entire period of the 1970s and 1980s, approximately constant hours of work.

Correlation does not mean causality, however; and we shall look into the topic in more detail. In the next section we describe the tax system. Section 3.3 is a survey of primarily Swedish research on tax incentives and labour supply. The Swedish transfer system and research on its behavioural effects are discussed in Section 3.4. The chapter ends with a short conclusion.

3.2. THE SWEDISH TAX SYSTEM, 1950–1991

Introduction to the Swedish Tax System

The Swedish system for personal income taxation has undergone several major changes since 1950. Some of these changes have simplified the

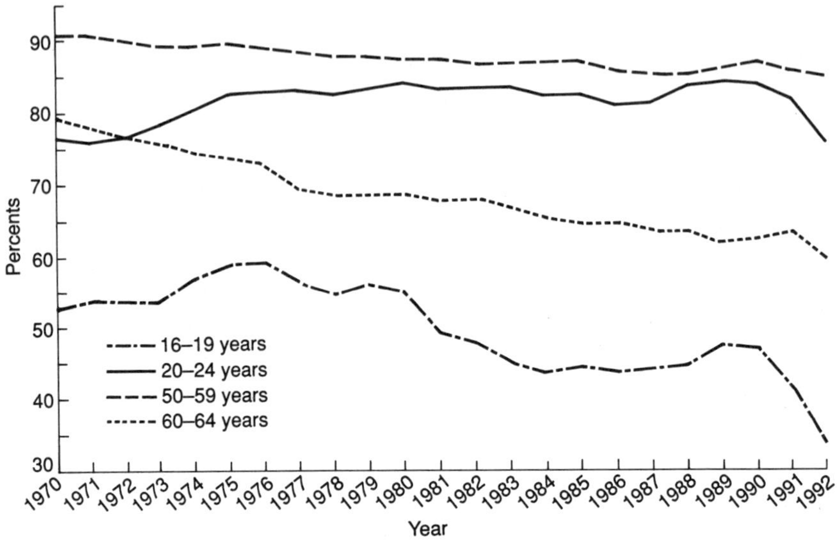

FIG 3.2. Labour Force Participation Rates for Selected Age Groups, Males, 1970–1992
Source: Labour Force Surveys, Statistics Sweden.

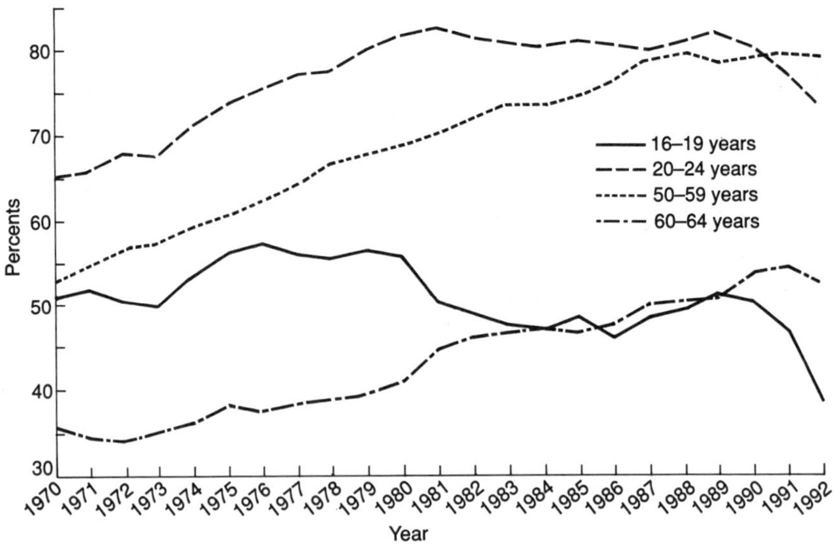

FIG 3.3. Labour Force Participation Rates for Selected Age Groups, Females, 1970–1992
Source: Labour Force Surveys, Statistics Sweden.

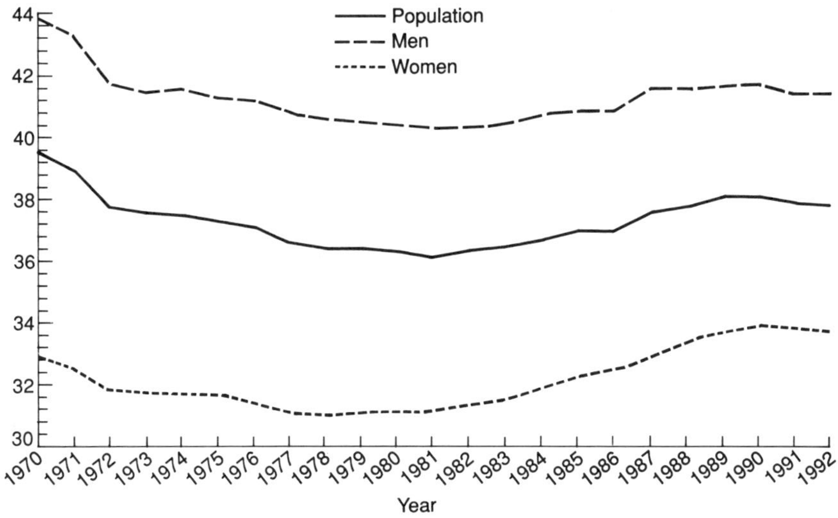

FIG 3.4. Average Weekly Working Hours for Employed Persons
Source: Labour Force Surveys, Statistics Sweden.

system, for instance the replacement of regional deductions (*ortsavdrag*) by a general basic deduction (*grundavdrag*) and the introduction of separate taxation rather than joint taxation of spouses. The procedure of filing an annual income declaration has also become much simplified for many taxpayers, because the burden of supplying income data to the tax authorities has been shifted from the individual taxpayer to the employers and the banks.

However, as the average tax burden increased (see Fig. 3.5), the need to eliminate legal but unintended (and illegal) means of tax evasion also increased. This was a gradual and piecemeal procedure, creating new loopholes which made new additions to the tax laws necessary, etc. This process resulted in an income tax system characterized by high tax rates, a rich variety of detailed rules, each applying to one or more categories of taxpayers, and an unequal treatment of various types of income. Jakobsson and Normann (1974) made an attempt to find homogeneous groups of taxpayers for which the same deduction rules and tax and fee schedules would apply. (For 1965 they found that they would have to work with more than 135 groups of taxpayers.) For instance, income from capital was favoured relative to income from employment, and non-cash benefits were favoured relative to cash wages and salaries. The system meant that tax planning and tax evasion become profitable compared to

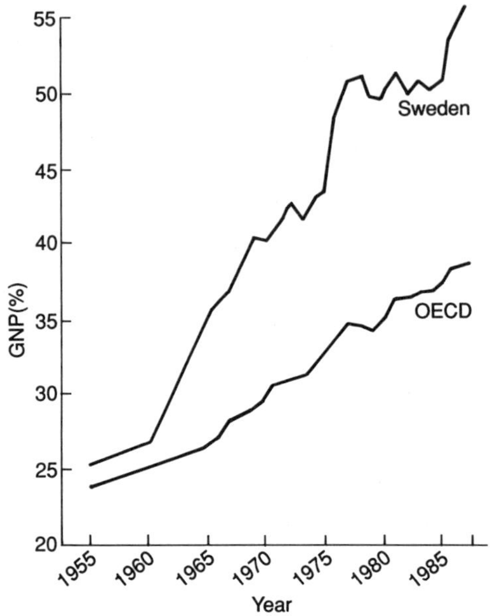

FIG 3.5. Total Taxes as Percentage of Swedish GNP, 1955–1987
Source: OECD revenue statistics 1965–87, quoted by Nordling (1991: 121).

productive work. Although the tax schedules were strongly progressive, the distributional effect of the entire income tax system became to some extent arbitrary and much less effective than politicians had intended, because certain high-income groups were able to take advantage of the system and decrease their tax base. The unequal taxation of various types of income also resulted in macroeconomic distortions. These circumstances resulted in the 1990/1 tax reform, which broadened the bases for taxation, lowered both the average and marginal income tax rates, and gave a more uniform treatment of incomes from various sources.

In the following section a brief review of the 1950–91 income tax systems is attempted. It starts with the introduction of a few necessary concepts, followed by a scheme for calculating the tax for an individual in 1989 given certain tax bases. 1989 is chosen as the starting-point rather than 1950 because in 1989 there was no joint taxation of incomes and the scheme was, for this and other reasons, less complicated than that of 1950. 1990 and 1991 are the first two years of the new tax system, which differs so much from the old one that it deserves a separate discussion at the end of this review.

We not only include the personal income taxes in this review, but also briefly mention the wealth tax and the property tax. The latter is a fairly recent addition to the Swedish tax system.

The Pre–1990 Personal Income, Wealth, and Property Taxes

The income tax system can be described as a number of tax rates which are applied to (and also are functions of) a base. Both the tax rates and the base might depend on the type of taxpayer. In calculating a base, certain incomes are added and deductions are made. These deductions are also often obtained by applying a rate or an amount to a base. Frequently, floors and ceilings apply to the base or to the deduction itself. These deductions are called income deductions. There are also tax deductions, i.e. the calculated tax is reduced.

In the pre–1990 tax system there were several income sources: income from employment, business income, income of capital, capital gains and losses. The sum of the following incomes,

income from employment
income from capital
imputed rent on owner-occupied home and secondary home
incomes from other real estate than farms
capital gains (losses)
income from farming, etc.
income from business

was called *total income* (*sammanräknad inkomst*). From this sum one deducted deficits and losses accrued in any of these sources of income. The resulting balance was *total net income* (*sammanräknad nettoinkomst*). From total net income were deducted 'other general deductions' (*övriga allmanna avdräg*), primarily life-insurance premiums and costs of maintenance for dependants who did not belong to the taxpayer's household, and retained business losses not previously deducted. The result was the *tax-assessed income* (*taxerad inkomst*). For incomes earned before 1987 there were separate tax-assessed incomes calculated for national and local taxation respectively. In order to obtain the base for the national and, after 1986 (in almost all cases), the local tax, the tax-assessed income was reduced by

a basic deduction (*grundavdrag*)
an extra deduction for those who had a general old-age pension (*extra avdrag för folkpensionärer*)
an extra deduction because of illness or poor health (*extra avdrag p. g. a. sjukdom*, etc).

The result was *taxable income* (*beskattningsbar inkomst*), which was the income tax base.

National income tax

In 1953–70 there were separate schedules for single persons without children and for married and single persons with children.

In 1950–65 married spouses were jointly taxed. Starting in 1961, this also applied to people who lived together without being married if they had children together. In 1966–70 one could choose between separate and joint taxation of incomes from work (*A-inkomst*). Beginning in 1971, separate taxation of income from work (*A-inkomst*) was introduced for everybody. Separate taxation was also the rule for small non-work incomes (*B-inkomster*), i.e. if the sum of these incomes of the two spouses was less than 2,000 SEK. This threshold was later increased. Thus income from capital and capital gains exceeding this threshold was until 1986 added to the income from work of the highest income-earner and taxed at his/her marginal tax rate. Joint taxation of the incomes of spouses was thus completely discontinued in 1987.

In the period 1949–82 there was only one national income tax, but in 1983–90 this tax was divided into two components, a basic national income tax and a supplementary national income, tax. The base of the basic tax was taxable income, while deductions made for interest payments, etc. were added to taxable income in the base of the supplementary tax. This was done in an attempt to penalize high income-earners, who were able to reduce their taxable income by taking out large mortgages and loans or running a business operation at a loss. In 1989 the tax rate of the basic income tax was 5% for taxable incomes below 75,000 SEK and the marginal rate was 17% for incomes above this threshold. The tax rate of the supplementary income tax followed a progressive scale. In 1989 the rate was 14% for a base between 140,000 and 190,000 SEK and the marginal rate was 25% for bases above 190,000 SEK. For instance, the marginal effect of the national income tax for someone with an income above 190,000 SEK was thus 17 + 25 = 42% (in May 1993 the exchange rate was 9 SEK for 1 ECU).

Local income tax

In 1950–86 the base of the local income tax differed from the base of the national tax, i.e. there was a separate taxable income for local taxation. From 1987 there was in general a common base, taxable income, for the local and national income taxes. Before 1987 a taxpayer could pay local tax to more than one municipality, for instance if the taxpayer owned a secondary house located in another municipality than his/her home municipality. Beginning with incomes earned in 1987, all taxes are paid to the municipality where the taxpayer lives. The flat tax rate of the local tax was determined locally. The average local tax rate increased from approximately 10% in 1950 to 30.9% in 1989.

Wealth tax

The base of this tax is taxable wealth. There is joint taxation of spouses and dependent children. Also, people who live together without being married are jointly taxed if they have common children. The tax rate follows a progressive scale. In 1989 the wealth tax started with 1.5% at a tax assessed wealth of 400,000 SEK and then increased to 3% for wealth above 1,800,000 SEK. The maximum wealth tax increased from 1.8% in 1950 to 4% in 1983, but was then in 1984 reduced to 3%.

Social-insurance taxes, etc.

The base is income from business. Employees who have no business income thus do not pay these taxes, the employer does; but the self-employed and employees who run a business as a side activity have to pay their own social-security taxes (see Table 3.1).

TABLE 3.1. Social-Insurance Taxes, 1989

Tax	Rate (%)
Sickness insurance	9.60
Basic old-age pension	9.45
Supplementary old-age pension	11.00
Partial pension	0.50
Child care	2.20
Work-injury insurance	0.90
Work-protection activies	0.20
General wage bill tax	0.34
TOTAL	34.19

The number and size of 'wage bill' taxes have increased in parallel with the expansion of the social-security system. In 1950 there was only a basic pension tax of 1%, by 1975 they had increased to 25.95% and by 1985 to 34.3%.

Real-estate tax

The real-estate tax was introduced in 1985. The tax rate and the base depend on the kind of property:

a) Owner-occupied houses and secondary houses (*schablontaxerade fastigheter*). In 1989 the tax was 0.014 x 0.33 x tax-assessed value.

b) One or two family houses which are part of a business operation (*icke schablontaxerade fastigheter*). In 1989 the tax was 0.020 x 0.33 x tax-assessed value.

c) Other real estate. In 1989 the tax was 0.025 x 0.55 x tax-assessed value.

The tax rates have increased since 1985. For instance, for owner-occupied houses and secondary houses it was 0.5% in 1985, 1% in 1986, and 1.4% thereafter. There was in 1990 a major increase in the tax-assessed values which increased the importance of the real-estate tax.

The real-estate tax did not immediately replace the taxation of an imputed income from owner-occupied houses and vacation houses which was part of the old tax system. Before 1990 imputed income was a progressively increasing percentage of the tax-assessed value of the property, but in 1990 it became a flat rate of 1.5%. In 1985–90 house-owners had to pay both taxes. They were, however, allowed to deduct from the imputed income and other incomes all interest paid on mortages. Not until 1991 and the new tax system did the property tax replace the tax on imputed income. The effective tax rate was then increased, and interest paid could not be deducted to the same extent.

In addition to real-estate tax, owners of a forest for commercial use have to pay a forest protection tax. In 1950 the rate was 0.15% of the user value of the forest (*skogsbruksvärdet*). Since 1984 the tax rate has been 0.8%.

Tax deductions

In 1983 a tax deduction for membership in a labour union was introduced: 40% of the fees paid during a year, with a maximum of 1,200 SEK.

In the period 1979–83 the government had a tax-favoured savings programme. Savings on a special account entitled the taxpayers to a tax deduction. It could never exceed 1,440 SEK.

In certain years during the period 1975–85 a special tax rebate was given to people with low incomes to smooth the marginal effects of the income tax schedule. These rebates were thus income-dependent, but never exceeded 1,060 SEK.

In 1971–90 there were also special tax reductions for single parents and for married taxpayers with a spouse with no or a very low income. The maximum reduction was 1,800 SEK.

Changes in average and marginal tax rates, and in progressivity, 1950–1989

Fig. 3.6 shows the dependence of the marginal tax rate on taxable income for a few selected years from 1953–91. For each year the kink points of the tax segments were deflated by the consumer price index to the 1980 price level. In this way inflationary income increases will not make people move to the right in the diagram, and make comparisons between the curves difficult. The figure gives a very clear picture of the increase in marginal taxes until the middle of the 1970s and early 1980s, a period which coincides with the expansion of the public sector in Sweden. It also shows the subsequent decrease at the beginning of the 1990s, which reflects the increasing concern about bad incentives and tax distortions.

It is not altogether simple to illustrate how the changes in the tax system described above have resulted in new average and marginal taxes and how the progressivity of the tax system has changed. The share of people liable to pay taxes has increased, the rules to calculate the tax bases and deductions have changed, nominal and real wages have changed, and people may have adjusted their hours of work. Although the tax schedules have undergone major changes, as illustrated in Fig. 3.6, the effective marginal income tax rates may in principle show a different pattern.

Table 3.2 shows an attempt to illustrate the trends in the average and marginal income taxes and in the progressivity of the system, taking changes in income levels into account. Estimates of median total (net) income and the corresponding quartiles, etc., were computed from published tables. Using certain assumptions about the relation between total (net) income and taxable income and the tax schedules for unmarried taxpayers, the average and marginal taxes were obtained for each median, quartile, etc.

These tables show that the marginal tax rates for the low- and middle-income groups increased until the beginning of the 1970s and then decreased a little, increasing again at the end of the 1980s to reach the same level as at the beginning of the 1970s. For the high-income groups the peak was reached in the mid- and late 1970s. Also, for this group marginal tax rates decreased in the middle of the 1980s and increased at the end of the decade, but they never reached the previous peak level. At the end of the 1980s low- and middle-income groups had relatively high marginal tax rates, while high-income groups had experienced a relative decrease, although small. It is important to note that changes in the effective marginal tax rates may occur for at least three reasons: tax rules, nominal and real wages, and changes in the number of hours worked.

Panel C of Table 3.2 shows the ratio of the marginal to the average tax rates, which is a measure of the degree of progressiveness of the tax schedule and an elasticity. It gives the percentage tax increase which follows from an income increase of 1%. For people with incomes at the first quartile, progressivity has decreased. There is no unique trend for

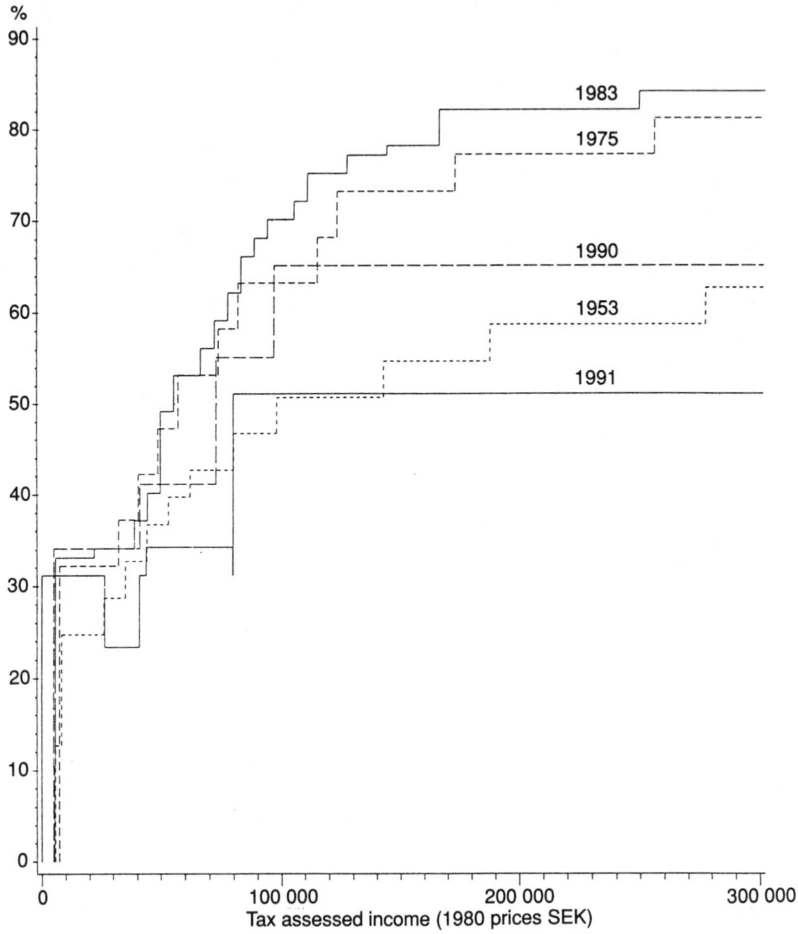

FIG 3.6. Marginal Income Tax Rates in Sweden
Source: Own calculations based on Swedish tax legislation.

those who had higher incomes. We may also note that there were no great differences in progressivity between low- and high-income earners.

Fig. 3.7 shows the marginal income tax rates calculated for an 'average' unmarried blue- and white-collar worker respectively. This figure shows that the marginal tax rate peak was reached in the 1970s for blue-collar workers, a few years before white-collar workers. In the 1980s successive tax reforms decreased the marginal tax rates. The data on which this figure is based are exhibited in Table 3.3, which also gives estimates of

TABLE 3.2. Average and Marginal Income Tax Rates and Measures of Progressivity for Median, Quartile, and 90th Percentile Income-Earners, Sweden, 1952–1990

Year	First quartile	Median	Third quartile	90th percentile	Income-earners as a share of the Swedish population above 15 years of age (%)
A. *Average tax rates (%)*					
1952	9	11	11	29	68.5
1955	14	20	24	26	70.9
1960	14	21	28	33	72.8
1965	17	27	33	40	75.0
1970	23	34	41	47	77.8
1975	23	29	37	41	88.1
1980	24	28	36	41	98.3
1983	26	30	34	39	98.6
1985	28	31	36	38	99.3
1987	28	32	37	40	99.8
1990	29	33	35	39	99.9
B. *Marginal tax rates*					
1952	23	23	22	40	
1955	25	31	36	40	
1960	25	36	44	51	
1965	28	42	54	59	
1970	36	48	57	65	
1975	32	43	58	64	
1980	32	41	55	68	
1983	34	40	53	62	
1985	35	45	51	51	
1987	36	50	50	55	
1990	34	41	55	55	
C. *Progressivity*					
1952	2.56	2.09	2.00	1.38	
1955	1.79	1.55	1.50	1.54	
1960	1.79	1.71	1.57	1.54	
1965	1.65	1.56	1.64	1.48	
1970	1.57	1.41	1.39	1.38	
1975	1.39	1.48	1.57	1.56	
1980	1.33	1.46	1.53	1.66	
1983	1.31	1.33	1.56	1.59	
1985	1.25	1.45	1.42	1.34	
1987	1.29	1.56	1.35	1.38	
1990	1.17	1.24	1.57	1.41	

Notes: (1) 1952–70 locational measures were obtained for total income (*sammanräknad inkomst*) and these were then transformed into taxable income for the unmarried. 1975–90 locational measures were obtained for total net income (*sammanräknad nettoinkomst*) and then transformed into taxable income.

(2) By income-earner we mean a person who has completed a tax assessment form. People with a total (net) income of zero are included. Children below the age of 15 can be income-earners although it is unusual.

Source: Own calculations, based on tax schedules and official income statistics.

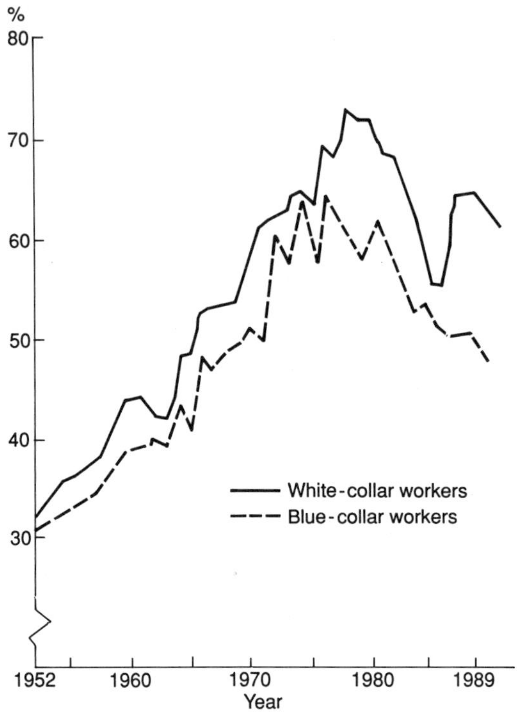

FIG 3.7. Marginal Income Tax Rates for Blue- and White-Collar Workers in Swedish Industry
Source: Nordling (1991: fig. 5.2, table 5.2).

the total tax wedge, i.e. the wedge between what the employer has to pay for an hour of work and the consumption value the employee obtains from the income he earns. In addition to the marginal income tax, this concept thus includes wage bill taxes and indirect taxes net of commodity-based subsidies. The very high tax wedge, of about 80% of the sum of the wage and wage bill taxes, for white-collar workers at the beginning of the 1980s implies, for instance, that a Swedish employer who is considering recruiting a white-collar worker from another country, where the tax wedge is only 50%, would have to pay him 2.5 times as much as he is paid in his home country to compensate him for the increased tax burden in Sweden (0.5/(1–0.8) = 2.5). It also implies that the production value of an additional hour of work must be five times the worker's consumption value.

The 1990–1991 Income Tax Reform

The motives behind the 1990–1 income tax reform can be summarized as follows. There was a need to:

- decrease the economic distortions created by tax wedges giving the wrong incentives in people's decisions to allocate time between work and leisure and incomes between consumption and savings, and making people engage in tax planning and tax evasion;
- harmonize the taxation of labour and capital to decrease any distortions in the allocation of resources;
- create a tax system which was effective in redistributing incomes, i.e. without having loopholes which would make redistribution arbitrary and smaller than intended;
- create conditions for smaller wage increases and thus less inflation;
- harmonize the Swedish tax system and tax rates with those of most Western countries in view of the increased internationalization;
- create a simple and transparent tax system.

The proposal was to reduce the six categories of incomes of the old tax system to three—incomes from employment, incomes from business, and income from capital—broaden the tax bases, and decrease the tax rates.

Income from employment would include not only wages, salaries, and pensions but also all kinds of employment-related cash and non-cash benefits. These benefits were previously given a favourable tax treatment but would now be taxed at market values. The state tax was reduced to zero for 90% of taxpayers and to 20% for the 10% who in 1991 had an employment income exceeding a threshold just below 200,000 SEK (approximately 22,500 ECU in May 1993). In effect, about 90% of all taxpayers only had to pay the flat-rate municipal income tax, which averaged a little over 30%. According to the proposal, the marginal tax rates would thus become about 30% for incomes below the threshold and about 50% above it. As the result of a political compromise when the reform passed through Parliament, the basic deduction (*grundavdraget*) was made income dependent: it first increased and then decreased with increasing income. The effect was the same as an adjustment of the tax scales for people with low incomes, which resulted in somewhat higher marginal rates for these groups (see Fig. 3.6). The proposal also included the suggestion that both the threshold and the basic deduction would be indexed and would follow the general increases in the price level.

Tax reductions for trade union fees were reduced, and reductions for the support of non-resident children, housewives, and single parents with children, and for people with special sickness costs and very low incomes, were all removed.

TABLE 3.3. Marginal Income Taxes and Tax Wedges, 1952–1989, for Blue- and White-Collar Workers with Average Wages in Swedish Industry

Year	Blue-collar worker			White-collar worker		
	Annual earnings (SEK)	Marginal tax (%)	Wedge (%)	Annual earnings (SEK)	Marginal tax (%)	Wedge (%)
1952	8,300	30.8	36.5	12,300	32,2	37,8
1955	9,700	32.6	39.7	14,400	35.4	42.2
1958	11,900	35.0	42.3	17,600	38.2	45.2
1960	13,500	38.5	48.4	20,000	43.3	52.2
1961	14,500	38.8	49.3	22,200	43.5	53.2
1962	15,600	39.5	50.9	23,800	41.3	52.4
1963	16,600	38.4	50.6	25,200	41.2	52.9
1964	17,800	43.0	54.6	26,800	47.4	58.1
1965	19,500	40.1	58.1	28,700	47.8	59.1
1966	21,300	48.1	59.9	31,100	52.0	62.9
1967	22,400	47.0	59.7	33,100	53.0	64.3
1968	23,300	48.9	62.0	35,000	53.0	65.0
1969	24,600	49.7	62.7	37,000	53.7	65.6
1970	27,500	50.3	62.7	40,000	57.6	68.2
1971	30,300	49.5	63.6	43,000	60.6	71.6
1972	32,200	60.9	71.6	46,500	62.1	72.4
1973	34,600	57.5	69.2	50,200	62.3	72.7
1974	38,800	64.1	74.2	56,100	64.1	74.2
1975	45,500	58.2	71.3	63,500	63.2	74.7
1976	51,200	64.1	76.0	72,200	69.1	79.4
1977	54,600	61.8	75.2	78,000	67,5	78.9
1978	59,000	59.7	73.6	83,900	72,5	82.0
1979	64,000	50.0	72.6	90,700	71.6	81.5
1980	71,000	62.1	75.4	98,100	71.7	81.7
1981	77,200	58.6	73.5	106,600	68.5	79.9
1982	82,200	55.7	71.7	112,600	68.4	79.8
1983	88,200	53.1	70.5	119,700	65.1	78.0
1984	96,100	53.3	71.4	130,700	61.0	76.1
1985	103,400	50.4	69.8	139,500	55.4	72.9
1986	111,000	50.3	70.5	150,100	55.3	73.4
1987	118,200	50.4	70.8	159,300	64.4	79.0
1988	127,500	50.6	70.9	170,900	64.6	79.2
1989		47.8			61.8	

Notes: Concerns single male income-earners from SAF area (Svenska Arbetsgivar Föreningen, the Swedish Confederation of Employers). Deficit reductions for white-collar workers 11% all years. Travel expenses 1.5%. Other expenses from income of employment 0.5%. Tax wedges include marginal taxes, wage bill taxes, 87% of all indirect taxes less food and housing subsidies (*räntesubventioner*) and less 50% of other subsidies to business.

Sources: (1) Calculations made by Gunnar Du Rietz;
(2)Nordling (1991: 166).

Income of capital includes interest, dividends, realized capital gains, and rental incomes. Deductions for interest paid and capital losses are permitted, but for capital losses and for interest paid in excess of interest received above 100,000 SEK (approximately 11,000 ECU) only 70% can be deducted. The tax rate is a flat rate of 30%. If the net income from capital is negative, 30% is deducted from the sum of all taxes gross of other tax deductions.

In the old tax system a progressively increasing imputed income was assigned to owners of owner-occupied houses and secondary houses, based on the tax-assessed value of the property. This is not done in the new tax system; instead, the flat-rate real-estate tax, already introduced in 1985, was increased.

The tax rate on *income from business* was decreased to 30%, but at the same time the possibilities of setting aside reserve income was limited in order to broaden the tax base and achieve a uniformity with the taxation of incomes from capital. The base of the social-security taxes was also broadened as a result of the new evaluation of non-cash benefits.

The *local tax* is still a flat-rate tax. The average tax rate in 1991 was 31.15%.

In 1990 the *wealth tax* was decreased for families with small amounts of wealth by an adjustment of the tax brackets. Large fortunes are still taxed at a rate of 3%.

The *real-estate tax* was changed in 1991. For people who only had an owner-occupied house or a secondary house, the tax rate for old houses (built before 1986) was decreased to 1.2% and for new houses (built after 1985) to 0.6%. These adjustments were made to balance new and considerably increased tax-assessed real-estate values.

With one exception, the *social-security tax* rates remained unchanged, while the base increased as mentioned above. The exception was a decrease of the general wage bill tax from 1.64% to 0.16% by July 1991.

The reduction of the marginal tax rates alone would lead to an increased income inequality. However, the total reform package, which also included substantially increased child allowances, would, according to government projections, lead to increased disposable incomes for all socioeconomic groups. These estimates showed that households with the highest incomes gained less than the average, and that the relative status of families with children was improved. People with substantial wealth were predicted to pay significantly higher taxes. These results have, however, been much debated in the media. An independent study, Schwarz and Gustafsson (1991), which simulated the effects of the tax reform, by and large confirmed that the net redistribution would be small.

Although tax bases were broadened and indirect taxes were increased at the same time as income taxes were decreased, the tax reform was not fully funded. Decreased tax rates were estimated to give an annual deficit of about 63 billion SEK in 1991–3, and decreased social-security taxes, increased child allowances, decreased support to milk production, and a few additional tax and transfer adjustments to give a deficit of almost 7 billion SEK. Broadened tax bases were estimated to increase the tax revenues by 43 billion SEK, increased indirect taxes by 19 billion and increased corporate business taxes by 3 billion. The balance of 5 billion SEK was assumed to be covered by so-called dynamic effects, i.e. changes in behaviour, primarily an increase in labour supply, which would increase the activity level of the economy and thus also the tax revenue. An increase in the labour incomes of Swedish households by approximately 2.5% would result in an increased annual tax revenue of 5 billion SEK (table 4.6 in RINK, I)

3.3. A NEW TAX SYSTEM AND NEW INCENTIVES?

The general purpose of the tax reform was to increase the incentives for market work and saving, decrease the perceived need of unions to demand high nominal wage increases and in this way decrease cost inflation, and as a result increase the capital formation and growth of the Swedish economy. A key mechanism of this scenario is the increase in labour supply. The decreased marginal tax rates increased the price of leisure for those who belonged to the income brackets where a tax decrease took effect. The simultaneous broadening of the tax base and the increased indirect taxation should have neutralized the income effect of the tax cut. The whole reform was almost fully funded, and as an approximation one might expect that the net effect would equal the substitution effect. As described in the following sections there is, however, a genuine uncertainty about the size of the substitution effect. (It might hold as a good approximation that the net effect of the tax reform equals the substitution effect, but even if the reform had been fully funded it does not necessarily mean that the real income of each household was unchanged, and the existence of an aggregate income effect will depend on the covariance between household income changes and their income elasticities. For instance, if households which increase their incomes tend to have higher income elasticities than those who experience an income decrease, there will be a non-zero aggregate income effect.)

As the marginal tax rates did not change much for low-income groups, they should not have experienced great incentives from the new income tax system to adjust their hours of work *marginally*. To the extent that their real income after tax decreased as a result of the increased indirect taxation, there might have been an incentive to compensate by more work hours. Those who had low incomes because they only worked part-time might have experienced an incentive to take a major step and switch to a full-time job. Most of them are women, and part-time working women have been mentioned as a group which could potentially react to the incentives of the tax reform and increase their supply of labour. Part-time work among women had decreased already before the tax reform, and it is possible that the reform provided additional stimulus for women to take a full- time job; but it is also true that women, and in particular those who had part-time jobs, tended to have low-paid jobs and thus relatively low incomes. For this group the tax reform will not give any major decrease in the marginal tax rate. To the extent that they are married to husbands who have well-paid jobs and thus experienced a decrease in their marginal tax rates, the incentives should rather have become the opposite. It should have been efficient to shift relatively more market work towards the husband and less towards his spouse.

Any major increase in labour supply would thus have to come from people in the upper half of the income distribution. Given the high labour force participation rates for both males and females in Sweden, and given that the participation rate is likely to be especially high among those well-educated groups who would benefit from the tax cut, no large effect can be expected from an increased participation. The increased labour supply would instead have to come from relatively well-paid groups who would increase their hours by more overtime, secondary jobs, and by not staying at home as much because of sickness and child care. It is an empirical issue to what extent this is possible, but it might be indicative that the groups who experienced the greatest incentives to increase their labour supply were those who already had a high activity in the labour market. All these adjustments presuppose that there is a demand side which is able to accommodate an increased supply. Suppose, for instance, that the average share of the workforce reporting sick permanently decreases from 20% to 10%. Employers can now get the same amount of work done by a smaller workforce than before, and it is not obvious that their reaction will be to increase the demand for labour to absorb all of the now redundant 10% of the workforce.

Independently of any effects on the supply of hours, the decreased marginal tax rates might give new incentives to young people to invest in human capital, both in the form of formal education and in the form of on-the-job training. The new tax scales imply that the return after tax to investments in human capital have increased (see Ch. 2). The tax reform might also change the wage structure before tax and in this way influence the return to human capital too, but the direction of this change is debated. It has been argued that wage increases could be exchanged for tax decreases, and that high-income earners who have the benefit of the largest tax cuts should be willing to hold back their demand for wage increases more than low-income earners. Cuts in marginal income taxes are therefore supposed both to hold back union demands on wage increases, and thus to ease cost inflation, and to decrease before-tax wage differences. This was, for instance, the motive behind the income policy in the 1970s called 'Haga agreements'. (These agreements were named after the Haga palace outside Stockholm, where representatives of the government, political parties, and unions negotiated them.) It is doubtful if any effect of this kind can be verified empirically. On the contrary, one could also argue that tax reform will increase wage differences before tax. When the marginal income tax is in the range 70% and above, it becomes very expensive for an employer to give incentive increases of a magnitude which is likely to have any effect. The wedge between the marginal product of an increase in labour input and the corresponding increase in labour cost is too large. When the old tax system was in effect, employers for this reason either found ways to give incentives in the form of fringe benefits which were less heavily taxed or just refrained from giving incentives at all. It is thus likely that the high marginal taxes in the old system prevented work effort which might have been carried out with another tax system. As a consequence, the new tax system will induce employers and employees to turn fringe benefits into cash wages and in this way increase 'reported' wage differences, but it is also possible that wage differences will increase even more, because on the margin it is now profitable to give more incentives.

When wage differences increase, it becomes more profitable to invest in the kind of human capital which makes it possible for workers to take more qualified jobs with more responsibility and which is rewarded by the market. The incentives to enter this process are, of course, greatest for young people and it is a process which will take time, but it might well become one of the most important effects of the income tax reform.

This conclusion gets some support from the Edin and Holmlund (1992) study of the Swedish wage structure, which demonstrated that the return to higher education decreased in the 1960s and 1970s and then increased in the 1980s. This increase was the combined result of somewhat widening wage differentials in the 1980s and decreased marginal taxes. They also showed that demand for higher education was highly responsive to the returns to university education. They found an enrolment elasticity for males with respect to the relative wage rate of about 2, i.e. the share of 20–4-year-old men enrolled in schools and universities will increase by 2% if the after-tax university-to-high-school wage premium increases by 1%.

The tax reform will also influence other aspects of people's behaviour apart from labour supply. The changes in the taxation of income from capital will change people's incentives to save, and in particular their portfolio choice. In the old tax system there was a differential treatment of various assets which implied that the tax system to a large extent determined the return (after tax) of an asset. High marginal taxes also made profitable the financing of housing consumption and consumption of durables by loans. As a result, Swedish households invested heavily in real estate and consumer durables during the 1980s. The new (almost) uniform tax rate of 30% of capital incomes and the reduced possibilities of deducting interest payments against income will first induce people to pay off their mortages and loans and then most likely shift their capital investments away from real estate and consumer durables and towards financial assets. A short-run effect of the tax reform of which we have already seen evidence is thus that people reduce their debts by a combination of reduced consumption and reallocation of their portfolios. Whether the tax reform will give people the incentive to increase their saving in the long run is not as clear (cf. Agell 1990). Another change which was also predicted as a result of the tax reform, and which we have already observed, is a substantial decrease in real-estate prices. As the owner-occupied house or apartment is the major asset of Swedish households, this price fall will make many households less well off and reduce their future consumption possibilites (cf. Persson 1989).

We have until now discussed the first two 'layers' of effects from the tax reform, i.e. direct effects on people's incomes and the individual adjustment effects, such as the changes in labour supply studied in most microeconometric studies. There is also a third layer: the general-equilibrium effects when all markets have adjusted. It would be very difficult to get reliable estimates of the size of the general-equilibrium effects, and there is no comprehensive study of these effects from the Swedish tax reform. Attempts have been made, however, to capture at least some aspects. Olofsson and Söderlind (1990) who use an intertemporal general equilibrium model of the same type as Auerbach and Kotlikoff (1987). A basic assumption in their simulations is that there is a large substitution effect on labour supply of the cut in the income taxes. The decrease in marginal taxes thus increases labour supply and private consumption and initially decreases the wage rates. Production will increase, as will the capital stock with a few years' lag. The increase in indirect taxes has the opposite effect. As consumption becomes more expensive, households shift towards more leisure and less work and consumption. An increase in the tax rate on capital income, which is an increased tax on future consumption, will initially increase and then decrease consumption and leisure. The net effect of all three changes is, in this model, dominated by the labour supply effects from the change in marginal income taxes. One has, however, to ask whether there is empirical evidence to support such hypothesized effects. This is the subject of section 3.4.

3.4. RESEARCH ON TAX INCENTIVES AND LABOUR SUPPLY

Introduction

Labour supply is probably the most researched area in applied microeconomics and microeconometrics. In the last decade, in which tax reforms have been planned and implemented in several countries, the empirical results from this kind of research have attracted considerable interest. Do increased marginal tax rates stimulate labour supply? How much distortion does the progressive income tax system create? To what extent is a tax cut self-financing? Estimates of labour supply responses to wage rate changes (net of marginal taxes) and income changes are needed to provide answers to these questions. There is, however, a wide variety of results, and politicians have been able to pick those which fit their policy. Although there are several good reviews of the labour supply literature (Killingsworth 1983; Blomquist 1985; Killingsworth and Heckman 1986; Pencavel 1986; Blundell 1987), they concentrate on results from the United States and to a lesser degree from the United Kingdom. Recent results motivate another quick retrospective view to highlight a few major points. This section does not discuss the whole issue of evaluating or predicting the effects of a tax reform. The topic is more narrowly restricted to certain aspects of modelling and estimating labour supply functions. Complete coverage is not attempted, and the discussion concentrates on results for Sweden.

A Retrospective View

Most labour supply studies are based on the assumption of myopic utility maximization: there is no planning ahead, and the budget constraint is completely determined by the incomes obtained in the current period (see Ch. 2). These assumptions a priori must lack in realism. Labour supply decisions belong to the most important decisions we make, and usually have consequences for the future. However, the assumption of myopic utility maximization simplifies the analysis considerably and is in frequent use.

Within this group we might distinguish between three subgroups, depending on how taxes have been incorporated into the budget constraint. In the first subgroup, usually consisting of very early studies, taxes have been ignored altogether. In most countries, and in particular in Sweden, progressive income taxes have made the budget set non-linear (see Fig. 2.6). If we also take various income-dependent benefits and social-security programmes into account, the budget sets become highly non-linear and also non-convex (Andersson 1989; see also Figs. 3.11–13 and the discussion of Fig. 2.6 in Ch. 2). For this reason these early results are less interesting.

In the second group of studies, the non-linearity of the budget set is recognized but the econometrics is simplified by a linearization of the budget set. As explained in Chapter 2, the variables used to characterize the budget set are the marginal wage rate, i.e. the wage rate multiplied by one minus the marginal tax rate, and 'virtual income', which is a theoretical construct obtained as the intersection of the earnings axis in an earnings – hours diagram and the extended linear budget segment on which the individual finds its optimum. Estimates of the uncompensated wage elasticity, usually based on US data, are typically negative but close to zero for males. For females they vary from small negative estimates to large positive. In the survey of the international literature by Blomquist (1985), the estimates for males range from –0.42 to –0.02 and for females from –0.31 to 2.3. The income elasticities are generally negative and of a magnitude such that the compensated elasticities measuring the substitution effect are positive, i.e. in agreement with conventional consumer choice theory. As pointed out by, for instance, Blomquist (1985), the effect of a change in the marginal tax rate is in these models not only inferred from the marginal wage elasticity but also from the income elasticity, because virtual income depends on the marginal tax rate. Thus a small net wage elasticity does not necessarily imply a small effect on labour supply of a change in the marginal tax rate, because we might have a high income elasticity. Surprisingly, we have not been able to find any contemporary study of this kind using Swedish data. Recently Flood and MaCurdy (1992) compared different approaches (see below).

The approach with a linearized budget set is able to explain why an individual chooses a particular point on the observed budget segment, but it does not explain why this segment was chosen rather than another one. Although the econometrics becomes more involved, a natural extension is to specify the whole budget set and allow the consumer to find a global maximum. This approach also 'solves' another problem of the second approach, namely that marginal taxes are endogenous. The marginal tax rate is a function of taxable income which includes earnings and thus depends on the number of hours worked. In the second approach this problem is usually dealt with by an instrumental variables approach, but the difficulties in finding good instruments in microeconometric applications is well known among econometricians. A complete specification of the budget set and the application of the maximum-likelihood method avoids this problem.

The third group of studies is exactly of this type. They specify a budget set which covers the whole choice range, but it usually only includes non-linearities caused by the income tax system. Non-linearities (non-convexities) caused by income-dependent benefits, etc., are frequently neglected. Results for males are usually small, uncompensated wage elasticities around zero, negative income elasticities, and positive compensated elasticities with respect to the net wage rate after marginal tax. For females, the uncompensated marginal wage rate elasticities range from small to large positive values and the income elasticities are clearly negative. Most of these studies thus give sizeable effects on the female labour supply of a decrease in the marginal tax rate.

In a series of papers Blomquist has analysed the labour supply of married prime-age Swedish males. (His data set is a sample of males aged 25–55, excluding those who were retired, in military service, sick for more than four weeks, self-employed, and unmarried.) In Blomquist (1983) preference parameters are estimated subject to a non-linear budget set determined by the Swedish tax schedules. He obtains a wage rate elasticity of approximately 0.08 and an income elasticity of –0.04 for an average individual. These results are extended in Blomquist and Hansson-Brusewitz (1990) and Blomquist (1989), where the functional form of the labour supply function is somewhat more general and the marginal effects of housing allowances (*bostadsbidrag*) are allowed to influence the budget set. They also assume that individual differences in preferences are random and generated from a normal distribution. Depending on model variant, the wage rate elasticity now varies between 0.05 and 0.13 and the income elasticity between –0.01 and 0.01. All these elasticities may appear to be very small. They show the labour supply effect of a very (infinitely) small change in the wage rate or virtual income at a given budget segment. They cannot be used to calculate the effect of finite changes, because in a model of the Hausman–Blomquist type the whole budget set will change when the wage rate, non-labour income, or tax parameters change. These small elasticities are thus not inconsistent with relatively large supply effects of changes in the tax system. (In general it is difficult to compare elasticities from different studies, because they depend on the particular model specification and can be calculated in a number of ways.)

An early unpublished study is Jakobsson (1982). Labour supply functions similar to those used by Hausman and Blomquist, but with preference differences somewhat more explicit, were estimated separately for males and females. As in the case of Blomquist (1983), the 1974 Level of Living Surveys (LNU) of the Institute of Social Research, University of Stockholm, were used. For males Jakobsson got a marginal wage rate elasticity of 0.06 and an income elasticity of –0.027. For females the estimates were 1.2 and –0.14 respectively. All elasticities were calculated at the sample mean point.

Another very interesting sequence of papers has been produced by Strøm and collaborators. The theoretical-model structure is explained in Dagsvik (1988) and Dagsvik and Strøm (1988). Their models have been applied to data from several countries. Results for Sweden can be found in Ljones and Strøm (1987), I. A.-K. Andersson *et al.* (1988), I. A.-K. Andersson (1989), and Aaberge *et al.* (1989). Their approach has a few attractive features. The basic story which motivates the model is one of the consumer choosing a 'job package' of a wage rate and a certain number of hours. These packages might not be available in any combination of wage rate and hours. They thus recognize that the distribution of hours might be concentrated to certain hours and have more than one mode. Their model is also a household model, which in principle explains both the decision to work and the number of hours worked. In Ljones and Strøm (1987) the model was applied to a relatively small research data set from 1981. Data did not permit the complete household model to be estimated. They found that if all working men got a pay increase of 1% the labour supply of men increased by 0.02%. Changes in the female wage rate had no effect on the labour supply of men. Females were, however, more responsive to changes in their wage rates. An increase in pay of 1% increased the number of hours with about the same percentage. 40% of this effect came from increased participation and 60% from longer hours. The model has also been applied to another Swedish data set from 1981, a survey which combines register data on incomes and taxes with interview data, called HINK and administered by Statistics Sweden. In a model with complete cross-effects between the spouses, the study found an uncompensated elasticity of 0.08 for males and 0.13 for females. The cross-wage elasticities were –0.07 and –0.11 respectively and the income elasticities were –0.39 and –0.11. If labour supply functions were estimated separately for males and females, the uncompensated elasticities increased to 0.23 for males and 0.33 for females and the income elasticities became close to zero.

While the estimates of the uncompensated elasticities from the second approach, i.e. with linearized budget sets, varied a great deal for both males and females, permitting both forward- and backward-sloping supply curves, the results from the third approach are more homogeneous. The uncompensated elasticities for males are small positive numbers. For females they are also positive but usually somewhat larger. One might also note that the compensated elasticities are non-negative, i.e. they do not violate the Slutsky conditions.

Have we now reached a consensus? The trend of research is towards a more complete and detailed specification of the budget set and more efficient maximum-likelihood estimation methods. Can we thus be more confident in these more recent studies than in those of previous generations? Not necessarily! There are a few contradictory results, and we have also reason to believe that serious specification errors remain in those studies which have here been called the third approach.

MaCurdy *et al.* (1988) has reviewed the econometrics of the third approach. They show that if the budget set is piecewise linear (as in Fig. 2.7), the Slutsky conditions are implicitly enforced on the estimates at all interior kink points which represent a feasible option for some individual in the sample. If the budget set is continuously differentiable there is a similar but less stringent constraint on the preference parameters. Estimates of compensated elasticities may have the theoretically wrong sign, but they cannot deviate too much from a positive value. Their empirical analysis using US data also shows that these implicit constraints drive the results. Using the same data source as Hausman (1981), they found a small positive uncompensated wage elasticity and a small negative income elasticity when the Slutsky conditions were enforced, while they got a backward-bending supply curve when the constraints where not enforced. Although there was no formal test, the data seemed to reject the Slutsky condition. If the constraints of the models used by Hausman, Blomquist *et al.* are enforced, the estimates cannot violate the Slutsky conditions. It is thus of some importance whether the constraints are binding or not. In the case of MaCurdy *et al.* they were. Replications made on Swedish data for males by Flood and MaCurdy (1992) showed that the constraints were *not* binding. They obtained results very similar to Blomquist (1983). (When the Slutsky constraints are *not* enforced the estimates are not proper ML estimates and do not necessarily have the same properties as ML estimates. Unconstrained estimates may, in particular, have a different asymptotic covariance matrix.)

In his study of the robustness of estimates of labour supply functions for women in the United States, Mroz (1987) showed that estimates obtained by the instrumental-variable approach are very sensitive to the choice of instruments. Flood and MaCurdy (1992) were able to get almost the same estimates as those typically obtained when the maximum-likelihood method is applied to a Hausman-type model, if they included the marginal wage rate and virtual income among the instruments; but if they only used demographic variables they obtained negative compensated and uncompensated wage elasticities and a positive income elasticity, i.e.

estimates which violated the Slutsky conditions. Flood and MaCurdy drew the conclusion that wage rates and incomes are endogenous. If this is true, it might have far-reaching consequences for any analysis of labour supply. The budget set cannot be taken as given. Although it is not entirely implausible that people make joint choices about hours, wage rates, and non-labour incomes, this might not have caused the endogeneity of the wage rate and income variables found by Flood and MaCurdy. It could also be a measurement error problem. The wage rate measure was the ratio between annual earnings and an estimate of annual hours. It is conceivable that measurement errors in the hours variable could have made them reject the hypothesis of an exogenous wage rate. If this is true it shows the importance of a carefully specified and measured budget set. The 'parameters' of a labour contract (a piece rate, an hourly wage rate, a monthly salary, overtime premia, etc.) might thus be exogenous to the labour-supply decision, while any simplified summary measure which involves hours of work might not be treated as exogenous.

Using the Hausman–Blomquist framework, and thus assuming that the gross wage rate, taxable non-labour income, and non-taxable non-labour income are exogenous to the labour supply decision, Blomquist (1992) did a simulation study to compare various estimation methods. Given that the basic assumptions underlying the Hausman–Blomquist model are true, his results showed that the maximum-likelihood method performs well for a sample size as small as 600. The instrumental variable method with the gross wage rate, taxable non-labour income, and non-taxable non-labour income as instruments gave almost as good results, which agrees with Flood and MaCurdy (1992), while an instrumental-variable estimator with truly exogenous socioeconomic variables as instruments gave a large bias. Blomquist conjectured that the consistency property of this estimator would show up only for sample sizes which by far exceed what we usually have. These simulation results offer an alternative interpretation of what causes the differences in estimation results, but they do not necessarily contradict or invalidate the conclusions of Flood and MaCurdy (1992) because Blomquist's results have nothing to say about the properties of estimates when the gross wage rate and the income variables are endogenous.

There are thus several reasons to be sceptical about estimates obtained with the Hausman–Blomquist approach as well as with alternative approaches. Although the Slutsky conditions have been rejected before (examples can be found in the literature on consumer demand), most economists would probably not like to reject this theory altogether. These results suggest, rather, that serious remaining specification errors have produced the rejection of the Slutsky conditions. We will now turn to a discussion of some of these problems.

Measurement Problems and the Estimation of Budget Sets

Data used for labour-supply studies are usually based on surveys in which the respondents have been asked about their normal or stipulated working hours per week and about the number of weeks worked in a year. At least for Sweden, these data tend to give distributions of working hours which for males are highly concentrated around 40 hours per week (1,800 hours per year), while the distribution for females may have more than one mode. People do not report temporary sickness, child care, or 'non-work at work'. These distributions are thus far from normal, which suggests that conventional assumptions about normal errors in labour-supply models are not realistic. Strøm and his collaborators have recognized this problem, and assume non-normal distributions which allow for the possibility of more than one mode. They also attach a particular interpretation to these distributions, as they suggest that the concentration on certain hours is the result of institutional restrictions and inertia in the labour market. Job openings tend to come in the form of full-time or half-time jobs, while it is difficult to find 30% or 80% jobs. Although this interpretation is plausible, it is not the only one possible. The models of Strøm *et al.* do not use any data or external information about the labour market restrictions they have in mind, and it is thus not possible to distinguish the effects of restrictions from those of, for instance, people's way of answering particular survey questions. Independently of the particular explanation of concentrated distributions of hours and several modes, it is basic to any econometric analysis and interpretation that we have a good statistical model which is able to predict well the observed distribution of hours.

An even more basic issue is what measure of labour supply we ideally would like to have. For most purposes we would like to measure the number of hours people actually work, not their stipulated hours or the number of hours they believe they normally work. Data which come close to this ideal are time-use data. As these data measure the details of adjustment by people to economic and non-economic incentives, and the resulting distribution of hours is much less concentrated in full-time and half-time jobs, one might expect that estimates based on time-use data should show higher responses to changes in incentives than 'ordinary' survey data do. There are, however, problems also with time-use data. They are usually obtained in interviews or by self-reported diaries covering only a few days. Obviously such data do not give good estimates of annual hours worked, which for many purposes is the most interesting variable. This also implies that one cannot use a model with an explicit budget constraint, because there is no binding budget constraint for such a short period as a few days or a week.

Using a model of the self-selection type with a labour-supply function which was a mongrel of preference and budget set variables, Flood (1988) compared estimates obtained from time-use data with those from ordinary survey data on 'normal hours including overtime'. His results indicated a backward-bending supply curve for males as well as for females. Contrary to what one might have expected, for males there was no significant difference between the two types of data in the marginal effect of the wage rate variable, and for females the estimate from time-use data was smaller in absolute value than the estimate from ordinary survey data. Thus, at least for this particular model, time-use data did not show a greater sensitivity than survey data to changes in the wage rate.

Measurement errors, not only in hours worked but also in wage rate and income variables, create difficult problems in the estimation of budget sets. The wage rate variable is a key variable in the construction of a budget set. It is obtained either as the ratio of annual labour income divided by an estimate of annual work hours or from direct survey estimates of hourly, weekly, or monthly wages. Annual labour income could either be obtained from survey data or from taxation data, i.e. from self-assessment forms. It is obvious that all these estimates are error-prone. An evaluation study which compared survey estimates with company records is the validation study done by the Survey Research Center at the University of Michigan (Duncan and Hill 1985; Bound *et al.* 1990; and Rodgers *et al.* 1991). They did not find any major bias in the wage rate estimates, calculated in three alternative ways, but the error variance was as high as 70% of the total variance, somewhat smaller for estimates based on annual earnings than for responses to questions about previous pay period and usual pay. There is not yet a similar study in Sweden.

In his simulation study Blomquist (1992) demonstrated the importance of measurement errors. If the gross wage rate is estimated as the ratio of labour income to hours of work and both are error-prone, the ML method gives a strong bias towards zero of the estimate of the wage rate coefficient. Furthermore, if there are measurement errors in taxable non-labour income the ML method breaks down. The latter result is intuitively plausible because, if there are errors in taxable non-labour income, all kink points and segments of the budget set are displaced.

The shape and location of a budget set do not only depend on labour income and income taxes but also on various types of benefit and transfer, as reviewed at some length in section 3.5. To properly include them as part of the budget set one needs quite detailed data at the individual and household level. For instance, to calculate housing allowances for someone who lives in an owner-occupied house, one needs to know the size of the house, the amount of interest paid on mortages and expenditures for heating, etc. To calculate the size of support to children in a previous marriage, one needs to know the number of children, how old they are, and the income of the former spouse. There are few data sets, if any, which have all the background information needed to calculate proper budget sets. In practice one thus has to work with simplifications based on more or less realistic assumptions, which will result in errors.

In the few cases when it has been feasible to include at least a few benefits or transfers, the resulting budget sets do not resemble those we are used to from the textbooks. They are non-convex, and sometimes there are frequent changes in the composite marginal tax rate (see Figs. 3.11–13). This raises the questions: what degree of detail is needed? how well does a single individual know his own budget set? It has been argued that most people do not even know their current marginal tax rate (see Wahlund 1987), and their knowledge of the details of the total composite marginal tax rate should then be even less. To model the labour-supply decisions it would be helpful to know if people are well informed or base their decisions on fragmentary information.

Life-Cycle Models

Most empirical work has explicitly or implicitly been based on myopic utility maximization. It is natural to relax this assumption and allow for the possibility that people are forward-looking and taking into account the likely future consequences of their decisions.

As explained in Chapter 2, one usually assumes in life-cycle models that an intertemporal utility function is maximized subject to a life-cycle budget constraint. Given initial wealth, wage rates, and interest rates, the consumer chooses a consumption and work path such that utility is maximized without violating the requirement that end-of-life wealth is non-negative. In this model, labour supply becomes a function of current assets, the current wage rate, and expected future wages and non-labour incomes. In practice, variables like schooling, experience, and age have been used to model the accumulation of human capital and thus also to control for future evolutionary wage changes, while non-earned income has been used to capture the effects of current assets.

Most life-cycle models of labour supply have assumed intertemporal separability of utility. The resulting labour-supply functions come in two alternative formulations, one which conditions on marginal utility of wealth and one which conditions on 'full income'. (Full income is the sum of unearned income, asset decumulation, and the value of the consumer's time endowment.) In these models the marginal utility of wealth and full income respectively summarize all intra-period allocations. Although unobserved, with panel data these summary statistics can be differenced out and therefore a relatively simple life-cycle-consistent structure estimated. (For an extensive discussion see Blundell 1987).

The assumption of intertemporal separability of utility is thus very convenient, but there is no strong theoretical reason to justify it. Equally, or more, plausible are assumptions of learning behaviour, habit persistence, and inertia due to transaction costs and institutional restrictions. One way to model these alternative assumptions is to include past behaviour as a determinant of current utility. This will in general lead to models with current labour supply explained by lagged labour supply. Blundell (1987) suggested that choices about family composition, labour supply, and purchases of major consumer durables are jointly determined, and that past behaviour should be reflected by current family composition, current stocks of consumer durables, and other household characteristics. In cross-sectional studies and in short panels these variables could therefore be used to control for past behaviour or to supplement data on past behaviour if the observed lag is short.

The simple life-cycle model only allows for the effects of investments in human capital in a rather primitive way. Expected future earnings are a function of present schooling and experience. However, decisions about work today influence the accumulation of human capital and thus also future wages. A tax reform which is expected to decrease future marginal taxes should thus stimulate investment activities today: people, and in particular young people, should tend to shift from consumption activities or non-investment activities to market work which involves investments for the future. A budget constraint which includes these incentives would thus be a function not only of the present income tax scales operating on current incomes but also of future scales operating on expected future incomes. It would also be a function of the taxation of non-earned income and wealth, not only of income taxes. An analysis of this scope has not yet been made. In many studies of life-cycle labour supply, taxes have been ignored altogether. An exception is Blundell and Walker (1986), who use marginal wage rates in their empirical work. The tax structure is, however, not part of their model framework. Blundell (1987) concludes that the intertemporal labour-supply elasticities reported in studies of life-cycle behaviour are small and unreliable for prime-age men. For women they are larger but more varied.

There are only a few Swedish studies using life-cycle-consistent models. One is Aronsson and Wikström (1991), who use the assumption of an intertemporally separable family utility function which is maximized subject to a dynamic budget constraint which takes the Swedish income tax system into account. Their assumptions imply that current saving contains all the information about the future needed to determine current hours of work. They thus condition the labour-supply functions of the two spouses on family saving, and estimate these functions by the maximum-likelihood method in the Hausman–Blomquist framework. Their estimates, based on the 1981 cross-section of the Level of Living Survey (LNU), show that women are more responsive than men to wage rate and income changes, and that cross-effects between the two spouses are important. Own wage rate elasticities at sample mean were 0.45 and 1.1 for men and women respectively, and the cross-elasticities –0.35 and –0.7. These estimates imply that a decrease in marginal taxes will result in a reallocation of market work hours within the household away from the wife towards the husband. As the husband will usually experience the largest tax cut and the wife's response to this is estimated to be relatively strong, the net result is a small decrease in family supply of work hours.

In a recent interesting dissertation Hansson-Brusewitz (1992) extends the labour-supply analysis to include the joint effects of the tax and pension systems. Two models are estimated, both in the Hausman–Blomquist tradition. One is a life-cycle model which takes into account that current labour supply will affect future pensions, and allows for the possibility of partial pension and a varying pension age. The other model is an atemporal model which only includes current pension benefits in the budget set. The life-cycle model gave an uncompensated own-period wage rate elasticity of about 0.1. The income effect was not significantly different from zero. In a simulation experiment Hansson-Brusewitz showed that a 10 percentage point decrease in the marginal taxes increased labour supply of the elderly (above 55 years) by about 3%. Most of them increased their hours of work, but some reduced pre-retirement hours of work and increased the retirement age.

The wage rate elasticities of the atemporal model was about twice those of the life-cycle model and a 10 percentage point decrease in the marginal taxes yielded a 5.5% increase in average hours of work. Hansson-Brusewitz recognized that his results relied on a number of untested assumptions which might be restrictive, and that 'the phasing-out of elderly men's labour supply to a large extent is caused by ageing per se and that a poor state of health may accelerate the process', but he also found important incentive effects on labour supply from the tax and pension systems (cf. section 3.5).

The time-use study by Flood and Klevmarken (1990) uses a completely different approach, but one which might still be viewed as a crude life-cycle approach. Because of the short period of observation, only two days, time-use data did not permit a model which enforced a budget constraint; one has to estimate a kind of reduced form. They used a self-selection type of model with two equations, one to explain the probability of observing non-zero working hours and one to explain hours of work given that the respondent worked. It was estimated separately for males and females. Variables like schooling, experience, the household's present net wealth, the wage rate net of marginal income tax, and non-labour income were assumed to index the life-cycle budget constraint. In addition, preference differences were modelled by marital status, age, number of children, household size, if the household owns the house/apartment in which they live, and region. The problem with an endogenous marginal tax rate was circumvented by the assumption that people base their decisions on last year's marginal tax rate. The authors argue that this might be a realistic assumption, as people in general cannot know their marginal tax rate until they have completed their self-assessment form in February the year after the incomes accrued. This assumption has empirical support in the interview study by Wahlund (1987), which showed that people learn about their marginal tax rate with a lag of about one year. All results indicated a backward-bending supply curve for males as well as for females. The uncompensated wage rate elasticities were –0.23 and –0.38 respectively. Non-labour income gave strong negative effects for both genders, while the wealth effect was positive for males and insignificantly negative for females. A positive wealth effect might be the result of an intertemporal exchange of current work hours for future leisure.

Labour Supply Is a Joint Family Decision

Most labour-supply studies have treated single persons and married/cohabiting couples alike and ignored the fact that labour supply is a joint family decision (see Ch. 2). Separate labour-supply functions were fitted for males and females. For males this might historically not have been a very unrealistic assumption, but for Sweden today it most certainly is. In an attempt to stay in the utility framework of one individual, people have sometimes conditioned on the spouse's earnings by adding it to non-earned income. Again, this might have been a reasonable thing to do when analysing female labour supply, but it does not appear to correspond to the behaviour of Swedish families today. (Although S. Gustafsson (1992*a*) assumes that the husband's income is exogenous in her interesting comparison of the labour supply of women in Germany and Sweden, she is able to demonstrate that the policy choice between joint and separate taxation of spouses is important for the labour supply of women (see the discussion of this article in Ch. 6).

Relatively few studies have attempted to model the joint decisions of two spouses. Examples are Hausman and Ruud (1984) and for Sweden the work by Strøm *et al.* and Aronsson and Wikström (1991) referred to above. These studies assume a 'family utility function'. The problem with this approach is that the axioms which lie behind a utility function only apply to a single individual. We thus do not know what properties a 'family utility function' should have, and in particular there is no reason to assume that the Slutsky conditions hold. To find a solution to this problem people have assumed individual utility functions, but embedded in an objective function for the family. Again, we know very little about the properties of this objective function. We have to impose some structure in order to get any predictions from our theory. A frequent assumption is that of weak separability of the individual utilities. This is a convenient assumption, but a priori unrealistic. There are also interesting game-theoretical approaches which impose a structure on the problem. The truth is, however, that we have no satisfactory framework for modelling joint family decisions about work and consumption. Only by collecting information, data, about family decision-making are we likely to obtain such a framework.

The presence of small children and their effect on decisions about market work is another aspect of joint family decisions. Flood (1988) and Flood and Klevmarken (1990) show that in families with small children *both* the male and female shift their time from the market to child care and household work. Their estimates suggest that males with a child 3 years old or younger work on average about 6 hours less per week in the market and females about 13 hours less. Although not explicit in their model, these relatively large effects are probably a result of the generous benefits parents of small children get from the Swedish social-security system. In other studies the wage rate effect has been differentiated in terms of the presence of children. For instance, using the Michigan Panel Study of Income Dynamics, Wales and Woodland (1977) found uncompensated wage rate elasticities for females in families without children in the range 0.13–0.39 and in families with children in the range –0.01–0.13. Blundell and Walker (1982) found a relatively high positive elasticity for British females with no children and a negative elasticity for those with 2 children. The labour supply of women with children is thus less responsive to wage rate (and tax) changes than childless women. Flood's and Klevmarken's result that not only women but also men with small children reduce their hours is, to our knowledge, unique to Sweden, however.

In a life-cycle perspective the number and spacing of children is not exogenous; decisions about work and children are joint decisions and should be modelled and analysed jointly. This is a relatively new area for economic research; see e.g. Hill and Stafford (1985).

How Much Do We Know about Tax Incentives and Labour Supply?

What do we know about labour-supply responses in Sweden to changes in wage rates, marginal tax rates, and incomes? Most, but not all, studies give positive uncompensated wage rate elasticities, in particular for women, and negative income elasticities. However, a truthful answer based on evidence from microdata is, unfortunately, that we do not know very much! As pointed out, there are good reasons to disbelieve the estimates of a slightly forward-bending supply curve obtained in the static approach with a 'completely' specified budget set. We have also presented cross-sectional results obtained by different methods which indicate backward-bending supply curves for men and women. Research on the incentive effects of labour supply has still a long way to go before we can expect any solid empirical evidence.

Much of the discussion above has concentrated around the slope of the labour-supply curve, and one might object that interest should be more focused on the substitution effects, which tell us something about the distortions of a progressive tax system, and less on the income effect. The tax system will create distortions independently of the particular choice between work and leisure, and one might argue that the sign of the income effect is of secondary interest because people know best if they increase their well-being by increasing their leisure or their consumption of goods and services. It is unfortunate, then, that estimates of the substitution effects depend very much on the assumptions made about preferences and the specification of the budget set. We know even less about compensated elasticities than about uncompensated. It is also a very one-sided view to concentrate only on the substitution effects. Everyone knows that politicians are interested in the distribution of leisure and incomes, and thus in the size and magnitude of the income effects for various groups.

Given the lack of consensus about these incentive effects within the profession, it is remarkable that a few of the Swedish studies were so influential when the 1990/1 tax reform was decided. In particular Blomquist's analysis, which suggested relatively large incentive effects on labour supply, contributed to the decision not to fund the reform fully. It is also interesting to note how the members of the committee which designed the tax reform chose among the results of the studies presented to get arguments which would fit their political views. (See the report from the committee part one, SOU 1989:33, in particular the declaration of dissenting opinions at the end of the report.)

Realistic labour-supply models would seem to become very complex, in particular if we take a life-cycle perspective. How can we find a balance between realism in details and useful applicability? How much a priori structure should we impose on data? Assumptions about more or less sophisticated utility functions has the advantage of suggesting functional forms which involve economic parameters of interest. They have the disadvantage of imposing constraints on data which are not always that obvious, and might have been rejected by data if properly tested. One lesson we have learned is that a model must be exposed to very careful misspecification testing. A model which does not explain data well in a statistical sense is not a good basis for economic analysis.

Realistic modelling of people's true budget set should involve major features of income-related and means-tested transfer programmes, in particular those of the social-security system. It would also involve modelling of multi-period budgets to accommodate a dynamic analysis. It is obvious that a model which tracks all details would be very data-demanding and cumbersome to handle. The degree of detail needed is an open question. We need to know more about the information set people use when they decide about their labour supply.

The dynamics of labour supply and joint family decisions must also become central themes in future research. From a theoretical point of view, it is obvious that the full apparatus of the life-cycle model is needed, but the idea of an average life-cycle path from which there are individual and temporary deviations might be useful. Given that our theoretical position with respect to joint family decisions and the dynamics of labour supply is relatively weak, it might be preferable to put less a priori structure on the problem compared to the approach which currently tends to be adopted.

We must also become more critical and demanding as to the data we use. We too often use much effort in accommodating theory and models to the data we happen to get access to in the faint hope of being able to say at least something. The labour-supply literature gives many examples. There is a lack of experimental planning in our science. Why not spend more resources on carefully planned data collection operations rather than on complex econometric modelling to compensate for deficiencies in data collected for other purposes? The Swedish Parliament has commissioned new data collection and a number of studies of the effects of the Swedish tax reform, which it is hoped will be able to provide new evidence on the incentive effect. Unfortunately, the Swedish economy has gone through major changes unrelated to the tax reform—in particular unemployment has skyrocketed—which are likely to influence severely our chances of disentangling the effects of the tax reform.

3.5. THE SWEDISH TRANSFER SYSTEM

In this part of the chapter we describe various transfer programmes targeted at persons of active age, and survey research on their effects on labour supply. In some cases we also examine new empirical material for possible relevance to the issues. There are many transfer programmes, and we group them under the headings (*a*) sickness cash benefits and early exit programmes, (*b*) transfers to families with children, (*c*) unemployment benefits and related transfers.

When comparing transfer programmes and research on their effects in countries surveyed in this book, some differences are noteworthy. Up to the 1990s open unemployment was not much of a social problem in Sweden. Thus we have nothing to say here on long-term unemployment and programmes targeted at this group. This is in contrast with, for example, Denmark where special programmes have been instutionalized (see Ch. 7). Also, because of the high labour force participation by females in Sweden, the issue of analysing non-participation in the labour force of the wives of unemployed men addressed in British research (see Ch. 5) has not been analysed in Sweden. Instead one finds research on the effects of active labour market policy and of family policy. Sweden's family policy deviates from those in other countries in some respects because large sums are paid as cash benefits to parents and the public sector provides day care for an increasing proportion of young children. More material on how Sweden compares to other countries in this respect can be found in Chapter 6 on Germany.

Sickness Cash Benefits and Early Exit

Total sums transferred as cash to households in the system of sickness insurance, work injury, and early-retirement pensions (*Sjukförsäkring*, *Arbetsskadeförsäkring* and *Förtidspension*) expressed as GDP proportions are illustrated in Fig. 3.8. Together these payments amounted to 5.5% of GDP at the beginning of the 1990s—a higher proportion than during the 1970s and 1980s. (The large expansion in 1974 was due to increased benefit levels, when the benefits were simultaneously made subject to income tax.) When disaggregating, we see that amounts of disability pensions have increased more or less continuously, and those in the system of occupational/work injury insurance increased strongly during the second half of the 1980s. On the other hand, payments in the sickness insurance system have not trended upwards since 1974.

The benefits we are discussing in this section have a rather pronounced age profile (see Table 3.4). Among households having a head aged 55–64 years, sickness cash benefits account for 6% of gross income, but for only 3 per cent among households having a head younger than 45 years of age. In absolute terms differences are even greater, as older households have larger gross income than younger households. Most households in active ages receive some sickness cash benefit during a year. Older persons receive benefits for more days compared to young persons. The pension

FIG 3.8. Transfers Due to Sickness, Disability, and Occupational Injuries as a Percentage of GDP, 1970–1992
Source: National Accounts, Statistics Sweden.

TABLE 3.4. Sickness Cash Benefits and Pensions for Families with Heads of Various Ages, 1985

	Age of household head					All households (incl. aged)
	‹24	25–34	35–44	45–54	55–64	
Yearly averages (SEK)						
Sickness cash benefits	2,271	4,892	4,894	9.147	9,515	4,527
Pensions	288	1,286	2,737	7,272	33,044	23,612
% households receiving						
Sickness cash benefits	67	78	75	76	64	55
Pensions	4	5	8	18	55	38
Averages as % of gross income						
Sickness cash benefits	3.2	3.5	2.7	5.4	6.1	3.5
Pensions	0.4	0.9	1.5	4.3	21.2	18.2

Source: Unpublished data from the Household Income Survey (HINK), Statistics Sweden.

payments are even more strongly related to age of household head. Less than 10% of households having a head below 45 years receive pension payments during a year. (Table 3.4 includes all form of pension payments, thus also pensions to widows and children.) More than half of those households with a head aged 55–64 have pension income, and for the average household in this age group pension payments make up 21% of gross income.

First we discuss the system of sickness cash benefits and studies of its effect on utilization and labour supply. Sickness cash benefits were paid in Sweden for the first time by local mutual associations more than one hundred years ago. Gradually these bodies united and involvement from the public sector increased. At the beginning of the 1930s fewer than 1 million persons were insured in publicly recognized societies covering a minority of the population in active ages. At that time the coverage rate was lower than in many of the present OECD countries. But two decades later more than 3 million people were covered by sickness insurance. In 1955 the sickness insurance was made universal for those of working age, with only a few exceptions, and the number of insured increased to 5.5 million persons. (For the history of the Swedish sickness insurance system, see Lindqvist 1990.)

Sickness cash benefits are paid in different systems. All those insured can receive benefits from the public benefit system. Employees might receive additional payments. In the case of a work injury, compensation starts to be paid in the sickness cash benefit system but after a predetermined period is taken over by the employment injury/work injury insurance (*Yrkesskadeförsäkringen*/ *Arbetsskadeförsäkring*, the former covering accidents that occurred before July 1977, the latter more recent accidents). Benefits in the sickness insurance system are related to present income. In 1955 benefits were paid after three 'waiting' days, and the replacement rate was relatively low. After 90 days of a period the replacement rate fell, and compensation was exhausted after two years.

Most changes in the system of sickness insurance following the introduction of general insurance meant higher expenditures for the public sector. Starting in 1963, benefits are paid for an unlimited period. Two waiting days were removed in 1967, when the replacement rate was also increased. Originally, sickness cash benefits were not subject to income tax, but this was changed in 1974 when benefit levels were increased. By this reform the compensation rate increased to about 90% for most wage earners. The last waiting day was removed in December 1987, and at the same time the method for calculating benefits was changed, with the purpose of targeting compensation better to part-time workers and shift-workers.

Recent reforms of the sickness insurance and work injury insurance systems aim to decrease public expenditure. Benefits were lowered in

March 1991 to a replacement rate of 65% for the first three days, and the replacement rate is 80% up to day 90 after which it is 90%. The compensation from public systems is regularly topped with additional payments from contractual insurances. Starting in January 1992 and following the example of the UK, payments during the first fourteen days of a sickness period have been shifted to the employers. Employers now have to pay a 'sickness wage' (*Sjuklön*) which is not refunded by the public sector.

During the Parliament session of spring 1993, further cuts were suggested by the government. It has been proposed that the concept of 'work injury' is redefined. This is estimated to decrease public expenditure by 2 billion SEK in 1996. The government has further suggested a reintroduction of the first waiting day in the system of sickness insurance, and reductions in benefit levels have been proposed. The following replacement rates have been suggested: 65% for the first two days (after the waiting day), thereafter 80% up to day 365, followed by the level 70%.

Evidence on effects from the sickness cash benefit system

Do sickness payments make people work less? Of course, there are situations in which staying at home from work is simply because of health status, and not subject to individual choice. In addition, room for decisions are restricted by the insurance-system. For example, for periods longer than a week a certificate from a physician must be provided to the social-security office, where it is decided if the person is eligible for a benefit.

But in several cases there are various options for the individual. By compensating for income loss, the system of sickness insurance makes the alternative of refraining from work more attractive. Therefore one would expect utilization of the sickness insurance benefit to be positively related to the replacement rate. A longer waiting period makes it more expensive to start an episode with sickness insurance payments. However, waiting periods also increase expected costs of returning to work in case there is uncertainty of health status. Increasing waiting periods can therefore be expected to lead to fewer but longer sickness periods. Also, administrative practices in the social-security office might influence utilization.

What do empirical studies on the relation between sickness insurance and labour supply indicate? Studies of Swedish experiences are few, and we start with findings from a cross-country investigation. Cross-country studies of social-insurance utilization are difficult to make because of difficulties in obtaining comparable numbers on the relevant phenomena, and in a cross-section the number of observations is often small. The study of Kangas (1991) uses the average number of sickness insurance utilizations per insured (*Sjuktalet*, the sickness number) during a year as a dependent variable. For a pooled cross-section sample of seven countries (including Germany, Sweden, and the United Kingdom) and for six years of observations, he was not able to find a significant relation between the replacement rate and the dependent variable. Kangas also analysed a cross-section of 18 OECD countries in 1985. In this data Sweden has, after Ireland, the largest sickness number, 21 days (the figures are 10 for Denmark, 19 for Germany and 16 for the UK). His estimates showed a negative effect of the number of waiting days, positive effect of the duration of benefit, and positive effect of the unemployment rate. While in the various specifications most of the coefficients had reasonably high t-statistics, this was not the case for the coefficient of the replacement rate. According to those results one single waiting day only (in 1985) and unlimited duration help to explain the relatively large average number of sickness utilizations in Sweden.

The time-series for the average number of days compensated by sickness insurance payments has been analysed by Lantto and Lindblom (1987) and Backman (1992), using different specifications. The former study covers the period 1956–85, the latter 1935–90. Changes in the insurance system were modelled by dummy variables. In both studies the coefficient for the reform in 1967 came out with a high t-statistic, and this also applies to the coefficient for the reform coming into full effect in 1988 analysed in the second study. (This also applies to a dummy for 1985, when an administrative change for public employees was made.)

Using the Level of Living Survey at the Institute of Social Research, Stockholm, Björklund (1991) studied the same dependent variable as above in a regression analysis, but with individual data. He made a cross-section analysis for 1981, restricted to persons employed in the private sector, and used ordinary least squares (OLS). Results show some effects of personal characteristics; in particular, females were found to have received sickness payments for more days. Various variables of self-reported work conditions were found to have strong effects. Especially repetitious tasks were found to have large effects. Large effects of industrial sector (28 classes) were also found, while it was difficult to find effects of firm size. Björklund's findings of strong effect of working conditions and sector can be used to justify the policy change of making employers pay the sickness wage. In the new system they have strong incentives to take measures to alleviate absence. However, the study was not designed to illustrate possible effects of the replacement rate.

Brose (1992) reports preliminary results from an ongoing study of sickness insurance utilization, using the HUS data base on all employed in 1984 and 1986, in a model including among the right-hand variables the marginal income loss when on sick-leave. When using variables measuring personal characteristics and variables for the industrial sector, the coefficient for the marginal loss variable was found to be negative and to have a t-statistic larger than 2. However, in specifications where variables on self-reported work conditions were added, some of them were found to have a high t-value; the value and significance of the marginal loss variable was reduced.

Given the relatively few studies of effects from the sickness insurance system, it seems worthwhile wide to look somewhat closer at the time-series. It seems as if possible effects have been evaluated only by analysing determinants of the number sick. There is no objection to this as long as the focus is on consequences for the public budget. However, when one is concerned with labour supply it is more useful to consider direct measure of absence. The rate of absence measures the proportion of the labour force that was absent during a week of measurement. As shown in Fig. 3.9, this fraction is higher for females than for males and increased steadily during the 1970s, when it reached a more or less stagnating level.

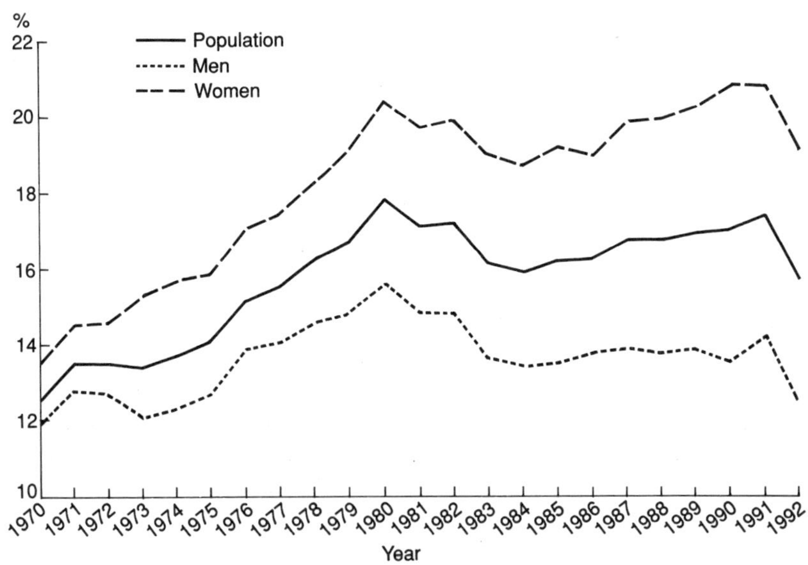

FIG 3.9. Absentee Rates, 1970–1991, by Gender
Source: Labour Force Surveys, Statistics Sweden.

There are many individual causes for absence: sickness, a holiday, birth of a child, military service, studies. A rudimentary theory of absence is that its occurence depends on its price, which most often is determined by the replacement rate in the system of sickness insurance and income. Waiting days in the system of sickness insurance makes staying off work because of sickness less attractive—which, however, might be counter-balanced by slower return to work in case of uncertainty of health status.

In order to investigate whether absence has been affected by those kinds of variable, we have run some regression models using OLS with the absentee rate as dependent variable. The replacement rate refers to a couple with typical income, and is obtained from calculations made by the Nordic Social Statistical Committee. As discussed in Chapter 5 when describing the system of unemployment insurance in Britain, a calculated replacement rate might depend much on individual circumstances. Thus one single figure for one point in time might give a less good description of how sickness insurance compensates the population in question. But if the structure of compensation does not change much over time, a time-series showing replacement rates for a typical case might give an adequate picture of how generosity of the system has developed. In addition to the compensation rate, right-hand variables are an index of GDP, the unemployment rate, and a measure of the minimum number of holidays. When interpreting effects from the latter variable, one should keep in mind that large groups in the labour market, because of collective agreements, have often obtained better rights than the legal minimum.

TABLE 3.5. Estimates of a Regression Model for the Absentee Rate (Sample Period 1970–1992)

Intercept	Replace-ment rate	Waiting days	GDP index	Unemploy-ment rate	Holidays	R^2 (adj)	DW
-1.95	0.16	0.23	0.14		0.09	0.893	1.58
(1.18)	(5.31)	(0.55)	(0.51)		(0.97)		
-1.53	0.14	0.27		-0.37	0.23	0.923	1.98
(1.20)	(5.53)	(1.02)		(2.71)	(2.67)		

Note: Replacement rates for 1970, 1972, 1974, 1978, 1981, 1984, 1987, and 1990 were obtained from Nordisk Statitistik Skriftserie nos. 24, 29, 34, 37, 43, 47, 50, 58.

The results (see Table 3.5) show surprisingly clear effects of the replacement rate on the rate of absence, and reading across specifications they are rather stable. The various point estimates imply that a general decrease of the compensation rate by 10 percentage points would decrease the absence rate by 1.4 – 1.6 percentage points. The coefficients for the waiting-day variable have a low t-statistic. A possible reason for lack of negative effect is that rules on waiting days have affected only some parts of the labour market, while thanks to collective agreements other groups have not been affected when a waiting day was removed.

Some comments can also be made on effects of other right-hand variables. The macroeconomc situation seems to influence absence, as there is a negative effect of the unemployment rate while the coefficient for the GDP index has a low t-statistic. Numbers of holidays have positive coefficients, which in one specification has a high t-statistic.

In order to investigate whether effects of the replacement rate vary in the population, supplementary analyses of the absentee rate in various demographic groups were run. It turns out that effects are rather similar for males and females. Somewhat more variation between age groups was found. The lowest coefficient for the replacement rate were obtained for the age group 45–54 and 55–9, the highest for the category 60–4. The relatively high sensitivity to economic incentives among those close to the general retirement age parallels results on early exit surveyed below.

The pension system

Let us now look at pension payments and research on their effects on utilization and labour supply. Pensions are paid from several schemes in Sweden. (Longer recent descriptions of pensions and early exit from the labour force in Sweden are found in Kruse and Söderström (1989), Ståhlberg (1990), Wadensjö (1991), and Olofsson and Petersson (1993).) The oldest is the basic pension scheme (*Folkpension*), which can be traced back to 1913 when the general retirement age was set at 67 years. Since 1948 benefits have not been related to income and almost everyone is eligible. (Exceptions are at present some foreign citizens, while in the future eligibility as well as benefits will be linked to the number of years a person has been residing in Sweden.) To benefit from this scheme, the benefits of the supplementary pension scheme has been added (*Allmän tilläggspensionering*). This latter system covers all wage-earners and the self-employed, and its benefits, are linked to individual earnings histories. Income earned in a certain year and declared on an income tax return gives 'pension points' but only within certain established limits. Persons not eligible for the ATP pension, or eligible only for small benefits, receive pension supplements (*Pensionstillskott*). The individual supplements are reduced in proportion to the amount of the individual supplementary pension, but not to other kinds of income. Thus benefits are not tested against present income, but against previous ones. Benefits in the basic pension scheme as well as the supplementary pension scheme are in law expressed as percentages of the 'basic amount' (*Basbeloppet*). The basic amount is regularly adjusted by Parliament. With some exceptions, this standard has followed the consumer price index.

In the basic pension scheme as well as the supplementary pension scheme, disability pensions (*Förtidspension*) can be paid. A person can be eligible for a full or partial disability pension depending on work incapacity. Most recipients have a full pension. Originally, eligibility was based on a concept of invalidity founded on medical factors. The criteria have, however, been widened. In January 1970 the rules were changed in order to put more emphasis on labour market prospects for people close to the general retirement age. The change was followed up already in 1972, when older persons who had used up their unemployment benefits became eligible independently of medical circumstances. The number of persons at early retirement was about 150,000 during the 1950s (or somewhat more than a one-year birth cohort) but started to increase in the mid-1960s, to reach double the size in the beginning of the 1980s. The expansion of the number receiving a disability pension still continues, but the flow into the system is not much higher than twenty years ago.

Several reforms of the pension system came into effect in July 1976. The general retirement age was reduced to 65. It was also made possible for a person to choose a starting date for receiving old-age pension within an interval starting at 60 years and ending at 70 years of age. Earlier utilization leads to lower benefits for all subsequent years and, conversely, later utilization to higher benefits. The adjustments of the compensation are approximately actuarly fair.

Also, since July 1976 pensions may be paid in accordance with the Partial Pension Insurance Act (*Delpension*). Eligible are those fulfilling certain conditions about part-time work; the person should not additionally receive any old-age or disability pension. These pension benefits are paid between the age of 60 and the general retirement age. The replacement rate was originally set at 65% of gross income, which due to progressive taxation means a considerably higher net replacement rate. However, the replacement rate was lowered in 1981 to 50% of gross income for new applicants by the Non-Social Democratic Government. From July 1987 the replacement rate was again set at 65% by the Social Democratic Government.

A recent reform puts more emphasis on rehabilitation, measures which might decrease public expenditure in the future. From 1992, employers were requested to start a rehabilitation investigation when an employee had been absent from work and drawing sickness cash benefits for more than four weeks. When engaged in rehabilitation the person is eligible for a special transfer payment (*Rehabiliteringspenning*) supposed to compensate for additional expenses because of rehabilitation. Other reforms aim to decrease public expenditures directly. Since October 1991 disability pensions cannot be paid, based solely on labour market prospects. During the parliamentary session 1992/3, a gradual increase in the general retirement age to 66 years, to take effect in 1997, is expected to be decided. (During the session 1992/3, cuts in the programme for part-time retirement have been suggested by the government. However, at the time of completing this text decisions have not been made.)

Besides public pensions there are contractual pensions (*Avtalspensioner*) covering most people employed in the Swedish labour market. Not covered are mainly those working in temporary or part-time jobs, and some workers employed by small firms not belonging to an employers' confederation. (For further details see Edelbalk and Wadensjö 1989.)

Where the public pension is low, a person can receive a municipal housing supplement (*Kommunalt bostadstillägg*). This is a means-tested benefit system in which scales decided by each municipal assembly are used. In the system there is considerable variation in generosity between locations. (However, a recent parliamentary committee (SOU 1992: 21), has suggested that national standards should be used.)

TABLE 3.6. Percentage of the Swedish Population Aged 60–64 Receiving Various Pension Benefits, December 1988

Pension benefit	Age					
	60	61	62	63	64	60–4
Full disability pension (incl. handicap allowance)	21.1	25.2	29.0	32.3	34.6	28.5
Partial disability pension	3.6	3.9	3.9	3.8	3.5	3.7
Early drawing of old-age pension	1.2	2.0	2.9	4.0	5.0	3.0
Part-time pension	6.5	9.4	9.7	9.4	8.8	8.8
TOTAL	32.4	40.5	45.6	49.6	52.0	44.1

Source: SOU 1989: 101, p.92.

How frequent are the different pension benefits used by the population under the general retirement age? Table 3.6 gives a snapshot for 1988. At age 60 one-third of the population received some kind of pension benefit, and the population share receiving a pension increased to about half immediately before the general retirement age occurs. The most often used benefit is a full early-retirement, which is received by somewhat more than one in four persons below the general retirement age. A part-time pension is received by less than 10% of these below 65, while early drawings are seldom made. Flow statistics show considerable variation in frequency for granting different pension payments. For example, the number of new part-time pensions granted decreased from 33,000 in 1980 to 13,000 the year following that, when the replacement rate for new pensions had been reduced. Early-retirement owing to labour market conditions has usually been granted to only a few thousand persons yearly. In 1985, however, two years after the unemployment rate peaked during this business cycle, new pensions for this reason amounted to more than 10,000.

Public pension payments are subject to income tax, but pensioners have a higher personal tax exemption than other persons. What can be said on replacement rates in the system of pensions? Over a long period benefits have increased faster than wages. According to Hedström (1980; 1987) the average disability pension increased in real terms by 340% from 1952 to 1976, during a period when the average real wage in manufacturing increased by 97%. Calculations of replacement rates for disability pensions for 1990 show the following figures (net of taxes) for a single person with various wages (Sosial trygghet 1992): half average wage: 89%; average wage: 70%; twice average wage: 59%. To this should be added benefits from contractual insurances. This leads to replacement rates in many cases close to 100%.

Evidence concerning behavioural effects

What does research on pension benefits and labour supply show? There are studies of utilization, but an investigation of numbers of hours in market work directly can also be found. An early attempt to address the issue was made by Berglind (1977), working with cross-sectional data on municipalities. The study used as dependent variables the stock of early retired in 1974, as well as the flow into early retirement the same year, both expressed as proportions of the total population. Results showed a positive effect of the relative unemployment rate. Also, a kind of replacement rate variable was found to have a positive effect. (The variable in question was defined as average pension income as percentage of average income in the population of the municipality.) Wadensjö (1985) used time-series data for men aged 60–4 for the period 1963–80. The estimates showed positive effects of a variable measuring replacement rate and of dummy variables indicating changes in the rules governing provision of disability pension.

Microdata studies have used the Level of Living Survey. Hedström (1980; 1987) related a dummy variable, indicating status as disability-retired or not, to unemployment the preceding year, own reported health status, and demographic variables. The same equation was run for 1968 and 1974. A considerably higher proportion disability-retired was observed in the later year. According to the estimates, this difference can be explained, not by changes in variables, but by changed coefficients which indicate increased propensities to retire. The rise of the disability pension during the 1970s might thus have been the result of legislative changes that increased benefits and broadened the definition of eligibility.

Hansson-Brusewitz (1992) modelled labour supply using a life-cycle model with the aim of incorporating the non-separable properties of budget constraint and non-linear income taxes (see also Section 3.4).

Hours of work and retirement age, as well as age of partial retirement, are choice variables in the model. The model is estimated by the method of maximum likelihood using data for 1973 and 1980 for married men aged 55–70. Data do not cover self-employed, farmers, and persons receiving a disability pension before 60 years of age.

What kind of results do simulations produce? Generally, the average age of retirement is only marginally affected. Increasing gross hourly wage increases hours of work, and increasing asset holdings decreases hours of work. While these effects are rather small, a cut in marginal tax rate by ten points on all levels of income is simulated to have a much larger and positive effect on hours of work. Abolishing partial pensions is simulated to increase the number of hours worked while part-time retired. However, the effect on number of hours worked as a full-time worker has the opposite sign, and is of the same magnitude. Thus, taken together, life-time hours of work are relatively unaffected. The partial pension system seems thus, according to the results, mainly to reshuffle hours of work over the life-span. However, this result is model-specific. In an atemporal model the partial pension is found to have a negative effect on hours of work.

Simulations of changes in the basic pension system and the system of supplementary pensions were also made. Abolishing the former marginally was found to decrease hours of work before partial retirement but to increase considerably more the corresponding number after partial retirement. Reducing the compensation rate in the supplementary pension system was found to have negative effects concentrated in the period before partial retirement. On the other hand, applying a new formula, making benefits stronger in relation to work history, increased hours of work. Thus effects were concentrated in the period as part-time retired.

Further evidence on the importance of the pension system for labour supply can be found in studies of Swedish plant closure. Storrie (1993) reports on subsequent labour market status for these employed by the Uddevalla Shipyard, which was shut down in the mid-1980s. Almost everyone over 58 years of age was found to have left the labour force with some kind of pension. Among persons aged 53–7 the proportion was much smaller. (However, measured closer to a shut-down the situation might have appeared different. According to rules prevailing in the mid-1980s, but now abandoned, a person aged 58 years and 3 months could almost automatically take early-retirement via a period of unemployment. Thus Edin (1988: Ch. 3) reports a large effect of being 58 years old on unemployment in a study of some hundred workers redundant because of closing a pulp plant in northern Sweden in 1977. Additional evidence on a fairly high incidence of unemployment shortly after shut-downs is provided in Edin (1988: Ch. 2). Here labour market status about five months after the shut-down is reported for 122 closures taking place from 1974 to 1980. In this data, one out of five were reported as unemployed, and the proportion is very clearly positively related to age.

Summary

What general conclusions can be drawn on the relation in Sweden between sickness benefits and pensions schemes on the one hand and labour supply on the other? The least research effort seems to have been devoted to the possible effects of sickness cash benefits. We therefore analysed the time-series for the absence rate 1970–92 from the Labour Force Survey. The results indicate quite clearly that replacement rates in the system of sickness cash benefits affect absence. In this respect there seems to be no difference between males and females.

The findings of studies surveyed here indicate that labour supply among those close to general retirement age is fairly sensitive to economic incentives. This is because absence was found to be affected by the replacement rate in the system of sickness cash benefits, in addition to the participation rates being affected by pension payments. But from the research (Hansson-Brusewitz 1992) we also learn that effects can be more complicated than one can assume from an atemporal model. For example, eliminating the partial pension scheme might increase hours of work before partial retirement, thus counterbalancing the fact that such an abolition would increase hours of work during partial retirement.

Transfers to Families with Children

The systems

Transfers targeted to families with children measured as a proportion of GDP are illustrated in Fig. 3.10, together with public expenditure on child care. As a package these expenditures increased from slightly less than 3% in 1973 to about 6% in 1991. Much of the expansion comes from the increased expenditures on public child care, as discussed below. However, cash transfers also increased, especially parents' cash benefits.

There are several transfer systems targeted at families with children in Sweden. Child allowances (*Almännt barnbidrag*) were introduced in 1948, and were paid at a flat rate for all children residing in the country. Since 1982 additional child allowances (*Flerbarnstilägg*) have been paid where there are at least three children in the family, making the benefits progressive in the number of children after the second child. For example, the schedule in effect in 1991 implies that a family with five children receives benefits eight times as large as a family with only one

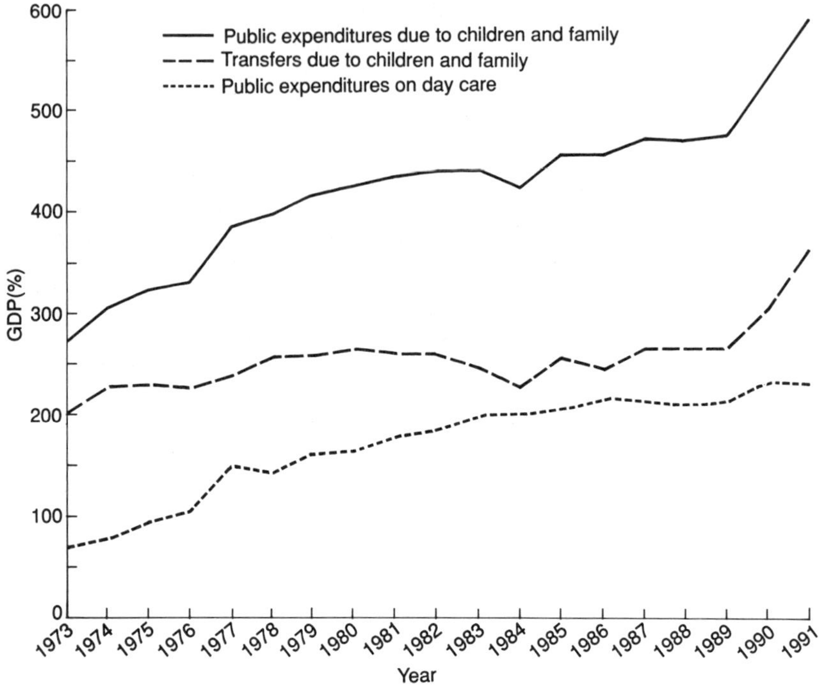

FIG 3.10. Child-Related Transfers, 1970–1992
Source: National Accounts and Social Statistics, Statistics Sweden.

child. Child allowances are paid for persons up to the age of 16. A similar benefit is paid to those attending secondary school.

The level of child allowances is *not* linked to the consumer price index, and the allowances are not subject to income tax. In order to compensate for the adverse income-redistribution effects of the recent tax reform, child benefits were increased rapidly at the end of the 1980s (for an analysis of the distributional consequences of Swedish tax reform, see Schwarz and Gustafsson 1991). For example, the benefit was set to 9,000 SEK per year for one child in January 1991, which in real terms is 50% higher than in 1980 (or not very different from an average monthly wage net of taxes for a full-time employed person). Because of the introduction of the additional child allowances to families with many children, the benefit increase has been much higher for large families. For example, in 1991 a family with five children received child benefits in real terms 2.4 times as high as in 1980.

Housing benefits (*Bostadsbidrag*) are income-tested and not subject to income tax. The benefits are administered by the municipalities but financed mainly by the central government budget. (Recently it has been suggested that the administration be transformed to social insurance offices; SOU (1992: 89). Families without children can also be eligible for housing allowances, but the majority of the recipients are families with children. Compared to the total sums paid as child allowances, resources channelled through the housing benefits system are small. Most single parents and couples with many children receive housing benefits. Thus, according to the household income survey, 70% of single parents and 57% of couples with at least three children were reported to receive a housing benefit in 1985. On the other hand, only 16% of the much more numerous category of couples with one or two children were reported as receiving a housing benefit. During the beginning of the 1980s the number of recipients decreased gradually. However, more generous scales motivated by the tax reform at the end of the 1980s increased the number of recipients.

The system of parent's cash benefits (*Föräldraförsäkring*) has several features. Most expenditures are due to the parent's cash benefit for childbirth (*Föräldrapenning i samband med barns födelse*), meaning that every family has the right to draw compensation for a maximum period. Although both parents are eligible for such benefits, the dominant part of days compensated goes to mothers. When the present system was introduced in 1974 the maximum period was 180 days. Later, the period expanded on several occasions. Since July 1989 the period has been 450 days. For the first 360 days the system compensates about 90% of income losses for most parents. Later days are compensated by a flat rate. After using up benefits for one birth, a parent can remain at the same benefit level for a second birth without going back to work, provided the second leave starts within a certain short period. The maximum interval between two births keeping the same benefit level has gradually been increased from about one year in 1974 to two-and-a-half years in 1986.

Parental cash benefits can also be paid during pregnancy (*Havandeskapspenning*), and in special cases when parents have to refrain from market work. These benefits are also motivated by goals of equality between sexes (Haas 1992). There are three kinds of special occasion entitling payments. First is the birth of a child, during which the father is eligible to benefits for ten days. The take-up rate is very high for this benefit. Second is the care of sick children. Such benefits can be paid up to 60 days per year and per child. Such benefits are mainly used by mothers, but about one-third of all days compensated relate to fathers staying home from work. Third, benefits can be paid one or two days per year and per child when parents of a child visit a day care centre or a school. These benefits are not widely used. (When the present government came to office in October 1991, it stated that a new transfer,

Vårdnadsbidrag, for young children should be introduced; but up to now no definite proposals have been laid before Parliament.)

Since March 1991 the replacement rates have been lowered to 80% for temporary care of children for the first two weeks compensated. After that, 90% of income losses (up to a ceiling) are compensated. The 90% compensation rate still applies to the other parent's cash benefits from the first day (although a cut has recently been proposed to Parliament by the government).

Maintenance allowances might affect labour supply by those paying as well as those receiving. In the case where a child's parents are living apart, the parent not having custody of the child usually pay a maintenance allowance (*Underhållsbidrag*). While it is up to the parent and eventually a court to decide upon sums, a central authority (*Socialstyrelsen*, the Department of Social Welfare) has issued guidelines on how to calculate an allowance. Maintenance advances (*Bidragsförskott*) have been introduced to prevent the recipients from being prejudiced by a parent's omission or inability to pay the allowance due. In 1990 maintenance advances were paid for 15% of all children in Sweden. The maintenance advance is paid to the custodian at a flat rate. This transfer is not subject to income tax, and the amount is guided by the 'basic amount'. (As discussed in the previous section the 'basic amount' is regularly adjusted by Parliament to reflect how consumer prices have developed. Thus benefits are more or less automatically adjusted to changes in the level of prices.)

According to the household income survey, 68% of single parents received maintenance advances in 1985. A child and its custodian are eligible for maintenance advances even if the custodian cohabits with another adult or even remarries. Thus, according to the household income survey, about 10% of all couples with children received some maintenance advance in 1985. (Before the recent tax reform, single parents were eligible for a special tax deduction. After this was abolished, a special transfer to single parents was temporarily decided in 1992. Benefits have been paid for 1991, 1992, and 1993. Changes in the system of maintenance advances has recently been suggested by the Ministry of Social Affairs (Socialdepartementet 1992). The reform implied, among other things, that the maintenance advance would have been income-tested. However, after much criticism the government decided in the autumn of 1992 not to follow those suggestions.)

If a maintenance advance is paid, the parent liable for maintenance allowance has to repay the advance. Such repayments are income-tested and are for some demographic categories not infrequent. Thus, according to the household income survey, somewhat more then one in three single males aged 35–44 paid some maintenance advances in 1985.

Public involvement in child care has increased steadily in Sweden during the last decades. At the beginning of the 1990s public resources used for child care were of the same magnitude as those for public schools, i.e. about 2% of GDP. The contribution of public day care to GDP is larger than the contribution from Swedish agriculture and comparable in size with e.g. the chemical industry. Public day care accounts for about 3% of total employment. It has many forms. Day care centres (*Daghem*) provide full-time as well as part-time care (*Play-schooling* or *Kindergarten*). Day care homes (*Familjedaghem*) are private homes where the care-giver (who most often is a mother with a young child) is contracted by the municipalitiy. The sector also covers facilities for younger schoolchildren (*Fritidshem*). At the beginning of the 1970s public child care covered about 10% of all preschoolers. At the beginning of the 1990s about two-thirds of children aged 3–6 had a placement in public child care, and the same applied to almost one in two aged 7–9. Full-time care has been expanding, while part-time care has somewhat decreased. While these coverage rates have trended upwards, the coverage rate for the youngest children peaked at about 30% in the mid-1980s. The deviant development of the coverage rate for the category of the youngest children is understandable, as parent's cash benefits have come to cover ever-longer spells of work absence due to newborns, as discussed above.

Public child care is provided by the municipalities and is mainly publicly financed. However, parents pay fees (*Barnomsorgsavgifter*) based on rates decided upon by each municipality. At prevailing rates, demand for public child care is larger than supply in many municipalities, and parents wanting public care for their children have to put them on a waiting list. There is a considerable variation in rates across the country. Most often payments increase with parental income, over a large interval of income. According to one survey (Svenska kommunförbundet 1990) about 80% of Sweden's 284 municipalities had adopted some kind of income-related rate; the rest used flat rates. One special measure adopted by one-third of all municipalities is rates which are a constant proportion, typically somewhat less than 10% of parental (gross) income. Thus there are striking similarities between fees for public day care and income taxes, making several observers looking upon the former as a kind of income tax. (For a comparison, see Gustafsson and Kjulin 1993).

Public financial aid to students has a long tradition. Earlier, such support was most often means-tested against parental income, but this has changed. Persons engaged in secondary education and older than 16 years receive a flat-rate benefit similar to the child allowance (*Studiehjälp*). University students and some other persons engaged in higher education may receive public funds (*Studiemedel*) in a system which came into effect in 1964. Benefits are tested against the applicants own present income and has two parts. The smaller is a stipend not subject to income tax (*Studiebidrag*), the other is a loan (*Återbetalningspliktiga studiemedel*). Presently there are about one million persons with debts resulting from such student loans, and they are thus fairly frequent among people of an economically active age. The amortizations of students loans has striking similarities with income tax. The terms of amortization differ between older loans and those granted since 1989. In the older system, a low income could after application lead to postponement of amortization and this occurs in approximately 20% of cases. The new student loans should be amortized yearly, with a sum calculated as 4% of the latest taxable income.

Affecting budget-sets

The various transfers to families with children affect a budget-set for a household in many ways, and might thus influence economic behaviour. First let us discuss how they can be incorporated into a model of atemporal choice between market work and leisure only. Various transfers modify a budget-set differently. Flat-rate benefits increase a budget-set uniformly; income-related benefits also change the shape of a budget-set. While the former have only an income effect on labour supply, the latter also have a substitution effect. Some benefit systems are fairly straightforward to model, others are much more difficult. We discuss the various programmes one after the other, leaving out those having only an income effect as they are relatively simple to include in standard labour supply analysis. (Attempts to include benefits when modelling marginal tax rates for 1991 are reported in Andersson and Gustafsson (1992*a*; 1992*b*), on which the following discussion draws.)

The housing benefit system adds a 'hump' to marginal income taxes (see Fig. 3.11, showing the situation for a single person). This hump is relatively small for such a person and related to income levels for persons working part-time. But existence of children increases the hump, which in the case of two children can be seen in Fig. 3.12. The hump increases by each child up to the third. Thus it affects many parents working full-time and having a moderate or even average wage-rate. The hump is also relevant for single earners with a high income if there are children in the family.

The system of student finance adds to composite marginal effects when the sums are paid but also when the loans are amortized. In the former case, an effect on behaviour is surely a deliberate property, as recipients are supposed to use much of the time for studies on which excessive market work might impinge. Amortization according to the old system leads to another hump on top of the marginal tax rate, because amortization can be postponed if income is low. For many types of family

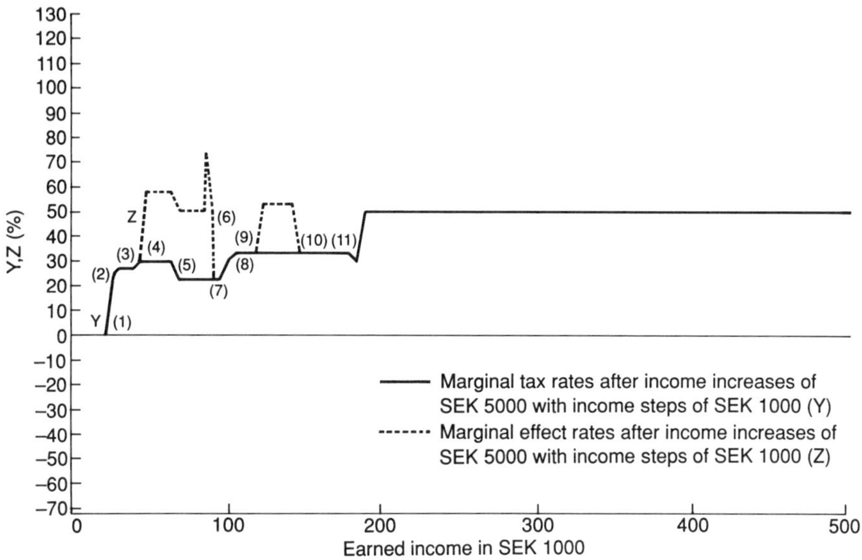

FIG 3.11. Marginal Composite Tax Rates for a Single Person, 1991

Notes: (1) The income-earner starts to pay income tax. (2) Maximum tax reduction for trade union dues. (3) Maximum standard deduction for costs. (4) The housing allowances start to decline. (5) The basic deduction starts to increase. (6) The housing allowances decline fully. (7) Maximum basic deduction. (8) The basic deduction starts to decrease. (9) The postponement of repaying student loans starts to decline. (10) The postponement of repaying student loans declines fully. (11) The basic deduction declines fully.
Source: Andersson and Gustafsson (1992*b*).

this hump is located at a somewhat higher income level than the hump from the system of housing allowances (see Fig. 3.11). However, amortization after the new system of student finance means that the marginal tax rate should be increased by a few per cent over the entire income range.

While it is possible to capture the housing benefits system and the system of student finance by algorithms applicable for most of the relevant population, it is much more difficult to model parental fees for public child care. Scales differ between municipalities and, more important, they are constructed in different ways. For example, the number of siblings can affect fees in many different ways; fees might depend on the number of hours the child is cared for; and there can be different scales for couples and single parents. In some municipalities parents have to pay a fee twelve months a year, in others they might be exempted during a summer vacation. Modelling problems are smaller if one focuses on couples with one child only in the relevant age. Unfortunately, this analytical alternative excludes most families with children.

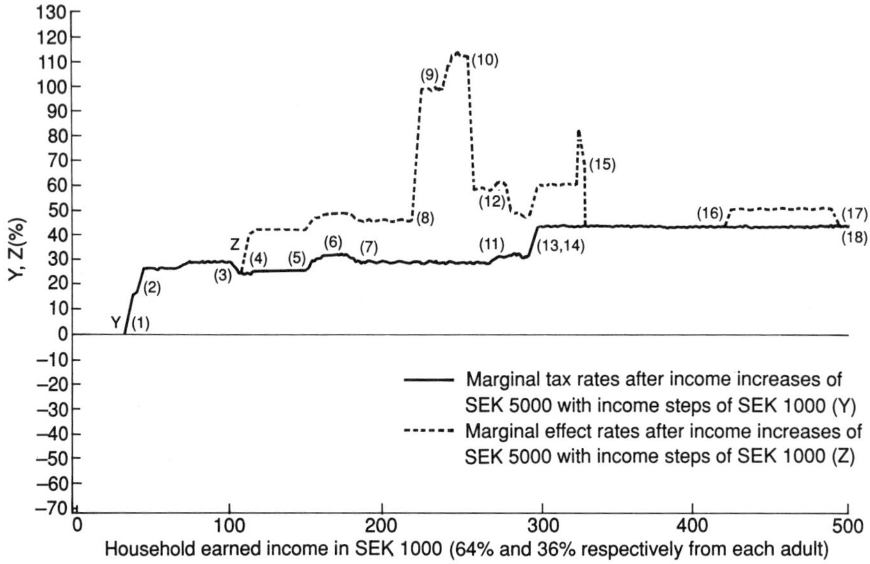

FIG 3.12. Marginal Composite Tax Rates for a Couple with Children Attending Public Day Care in the City of Stockholm, 1991

Notes: (1) The 1st income-earner starts to pay income tax. (2) The 2nd income-earner starts to pay income tax. (3) The basic deduction for earner 1 starts to increase. (4) The housing allowance starts to decline. (5) Maximum basic deduction for earner 1. (6) The basic deduction starts to decrease for earner 1. (7) The basic deduction for earner 2 starts to increase. (8) The disposable income is smaller than the norm for social assistance (216,000 SEK), leading to an income-tested fee for children's day care which is less than the ordinary fee. (9) The postponement of repaying student loans starts to decline for earner 1. (10) Testing disposable income against the norm for social assistance gives a full fee for children's day care, at the same time reaching the fee's maximum level. (11) Maximum basic deduction for earner 2. (12) The postponement of repaying student loans declines fully for earner 1. (13) The basic deduction starts to decrease for earner 2. (14) The basic deduction declines fully for earner 1. (15) The housing allowance declines fully. (16) The postponement of repaying student loans starts to decline for earner 2. (17) The postponement of repaying student loans declines fully for earner 2. (18) The basic deduction declines fully for earner 2.

Source: Andersson and Gustafsson (1992*b*).

Some scales for public child care produces rather large humps. For example, the scale in effect for the capital, Stockholm, in 1991 meant that a family whose income was below a certain threshold could be completely or partly relieved from paying a fee. This possibility augments the marginal tax rate to around 100% for a relatively short interval (see Fig. 3.12). For other scales the addition to the marginal tax rate is less dramatic. One not uncommon alternative implies an addition to marginal taxes by slightly less than ten percentage units over the entire income range.

One can discuss whether rules for paying child support and thus also maintenance advances should be thought of as modifying budget-sets and thus possibly affecting labour supply. The argument against this is that sums going from the absent parent to his (her) child have their counterpart in a nuclear family. When a parent receives a higher income, it is assumed that children in the household also benefit from it. If one talks about marginal effects from maintenance of an absent child, the argument goes, one should also talk about marginal effects from maintenance of present children. The counter-argument is that children in a nuclear family are in a much more difficult position if they try to assert a similar right to income. A child in a nuclear family is very seldom engaged in a legal process claiming its needs, while this is not infrequent for children with an absent parent.

Because decisions on child support and maintenance advance are made by parents and a court, taking many specific considerations into account, it is not easy to model them adequately. A less ambitious alternative is to make algorithms for the standards recommended by the Department of Social Welfare (*Socialstyrelsen*). When interpreting such results, one should thus bear in mind that those standards are not always applied. According to them child support provided by an absent parent increases with his (her) income provided it has gone over a certain threshold. For a given income of the threshold absent parent, child support decreases with the income of the custodian parent. What can be learned from such modelling efforts? One finds that a very sizeable hump should be added to the marginal tax rates for the absent parent when he (she) is due to pay child support. For example, when the custodian parent has a fairly low income, a hump of 377% is found for the absent parent having a very low income capacity and working full-time (see Fig. 3.13). The size of such a hump increases with the number of children an absent parent has to support. Where the custodian parent has a higher income the maximum size of the hump is lower, but it stretches over a longer interval. If the absent parent remarries and has children in the new relationship, the hump is pushed to a higher income level.

From the inspection of the various transfer payments targeted to families with children, some conclusions for modelling budget-sets can be drawn. The existence of the systems makes it difficult to specify the relevant budget-sets adequately for a considerable number of families. For atemporal modelling of choice between market work and leisure, such problems are large where there is a preschool child and particularly if a parent has to pay child support. When taking the system of transfer payments into account for calculating marginal tax rates, the highest ones

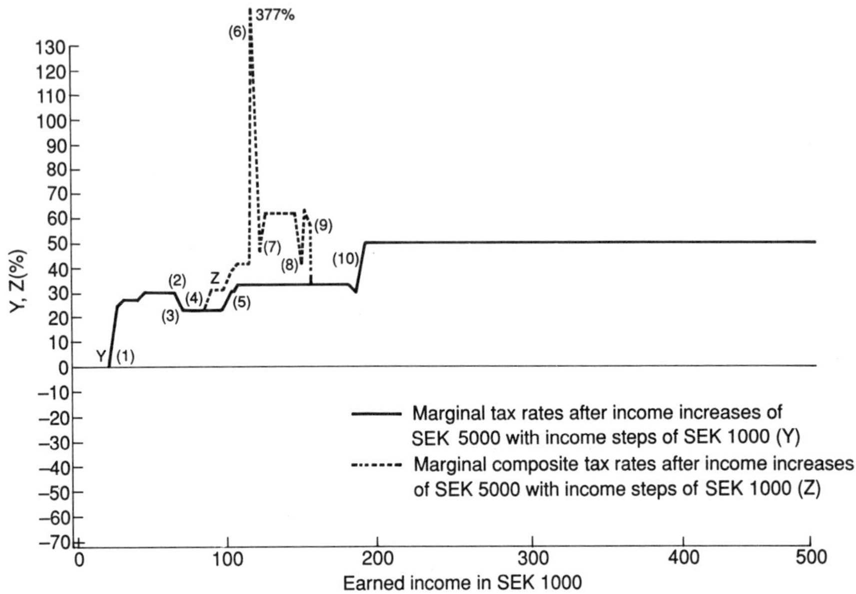

FIG 3.13. Marginal Composite Tax Rates for a Person Liable to Pay Child Support, 1991 (The custodian parent is assumed to have a low income.)

Notes: (1) The income-earner liable to pay maintenance starts to pay income tax. (2) The basic deduction starts to increase. (3) The housing allowance starts to decline. (4) Maximum basic deduction. (5) The basic deduction starts to decrease. (6) The earner liable to pay maintenance starts to do so. (7) The postponement of repaying student loans starts to decline. (8) The postponement of repaying student loans declines fully. (9) The housing allowance fully declines. (10) The basic deduction declines fully.

Source: Andersson and Gustafsson (1992*b*).

are not always found for the highest income levels. Actually the choice between work and leisure might be most distorted for persons with a relatively low income capacity.

Evidence on behavioural effects

To understand many of the decisions made by members in a household, other models than an atemporal choice between leisure and work are helpful (see Ch. 2). For example, modelling the effect of introducing subsidized public child care seems to require a household production framework. Important aspects of effects from parental insurance requires the analyst to take temporal aspects into account. This is so because the level of benefits during parental leave depend on how high the income was before the leave. Labour-supply effects are not only that the insurance benefits make the alternative of leave more attractive; the benefits also make the alternative of working full-time before leave much much more attractive. And the length of leave might have effects on subsequent wages because human capital is depreciated. The latter effect has been quantified by Sundström (1991*b*) using data on employees of the Swedish telephone company. According to the estimates, women having a parental leave of one year have *ceteris paribus* a wage increase about 2% lower during 1983–8 than women not on parental leave.

Parental-leave programmes and other benefits to families with children might have effects on other choice variables than hours of work. (1) As the public sector pays parents during parental leave, provides child care, and also pays child-related benefits, it becomes more attractive to give birth to a child. In addition, spacing of children can be thought of as affected. As parents can retain the level of compensation paid after one birth for the next, provided the interval between births is not too long, there is a 'speed premium' for close births. (2) The qualifications of the labour force might be affected, as recruitments to higher studies might be influenced by the system of student finance. (3) The alternative of staying or becoming single is made more attractive by support targeted to single parents. However, it should also be said that, compared to other possible alternatives, transfer systems in Sweden do not make it financially difficult to remarry; for example, a single mother can keep maintenance advances when remarried.

Those who believe that decisions on family formation are unaffected by changes in public transfer payments should be convinced to the contrary by Swedish experiences during the last month of 1989. In 1990 new regulations on widows' pensions came into effect. The general right to a widow's pension from the public system on the husband's death, regardless of the woman's income, was abolished. Instead, there is now a survivor's benefit that applies equally to both sexes. However, the old rules have been phased out, creating a better position for females who were married at 31 December 1989 than those cohabiting. Particularly women born in 1944 or earlier can receive the same benefits as in the old system if married, while terms are less favourable for younger females. Marriage reaction to the new rules came slowly, but in November 1989 there were 4,100 marriages, twice as many as in November 1988, and in December the figure exploded to 64,000 which is about 50% more than during a whole normal year (Hoem 1991).

While there are many possible ways in which transfer programmes to families with children can affect choices of families, little research has tried empirically to show the sensitivity of the choices. Let us start by discussing studies of labour-supply responses.

Sundström and Stafford (1992) made a cross-country analysis of female labour supply in twenty-one OECD countries at the end of the 1980s.

Right-hand variables were the total fertility rate and a set of policy variables. While the coefficient for the first-mentioned variable came out with a low t-statistic, this was not the case for coefficents of several policy variables. Public consumption as a percentage of GDP, which might serve as a demand-side variable and an indicator of services substituting for women's work at home, was found to have a positive effect. The result indicates that availability of an extensive public day care system increased the participation rate. Variables indicating parental-leave benefits were also found to have effects, with longer duration having a positive effect but shorter the reverse. Large public consumption, an extensive public day care system, and the long duration of parental-leave benefits all contribute to a high participation rate for females in Sweden.

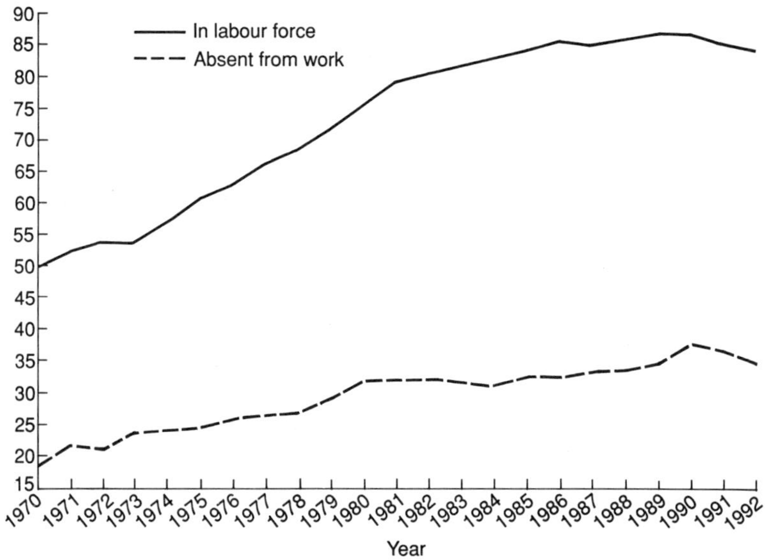

FIG 3.14. Participation Rates and Absentee Rates for Mothers with Young Children, 1970–1992
Source: Labour Force Surveys, Statistics Sweden.

Participation rates as well as absence rates for mothers with young children in Sweden have very much developed in accordance with what one might expect from the expansion of parental insurance and public child care. As shown in Fig. 3.14, the participation rate for mothers of young children increased from 50% in 1970 to somewhat more than 85% at the end of the 1980s. At the same time, the rate of absence increased from under 20% to a maximum of 38% in 1990.

What role has the increased number of days compensated at child birth played in the absence rate among mothers with young children in Sweden? We investigate this by running regression models for 1963–92. Right-hand variables are the number of waiting days and the replacement rate in the system of sickness insurance, maximum number of holidays, and unemployment rate. The results are shown in Table 3.7.

TABLE 3.7. Estimates of a Regression Model for the Absentee Rate, Mothers with Young Children, 1963–1992

Intercept	Replacement rate	Waiting days	Unemployment rate	Holidays	Length of compensation at birth	R^2 (adj)	DW
11.49	0.26	0.55	0.23	0.14	0.049	0.949	1.64
(2.86)	(5.05)	(0.76)	(0.47)	(0.39)	(4.25)		

Coefficient of two variables stand out by relatively high t-statistics: the replacement rate and the length of compensation at birth. The point estimate of the latter means that a difference in compensation of 100 days leads to a difference in the rate of absence of 4.9 percentage points. As the length of compensation at birth has expanded from 1963 by 180 days, this can be judged to have increased the absence rate by 9 percentage units. The increased length of compensation thus seems to explain much, but not all, of the increasing absence among mothers with small children.

Further evidence can be found in disaggregating the labour force survey, as it is possible to follow the labour market status of a woman over the period when she gives birth. Such data show that the proportion of first-time mothers who worked full-time up to the birth and then kept a full-time job while being absent have increased from a quarter of all first-time mothers at the beginning of the 1970s to about half at the end of the 1980s (Sundström 1991*a*).

Evidence of public child care affecting labour supply can be found in a cross-section study using microdata by Gustafsson and Stafford (1992). The authors specified female market work and utilization of public day care as a joint decision. Respondents' location in a particular municipality was used to obtain variables measuring price of public day care placement as well as an indicator of the availability of child care. Data for 1984 come from HUS (the Survey of Household Market and Non-Market Activities), and the analysis was restricted to two-parent households with only one young child, resulting in a moderate sample size. In one specification, which takes rationing of space in the municipality into account, a substantial negative price effect on female market work and utilization of public day care was found. From this it follows that the extent to which the system is subsidized will influence labour supply of females. However, this conclusion might not be 'portable' to another environment. As discussed in Chapter 6, it is much more difficult to establish a link between child care and female labour supply in the Federal Republic of Germany. One should, however, bear in mind that the emphasis of services provided there is much more on part-time care, while full-time care plays a larger role in Sweden.

Additional indications concerning the effect on female labour supply of increasing public expenditure on child care in Sweden comes from labour-supply analyses made in the Level of Living Survey. Sundström (1987) estimated labour-supply function in cross-sections for 1967, 1973, and 1980. Among right-hand variables were those indicating presence of preschool children in the family. It was found that coefficients for such variables decreased between surveys, which might be interpreted as an effect of increased supply of child care.

While it seems appropriate to conclude that transfers to families have increased female labour supply, the reverse can be the case for males. Using time-use data, Flood (1990) finds presence of preschool children to have a negative effect on male labour supply. It is not unreasonable to think that such effects would have been smaller in the absence of parents' cash benefits.

Has family policy affected the number of births and/or the spacing of births in Sweden? The crude birth rate increased during the late 1980s, and considerably more children were born than had been projected using demographic variables only (Statistics Sweden, 1986). While the total fertility rate during the same period did not increase in Germany and the UK, an increase similar to the one in Sweden also occurred in Denmark, although from a lower level.

Considerable research efforts have recently been made to analyse births in Sweden using microdata. In a series of papers Heckman and Walker (1990*a*; 1990*b*) used the 1981 Swedish fertility survey to estimate various birth process models for different birth cohorts. Results showed rather strong effects of the female wage rate. Female wages play an important role in postponing first births but only a minor role in explaining childlessness. Female wages substantially affect a third birth. It follows that taxes and transfers via the net wage rate affects births. Male wage effects are weaker. However, variables measuring family policy was not used in the estimations. Instead, parameter instability across cohorts showing weaker effects of female wages were interpreted as indirect evidence of policy effects.

Direct measures of family policy were used by Klevmarken and Tasiran (1991) and Tasiran (1993) using the HUS data. In their results, effects of female wages are smaller. As explanatory variables, measures of the supply of child care services as well as a measure of maximum number of days compensated for at childbirth were used. Estimated coefficients came out with an unreasonable negative sign. In estimates for higher birth transitions, however, parental benefit days came out with strong effects having high t-statistics. Additional evidence showing parent cash benefits affecting birth comes from Hoem (1992). This provides evidence that the speed of further childbirth was pushed up considerably in Sweden through the 1980s, consistent with what one would expect from changes in the system of parents' cash benefits.

Do transfer and tax policy affect qualifications of the labour force? One way of analysing this question is to compute internal rates of returns to higher education under various assumptions of taxes and transfer payments and then compare the results. Edin and Holmlund (1992), also referred in the previous section, report such calculations showing that progressive income tax substantially decreased internal rates of return before the recent tax reform but later had considerably smaller effects. On the other hand, payments from the system of student finance increase the rate of return, and in an example for 1991 the second effect is larger than the first. Taken together, income taxes and transfers thus increase incentives for a longer education. The same study also indicates that rates of return affect qualifications of the labour force, as the school enrolment rate among 20–4-year-olds from 1963 to 1991 was found to be positively affected by the size of the (net of tax) rate of return. The system of student finance did not affect the variable utilized, however, so we do not know to what extent this has affected recruitment. It might be that changed labour market prospects play the leading role and that changes in student finance have had only a small role. This kind of conclusion was drawn by Nilsson (1984: 145) when studying (without formal modelling or estimation) effects on recruitment after the introduction of the present system.

Evidence on the effects of systems of student finance on the qualification structure comes also from answers by respondents to direct questions summarized by Reuterberg and Svensson (1992) (see also Reuterberg and Svensson 1987*a*; 1987*b*). Evidence on decisions to start secondary education comes from questions posed relatively close in time to the choice made, and are from this perspective the most reliable. The answers indicate a positive but small effect of the transfer on choice of education, as only about 5% of respondents answered that they would not have started secondary school in the case of no specific benefit. This small reaction is quite understandable, as benefits are modest.

Questions whether the respondent would have attended higher education in the absence of the system of student finance were posed at a considerable later stage in life, and answers to those questions are, therefore, more difficult to evaluate. There is also another objection to the research strategy: if the public sector had not provided funds, one might assume that financial institutions such as banks would have provided loans for such purposes. But one does not know if the respondent had such alternatives in mind when answering. Questions were posed to respondents from the birth cohorts of 1948, 1953, and 1963. In each cohort, 11–17% of respondents indicated that they would not have started higher education if no system of public finance had existed. Those respondents make up a rather high proportion of all attending higher education. Taken at face value, those results support the argument that the system has had large effects. However, because of the methodological limitations one should not read too much into these figures.

Summary

There are many transfer payments targeted at families with children in Sweden, and resources used for public child care have increased strongly. Possible behavioural effects are many, and different effects require different modelling. Some programmes make it quite difficult to model the budget-set adequately in an atemporal model of market work and leisure only. Based on statistical evidence and a few studies, it seems reasonable to judge that increased expenditure on public child care and the expansion of parents' cash benefits have played a role in the increased labour force participation rate of mothers. However, on the evidence it is difficult to judge whether the role has been a major or minor one. Effects of the Swedish parents' cash benefits are of special interest, as the system seems to be unique. The system might affect parental choices in a number of ways: increased incentives to work before a birth, increased incentive to take a leave which seems to decrease further earnings, and a 'speed premium' on subsequent births. It is natural to think that increased public expenditure related to children in Sweden during the 1980s has increased birth rates. However, there is not much solid evidence quantifying the channels of influence. And when evidence is available, it might be limited to only one study. Further, transfers to families can be thought of as affecting the qualification structure of the labour force. But we do not have much empirical evidence which unquestioned supports this.

Unemployment Benefits and Related Transfers

The systems

Unemployment benefits and related transfers in Sweden as proportions of GDP in 1970–91 are shown in Fig. 3.15. The sum of unemployment insurance benefits (*Arbetslöshetsförsäkringsersättning*), cash allowances for the unemployed (*Kontant arbetsmarknadsstöd*), social assistance (*Socialbidrag*), labour market training benefits (*Utbildningsbidrag*) and earnings guarantee to people who have lost their jobs because of bankruptcy or shutdowns (*Lönegaranti*) were less than 0.5% of GDP in 1970, but had increased to about 2% in 1991. Largest of the total are the payments from the unemployment insurance system. Quite naturally, there is a pronounced cyclical pattern for the expenditures we discuss in this section. The largest change between two subsequent years occurred at the end of the period when expenditures increased by two-thirds. As the unemployment rate has continued to rise after that date, the expansion can be expected to have continued after the observation period.

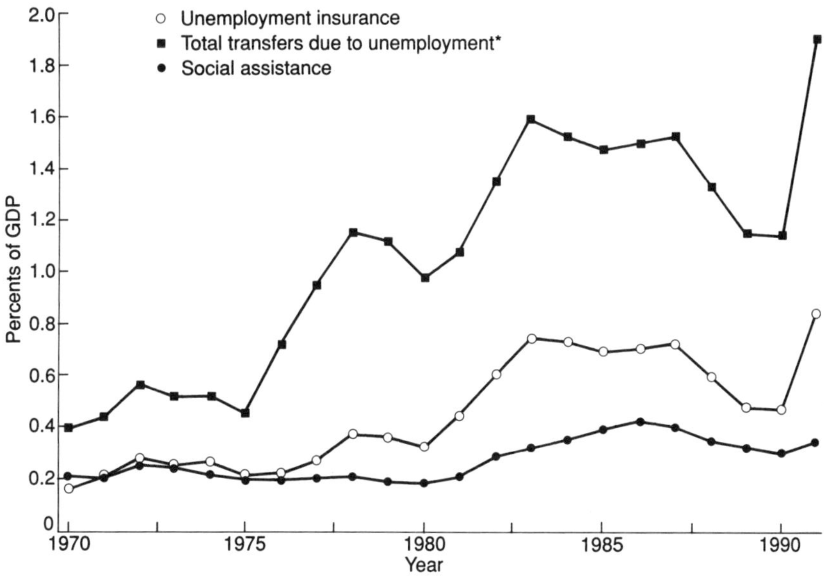

FIG 3.15. Transfers Due to Unemployment and Similar Compensation as a Percentage of GDP, 1970–1992

Note: 'Total transfers due to unemployment' includes unemployment insurance, social assistance, cash allowances for unemployment, labour market training, and earning guarantees.

Source: National Accounts, Statistics Sweden.

The origin of the system of unemployment insurance benefits in Sweden can be traced back to the 1890s, when a fund for typesetters and printers was institutionalized. During the following decades many new funds were created, and demand for public involvement was made. In 1935 the public sector subsidized unemployment insurance funds which satisfy certain requirements (*Erkända arbetslöshetskassor*). For the early history, see Edelbalk (1975; 1988). A fuller description of the system is given by Björklund and Holmlund (1991). Since then the public share of expenditure on unemployment benefits has increased from a minority to three quarters in the mid-1970s, and to about 90% at the beginning of the 1980s. Although the funds are formally associated with labour unions, it is the government which has determined the most important requirements, including benefit levels and criteria for receiving a benefit.

Unemployment insurance in Sweden has always been voluntary for individual employees. (However, on several occasions suggestions for compulsory unemployment insurance has been put forward. Another such suggestion is expected to come from a government committee in 1993.) Union membership is not compulsory for membership in an unemployment insurance fund; anyone who works in a field covered by a fund has the right to become a member. For many labour unions, on the other hand, membership of such a fund is obligatory.

To qualify for unemployment insurance benefits a number of requirements must be fulfilled, some of which are difficult to describe. A 'membership requirement' is imposed, meaning that a claimant must have been a member of the unemployment fund for at least twelve months prior to the claim. There is also a requirement of at least 75 days' gainful employment during the twelve months preceding the period of unemployment (the 'work requirement'). This leads to exclusion from benefits for entrance to the labour market, and of those with a weak attachment to it. Other requirements concern the unemployed person's 'search intensity'. To receive a benefit a person must be registered at the employment office as seeking work. There is also a work test, as an offer of 'suitable' work must be accepted.

Unemployment insurance benefits are paid five days a week. Earlier there was a waiting period, but this was abolished in January 1989. Since 1974 the benefits have been subject to income tax. Benefits do not depend on family status and have an upper limit in nominal terms. Replacement rates therefore fall with the worker's past income from employment. During the 1970s and 1980s, replacement rates of a typical unemployed person have increased. Calculations of replacement rates for 1990 give the following figures for a single person with various wages, net of taxes (Sosial trygghet 1992): half average wage, 91%; average wage, 85%; twice average wage, 54%. Earlier, benefits could not be paid for longer than 150 days. However, this period has been increased. In July 1968 it was prolonged to 450 days for those 60 years and older. In 1974 the period was generally increased to 300 days, and at the same time the age limit to be eligible for 450 days was reduced to 55 years. (The present government has indicated ambitions to cut expenditures on unemployment insurance. It has suggested an introduction of five waiting days and a reduction of benefit levels.)

The rules which apply to payments of unemployment insurance benefits mean that a considerable number of the unemployed are not entitled to a benefit. Some of them can obtain compensation from the system of cash benefits (KAS) which came into effect in 1974. The system is entirely financed by the government, and is administered by the social-insurance offices. To be eligible, either the same work requirement as for unemployment insurance benefit (but not the membership qualification) must be met or, alternatively, there is a schooling requirement. School-leavers can qualify after a waiting period of three months. Persons over 60 years who have used up their unemployment benefits are also eligible for KAS.

The maximum benefit period for KAS is 150 days, but people older than 55 can receive payments for 300 days and those over 60 are entitled to payments for 450 days. The KAS compensation takes the form of daily benefits subject to income tax, and the benefit level is much lower compared to the daily benefits in the system of unemployment insurance benefits. The same requirements concerning search intensity and work test as for unemployment insurance benefits apply to KAS.

Who is covered by unemployment compensation? For a long time only a minority of the unemployed in Sweden received some unemployment compensation. Around the mid-1960s, only about one in four unemployed were members of a certified unemployment insurance fund and could thus be eligible for a benefit. But nowadays a majority of the unemployed are members. Figures for 1988 (Björklund and Holmlund 1991: 122) show that 69% of the unemployed received unemployment insurance benefits and an additional 7% KAS. Nevertheless, 24% of the unemployed received no compensation at all. The coverage is very similar for females and males, but varies much with the age of a person. Older unemployed receive unemployment insurance benefits to a much higher degree than younger persons. Among those not receiving any unemployment compensation at all, persons who had used up their benefits were only a small minority. However, rising unemployment figures at the beginning of the 1990s might lead policy-makers to pay more attention to this group.

Unemployment compensation has traditionally made up only a small part of all public expenditures on labour market policy in Sweden. The number of persons directly affected by various labour market programmes was higher than the number of unemployed during the 1970s and 1980s. Out of all expenditure on labour market policy, only 10–15% related to unemployment compensation during the 1970s, but this increased to about 25% during the 1980s. During the 1990s expenditures on active labour market measures have not decreased in real terms, and many are still directly affected. However, as the number of unemployed has increased dramatically, active measures now make up a considerably smaller part of all expenditures on labour market policy.

Some labour market policy measures have the effect of moving people from unemployment to employment directly. Such measures include special measures for disabled (*Samhall, Offentligt skyddat arbete, Lönebidrag*), measures for youth (e.g. *Ungdomslag/Inskolningsplatser*), and temporary public employment (*Beredskapsarbete*). People engaged in labour market training receive transfer payments, not wages, although for some observers this distinction does not mean very much.

Although labour market training programmes have long existed in Sweden, their importance was only marginal up to the beginning of the 1960s, when an expansion started. Since the beginning of the 1970s the number of persons engaged in labour market training programmes has amounted to about 1% of the labour force. (People in labour market training are, however, not members of the labour force). People eligible for labour market training must either be unemployed or be at risk of becoming unemployed. Among trainees there are almost as many females as males. Immigrants, having higher unemployment rates than natives, are over-represented, and the same applies to persons residing in the northern part of Sweden. Trainees receive a benefit (*Utbildningsbidrag*) which is subject to income tax. Persons receiving an unemployment benefit when starting the training receive training benefits as high as the unemployment benefit. Others receive a minimum benefit.

Unemployed persons not receiving any unemployment compensation or only a low compensation may apply for social assistance (*Socialbidrag*). This is a means-tested transfer, having its historical roots in the system of poor relief. Social assistance is provided at social welfare offices (*Socialbyråer*) by social workers who decide on behalf of local politicians. The decision-making is directed by guidelines (*vägledande socialbidragsnormer*) issued by the municipal assemblies, and it is this local part of the public sector that finances social assistance.

According to the law, all persons with a low income who cannot make ends meet in any other way are eligible for social assistance. However, variations in judgement of applications between municipalities, as well as within parts of a municipality and between individual social workers, has been shown to exist (Gustafsson *et al.*, forthcoming). A simplified description of the decision-making is the following: eligible households which apply and have an income below thresholds laid down in guidelines receive assistance to an amount which closes the gap between the thresholds and income (before assistance). This implies a marginal tax rate on income before social assistance of 100%. Thus one would think of social assistance as exerting a strong disincentive to market work; but it seems that applicants are usually subject to a work-test which could counterbalance the disincentives.

While most recipients of poor relief are old persons, the typical recipient of social assistance is a young adult. Immigrants are over-represented among recipients. While asylum-seekers earlier were eligible to social assistance, this ceased to be the case in May 1988 when a new transfer (*Asylbidrag*) was introduced. Time-series studies show that the rate of unemployment strongly affects the rate of social-assistance recipiency, and that this effect lasts for more than one year. Analyses for age groups show that the rate of social-assistance participation in age group 16–29 is most affected (Gustafsson 1984). Also, a cross-section analysis indicated a relation between the volume of unemployment and payments of social-assistance. However, effects have been shown to be concentrated on uncompensated unemployment, while the extent of unemployment compensated by insurance benefits or cash benefits had no effect (Aguilar and Gustafsson 1992). This clearly illustrates that social assistance seems to act as a substitute for unemployment insurance benefits and cash benefits.

Effects on behaviour from unemployment compensation

What evidence can be found of a relation between unemployment compensation and labour supply? Unemployment compensation makes the alternative of becoming, as well as staying, unemployed less unattractive, and therefore unemployment benefits might increase unemployment.

At the macrolevel Layard *et al.* (1991) have studied unemployment levels in different countries for a cross-section in 1983–8 as well as over time. When interpreting these results one should remember that reliable cross-country comparisons are always difficult to make. One would expect problems to be particularly large regarding systems of unemployment compensation (Atkinson and Mickelwright 1991). In the cross-section analyses, right-hand variables include measures of unemployment compensation for the country in question. According to estimates, positive effects on unemployment having a relatively high t-statistic could be found for the duration of unemployment benefits as well as for the replacement rate. On the other hand, active labour market spendings were found to have a negative effect. In this sample Sweden had the lowest unemployment rate, which the comparatively high expenditure on active labour market policy helps to explain. The analyses using time-series for nineteen countries build on price as well as wage functions estimated for each country, which in turn are used to explain unemployment rates. In this manner unemployment compensation can affect unemployment by affecting parameters in the wage function. Actually, cross-country estimates of parameters in the wage function indicate roles played by the benefit duration as well as by the replacement rates (Layard *et al.* 1991: 418).

Several time-series studies have been made on possible effects of unemployment compensation on unemployment in Sweden. In an early study Ståhl (1978) used annual data for 1957–73, including a measure of the benefit level among the right-hand variables. No effects of the latter having a high degree of significance was found. Another early study, by Edelbalk and Wadensjö (1978), investigated possible effects of the abolition in September 1964 of seasonal limitations on benefits. For models explaining unemployment during February and March a positive effect from a dummy indicating year with no seasonal limitation having expected positive coefficient was found, but the degree of significance was not particularly high.

Björklund (1978) and Björklund and Holmlund (1989) based their analyses on time-series of escape rates from unemployment calculated from the labour force surveys. The former study covers 1965–76, the latter extends the period of observation to 1985. Effects of extended duration were modelled with dummy variables intended to capture extensions of the benefit periods in 1968 and 1974, and the second also capturing the introduction of cash benefits. A variable measuring the replacement rate was also used by Björklund and Holmlund (1989), but coefficients for this variable only rarely had an expected sign and a reasonable high t-statistic. Across specifications the coefficient of the dummy for 1968 was most often found to have a negative sign, in several cases, however, having a low degree of significance. The expected negative effects from the 1974 reform variable on the escape-rates could only infrequently be found. A possible reason for the lack of effect is that the introduction might have also led to increased search efforts: to be eligible for cash benefit, a person has to search for work using the employment offices, and the reform thus also increased incentives to search.

Let us take a fresh look at time-series evidence on the relation between unemployment compensation and unemployment, based on aggregated data from the labour force surveys 1970–92. As right-hand variables in a regression analysis we use replacement rates as calculated by the Nordic Social Statistic Committee on various occasions, a dummy for the reform in 1974 and thereafter, when KAS came into effect and the period of compensation was prolonged, a variable explaining the coverage rate of unemployment insurance benefits, and, finally, a variable measuring vacancies to capture the cycle. Results from OLS estimates are reported in Table 3.8. It turns out that coefficients for the replacement rate as well as the dummy for reform 1974 both have low t-

TABLE 3.8. Estimates of a Regression Model for the Unemployment Rate as a Function of Unemployment Compensation (Sample Period 1970–1992)

Intercept	Replacement rate	D74	Coverage	Vacancies	Trend	R^2 (adj)	DW
5.76	-0.03	-0.33	0.031	-4.85		0.761	1.61
(4.47)	(1.84)	(1.25)	(2.21)	(6.68)			
1.91	0.01	0.09	0.073	-4.70	-0.11	0.787	1.78
(0.78)	(0.19)	(0.26)	(2.73)	(6.80)	(1.81)		

statistics. This is very much in accordance with earlier time-series results. However, the coverage rate, which appears not to have been used in earlier Swedish studies, comes out with a positive effect and a rather high t-statistic. This result remains when a time-trend is added to the right-hand variables, but actually the size of the coefficient doubles. The point estimate indicates that an increase in the coverage rate by 10 percentage points increases the unemployment rate by (depending on specification) 0.3 and 0.7 percentage points.

We have implicitly assumed causality to run from unemployment insurance to unemployment. It is rather likely that influence in the other direction also exists: rising unemployment give people incentives to become members of an unemployment insurance fund.

Some studies have investigated possible effects on unemployment from unemployment compensation using microdata. In such data one can observe unemployed without any compensation and other persons receiving compensation from different programmes. By comparisons one arrives at figures which can be interpreted as 'effects of unemployment'. However, there is in this respect one general limitation to all studies surveyed below. No attempt seems to have been made to model the process leading to some persons being members of an unemployment insurance fund and others not. This might lead to erroneous conclusions, because differences in economic behaviour might be caused by the selection process, not necessarily by the unemployment insurance system.

Björklund (1981) investigated duration of unemployment in cross-sections of the level of living survey 1966/7 and 1973. According to model estimates, no effect of collecting benefit having a high t-statistic was present. On the other hand, Heikensten (1984) on the basis of microdata from the labour force survey, found that the propensity to remain unemployed for one subsequent quarter was higher for members of unemployment insurance funds. However, this effect was due to a lower probability of leaving the labour force, while the probability of moving from unemployment to employment was not significantly affected by membership of an unemployment insurance fund. Unemployment compensation thus seems to increase unemployment duration by reducing the propensity to withdraw from the labour force.

Other studies have used the 'Stockholm youth sample'. This covers about 850 persons aged 16–24 in 1981, when the sample was drawn from registered unemployed in the county of Stockholm (*Stockholms län*). The respondents' labour market histories were collected up to 1985. In a model explaining length of unemployment observed in 1981–2 Holmlund (1986) found receipt of unemployment insurance benefits to have a positive effect amounting to seven weeks. However, no coefficient for receiving cash allowances for unemployed having a high t-statistic could be found. According to Edin and Holmlund (1991), using data for the whole observation period, unemployment benefits prolonged transitions from unemployment to employment significantly. On the other hand, receipt of cash benefits had the reverse effect.

T. Korpi (1991), working with the same data but defining states and variables somewhat differently, came to similar but not identical conclusions. In his specifications receipt of unemployment compensation and related transfers were more elaborated, as receipt of unemployment insurance benefits and cash allowances for unemployed were defined for different lengths of time, and a variable receipt of social assistance was also introduced. The coefficient for receiving unemployment benefit for up to ten months came out with a negative coefficient having a relatively high t-statistic. According to the results, the destination 'temporary unemployment' was negatively affected by unemployment insurance recipiency, but not necessarily the alternatives 'permanent employment' or 'labour market training'. While no effects of receipt of cash benefits having a high t-statistic could be found, receipt of social assistance had negative effects on transitions to permanent as well as to temporary employment (but not on transition into labour market training programmes).

One way to escape unemployment is to move into another local labour market. Providing unemployment benefits might decrease such movements. It is possible to show effects from unemployment compensation on migration behaviour? Lundborg (1991) analysed propensities to migrate to Sweden by economically active people coming from other Nordic countries. For some decades there have been no legal obstacles preventing citizens of one Nordic country from moving to another. Data for this study was a combined cross- section and time-series data base on aggregates for 1965–85. Among explanatory variables were measures of maximum unemployment benefits at destination as well as origin. It turns out that estimates for those variables were somewhat mixed. For Finnish migration of both sexes, negative coefficients having a high t-statistic for the relation of benefits between origin and destination was found. On the basis of those estimates one can argue that increased unemployment benefits in Sweden have increased migration from Finland. However, estimates taken at face value indicate that the level of unemployment benefits in Sweden actually reduces immigration from Denmark, which is counter-intuitive, although, as expected, this migration propensity was found to be negatively affected by the level of benefits at origin. Finally, propensities for migration from Norway were not found to be significantly affected by benefit levels, whether at origin or at destination.

Effects on behaviour of active labour market policy

Many unemployment problems in Sweden during the 1970s and 1980s have been combated by active labour market policy. Has this been a success or only a way to disguise employment problems? Considerable research efforts have recently been made to illuminate this question. Here we will look very briefly at those studies concentrating on the results.

A possible negative effect of active labour market policy on employment can appear at the macrolevel. Unemployment puts pressure on wages, but this might be counterbalanced by labour market programmes in as far as they offer unemployed persons alternatives more favourable than living on unemployment compensation. This suggests that programmes might crowd out regular employment, which is undesirable. Various recent studies have investigated possible effects of labour market programmes on real wages in Sweden. Most have used time-series data in which the volume of labour market programmes have been measured in terms of the number of persons employed in temporary public employment and labour market training. However, there are striking differences in results between studies, and it is far from clear why those differences appear.

In a first group of studies, a positive effect from the volume of labour market programmes on real wages is found. This group of studies includes Calmfors and Forslund (1991), using time-series data for the private sector, and Skedinger (1990), basing his study on time-series for private-sector workers in mining and manufacturing, disaggregated by gender and occupation. This group also includes a coefficient estimate for a variable measuring public employment from Forslund (1992). This study is based on pooled cross-section and time-series information for twelve unemployment insurance funds. In a second group of studies, the main interpretation of results is no effect from the volume of labour market programmes on real wages. Such results are reported by Holmlund (1990), Calmfors and Nymoen (1990), and Löfgren and Wikström (1991). In the third group we find studies indicating a negative effect from the extent of labour market programmes to real wages. Such results are reported by Forslund

(1992) referring to labour market training programmes and also by Edin *et al.* (1993), using microdata matched with regional labour market variables.

Active labour market programmes move persons away from the state 'unemployment' to other labour market states such as 'temporary subsidized employment (relief work)' or 'labour market training'. But do such movements make things better in some sense? Actually the alternative states often require additional public funds. Therefore, in order to be successful a labour market programme should yield benefits during later periods.

To evaluate possible benefits of active labour market policy is not an easy task, for several reasons. Possible benefits are not only a better labour market status and higher wages but also other aspects of welfare such as health. Benefits can be evaluated at different points in time. A further problem is that participation in a programme is not decided at random. An outcome showing that persons who have taken part in a programme do no better than the unemployed does not necessarily mean that the programme has no treatment effect. It might be targeted towards persons having worse labour market prospects than others. Conversely, a programme has not necessarily had a positive treatment effect even if participants are doing better than unemployed.

Several studies on effects from labour market programmes in Sweden have been made. Here we concentrate on programmes which could be thought of as close alternatives to unemployment compensation. This means that we omit measures such as mobility grants and intensified employment services.

A first group of studies uses data drawn to show the situation for the entire country. Axelsson (1989) compared a sample of 900 persons who completed labour market training programmes in 1981 with various control groups (e.g. persons reported as job-searchers at the employment exchange). Outcomes one and two years after the training are evaluated by several different variables. Results show programmes to have a significant positive effect on annual income from employment, amounting to about 20% in 1983. This effect was found to be much higher for immigrants but lower for natives, and for some persons in the latter group it might be quite low. When interpreting the high effects recorded for immigrants, it should be remembered that these are not necessarily due only to labour market training but are due also to a process of assimilation in the new country. A study by Björklund (reported in Björklund 1990) belongs to this category. It covers persons who were trained during the second part of the 1970s and builds on the level-of-living survey. The general pattern for the results is a finding of positive but weakly significant effects of training.

A second group of studies is concentrated on youth. Sehlsted and Schröder (1989) used a sample of 500 young persons registered as unemployed in four cities in autumn 1985. The design of the study was to identify the 'strategies' chosen during a year and then compare labour market status two years later. Results showed that the strategy 'recruitment subsidy to an ordinary employer for a permanent or temporary job' provided a significantly better subsequent labour market outcome than unemployment. However, similar conclusions could not be drawn for the strategies 'relief work', 'labour market training' and 'education'. One possible reason for this is the relatively small number of observations recorded for some of the strategies.

Studies based on the 'Stockholm youth sample' indicate that effects of programmes are complex. On one hand, Edin and Holmlund (1991) found that participation in temporary public employment increased the period of transition to employment from unemployment. On the other hand, according to the size of future wages, temporary employment is preferable to unemployment for those who are at work (Ackum 1991). In addition, the duration of employment following unemployment can be used as an outcome variable. In analysing this T. Korpi (1992) distinguishes between number of spells of programmes and time spent in programmes. While the first is found to have a negative effect on employment stability, the second is found to have a positive effect.

Methodologically similar to the second group is the third group of studies. The difference is that the data cover displaced workers. There seems to be only one such data source analysed up to now. It covers about 300 workers displaced by the closing of a pulp plant in a small town in the north of Sweden 1977, whose labour market behaviour over some subsequent years was studied. Effects on subsequent earnings are analysed by Edin (1988) in a specification allowing for effects to vary over time. According to results, labour market training for a first period has a larger negative effect than unemployment, but this decreases in the future period. This can be interpreted as caused because persons with greater labour market difficulties were more often chosen for training. Also for this sample Edin and Holmlund (1991) found that temporary public employment increased the period to re-employment.

Summary

From an international perspective, unemployment has been low and active labour market programmes have been ambitious in Sweden. But at the beginning of the 1990s this changed drastically, as unemployment increased rapidly. Considerable recent empirical research has dealt with various aspects of active labour market policy. What has been learned? From estimates of real wage functions it is difficult to know whether active labour market policy has had adverse effects at the macrolevel. Several studies have been carried out with the purpose of illustrating this, but the results point in different directions.

Findings from microstudies of active labour market policy do not shed much light on whether the strategy of an active labour market policy has been a success or not. Instead, such studies evaluate different programmes by inspecting differences in outcomes which can be measured at various points in time. However, differences recorded do not necessarily originate from programmes, but can be caused by the mechanism of choosing candidates for a programme. Thus a finding that in a future period programme participants are not doing better than the unemployed does not necessarily mean failure of a programme, but can actually be used as an argument for the opinion that the measure has been well used, as it is targeted to those in most need.

However, the state of the art does not mean that the micro-approach to labour market policy evaluation is useless. What it does mean is that this research has to advance further before it becomes very relevant for policy-making. At present the contribution by the research work to the policy debate seems to consist of warnings against making definitive statements about the supposed effects of labour market policy. It should not be claimed that participants in labour market programmes have been shown to perform much better—or, for that matter, much worse—than the unemployed.

In some respects cash compensation to the unemployed in Sweden is not as developed as in some other countries. Several categories, especially young persons and other entrants to the labour market, are not covered by unemployment insurance benefits or by cash benefits, but have to rely on means-tested social-assistance. In addition, benefits are limited in duration.

Empirical studies of the possible effects of unemployment compensation on unemployment and other outcome states have been investigated. A limitation of such studies is that they have not modelled the process leading to people having different unemployment insurance coverage, including the compensation. In previous time-series analyses it has been difficult to find effects from replacement rates and extended benefit periods, and our analysis of time-series data is no exception. However, according to our results there is a strong positive relation between the coverage rate of the unemployment insurance system and the rate of unemployment which is in agreement with results from microstudies.

When summarizing various results it seems reasonable to distinguish between various forms of unemployment compensation. First, for the cash benefit system, having a low replacement rate, no adverse effects seem to have been reported. Second, there are signs indicating that unemployment insurance benefits, for which replacement rates can be rather high, affect behaviour. But such effects might not necessarily result only in longer unemployment periods but might also result in a higher propensity to remain in the labour market. Third, it seems reasonable that social assistance has a negative effect on labour supply because of the 100% marginal tax rate built into the system. However, empirical support for this hypothesis is limited to one single study on youth in the region of the capital. The situation is similar for possible effects on migration from unemployment compensation. While effects seem plausible the issue seems to have been addressed in one study only, which has produced mixed results.

Conclusions

Sweden has become known for many and generous transfer programmes, which expanded generally during several decades. However, the development has been reversed at the beginning of the 1990s. This occurs in a climate of high unemployment rates and large public-sector budget deficits. Further cuts covering most areas are now on the political agenda.

Considerable research efforts have been made in order to evaluate how transfer payments in Sweden affect labour supply as well as other variables. Progress has been made possible because of microdata being available, as well as techniques for analysing such data. Nevertheless, our present knowledge is limited on several subjects, and in many cases results only come from very few studies or from a single study.

We have little solid evidence on the effects of sickness cash benefits on labour supply. This made us look at numbers of absence in the labour force survey 1963–92. The statistical analysis indicated quite clearly that compensation rates in the system of sickness insurance affect absentee rates.

More research has been carried out on the effects of pension payments, and it seems fair to conclude that the findings show pensions as affecting labour supply. But when evaluating this one should remember that the effects might be intentional. Further, the research also shows that effects can be more complicated than predicted from an atemporal model, as workers adjust behaviour over several periods.

There are many transfers to families with children in Sweden, and the public sector has provided subsidized day care for ever-larger numbers of young children. The system of parental cash benefits has expanded, and can be thought of as affecting parental behaviour in many ways. The incentive to be absent from work increases, and time-series evidence indicates that the expanding periods of compensation at childbirth have been important for the rapidly increasing rates of absence among mothers with young children. But the existence of parental cash benefits also means a strong incentive to work full-time before parental leave, and data also show that increasing proportions of Swedish mothers have been doing so. From available evidence it seems reasonable to conclude that increased public spending on child care as well as increased parental benefits is one factor behind the rising participation rate among females in Sweden. Public transfers might also have increased the qualification of the labour force by providing funds to students, and might have led to closer spacing of births, as there is a 'speed premium' in the system of parental cash benefits. However, we do not yet have much solid evidence for the existence of those reactions.

Seen from the outside, systems of unemployment compensation are not particularly developed in Sweden. Instead, the active labour market policy is the unique feature. While several studies have had difficulties showing how unemployment compensation affects labour market behaviour, others have been more successful. When we analysed time-series we had difficulty finding effects from replacement rates or extended duration of benefits. However, the extent to which the unemployed are covered by unemployment insurance benefits was found positively to affect the unemployment rate. But our analysis did not allow for the possibility of causality running in the opposite direction, i.e. the extent of unemployment might affect motives for joining an unemployment insurance fund.

One reading of the various findings is that results vary between forms of compensation. There seems to be no support at all for adverse effects of the cash benefit system, while somewhat more signs can be found for the unemployment insurance benefits. This distinction seems plausible, since the unemployment insurance benefits are considerably higher than the cash benefits. Social assistance might negatively affect employment, and the high level of unemployment benefits might affect the tendency to migrate from other Nordic countries. But empirical evidence on such reactions is limited to one study of each issue, and for the latter case results are quite mixed.

Research on active labour market policy programmes have posed macro as well as microquestions. At the former level, the issue has been whether programmes affect real wages, which might crowd out regular employment. On this issue, despite intensive research efforts, no consensus has been reached. Microquestions address how programme participants subsequently perform in relation to the unemployed. Programme participation can be targeted at special categories, making programme evaluation more difficult than if participation were at random.

Subsequent performance can be evaluated as labour market status or wages, and at different points in time after programme completion. There are many different programmes. It is hardly instructive to talk about '*the* effect of labour market programmes', and thus to state whether active labour market policy generally is to be preferred to unemployment on economic grounds only. Instead, some programmes might be preferred to unemployment, while the reverse can hold for others.

3.6. CONCLUDING REMARKS

This review of Swedish research does not suggest strong general conclusions about incentive effects on labour supply at the microlevel, and there is even less to say about general equilibrium effects; but studies of more narrowly defined aspects of the tax and transfer system have revealed negative as well as positive effects. Studies based on behavioural models have given a variety of results; this is in particular true for analysis of tax incentives and, more generally, of the incentive effects on work hours of changes in the budget-set. When the analysis has been more focused on a particular aspect of labour supply, for instance the age of retirement and sickness absence, we find it easier to draw conclusions, although in these cases too there are problems of interpretation. Given the current state of the art there is ample room for interpretation of the results obtained and for speculative discussions about the causes of observed patterns. These concluding remarks belong to the same category.

Most Swedish studies have obtained positive wage rate elasticities for both males and females, which implies forward-bending supply curves and disincentive effects of increased taxes. Looking back at the major trend in labour supply of this century, we find that a large share of the increase in well-being has taken the form of increased leisure. For instance, the normal weekly hours (stipulated by law or in a labour contract) for blue-collar workers in Swedish industry decreased from 72 hours in 1860 to 50 hours in 1924, 48 in 1950 and 40 in 1973 (Tegle 1983). From this perspective, a backward-bending supply curve is not that implausible, which adds to the credibility of the studies which have obtained this result.

After the Second World War the trends in household time-use in Sweden, as well as in other countries, are that women are increasing their market work and decreasing their household work, while the reverse is true for men. The comparatively rapid increase in the market work of women, which is a particular feature of the Swedish labour market, has many explanations. Among them are the change from joint to separate taxation of spouses and the generous Swedish family policy. The comparison between females in Sweden and Germany by S. Gustafsson (1992*a*) gives convincing evidence that the differences in the tax systems of the two countries help to explain the differences in female labour force participation. This comparison, however, implicitly assumes that the sensitivity of females to economic incentives, as measured by the model parameters, does not change when such a drastic change in the tax system is imposed upon them. Generally, one might wonder if the estimated behavioural structures are stable when the tax and transfer systems are exposed to such large changes as the recent tax reforms in many countries. If not, most current studies have little to say about tax effects of these reforms. A successful analysis of behavioural change would at least need data before and after a major reform.

There are also reasons to believe that the behaviour of people shows a more gradual change as a response to gradual changes in their economic environment. (Most studies have used cross-sectional data.) One might, for instance, expect the behaviour of women to become more similar to that of men as they increase their involvement in the labour market and go into occupations previously dominated by men. The gender differences in estimated labour supply elasticities obtained in many studies, mostly on data which are almost fifteen years old, could thus be expected to decrease.

Although there is evidence that young cohorts of well-educated women have such high productivity both in market work and in household work that they can cope with both and still get some leisure time, the time constraint is probably perceived as more and more binding as less productive women are drawn into the hustling life of combined market and household work. It is not at all implausible that preferences for children and leisure are such that additional increases in real income will not increase the market work of women (or men). Aronsson and Wikström (1991) gave an interesting illustration of the potential shift in hours of work to the husband from his spouse as a result of an income tax reform of the Swedish type. This is an indication that the trend of increasing female labour supply might not continue. However, if this were not true, and if women actually continued to increase their market work, we still have to note the trade-off between women's hours and men's hours. If a woman increases her market work, her spouse has to decrease his if the quality of child care and other labour-intensive household duties is not to deteriorate. It is sometimes said that part-time working women compose the largest potential source of labour in Sweden. It might thus be much smaller than a simple count of hours would suggest.

We have argued that there is no conclusive empirical evidence for a major labour-supply effect of changing income taxes. Research and the public debate have perhaps concentrated too much on the tax incentives on the supply of annual or weekly hours of work. For the reasons already given, this might not become the most important effect of the tax changes. Although there is even less empirical evidence about the incentives to invest in human capital, increased investments in human capital might well become the most important result of the Swedish tax reform.

Our analysis of the system of transfers in Sweden has shown that there are labour-supply effects produced by a few such programmes. In comparison with other countries surveyed in this book, some features of the system stand out as special to Sweden. The active labour market policy gives transfers to people engaged in training activities. Parents receive cash benefits when children are young, and families with children can also benefit heavily from subsidized child care. Swedish family policy gives strong incentives for potential parents to enter early into the labour force and then stay there. The result has not only been an increased supply of hours, in particular from females; one might also conjecture additional investments in human capital and increased gender equality. These are examples of transfers which actually might increase rather than decrease labour supply.

However, there are other programmes which give people incentives to work less. Examples are programmes on early exit and sickness cash benefits. Results indicate that an increase of the replacement rate in sickness insurance and in the systems of early exit will increase absence from work and decrease labour supply respectively. One might note though, that a general-equilibrium analysis would be needed to capture fully the effects of early exit programmes, because they might enhance structural change and in this way favourably influence employment and economic growth in the long run.

The labour market policy in Sweden is a topical subject for empirical research. Although several studies have recently been completed, there is no consensus as to macroeconomic effects. Microstudies analyse how programme participants succeed after the programme is finished. For instance, the research surveyed indicates that membership in an unemployment insurance fund has adverse effects on unemployment. This conclusion must, however, be qualified, because these studies have not taken into account the selection mechanism which makes a person member of an unemployment insurance fund.

Although one might argue that research about the particular features and incentive effects of various transfer programmes has reached more specific results than have general studies of labour supply, the number of studies are still relatively few and they leave many questions without an answer. There is a long way to go before we have a complete picture of the incentive effects of the Swedish welfare system.

4

Taxation and Labour-Supply Incentives in the UK

RICHARD BLUNDELL

4.1. INTRODUCTION

In the UK over the 1980s, direct tax rates faced by individuals at the top end of the earnings distribution fell from over 80% to around 40%, with less dramatic, but well-publicized, reductions for basic-rate payers. Revenue neutrality was approximately achieved in the initial round of reforms by broadening the tax base and increasing the rate of indirect taxation. Although the impact on work incentives of these reforms differed markedly across individuals, it is equally clear that these policy experiments and those that have taken place in other industrialized countries over this period provide an ideal opportunity to assess our understanding of labour-supply responses. In the UK we are also fortunate to have detailed microdata available over the whole of this period with which to study such behaviour.

But what of the likely impact of such reforms on labour supply? As economists, our usual framework for analysis of behavioural responses is through the supply elasticity. However, this is not an appropriate means of analysis for labour-supply responses: as we will document below, wage elasticities and effective marginal tax rates in the UK diverge substantially across individuals. In particular, there are well-documented differences in elasticities between married men and married women, between part-time and full-time workers. Such differences are pervasive in many other dimensions and, in sum, there is no single representative elasticity. Moreover, even after the reforms of the 1980s, we still see different individuals facing significantly different effective marginal tax rates. The first task in tax reform analysis, therefore, is appropriately to associate individual labour-supply responses with corresponding marginal tax rates.

As the discussion in Chapter 2 has emphasized, labour supply itself is difficult to define. Typically we use the term to refer to both hours of work and labour market participation, although, (as I shall argue below) these are likely to respond to tax reform in rather different ways. As a result, attention in this chapter will be placed on hours of work, while in Chapter 5 the focus will turn to labour force participation and unemployment. Even so, a number of conceptual issues arise. Should we account for effort or just for hours? Should we take a life-cycle view or is a static single-period analysis sufficient? Does the choice of occupation or human capital dominate choices over labour supply? Do the collective demands of firms and/or unions dominate individual choices? Do individuals participate in untaxed activities—housework and black-economy work—when effective taxes are too high?

Labour-supply responses are commonly assigned a prominent role in the analysis of tax reform. For example, Hausman and Poterba (1987) and Bosworth and Burtless (1992), in their evaluation of the US tax reforms of the 1980s, emphasize the importance of labour-supply responses, especially those by married women. As we shall see below, this reflects a general view that labour-supply responses—at least as measured by hours of work—are likely to be largest for married women. This conjecture is also supported by the early work of Rosen (1976*a*; 1976*b*), suggesting that the perception of marginal tax rates among this group is good, and by the numerous empirical studies that have recovered relatively large elasticities from both experimental and sample survey data sources for married women. It should be added, however, that the divergence in predicted responses across these studies, even for married women, is large, and clearly calls for an assessment of overall robustness which will be part of the objective of this chapter. Indeed, as is well known, economic theory alone—even the simplest neoclassical framework—does not offer clear-cut predictions for the direction of responses, let alone their magnitude.

Although the appearance of a large number of potentially contradictory empirical measures of labour-supply responses may be cause for despair, recent attention to the robustness of such empirical analyses has pointed to a high degree of sensitivity with regard to statistical methods adopted and treatment of the after-tax income schedule facing workers. Given that reliable estimates from a representative sample will probably involve several thousand individual data points, for each of which a detailed analysis of the tax and benefit constraint is required, it is perhaps less surprising that progress in this area is slow and subject to error.

Our starting-point, therefore, is a description of the reforms to the tax system in 1980s' Britain as they have changed the level and distribution of effective marginal tax rates—most especially their incidence as far as married women are concerned. This is then used in Section 4.3 to assess the evidence on labour-supply responses. To the extent that these reforms are largely exogenous and independent of individual preferences, they provide an ideal setting for drawing more robust conclusions on the size (and sign) of responses. Section 4.4 presents an evaluation of response elasticities broken down by three groups of workers: married women, prime-aged men, and single mothers. In Section 4.5 we present an illustration to highlight the importance of microsimulation in the evaluation of tax reforms, and to emphasize the value of correctly modelling all income sources and marginal tax rates.

4.2. A PICTURE OF UK TAX REFORM AND LABOUR SUPPLY IN THE 1980s

Tax Reform

Over the 1980s the main 'in-work' benefits and tax allowances in the UK were maintained in real value, with the exception of the lump-sum child benefit, which by 1989 had lost 10% of its value in real terms. Basic income tax allowances showed a 20% real increase over this period. These are the allowances above which the basic rate of income tax is collected, and their increase has taken a significant number of taxpayers out of the tax system. Alongside the fall in the top rate of income tax ran a simplification of the system, with the number of higher-rate bands falling from nine in 1979 to just one by 1989. However, it should be pointed out that only some 5% of the UK taxpaying population pay income tax at the higher rate.

TABLE 4.1. Tax and Benefit Changes, 1979–1988

	1979	1980	1981	1982	1983	1984	1985	1986	1987	1988
Basic-Rate Income Tax	33->30	30	30	30	30	30	30	29	27	25
Top-Rate Income Tax	83->60	60	60	60	60	60	60	60	60	40
Basic Tax Allowances	+8%	–	-10%	–	+8%	+2%	+2	–	–	–
National Insurance Contributions	6.5	6.75	7.75	8.75	9	9	9	9	9	9
VAT (%)	9->15	15	15	15	15	15	15	15	15	15

Note: Tax allowance % denote real changes.

Source: Johnson and Stark (1989).

Clearly, we cannot separate the tax system from the workings of the welfare and social-security system, which also have an important impact on the shape of the budget constraint facing working individuals. Table 4.1 summarizes some of the main features of the UK tax and benefit system over the 1980s. It details the monotonic decline in basic and higher income tax rates. This is countered, to some degree, by the increase in the rate of national insurance contributions (NICs) which; although by name it is associated with unemployment and retirement payments, its real value is largely unrelated to the level of these contributions, and it is best considered as a non-discretionary tax on earned income. It applies to all earnings above a lower earnings limit that is close to the basic tax allowance, and below an upper earnings limit that is somewhat lower than the point at which the higher income tax bracket begins. For those above the lower earnings limit it clearly adds to the effective marginal tax rate, while at the same time removing a lump sum of income if earnings rise above that limit. Finally we should draw attention to the rise in the Value Added Tax (VAT) rate which applies to most goods, with the important exception of food, children's clothing, and domestic energy. The increase in the rate of VAT in 1979 displays the shift toward indirect taxation.

TABLE 4.2. Average Gains and Losses, 1979–1989

Income decile	Loss (%)	Gain (%)	Houshold type (£ per week)	Average gain/loss
			Single unemployed	-2.16
1	22	59	Single employed	7.02
2	26	56	Single parent	7.08
3	32	53	Single-earner couples	
4	32	53	with no children	13.25
5	22	60	with children	5.50
6	18	69	Two-earner couples	
7	14	73	with no children	9.80
8	15	73	with children	8.50
9	10	80	Single pensioner	2.31
10	12	78	Couple pensioners	2.04
Overall	20	65	Overall	7.18

Source: Johnson and Stark (1989).

It is clear from Table 4.2 that by 1989 the gains resulting from these changes were spread reasonably far down the income distribution, even though, for the majority of working individuals, the income tax reductions were mitigated by increases in indirect taxes and increases in the level of national insurance contributions. Nevertheless, for many earners, reductions in the marginal rates were significant. Moreover, at the bottom end, high rates of benefit withdrawal in excess of 100% were largely removed, although this often occurred at the cost of extending the range of earned income over which the lower withdrawal rates were effective.

Hours of Work and Earnings in the 1980s

Since empirical evidence on labour-supply responses suggests that they differ depending on hours worked, gross earnings, and a number of other characteristics that also determine marginal tax rates, it is important to note how changes in the effective marginal tax rates, noted above, affected individuals according to their position in the income and hours distribution. For example, Table 4.3 presents the average marginal rates faced by women married to employed men sampled from the UK Family Expenditure Survey, broken down by hours ranges. The reductions in marginal tax rates were clearly not restricted to women on higher hours but were present throughout the range of hours worked.

TABLE 4.4(*a*). Hours of Work for Married Women by Occupation Group (%)

Hours	Prof.	Admin.	Teach.	Clerical	Shop	Skilled	Semi-skilled	Unskilled
≤5	2.42	0.94	8.76	2.48	1.75	2.21	3.42	9.68
≤10	4.83	1.25	7.63	5.30	9.75	5.65	16.52	23.65
≤15	5.43	1.57	7.81	5.70	31.44	7.37	14.13	30.00
≤20	15.46	4.08	6.48	12.30	27.49	10.32	16.39	16.83
≤25	8.09	2.51	9.14	6.07	11.31	7.62	9.16	8.41
≤30	8.70	5.64	28.57	5.17	5.46	5.65	7.74	3.33
≤35	13.04	13.17	13.52	18.90	2.53	8.60	4.32	1.43
≤40	38.53	58.62	9.71	39.84	16.96	47.17	23.61	5.24
≤45	0.97	5.33	2.86	1.26	0.58	1.72	0.90	0.32
45<	0.72	3.76	3.24	0.29	0.19	0.25	0.77	0.00

Note: % figures. Armed forces were excluded throughout. Working women married to employed men.
Source: Bludell *et al.* (1993).

TABLE 4.4(*b*). Hours of Work for Married Women by Industry, 1981–1986 (%)

Hours	Public serv.	Prim. man.	Heavy man.	Light man.	Print.	Private serv.	Transp./ comm.	Financial serv.
≤5	2.06	1.64	2.14	2.65	4.32	3.28	0.72	4.50
≤10	5.18	1.64	4.28	5.04	4.94	11.72	4.35	9.24
≤15	11.55	8.20	3.83	5.80	7.41	18.60	6.88	8.53
≤20	10.57	5.74	8.11	11.22	8.02	18.88	10.14	11.49
≤25	14.99	4.10	5.63	8.32	6.17	9.07	5.43	4.38
≤30	8.59	0.00	3.15	6.81	4.32	6.43	2.90	2.96
≤35	10.55	9.84	8.78	11.85	17.28	6.20	10.14	36.37
≤40	8.12	68.85	58.45	40.73	40.12	19.43	48.19	19.08
≤45	26.04	0.00	0.56	1.26	0.62	1.50	7.25	0.47
45<	1.43	0.00	0.56	0.50	1.85	1.19	1.45	0.47
Total no.	3,783	122	888	793	162	2,193	276	844

Notes and Source: as for Table 4.4(*a*).

It is also important to note that there are significant proportions of married women in each of these hours ranges, except the very lowest, throughout the period. This contrasts quite strongly with the distribution

TABLE 4.3. Average Marginal Tax Rates by Tax Year for Married Women

Hours	Proportion	1980–1	1981–2	1982–3	1983–4	1984–5	1985–6	1986–7	1987–8	1988–9	1989–90
⩽5	0.03	0.01	0.00	0.00	0.00	0.02	0.00	0.00	0.04	0.03	0.00
⩽10	0.07	0.07	0.05	0.07	0.06	0.03	0.01	0.05	0.03	0.00	0.01
⩽15	0.05	0.36	0.33	0.26	0.24	0.22	0.12	0.26	0.18	0.16	0.17
⩽20	0.12	0.37	0.37	0.38	0.38	0.38	0.34	0.34	0.32	0.30	0.29
⩽25	0.09	0.37	0.38	0.40	0.39	0.39	0.38	0.36	0.34	0.32	0.32
⩽30	0.09	0.37	0.38	0.40	0.39	0.39	0.38	0.36	0.34	0.32	0.32
⩽35	0.14	0.37	0.38	0.40	0.39	0.39	0.39	0.38	0.36	0.34	0.34
⩽40	0.38	0.37	0.38	0.39	0.39	0.39	0.39	0.38	0.36	0.34	0.34
40<	0.03	0.39	0.38	0.39	0.39	0.37	0.40	0.37	0.35	0.33	0.34
Total		0.35	0.34	0.34	0.35	0.34	0.33	0.33	0.31	0.30	0.29

Notes: Average marginal tax rates. Women married to employed men.
Source: Blundell *et al.* (1993).

of working hours in other European countries—see, for example, the case for France in Bourguignon and Magnac (1991). For such married women the debate over hours-of-work responses seem most relevant. Their hours of work are spread over a wide range, and this is prevalent over most occupations and industries (see Tables 4.4(*a*) and 4.4(*b*)). Although the bunching in certain skilled and administrative occupations is suggestive of collective agreement on labour supply rather than pure individual choice, the wide spread of hours is also quite striking and may well warrant a labour-supply interpretation.

Finally, it is worth noting that the distribution of pre-tax earnings has changed significantly over this period. Table 4.4(*c*) shows the significant growth in inequality of full-time gross earnings. However, as Johnson and Webb (1992) have shown, the largest part of the growth in inequality over the 1980s can be attributed to tax and benefit reforms.

TABLE 4.4(*c*). Average Decile Earnings of Full–Time Employees

Decile	1979 (£ per week)	1988 (£ per week)	% increase, 1979–88
1	33.50	71.65	114
2	47.55	106.95	125
3	57.50	130.25	127
4	66.50	151.45	128
5	74.95	173.50	131
6	84.30	197.95	135
7	94.85	224.90	137
8	107.10	258.25	141
9	123.95	309.65	150
10	176.75	503.45	185
Population	86.80	212.75	145

Source: Johnson and Webb (1992).

4.3. EVALUATING WELFARE GAINS AND LABOUR-SUPPLY RESPONSES

Although there have existed brief periods of agreement among economists on the size of these response parameters they have turned out to be short-lived—especially for male labour supply. For example, in his exhaustive survey of male labour supply, Pencavel (1986) points to the small and negative responses by prime-aged men recovered in the early microeconometric analyses, especially in the USA. These results were subsequently challenged in the more coherent and elegant 'second-generation' studies developed in Burtless and Hausman (1978) and Hausman (1981). These studies pointed to positive wage effects and negative income effects resulting in non-trivial welfare losses due to taxation, hinting at some overall expansion in labour supply from the proposed reforms.

Although elegant and internally self-consistent, however, the results from studies using the Hausman procedure have been shown to be rather vulnerable to misspecification and measurement error. More robust estimation techniques for the USA appear to point to smaller elasticities for men (see MaCurdy *et al.* 1990) or at least to indicate sensitivity to the measurement of marginal tax rates and non-taxable other income. This conclusion is also reflected in the work on other countries; see Flood and MaCurdy (1992) and Blomquist (1992) for Sweden.

For married women these sensitivity issues are potentially more critical once it is recognised how influential, and yet unreliable, the estimated wage effect on participation can be (see Mroz (1987) for the USA and Blundell *et al.* (1987) for the UK). In the standard model a simple reservation wage condition is used to determine participation, in which an individual moves into employment if the market (after-tax) wage exceeds his or her reservation wage. It is easy to show that many of the large elasticities for female labour supply are simply an extrapolation of the wage effect on participation. Yet since we cannot know the true market wage for non-participants or correctly measure the size of fixed and search costs, such an extrapolation must be unreliable.

This distinction between participation and hours of work is an example of the potentially important features of the labour market that are often ignored in simulation models. They relate to fixed costs of work for women with children and the cyclical nature of demand-side constraints on job offers which make the participation decision so hard to analyse. They should also include the pay-off to on-the-job human capital investment and the impact on life-cycle wealth of taxation which focuses on the importance of future after-tax wage changes on current labour-supply responses.

Budget Constraints and the Distribution of Hours

If individuals can exert some degree of choice over their labour supply, the characteristics of a tax and benefit system should have implications for observed labour-supply behaviour. For example, if the tax and benefit system does not lead to a proportional tax, in which the effective marginal tax rate is constant, we should observe bunching in the hours distribution. As indicated in Section 4.2, the UK system of national insurance contributions (NIC) leads to such a situation, since at the lower earnings limit (LEL) or 'notch', the point at which NIC payments are made, there is an infinite effective marginal tax rate. As a result, we might expect part-time workers to attempt to locate themselves just below the LEL notch and relatively few to be found just above. Fig. 4.1, which focuses on a sample of part-time working women from the 1985 UK Family Expenditure Survey appears to confirm this prediction with the LEL notch or kink falling at around £34 per week for this sample.

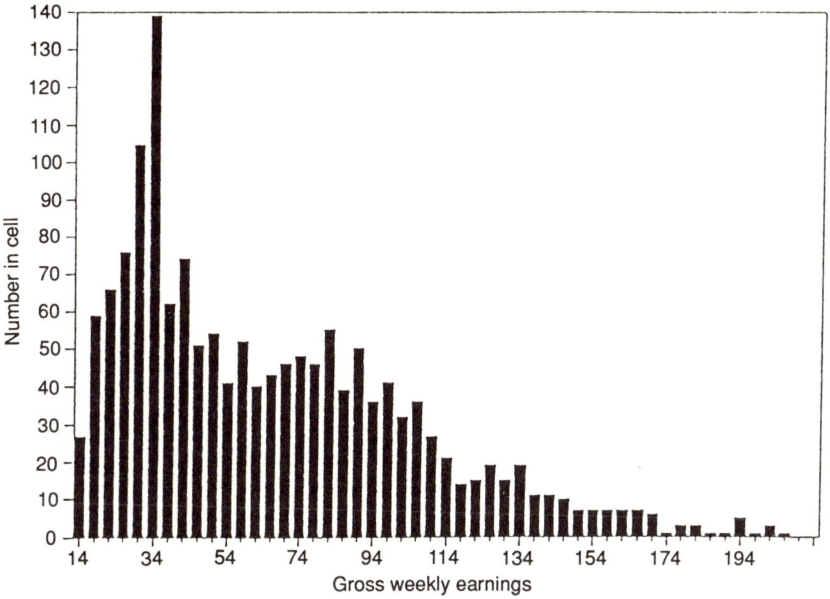

FIG 4.1. Married Women's Earnings and the NI Kink
Source: FES calculations, 1984 data.

Clearly, choice theory would suggest that if the LEL notch, in our discussion of NICs above, were lowered (raised) the bunching of hours would tend to move down (up). For similar reasons, choice theory predicts that bunching will also tend to occur where the marginal tax rate increases—say from 0 to 25%. However, for those individuals actually paying the 25% band, a cut in the tax rate may induce an increase or decrease in work effort. For those with taxable earnings just above the tax allowance the effect can only be positive, but for those on a higher income the response can go either way. A decrease in work effort in this case is commonly referred to as 'backward-bending' labour supply and is explained by the income effect (from the extra income) working against the positive incentive effect of the marginal tax reduction. Of course, even with backward-bending supply, direct tax increases would still induce an individual welfare loss in comparison to the lower tax situation although the supply of effort or hours is increased. In this case a more redistributive tax can also raise hours of work.

Measuring Labour-Supply Responses

What should be the shape of the labour-supply curve? Whatever the answer, it is unlikely to be linear. Chapter 2 of this volume has emphasized the importance of considering both income and substitution effects when analysing the total effect of wage changes on work incentives. Consider, as an illustration, an increase in the tax rate in a proportional tax system. Such an increase reduces the hourly wage for those in employment and reduces the pay-off to every extra hour worked. Those individuals free to enter the labour market would therefore be less likely to join. Those already in work may also be expected to reduce their work effort. However, from our earlier discussion this latter result is only a prediction from choice theory if those already in work are compensated for the loss in utility generated by the loss in leisure time. In the absence of such compensation, the income effect generated by the loss in earned income may increase desired work effort.

This latter effect is likely to be more important for individuals working longer hours, as is evident in the non-parametric regression presented in Figs. 4.2(*a*) and 4.2(*b*). These regressions are performed using the Kernel smoothing technique, and can be best thought of as estimating the relationship between hours and wages at each point in the data using only information on wages and hours that is local to that point. The plot then displays a moving average of these estimates. These graphs were produced using the interactive Kernel regression programme by Duncan and Jones (1991). Confidence bands (95%) have been placed round the Kernel regression lines. The first figure depicts the labour-supply behaviour for a sample of single working mothers above and below median income from the UK FES data source. This regression analysis places no restriction on the slope of the labour-supply curve at any point, but distinctly displays a decreasing slope with hours worked. It also displays a strong income effect with the labour-supply curve for mothers above-median other income nearly everywhere below that for the group with below-median income. Similarly, Fig. 4.2(*b*) presents two Kernel regressions of hours on the wage rate for our sample of married women. Again, the top regression line relates to a sample of individuals with other income below the median, while the bottom regression relates to individuals with other income above the median.

These Kernel regression results should be interpreted with caution, since no allowance is made for endogeneity of the marginal wage, of other income, or of sample selection. Moreover, we should note that, as the pointwise standard errors indicate, the data are sparse above hourly wage rates of around £6.00. Notwithstanding these points, the raw data do reveal a non-linear relationship between hours and wages, with labour

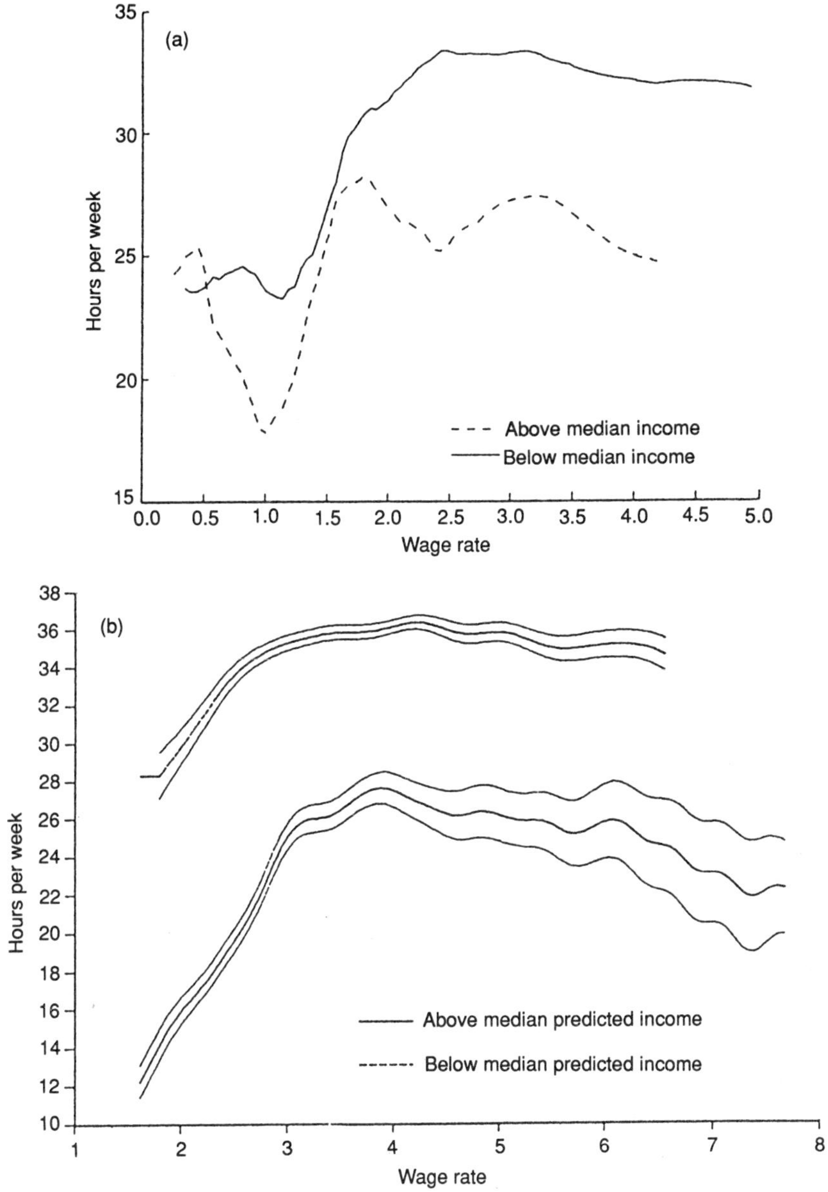

FIG 4.2(*a*). A Picture of Labour Supply, Lone Mothers (Kernel Regression: 1981–1986 Data)
Source: Blundell *et al.* (1992).

FIG 4.2(*b*). A Picture of Labour Supply, Married Women
Source: Blundell *et al.* (1993).

supply being forward-sloping at lower hours (initially quite steeply so) and then becoming backward-bending. The relative positions of the two graphs again reveal a strong negative income effect on hours. On this basis it would seem important to use a model to assess tax incentives that does not a priori rule out such non-linearities.

This picture of labour supply also provides a compelling example of the estimation methodology for tax reform simulation. By looking at individuals facing different hourly wages and other incomes, as in Figs. 4.2(*a*) and 4.2(*b*), we would hope to learn about the size of hourly wage and other effects and then be able to infer how particular individuals might change their behaviour in the face of reforms to the tax system.

When tax and benefit systems are complex, the budget constraint facing individuals in the labour market can be highly non-linear. As a result, the effective hourly wage rate facing individuals as they change their hours is far from constant. In order to evaluate elasticities or responses to tax changes, we need to know how labour supply adjusts to wage changes induced by tax changes. However, in any survey we will see individuals with same gross wage choosing very different labour supplies. This could happen because their preferences differ, but it may also reflect differences in their marginal tax rates. Separating these two influences is highly problematic.

Reforms to the system of means-tested benefits may also be treated in the same framework, since they usually combine an hourly wage change, through the movements in benefit withdrawal rates, with a change in the level of unearned income. However, since benefit systems often act to support family income, withdrawal rates will often be effective on all workers in the household. This can produce quite complex interactions in household labour supply, most notably in the UK for the labour supply of women married to unemployed men, a group which displayed persistently lower rates of labour market participation during the 1980s (see Kell and Wright 1990).

An advantage of the move to simplification of the tax system of the 1980s has been the opportunity to select large groups of numbers for whom the tax rate is essentially constant. Indeed, Figs. 4.3 and 4.4 show the proportion of lone mothers and women married to employed men in the UK Family Expenditure Survey (FES) who pay tax at the basic rate. For women married to employed men the budget constraint can be reasonably described by Fig. 4.5: apart from a range around the NIC notch (NI) and the basic tax rate kink (IT), marginal tax rates are effectively constant. The full details of this are presented in Table 4.5. Those individuals on the long linear segments, who are well away from the tax kink point, have an effectively constant composite tax rate. Indeed, as will be illustrated below, it is the rationalisation of behaviour by individuals at or near tax kinks that

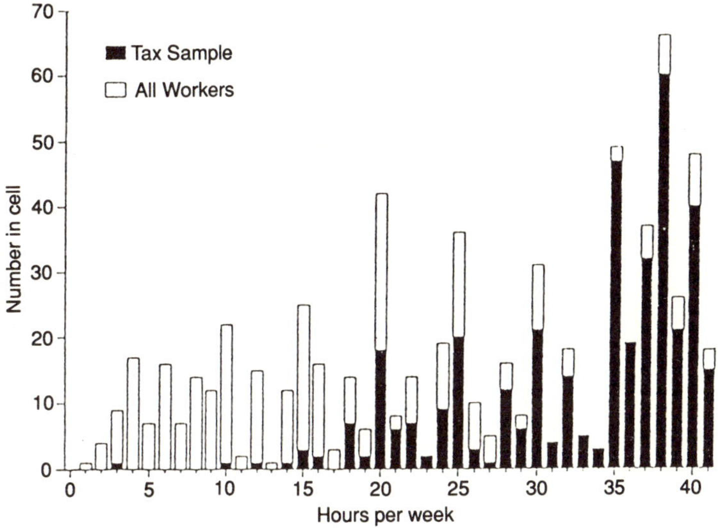

FIG 4.3. Hours Distribution, Lone Mothers
Source: Bludell *et al.* (1992).

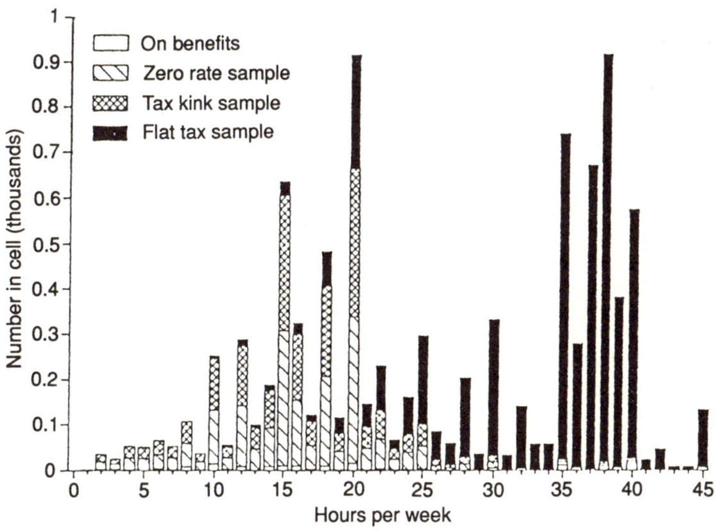

FIG 4.4. Hours Distribition, Married Women
Source: Blundell *et al.* (1993).

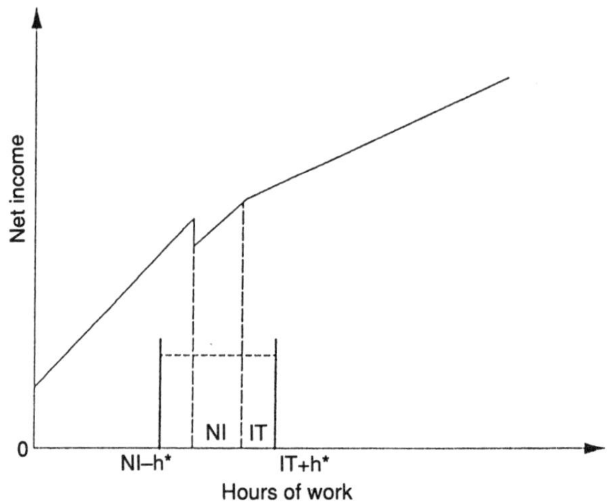

FIG 4.5. Married Women and the UK Tax System
Notes: NI = National insurance contribution notch; IT = basic tax allowance.
Source:

induces the sensitivity in the Hausman procedure for estimating labour-supply responses in the presence of nonlinear taxation. By selecting workers 'deep' inside the long linear segments (and correcting selection bias) we can avoid this sensitivity. This 'deep selection' approach is developed in the Blundell, Duncan and Meghir studies described in more detail below.

Another disadvantage of systems with many different tax rates is the problem of grouping at (or near) kink points. As argued above, choice theory suggests that grouping should occur and, moreover, for individuals at these points, that desired labour supply should be below the tax kink when evaluated at the after-kink tax rate and above the kink when evaluated at the before-kink tax rate. Only in this case will those individuals bunched near the kink point be following rational choice behaviour. However, this can also be shown to imply that the compensated wage elasticity is positive. In other words, optimization theory holds at these points. If there are many such tax kinks, as in the complex budget constraint case, empirical results can be misleading, in so far as the data is not given a free hand in determining the labour-supply relationship.

To illustrate this point briefly and to stress its significance in the debate over tax policy and labour supply, let us consider the linear labour-supply model, popular in tax reform analysis (see Hausman 1981; Blomquist

TABLE 4.5. Tax Benefit Combinations (Married Women)

	IT	NI	FIS	SB	RR	HB	Total	%
1.	–	–	–	–	–	–	3,083	26.72
2.	IT	–	–	–	–	–	106	0.92
3.	–	NI	–	–	–	–	597	5.17
4.	IT	NI	–	–	–	–	7,591	65.80
5.	–	–	FIS	–	–	–	10	0.09
6.	IT	NI	FIS	–	–	–	3	0.03
7.	–	–	–	–	RR	–	13	0.11
8.	IT	NI	–	–	RR	–	17	0.15
9.	–	–	–	–	–	HB	55	0.48
10.	–	NI	–	–	–	HB	6	0.05
11.	IT	NI	–	–	–	HB	33	0.29
12.	–	–	FIS	–	–	HB	5	0.04
13.	–	–	–	–	RR	HB	12	0.10

Notes: Only those combinations with more than one observation are presented. Results are derived from the Family Expenditure Survey 1980–9. Marginal tax rates are calculated using information on taxes paid and benefits received by each individual in the sample. Thus we avoid the problem of modelling benefit take-up when marginal rates are calculated on the basis of entitlement. The codes to tax deductions and benefit receipt are as follows: IT = Income Tax; FIS = Family Income Supplement; RR = Rate Rebate; NI = National Insurance; SB = Supplementary Benefit; HB = Rent Rebate/Housing Benefit.

Source: Blundell *et al.* (1993).

1983). In the context of the model for hours of work we may write this model as

$$h = \mathrm{a} + \mathrm{b}w + \mathrm{c}y$$

where h, w, and y represent measures of hours, hourly wages, and other income respectively while a, b, and c are the unknown constants, the latter two of which represent the response coefficients for the wage and other income variables. Together they determine desired labour supply for any wage and income combination.

When marginal tax rates increase, an individual will decide to remain at a tax 'kink' if his desired hours at the higher tax rate would be below the tax kink. For this to be true the parameters b and c have to be restricted. In particular they must accord with choice theory which requires b–ch to be positive. Since, with many kink points, this must be true for a wide range of hours, b will have to be positive and c negative. However, with b positive there is *forward-sloping* labour supply everywhere. So restrictions from theory become a constraint on the empirical evidence. A negative b cannot be recovered even if for a large section of the data the slope is close to zero or negative! The MaCurdy *et al.* (1990) results show that these restrictions appear to have been binding in the influential Hausman (1981) results, and may explain the vulnerability of this model to small changes in specification.

Any realistic empirical model has to allow measurement error and optimization error. When added to the model above, this allows individuals who would like to locate at the tax kink (or notch) to be observed off this point, and consequently 'smooths' out the resulting distribution of working hours. This makes the estimation more complex (see Hausman 1985), but does not change any of the arguments raised in the context of the linear labour-supply model above.

There are two possible responses to these issues. One is to derive a model that is more flexible than the linear case. This has been a line followed in our own research (see e.g. Blundell *et al.* 1992). There the non-linear labour-supply model due to Heckman (1974*c*) was found to fit the data well, satisfying rational-choice behaviour and producing a shape for the labour-supply curve not unlike Fig. 4.2. The second response has been to adopt more robust, if less efficient, estimation techniques that allow for measurement error and do not impose choice theory restrictions on every individual. MaCurdy *et al.* (1990) adopt such an option in the linear labour-supply case for the US data on male labour supply. In Blundell *et al.* (1993) we have pointed to the simplification of the tax schedule as a device for achieving robust estimates. With only one effective tax kink for large groups in our data, by choosing individuals well away from the kink (in the range NI–h^* to IT + h^* of Fig. 4.5 above), a simple estimator can be used which does not necessarily require optimal behaviour for all individuals in the sample. Moreover, Blundell, Duncan and Meghir (1993) show that the tax policy experiments of the 1980s, referred to above, can be used to pin down responses quite precisely. The impact of these robust estimation techniques on our understanding of labour-supply responses is discussed below in the context of the literature on labour-supply estimates.

4.4. SOME LABOUR-SUPPLY ESTIMATES

As has already been noted, the size of income and wage responses is still the subject of some debate among empirical economists, even after more than twenty years of detailed statistical analysis. By far the most reliable picture of labour-supply responses concerns married women, although, as can be inferred from Table 4.6, the range of estimated elasticities is large. Table 4.6 provides a comparison across a number of empirical studies. It is not exhaustive but it is representative. In general, the results point to a positive uncompensated-wage elasticity (Uncomp. wage) and to a negative income effect as choice theory would suggest. This results in reasonably large compensated-wage effects (Comp. wage), and indicates that efficiency gains from lowering tax rates on these women would be non-negligible.

TABLE 4.6. Some Elasticities for Married Women's Labour Supply

Author	Sample	Uncomp. wage	Comp. wage	Income
Cogan (1981)	USA	0.65	0.68	-0.03
Hausman (1981)	USA	0.45	0.9	-0.45
Arrufat and Sabalza (1986)	UK	0.68	0.62	-0.06
Blundell and Walker (1982)	UK	0.43	0.65	-0.22
Blundell, *et al.* (1993)	UK	0.33	0.52	-0.19

Source: Killingsworth (1983: 193) and own calculations.

As mentioned earlier there is still some debate as to the sensitivity of these estimated labour-supply models to small changes in specification, and it is clear that studies adopting more robust procedures tend to find slightly smaller elasticities. For example, Mroz (1987) suggests that the wage elasticity on hours for women in work in the USA is as small as 0.2, while Blundell *et al.* (1993) place this estimate at around 0.3 for married women in the UK. However, the latter study deliberately utilizes a non-linear labour-supply curve following the discussion of Figs. 4.2(*a*) and 4.2(*b*) above. As a result, the wage response depends critically on the hours of work at which it is evaluated. For some women there are large positive responses, while for others the response to an increase in the hourly wage is very small or even negative. This can also be seen in the work of Arrufat and Zabalza (1986) in their study of married women's labour supply in the UK. Again the elasticity falls significantly with hours worked, highlighting the importance of microsimulation in the evaluation of tax reforms, since different tax reforms will affect individuals differently depending on their wage and hours of work.

There is much less variation in the labour supply of married men, and generally empirical studies have avoided a separate analysis of non-participation, partly because of the relatively (in comparison to married women) high participation rates. It is also reasonable to suppose that the majority of prime-aged men are likely to be found in occupations/industries in which labour supply is determined by a collective agreement of some kind. As a result there are many fewer believable studies of male labour supply, and those that have been made find smaller and often negative wage elasticities. Table 4.7 documents some illustrations from the literature. The first point to note is that, because men are generally found in full-time employment, these results are not completely out of line with the results for women, especially those in full-time employment. However, the lack of variation in working hours generally leads to a lack of precision. Indeed, the Atkinson and Stern (1980) study of household heads restricts analysis to full-time employees.

TABLE 4.7. Husbands' Labour-Supply Elasticities

Author	Sample	Uncomp. wage	Comp. wage	Income
Hausman (1981)	Husbands USA	0.03	0.95	-0.92
Ashworth and Ulph (1981)	Husbands UK	-0.33	0.29	-0.62
Atkinson and Stern (1980)	Household heads UK	-0.16	-0.09	-0.07
Blundell and Walker (1982)	Husbands UK	-0.23	0.13	-0.36

Source: Killingsworth (1983: 193) and own calculations.

It should also be pointed out that the larger income effects in Table 4.7, especially in the case of Hausman (1981) for the USA, imply large compensated effects and therefore correspondingly sizeable efficiency losses from taxation. However, the recent results of MaCurdy *et al.* (1990) suggest that this income effect is probably overestimated.

In sum, it is usually felt that the response to tax reductions in terms of working hours by prime-aged men is small and possibly negative, with working hours probably determined in some collective manner. This coincides with the idea put forward in Lazear (1983) that unions/collective agreements are more likely to be found where there are small supply elasticities and more homogeneous groups of workers. Moreover, there is evidence from Ham (1986*a*; 1986*b*) that men, especially non-participants, are off their labour-supply curve.

TABLE 4.8. Lone Mothers' Labour-Supply Elasticities

Author	Sample	Uncomp. wage	Comp. wage	Income
Hausman (1980)	USA	0.53	0.65	-0.18
Bingley *et al.* (1992)	UK	0.76	1.28	-0.52
Jenkins (1992)	UK	1.44	1.68	-0.24

Source: Killingsworth (1983: 193) and own calculations.

For lone parents the position is somewhat different. In the UK, these are mainly women who face child care costs and a benefit system that makes part-time work, at least for those on low wages, unattractive. As a result many fewer of these women work part-time, especially in comparison to women married to employed men. However, they are a group whose importance in the labour market and in the benefit system is growing rapidly. Empirical results for this group tend to be more recent, and in Table 4.8 some elasticities are presented. Since fewer of these women work part-time, the elasticities tend to be dominated by the participation effect, and the large elasticities in the studies by Bingley *et al.* (1992) and Jenkins (1992) for the UK certainly reflect the strong wage effect on participation. Once working hours alone are considered, as is the case in Blundell *et al.* (1992), we find the characteristic fall in the wage elasticity, with values for the uncompensated elasticity around 0.2. Again, this probably reflects an underlying labour-supply curve much like that depicted in Fig. 4.2, in which elasticities around the point of participation are large but fall off rapidly with increases in working hours.

4.5. 'REAL WORLD' CHARACTERISTICS OF THE UK LABOUR MARKET

Before turning to a practical microsimulation of tax reforms, we briefly focus our attention on certain caveats in the above approach to the measurement of labour-supply responses which reflect features of the 'real world' that are likely to interfere to a lesser or greater extent with predictions from the choice-theoretic framework outlined above. Some of these concerns have been raised in Chapter 2, and here stress will be placed on how they may influence our interpretation of the results presented above.

Fixed Costs of Work

These have already been the focus of some discussion above in the context of the participation decision for women with children. In general, fixed costs take the form of time or money costs, and may even arise as part of the tax and benefit system itself. For example, benefit systems seeking to keep family income above a minimum level can severely reduce the incentive to accept a job offering less than the amount of income that takes family income over the minimum threshold. For women on low hourly wages, part-time jobs become less attractive and choice is restricted to non-participation or jobs with full-time earnings. Child care costs may make part-time employment less attractive. However, there is some evidence that child care availability positively affects participation of women with young children; it is often available on a daily or hourly basis and as a result may often act like a proportionate tax (or subsidy) on earnings. These effects are not restricted to young children: the presence of older dependent relatives in the household is also found to be negatively correlated with participation.

The presence of fixed costs influences the trade-off between work and non-work, and reduces the effectiveness of marginal wage increases at the point of participation as an encouragement to work. For example, earnings disregards which in effect raise the marginal wage for those with very low weekly earnings, although still encouraging work through an income effect, would be far less effective in the presence of fixed costs.

All this suggests that labour market participation is likely to be decided on in a rather different way from choices over increasing or decreasing labour supply for those in work, for whom the fixed cost is a sunk cost—simply reducing income whatever hours are chosen. Empirically, we should model the wage (and tax) effects on participation separately. It is interesting to note that almost all studies of tax reform *do not* do this, despite the clear empirical evidence (e.g. Mroz 1987) that wage and income effects are highly sensitive to this separation.

The Cogan (1981) study for the USA showed the elasticity falling from almost 2 to around 0.5, once fixed costs were included, for the married women in his sample whose fixed costs averaged some 28% of annual earnings. Similarly, the study by Blundell *et al.* (1987) of married women in the UK showed a significant downward shift in the wage response after fixed costs were allowed for. As mentioned above, this distinction does not tend to be made in models used in tax reform simulation. The reason for this is simple but not convincing—unless fixed costs can actually be measured, the effects of tax reform on *participation* in these models is more difficult to predict. Nevertheless, it is critical in our understanding of participation effects of tax and benefit reforms. As a result, there is a tendency to extrapolate a strong wage effect on participation across the whole-hours distribution. This is further exacerbated in a linear model where a strong wage effect at low hours, as in Fig. 4.2, for example, would produce highly misleading predictions at higher hours.

Life-Cycle Savings, Demographics, and Wealth

In a life-cycle model, individuals may supply labour in order to save for future periods where the relative value of non-work activity is higher. In general this will cover retirement, periods of ill health, and periods of unemployment. For women (and men to some extent) this will also cover periods of family formation. As a result, two otherwise identical individuals may supply very different levels of labour reflecting their different expectations of future needs and uncertaintics. The individual with higher future needs or a more uncertain future income stream is correspondingly less well off and will supply more labour. To allow for this, a life-cycle-consistent labour-supply model has been introduced into the literature (MaCurdy 1983; Blundell and Walker 1986) in which consumption expenditures are used to correct unearned income for savings. The UK FES data are ideal for this, as they include consumers' expenditure records for all households as well as their weekly labour supplies. The general effect of this adjustment to income is to increase the size and precision of income effect on labour supply, the former *increasing* the compensated elasticity and the welfare costs of tax distortions.

It is clear that a change in marginal tax rates will have an impact on future earned income and therefore on expected wealth. Savings will adjust to reflect this. When a tax reform occurs it is usually considered permanent and is often unexpected. As a result it can have a large wealth effect. For example, if a marginal tax reduction reduced the need for saving, the wealth effect may add to the usual income effect, initially reducing the effectiveness of the incentive to supply more effort. On the other hand, if this is coupled with an expected decline in the real value of state pensions and unemployment benefit, it may encourage the supply of effort by workers.

Most empirical analyses of intertemporal labour supply focus on the intertemporal elasticity of substitution, which measures the response to an *anticipated* change in the real wage in one period, holding all future real wages constant and maintaining the marginal utility of income (see Altonji 1986; Browning *et al.* 1985). It is not surprising, at least in a world without uncertainty, that a fall in the *real* wage for one period would reduce labour supply during that period given the knowledge that it is a one-off change. Uncertainty and risk aversion reduce this effect, but elasticities for women are often large and can be in excess of 1 (see Heckman and MaCurdy 1980). However, a tax change is usually neither temporary nor anticipated. Moreover, marginal utility cannot be maintained, since tax increases (decreases) reduce (increase) wealth and therefore increase (reduce) marginal utility. The upshot is that this large intertemporal elasticity can be significantly reduced once unexpected wealth effects are acknowledged. Card (1991) finds an intertemporal substitution elasticity reduced by more than 50% once wealth effects are accounted for. It is likely that the standard life-cycle-consistent elasticity provides an inflated view of responses after wealth effects are accounted for (see Bover 1989 for a useful presentation of elasticities for the USA). It may well be the case that the standard uncompensated-wage elasticities provide a more accurate guide to responses.

On-the-Job Human Capital and Seniority

It is well documented that for some groups of individuals there is a significant pay-off to participation in terms of wage growth. In other words, interrupted labour market histories reduce wages; (see e.g. Eckstein and Wolpin 1989; Shaw 1989). This can occur in a neoclassical model with on-the-job human capital or in a collective-bargaining model with seniority-related pay. In either case the pay-off to continuing in employment may induce participation where 'simple' choice theory would suggest otherwise. Short-run (temporary) fluctuations in income or marginal wages are less likely to result in movements in and out of the labour market, and the impact of short-run changes to taxes and benefits is thus reduced.

In terms of encouraging investment in human capital, a linear proportional tax is clearly preferred to a system with an increasing marginal rate (see Heckman 1976). In terms of the impact on our labour-supply elasticities, the evidence for married women seems to point to a larger experience effect for professionals and those with high educational qualifications. It is unlikely, therefore, that the 'simple' labour-supply model would provide reasonable predictions for such groups.

Job Queues, Unions, and Collective Bargaining

If unions bargain over employment and wages, there will be unfulfilled supply at the going wage and not all individuals who would like to supply work will receive a job offer. More generally, with information asymmetries and a continuously changing environment there will be individuals who would like to work but who do not receive job offers. This again suggests that the participation effects of wage changes will not simply reflect individual choice.

For groups of workers in industries or occupations where unions negotiate over hours of work, as well as employment and wages, the consequence of bargaining will in general be a restriction on supply. This may well result in a spurious negative correlation between hours of work and real marginal wages. This is why researchers have often been reluctant to fit standard labour-supply models to data on men (or women) in highly unionized sectors, and is yet another reason why the focus has often been on female labour supply, particularly, in non-professional occupations.

Benefit Take-Up and Effective Tax Rates

Although means-tested benefits induce a 'tax rate' on earned income through the withdrawal mechanism, they are also invariably subject to a lower than 100% take-up among eligible households. Housing benefit (see Blundell, Fry, and Walker 1988) and family credit (see Dorset and Heady 1991), are two examples. As Fraker and Moffitt (1988) point out, an increase in the withdrawal rate can exhibit two opposing responses.

The increase in the rate will induce a higher tax rate for those continuing to take up but, as the benefit is now worth less, some eligible individuals may decide to stop taking up, and for them the effective tax rate in earned income is reduced. Indeed, in their study of food stamps in the USA, Fraker and Moffitt find these effects almost completely cancelling out in aggregate. In the UK, take-up is responsive to the *value* of the benefits (see Blundell, Fry, and Walker 1988), and this observation can be expected to reduce the impact of withdrawal rate changes on overall labour supply.

4.6. SIMULATING THE UK TAX REFORMS OF THE 1980S

The 1980s have seen a number of policy experiments that may be expected to have influenced labour-supply behaviour. They provide an ideal opportunity for counterfactual simulation, and in what follows we consider one aspect of these reforms in the UK. As was discussed in Section 4.2 above, the three main features have been the cut in basic rates, the increase in the real value of the basic income allowance for tax, and the shift toward indirect taxation from the increase in VAT. We will focus on the basic-rate changes. It could be argued that the introduction of independent taxation was a major feature of tax reform in this period. However, its impact on labour supply, at least for the groups on which we are focusing, was probably rather limited. In particular, taking a recent year of FES data (1989), we consider the increase in the basic rate from the 25% level to the 33% level that existed before 1980. In exploring this counterfactual, the increase in real value of tax allowances will be ignored. The pre-1980 levels in the tax allowances would also have implied higher tax rates for many workers—especially women in part-time employment. Similarly, we ignore the offsetting increase in VAT rates. This is not to say that the microsimulation model used in this analysis cannot account for these changes; but to understand the pattern and magnitude of likely reactions it is useful to move systematically though the individual components of any tax reform.

To illustrate the issues involved, attention will be focused on the group of married women with employed husbands. Analysis of this group has two advantages. Firstly, the tax and benefit system for them is relatively straightforward. Secondly, we can contrast the differential impact that occurs whether husband's income is held constant or allowed to be affected by the tax reform—as it indeed was. The latter point will emphasize the importance of modelling income effects within the household in addition to substitution/incentive effects for individual household members.

TABLE 4.9. Simulating an Increase in the Basic Rate of Income Tax for Married Women: A Cross-Tabulation of the Impact on Working Hours

	Post–reform hours												
	0	<4	<8	<12	<16	<20	<24	<28	<32	<36	<40	<44	44+
0	147	–	–	–	–	–	–	–	–	–	–	–	–
<4	–	49	–	–	–	–	–	–	–	–	–	–	–
<8	–	–	33	1	–	–	–	–	–	–	–	–	–
<12	1	–	–	49	1	–	–	–	1	–	–	–	–
<16	–	–	–	2	186	1	4	1	–	1	–	–	–
<20	1	–	–	–	3	78	1	1	–	–	1	–	–
<24	–	–	–	–	–	7	74	–	–	1	–	–	–
<28	–	2	–	1	5	–	3	72	–	–	–	–	–
<32	–	–	–	–	–	–	–	4	63	–	–	–	–
<36	–	–	1	–	–	1	–	1	5	81	–	–	–
<40	–	–	–	–	1	–	–	–	–	14	178	–	–
<44	–	–	–	–	–	–	–	–	–	1	8	14	–
44+	–	–	–	–	–	–	–	–	–	1	–	–	21

Note: Women married to employed husbands.

Source: Blundell *et al*. (1993).

Table 4.9 provides a cross-tabulation of hours before and after reform for our sample of married women. For the bulk of women there are small decreases in their hours of work in response to the basic rate increase, as we might expect from the small but generally positive uncompensated wage effects estimated in our models. The backward-bending effects are also apparent for a few women reflected in points above the leading diagonal in Table 4.9. These latter effects are magnified in Table 4.10 once husband's income is reduced in line with the basic rate increase. There are now many more responses lying above the diagonal in Table 4.10 which highlight the importance of modelling the impact of tax reform on total household resources. There are even non-working women who now want to supply positive labour supply given the reduction in household disposable income.

4.7. CONCLUSIONS

The aim of this survey has been to highlight the central role played by labour supply in tax reform evaluation, and to stress the importance of microsimulation analysis. The illustrative reform simulations in the last section help to focus attention on the importance of correctly associating individuals with differing wage and income responses to appropriate points on the tax and benefit schedule. Microsimulation allows the distinction between the many types of individual supplying labour in the

TABLE 4.10. Simulating an Increase in the Basic Rate of Income Tax for Married Women: Allowing Husbands' After-Tax Income to Change

	Post-reform hours												
	0	<4	<8	<12	<16	<20	<24	<28	<32	<36	<40	<44	44+
0	118	1	2	–	11	10	3	1	–	–	1	–	–
<4	1	48	–	–	–	–	–	–	–	–	–	–	–
<8	–	1	28	5	–	–	–	–	–	–	–	–	–
<12	–	–	–	45	5	–	–	–	1	1	–	–	–
<16	–	–	–	2	181	5	7	10	–	–	–	–	–
<20	–	–	–	1	1	72	1	–	–	–	1	–	–
<24	–	–	–	–	–	4	73	1	–	1	–	–	–
<28	–	–	–	1	6	1	3	72	–	–	–	–	–
<32	–	–	–	–	–	–	–	–	65	1	1	–	–
<36	–	–	–	–	–	–	–	2	2	85	–	–	–
<40	–	–	–	–	–	–	–	–	–	8	183	2	–
<44	–	–	–	–	–	–	–	–	–	–	6	17	–
44+	–	–	–	–	–	–	–	–	–	–	–	–	22

Note: Women married to employed husbands.
Source: Blundell *et al.* (1993).

economy and the variety of economic and demographic circumstances they face. The large and wide****ranging tax reforms of the 1980s provide a sequence of important policy experiments with which to evaluate tax reform responses. From the standpoint of the usual framework for measuring labour-supply responses, we have shown that married women appear to be the group most responsive to such reforms. However, this is also the group for which tax reform usually brings significant family income effects as well as marginal wage changes. Our simulation results have shown that these income effects can go a long way towards cancelling out labour-supply increase from this group, and stress the importance of analysing tax reform in a household context.

The labour-supply results referred to in Section 4.3 have also stressed that care is needed in both estimating and interpreting labour-supply parameters. The overall picture of labour-supply responses, especially for married women, is now fairly well understood, but the importance of distinguishing between participation and hours of work, reflecting the importance of fixed costs and job opportunities, is much less well researched. This is also the case with regard to the precise shape of the labour-supply curve over the range of hours worked. The microsimulation examples illustrate how important these aspects of labour supply are when evaluating tax reform, as some reforms are designed to encourage participation (changes to the benefit structure, for example) while others appear designed to encourage more work from those already in employment (reductions in basic and higher rates of tax, for example).

Our discussion of results for the UK points to a reasonably robust picture now emerging with regard to labour-supply responses. These seem to suggest that wage and tax response parameters have typically been overestimated by confounding the participation and hours-of-work decisions and by forcing a tight optimization structure on individual responses. More robust results indicate that responses can be relatively large, especially for married women, but such large responses tend to be concentrated among those working relatively low hours. For women and men on close to full-time hours, the overall response appears small if not negative.

Of course, small wage elasticities do not necessarily suggest insignificant welfare loss from taxation, since compensated responses can still be large for all groups. Indeed, in the Blundell *et al.* (1993) study of married women's labour supply in the UK we find a large accordance with positive compensated-wage effects despite the occurrence of backward-bending labour-supply effects for some individuals. Moreover, for some groups it may be that productivity is poorly measured by working hours. However, the analysis of top-rate tax cuts by Dilnot and Kell (1989) found little evidence to attribute the increased tax revenues from such taxpayers to large behavioural responses. For other groups, therefore, although the results are less precise because of less variation or smaller sample sizes, the picture is probably somewhat similar. Most prime-age men work full-time and have small wage responses. For single parents the responsiveness is probably greatest at the participation margin, and the remaining shape of the labour-supply curve is probably similar to that of other groups.

Putting this together with the reforms of the 1980s, it is difficult to believe that the reduction in marginal rates of income tax could have induced large (positive) labour-supply responses. The direct responses by the types of individual for whom the tax reforms were primarily directed appear small. Moreover, the income effects on other groups such as part-time married women are likely to have had an offsetting effect.

5

Have Social-Security Benefits Seriously Damaged Work Incentives in Britain?

A. B. ATKINSON

5.1. INTRODUCTION

A major role has been played in the debate about the welfare state in Britain by the view that generous social-security benefits have seriously damaged work incentives. According to this view, in addition to the cost of financing large-scale transfers and the consequent levels of taxation (the subject of the previous chapter), the structure and level of benefits is such as to discourage recipients from taking steps to improve their own position. It is with this view that the present chapter is concerned.

The principal elements of the British social-security system are outlined in Section 5.2. Two features have led to particular concern about incentives. The first is the fact that social insurance largely provides flat-rate, rather than earnings-related, benefits. Unemployment benefit is now flat-rate and, as a result, the ratio of benefit to earnings in work is higher for low-paid workers. Combined with means-tested benefits (see the next paragraph), this has led attention to be drawn to the *unemployment trap*, whereby people may find themselves not a great deal better off financially if they return to work.

The second feature of the United Kingdom social-security system is heavy reliance on means-tested benefits. This applies to those not in work who are eligible for social assistance, housing benefit, and relief from local taxes. It applies to those in work through means-tested family assistance, and, again, housing benefit and relief from local taxes. For those in work, the withdrawal of benefits as income rises involves a high composite marginal tax rate on additional income. (The term 'composite marginal tax rate' is used to denote the combined effect of extra taxes paid and benefits lost as a result of an increase in income.) This has led to concern about the *poverty trap*, whereby a person or family is little better off as a result of earning additional income.

These potential disincentives have been stressed in government statements. The White Paper of 1985, setting out proposals for reform, said that

> social security can leave too many people trapped in poverty or unemployment. People can still find themselves worse off in work than if they were unemployed. Others can find that a pay rise in work has at best a marginal effect. (Department of Health and Social Security 1985: 1).

The attempts which have been made to resolve this problem are described in Section 5.2.

The potential impact of benefits on the work decisions of individuals is the subject of Section 5.3. This examines the effect of the social-security system at the level of the individual budget constraint, where 'individual' refers to the decision-making unit, which may be a single person, a couple, or a wider household unit. The interrelation through the benefit system of the decisions of different people is an important part of the story. It is also essential to remember that, even if social-insurance benefits are largely flat-rate, benefit payments vary considerably with individual characteristics and past experience. The institutional details of social security, and the way in which the benefit system is administered, are often disregarded by economists but may be of material importance. Unemployment benefit, for example, is often treated as though it is paid automatically to all who are unemployed. In reality, benefit in many countries is paid subject to conditions which mean that coverage of the unemployed is less than 100%. Similarly, the extent to which means-tested benefits generate a poverty trap is less than appears at first, on account of the fact that there is significantly less than 100% take-up of these benefits.

The institutional structure of benefit is necessary background for the analysis in Section 5.4 of the empirical evidence concerning the impact of benefits on work decisions. There are many dimensions of such decisions, and here attention is focused on six possible types of disincentive effect: delayed return to work by the unemployed, voluntary quitting by those in employment, non-participation in the labour force by the wives of the unemployed, non-participation by single parents, increased sickness absence, and early retirement. As in the rest of the book, we do not consider the position of those over the state pension age, which in 1993 is 60 for women and 65 for men (plans to harmonize these ages are under consideration).

5.2. THE SOCIAL-SECURITY SYSTEM IN GREAT BRITAIN

The present British social-security system has a long history. While it is common to trace the national insurance system back to the Beveridge Report of 1942 and the consequent post-war legislation which came into effect in 1948, this oversimplifies the story in several important ways. In particular, we need to distinguish between social insurance and social assistance, and to consider separately categorical benefits which can be classified under neither heading, including family allowance and benefits for the disabled.

The following account of the social-security system, and its recent evolution, is highly simplified; and the details require qualification in many respects (see e.g. Matthewman 1992). It should also be stressed that the system is subject to frequent modification. The attention of the reader is drawn to the following changes of name:

Social assistance was called *national assistance* from 1948 to 1966, *supplementary benefit* from 1966 to 1988, and has been called *income support* since 1988.

Family means-tested benefit was called *family income supplement* from 1971 to 1988, and has been called *family credit* since 1988.

Child allowance was called *family allowance* from 1946 to 1977, and has been called *child benefit* since 1977.

It should also be noted that much of the discussion concentrates on the situation in Great Britain, which consists of England, Wales, and Scotland; at some places explicit reference is made to the United Kingdom, which also includes Northern Ireland.

Social Insurance

The report written by Beveridge (1942) during the Second World War set out proposals for a unified system of social insurance or contributory benefits, providing income replacement in both the short and the long term. The legislation which came into effect in 1948 was in this respect true to his intentions, and remains today largely intact. A wide range of contingencies are covered by the same scheme, called *national insurance* (NI), which provides (in 1993) retirement pensions, widows' benefits, unemployment benefit, invalidity benefit, and residual sickness and maternity benefits. These benefits account for around half of total social-security spending in Great Britain.

Of the national insurance benefits, retirement pensions are the single most important in terms of total spending. Fig. 5.1 shows the development of spending on these and other programmes in real terms over the past twenty years. Under the retirement pension provisions, a person reaching the minimum state pension age who satisfies the contribution conditions receives a flat-rate basic NI pension, in 1993–4 approximately equal to 20% of national average earnings net of tax for a single person. The pension is taxable. A married woman may qualify for a (reduced) pension as a derived right from her husband's contributions (there are also dependents' allowances).

The intention of Beveridge in recommending flat-rate benefits was that individuals should supplement the state benefits with private provision. In

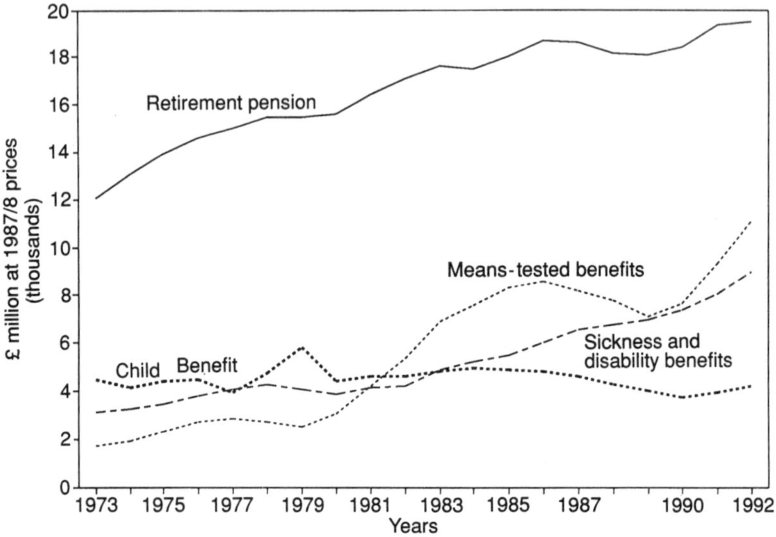

FIG 5.1. Spending in Real Terms, Great Britain

Notes: (1) The 1992–3 figure is the estimated out-turn. (2) Sickness and disability benefits include sickness benefit (including statutory sick pay), invalidity benefit, industrial disablement benefit, industrial death benefit, attendance allowance, invalid care allowance, invalid pension/severe disablement allowance, mobility allowance, disability living allowance, and disability working allowance. (3) Means-tested benefits include here supplementary benefit/income support, net expenditure from the social fund, and family income supplement/family credit; housing benefit is not included. (4) Retirement pension does not include the Christmas bonus.

Sources: 1973–4 to 1988–9 from Hills (1990: table 7A.1). 1989–90 to 1992–3 from Dept of Social Security (1933*a*: table 1), applying a GDP deflator (HM Treasury 1993: table 2.1) of 86.6/75.8 for 1989–90, of 93.5/75.8 for 1990–1, of 100/75.8 for 1991–2, and of 104.3/75.8 for 1992–3.

the case of retirement pensions, this, together with the favourable income tax regime, led to a growth of occupational pensions provided by employers. The coverage of occupational pensions was, however, far from complete, leading Titmuss (1955) to describe the situation as one of ‘two nations in old age’. Moreover, there was considerable variation in the generosity of the benefits of these occupational schemes, ranging from a guaranteed benefit based on final salary, through schemes which had a final salary target but no guarantee that this would be attained, to those that were defined contribution schemes with no target benefit level.

There followed a succession of official plans, some enacted, to provide a complementary state earnings-related pension scheme (SERPS), from which employers were allowed to ‘contract out’ if they provided occupational benefits to a specified standard. In 1987 43% of employees were contracted out in this way (Government Actuary 1991: 4–5). The current scheme, SERPS, was introduced in 1978, but the benefits were scaled down with effect from 1988. When SERPS reaches maturity, a person with lifetime average earnings equal to the national average for males will have a total state pension equal to 42.5% of net earnings at retirement (Atkinson 1991: 125). The 1986 Social Security Act also introduced the possibility that people could contract out of SERPS, not only into an occupational scheme but also into a 'personal pension'. Such a pension operates on the basis of a defined contribution rather than a defined benefit.

It is benefits for those below pension age that are of particular concern here. Britain is unusual among European countries in having flat-rate benefits for sickness and unemployment. Short-term earnings-related benefits *were* introduced in 1966, with the intention of encouraging labour mobility, but they were discontinued in 1982. The main earnings-related benefit which remains for those below pension age is the additional pension payable under invalidity benefit. Invalidity benefit is payable after twenty-eight weeks of sickness, subject to an indirect contribution condition (claimants previously having received short-term sickness benefit).

The abolition of earnings-related short-term benefits was one important policy development of the 1980s; a second was the transfer to employers of the responsibility for paying sickness and maternity benefits. In 1983 employers became responsible for paying the first eight weeks (since 1986 the first twenty-eight weeks) of sickness benefit (statutory sick pay), with the payments being refunded (the refund is now only 80%) via deductions from income tax and contributions forwarded to the Inland Revenue. Statutory sick pay is currently at one of two flat rates, depending on the claimant's normal weekly earnings. A similar scheme was introduced for maternity benefit in 1987.

One consequence of the transfer to employers is that public expenditure and taxation appeared to fall. In the total for public spending in Fig. 5.1, the cost of statutory sick pay is included on a gross basis, in order to ensure comparability across years. It may be seen that the cost of sickness, invalidity, and disability benefits (see below) has increased substantially in proportionate terms over the past twenty years, and is now approaching half that on retirement pensions.

Total spending on social insurance has increased in real terms by about 50% over the past twenty years. The sources of this rise may be found in changes in: (i) the number of potential beneficiaries, (ii) the rate of coverage (actual divided by potential beneficiaries), and (iii) the real amount received per beneficiary. The number of potential beneficiaries certainly increased, and, in the case of those over minimum retirement age, the coverage also increased. The number of people receiving national insurance retirement pensions in Great Britain is now some 10 million, compared with some 7 million at the beginning of the 1970s.

The position with respect to the unemployed is more complicated. Recorded unemployment is certainly higher. In Great Britain, unemployment did not exceed 600,000 in the 1960s; in the 1980s it did not fall below 1.5 million. But the effective coverage of national insurance was reduced. Atkinson and Micklewright (1989) list seventeen legislative changes in NI unemployment benefit between 1979 and 1988. Two of these were favourable to the unemployed; four could have had either a positive or a negative effect; and no fewer than eleven were unfavourable to the unemployed, including the tightening of contribution conditions, the abolition of lower-rate benefits, and the lengthening of the disqualification period for voluntary quitting, dismissal on account of industrial misconduct, or refusal of a job offer. These have all led to a reduction in the proportion of those registered as unemployed in Britain who actually receive NI unemployment benefit (Micklewright 1990).

The third element is that of changes in the real value of benefits. With largely flat-rate benefits, the issue of uprating is an important one, there being no inbuilt assurance that benefits will keep pace with rising earnings. When national insurance was introduced, there was no automatic machinery to adjust benefits, but over the 1950s and 1960s there came to be a general acceptance that benefits should be adjusted with the rising real incomes of the working population. In the 1970s this practice was formalized, with retirement pensions guaranteed to increase at least in line with average earnings, and short-term benefits given statutory price indexation; but the latter provision was subsequently abolished, and the indexation of pensions limited to prices. Benefits have, in fact, not risen in line with average earnings: over the 1980s the basic retirement pension fell from some 30% of net average male weekly earnings to around 20%.

The failure to increase benefits in line with average earnings, and the reductions in coverage, have meant that total social insurance spending has risen less in relation to GDP than would be expected on the basis of the demographic and other changes in the beneficiary population. Between 1973–4 and 1992–3, expenditure on contributory benefits rose from 5.2% to 6.2% of GDP (Hills *et al.* 1990: table 7A.1; Department of Social Security 1993*a*: 37). Spending on social insurance has risen less than that on means-tested assistance and on non-contributory benefits, to which attention is now turned.

Social Assistance

As is illustrated in Fig. 5.1, expenditure on means-tested benefits has grown very substantially; the greater part, but not all, is accounted for by social assistance (called initially national assistance, then supplementary benefit, and now income support). This is contrary to the original intention. It had been the objective of Beveridge in his plan of 1942 that the social-insurance benefits would be sufficient in their own right for the great majority of recipients, and that the need for means-tested supplementation would be residual and decline over time. He took this view on account of 'the strength of popular objection to any kind of means test' (1942: 12) and of the way in which it penalized individual efforts (through the high composite marginal tax rate).

Beveridge's hopes were not in this respect realized. The insurance benefits enacted in 1948 were not, in fact, set at a level which ensured that people could live independently of means-tested assistance in all but exceptional cases. As a result, many had to rely on national assistance. This differed from the old poor law in being a nationally unified scheme, and in being assessed on the basis of the resources of the benefit unit (inner family) rather than the whole household; but it remained a means-tested benefit. Under present-day income support, cash assistance is paid to those families which are not supported by a person in work, where the capital assets are below a specified level, and which have income below an 'applicable amount', which depends on the family composition. For those who are unemployed, further conditions apply concerning availability for work, etc. The amount paid is equal to the difference between the family's net income and the applicable amount. People may receive assistance in addition to national insurance benefits. Social assistance in the UK is administered by specialist benefit offices, not by social workers, and there is very little local discretion (apart from the Social Fund—see below).

The growth in the role of social assistance is illustrated in Fig. 5.2, which shows how the proportion of the population living in families receiving cash assistance rose steadily over the post-war period and then jumped in the 1980s. At the beginning of the 1990s, around 40% of those in receipt of income support were elderly, about 30% were unemployed, and 20% were single-parent families.

In addition to regular weekly payments, national assistance at the outset provided for lump-sum grants to be made to recipients for exceptional needs, such as the replacement of household equipment or clothing. Under supplementary benefit, the proportion of claimants in receipt of such exceptional-needs payments rose to over a third (in 1976). Although at that time they only accounted for a small percentage of total expenditure, they attracted a great deal of attention; and in the first half of the 1980s there was a further rapid growth in the number of claims and in expenditure. The response of the government in the 1986 Social

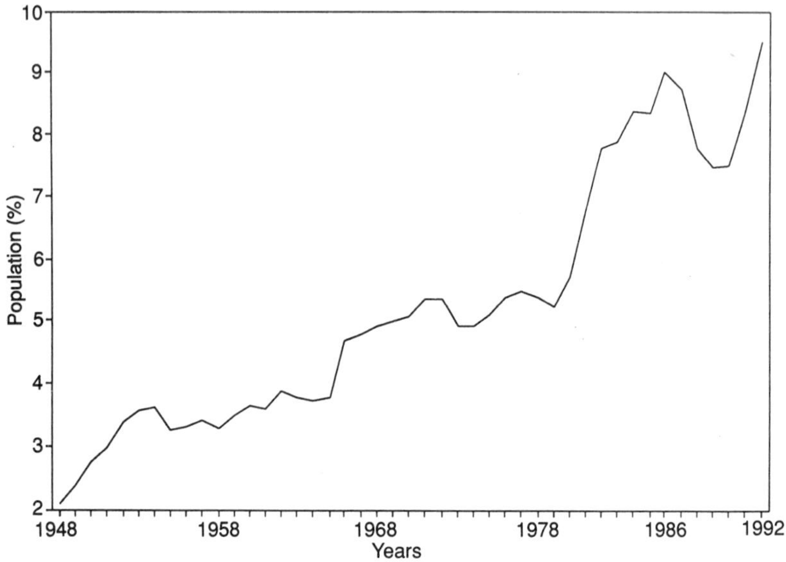

FIG 5.2. People Dependent on Means-Tested Benefits, Great Britain
Sources: 1948–65 (national assistance) from National Assistance Board (1966: 54), figures for Dec. of each year. 1966–87 (supplementary benefit) from Dept of Health and Social Security (1990: table 34.29), figures for Nov. or Dec. 1988–92 (income support) from Dept of Social Security (1993*a*: table 6). The population figures are the mid-year estimates from Central Statistical Office (1992: table 2.1; 1961: table 6; 1952: table 6).

Security Act was to replace lump-sum grants under social assistance by the Social Fund. This has increased the degree of discretion on the part of the awarding officers; it has imposed a fixed budget at local-office level (so that the probability of receipt depends on where and when a claim is made); and many payments are loans rather than grants.

Child Benefit and Family Credit

The increased role of means-testing applies not just to benefits paid to those not in work but also to transfers to families with children. Following a long campaign in the 1920s and 1930s, the government introduced in 1945 a cash allowance for all children apart from the first in the family, payable to the mother. In 1975 the Child Benefit Act (taking effect in 1977) combined family allowances with the income tax allowances for children. Child benefit is a cash payment for all children, including the first, paid without regard to means and not subject to income tax, and payable to the mother. (The amount of income tax paid is now no longer dependent on the number of children.) Fig. 5.1 shows the evolution over time of the real spending on child benefit, where the value of the earlier income tax allowances is included for the sake of comparability.

The level of child benefit has been a subject of considerable political debate, especially since the identification of the persistence of poverty among working families in *The Poor and the Poorest* published on Christmas Eve 1965 by Abel-Smith and Townsend (1965). Successive governments have shied away from the cost of significant increases in child benefit, and the Conservative Government in 1970 introduced a new means-tested benefit for families with children, then called family income supplement. The aim was to concentrate transfers for children on those with low incomes, the benefit being withdrawn at a rate of 50% of additional gross income, until totally extinguished. The application of the withdrawal rate to gross income meant that the composite marginal tax rate on net income was substantially higher, since the withdrawal rate was additional to the loss of income in income tax. If we denote by t the rate of income tax and by w the rate of withdrawal, then the overall composite rate was $(t + w)$, and there was nothing to stop it exceeding 100% even if both t and w were less than 100%.

In 1988 the income-tested family benefit was replaced by family credit, with a rate of withdrawal of 70%, but applied to *net* rather than gross income. This means that the composite marginal rate became, in principle, $[t + w(1-t)]$, which cannot exceed 100% where both t and w are below 100%. The extreme form of the poverty trap was therefore abolished. At the same time there was added a capital test, so that families with savings in excess of a specified amount do not qualify. It should also be noted that the withdrawal of benefit only takes place when the benefit is reassessed. Family credit is awarded for a twenty-six-week period at a fixed rate, regardless of changes in circumstances. A temporary rise in earnings may not therefore be subject to the high composite marginal rates of tax.

The policy of 'targeting' transfers on those with low incomes led the Conservative Government in the second half of the 1980s to freeze the rate of child benefit in money terms, and to expand the means-tested programme. From Fig. 5.1 it may be seen that total real spending on child benefit fell in this period, although child benefit was increased in 1991 and a higher rate introduced for the first child.

Low-income working families, and others on low earnings, may in addition be eligible for housing benefit, as may be those not in work. Provision for the housing costs of those on low incomes has been a problem throughout the post-war period, and there have been frequent changes in legislation. At the outset, housing costs were met either via national assistance or via local-authority rent rebate schemes. The latter have evolved over time, moving to a national scheme for rent rebates and bringing in private tenants. In parallel has come the introduction of rebates for local taxes (rate rebates), currently in the form of council tax benefit. (The local tax in Britain was for many years known as the *rates*. In 1990 (1989 in Scotland) this was replaced by the *community charge*, generally known as the poll tax. This in turn was replaced by the *council tax* in April 1993.) These benefits are automatic for recipients of income support, but for other claimants involve a similar income test, with the excess of income over the qualifying level reducing the amount of the housing benefit. These schemes therefore involve an additional marginal rate of withdrawal (currently 65% for housing benefit and 20% for council tax benefit). (Expenditure on these means-tested benefits is not included in Fig. 5.1.)

Other Non-contributory Benefits

The past two decades in Britain have seen the introduction and expansion of benefits for people who are mentally or physically disabled. In the past the benefits have included attendance allowance, payable to those who require constant or regular nursing or attendance, mobility allowance for those who have difficulty walking, and invalid care allowance, paid to those who have to stay at home to look after a severely disabled person. A recent review by the government of provisions for the disabled has led to the introduction in 1992 of a disability living allowance, in place of attendance and mobility allowances, and a disability working allowance for those with a physical or mental disability who are in full-time work but with low earnings. The latter is means-tested on a similar basis to family credit (to which it is an alternative).

The introduction of the disability working allowance represents a fifth major means-tested benefit (the others being income support, family credit, housing benefit, and council tax benefit). There are in addition other benefits to which receipt of one of those listed above acts as a 'passport', just as receipt of income support allows a person to receive housing benefit, so that a person receiving one of the five means-tested benefits may automatically qualify for other help. This applies to payments from the social fund for maternity expenses, funeral expenses, or cold-weather payments. It applies in the case of recipients of income support and family credit to exemption from prescription charges, free dental treatment, free eye tests, and fares to hospital. Recipients of income support receive free milk and vitamins and free school meals. In addition there are a number of other means-tested benefits, which allow people not otherwise qualified to receive exemption from prescription charges, free dental treatment, free eye tests, and fares to hospital, free milk and vitamins, grants for school uniforms, and educational maintenance allowances. It is not perhaps surprising that the Child Poverty Action Group's *National Welfare Benefits Handbook* dealing with means-tested benefits for 1993–94 (Webster *et al.* 1993) runs to 488 closely printed pages.

5.3. BENEFITS AND THE INDIVIDUAL BUDGET CONSTRAINT

The main thrust of policy towards social security in the United Kingdom in recent years has been to

switch from state to private provision, as in the encouragement given to occupational and personal pensions, and the introduction of statutory sick pay and maternity pay;

give greater emphasis to means-tested benefits, with the expansion of schemes such as family credit, the introduction of new benefits such as the disability working allowance, and the increased dependence on income support; as a result of moves to

reduce coverage of social insurance benefits.

All these measures served to reduce the overall level of public spending, as did the fact that the levels of benefits were not adjusted in line with average earnings. This contributed to restraining the rise in tax and contribution rates which would otherwise have been necessary to meet demographic changes, and to provide for the increased number of families without work income. At the same time, the switch towards means-tested benefits has tended to *increase* the seriousness of the unemployment and poverty traps, in the sense that more people are affected, so that there are reasons to fear that the disincentive effects of the benefit *structure* have become more, rather than less, serious.

This section examines the *potential* impact of the social-security benefit structure in Britain on the work decisions of recipients. (In the next section we examine the evidence concerning the *actual* impact.) How do benefits affect choices open to the individual and his or her family? What is the impact on the budget constraint?

In seeking to answer this question, attention is focused on certain dimensions of labour supply. As we have seen in Chapter 2, there are many decisions which may potentially be affected, and only some are treated here. Moreover, we concentrate on the position of the worker, although the incentives affecting employers may be equally important. The shift from state to occupational provision of a final salary pension, for example, could leave the employee virtually unaffected but alter seriously the incentives faced by the employer. Employers may find the pension costs of older workers to be much higher than those of younger workers. Unemployment insurance without experience rating may provide an incentive for employers to place workers on temporary lay-off. These are potentially important issues which are not discussed here.

Net Income of Working Families

In Chapter 4 reference was made to the poverty trap and the impact of benefit withdrawal on the trade-off faced between net income and leisure. The reduction of benefit adds to the composite marginal tax rate faced by workers in low income families. This is illustrated below by calculations for April 1991 taken from the Department of Social Security (1991) *Tax/Benefit Model Tables*. The levels of earnings have been expressed relative to the median gross earnings for all workers (male and female) paid on adult rates, whose pay was not affected by absence, which was then £247 a week.

Fig. 5.3 shows the budget constraint faced by a couple with two children aged four and six, living in accommodation rented from the local authority, where only one of the husband or wife is in employment, and they have no capital. The person is assumed to be working full-time (sixteen or more hours a week). The budget line starts at 40% of median earnings (only some 2% of full-time workers earned less than this amount).

The family is entitled to child benefit, which is equal to 6.3% of median earnings, and this does not change with the level of earnings. In addition, at earnings of 40% of the median, the family was in April 1991 entitled to family credit (FC), housing benefit (HB), and community charge benefit (CCB). (The CCB has now been replaced by council tax benefit.) The net effect, allowing for income tax, NI contributions, and local taxes paid, is to leave the family with a net income some 50% higher than their gross earnings—see Fig. 5.3.

If the family increases its gross earnings, for example by working additional hours, then this leads to higher income tax and NI contributions. At this date, the marginal tax rate over the relevant earnings range was 34%, so that there remained in net terms a proportion $(1-0.34)$. For the low-paid family receiving family credit there would in addition be the withdrawal of means-tested benefits, so that the net gain became:

$$(1-0.34)(1-0.7)=0.20 \quad \text{if FC received}$$

$$(1-0.34)(1-0.7)(1-0.15)=0.17 \quad \text{if FC and CCB received}$$

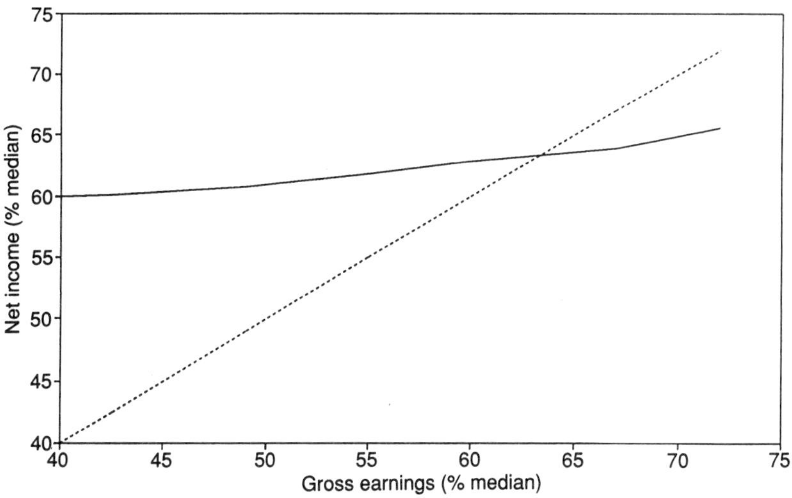

FIG 5.3. Budget Constraint, Couple with Two Children, Great Britain

Notes: (1) The position relates to that in Apr. 1991. (2) The family is assumed to rent local-authority accommodation appropriate to its size, and to pay average rent and poll tax. (3) The family is assumed to take up all entitlement to means-tested benefits. (4) The earner is assumed to be not contracted out of the state earning-related pension scheme. (5) There are assumed to be no tax allowances other than the personal allowance. (6) The family is assumed to have no income from capital. (7) All earnings are of the main breadwinner. (8) The children are assumed to be aged 4 and 6.

Source: Dept of Social Security (1991).

$$(1-0.34)(1-0.7)(1-0.15-0.65) = 0.04 \quad \text{if FC, CCB and HB received}$$

(the calculations have been rounded to two figures). The post-1988 structure of means tests, applied to net income and taking into account benefits earlier in the chain, ensures that the composite marginal tax rate cannot exceed 100%, but it reaches 96% where all three benefits are received. As a result, the budget line in Fig. 5.3 is virtually flat for a wide band of earnings. Eligibility to CCB does not, in fact, end for this family until it reaches earnings of some two-thirds of median earnings. In money terms, the gain in net earnings from moving from £100 to £161 a week is only £8.94. The 'break-even' point, where net income is equal to gross, is passed a little before this level of earnings. Eligibility for family credit ends at 72% of overall median earnings; and around a quarter of all full-time workers earn less than this amount.

There is, therefore, a significant range where composite marginal tax rates are potentially high. How many people are in fact affected depends, however, on the joint distribution of earnings and family characteristics.

After all, the calculations underlying Fig. 5.3 are based on a large number of assumptions about the family circumstances. Variation in these assumptions can affect substantially the conclusions. For example, the level of rent determines the range over which there is eligibility to housing benefit. Or the family may have savings which reduce their entitlement to benefits or disqualify them totally.

Two of the most important considerations missing from Fig. 5.3 are the joint effect of the earnings of husbands and wives and the incomplete take-up of means-tested benefits. The hypothetical calculation assumes that there is only a single earner, an assumption which does not apply in many cases and which fails to draw attention to the implications of means-tested benefits for family decisions. Since the test is applied to the joint earnings of husband and wife, they in effect face the same composite marginal tax rate as far as benefits are concerned. The situation is in this respect different from that which applies to income tax and NI contributions, which are essentially operated on an individual basis. Therefore, a married woman considering taking a part-time job which pays less than the income tax and contribution thresholds will face a composite marginal tax rate which depends on the family credit and other benefit withdrawal rates. In the 'flat' range in Fig. 5.3 for the husband's earnings, this can mean a composite marginal tax rate of between 70% and 91%. The poverty trap affects not just the main breadwinner but also his or her partner.

The hypothetical calculations assume that all those eligible for means-tested benefits do in fact claim. Experience has shown that there is in fact a significant problem of incomplete take-up: people who are eligible do not in fact claim, or are not awarded, the benefit. When family income supplement was first introduced, concern was expressed about the problem of incomplete take-up and the government set a target take-up rate of 85%. The early numbers claiming did not suggest that this had been attained, and examination of the time-series of numbers in receipt indicated no trend towards improved take-up (Atkinson and Champion 1989). The official estimates (HM Treasury 1990: table 14.16) for 1985–6 showed that only 48% of those eligible for family income supplement were claiming.

One of the aims of family credit, which replaced family income supplement (FIS) in 1988, was to improve take-up. At the same time, the new scheme widened the field of eligibility, so that nothing can be deduced from the rise in the number of families in receipt, which went from 220,000 families receiving FIS in 1987–8 to 280,000 families receiving FC in 1988–9 (Department of Social Security 1993*a*: 45). The official estimate of take-up of FC in 1988–9 is that 57% of families were claiming and that the amount of benefit claimed was 67% (Department of

Social Security 1993*a*: 7). The difference between these two figures reflects the fact those with larger entitlements were more likely to claim. The same source quotes an estimate for 1991 by the Policy Studies Institute that 64% of families were claiming and that 70% of the benefit was claimed. It appears that non-take-up remains a serious problem.

TABLE 5.1. Working Families Facing High Composite Marginal Tax Rates, Great Britain

Composite marginal tax rate	Nos. with composite marginal tax rates at or above specified level (000)	
	1985	1992–3
100% and over	70	0
90% and over	130	75
80% and over	290	250
70% and over	290	500

Note: 1985 figures refer to tax units where at least 1 partner works 24 hrs. a week or more; 1992–3 projections refer to tax units where at least 1 partner works 16 hrs. a week or more.

Source: Department of Social Security (1993*a*: 11)

Incomplete take-up, and the aggregation of family earnings, mean that fewer families are affected by the poverty trap than may appear from Fig. 5.3. Some light is cast on this by estimates based on sample surveys of the distribution of composite marginal tax rates faced by families if they earn more. Official estimates for 1985 (based on data from the 1982, 1983, and 1984 Family Expenditure Surveys (FES)) and for 1992–3 (projections based on the 1986, 1987, and 1988 surveys) are shown in Table 5.1. In 1985 there were a small number of families with composite marginal rates in excess of 100%; this has now fallen effectively to zero with the 1988 reforms of social security and the elimination of the notches in NI contributions. At the same time there has been an increase in the number facing composite marginal tax rates in excess of 70%. Overall the numbers are small in relation to the total number of tax units in the UK of some 30 million. At the same time, it has to be remembered that people may have been led by the existence of the poverty trap to choose a level of work effort outside the range where the composite rate is high. As explained in Chapter 2, people may reduce, or increase, their work effort in order to avoid this section of the budget constraint.

Income of the Unemployed

The second comparison for which hypothetical calculations are frequently employed is that of incomes in and out of work, the ratio of the two being referred to as the replacement rate. The Department of Social Security model tables show the replacement rates corresponding to different levels of earnings and these are depicted (for April 1991) in Fig. 5.4 for a range of different family types. The calculation compares (*a*) net income after housing costs (rent and local taxes) when the main bread-winner is unemployed and receiving income support (IS), including where applicable free school meals and welfare foods, and (*b*) net income after housing costs when the main breadwinner is employed. The earnings level is expressed, as in Fig. 5.1, as a proportion of the overall median gross earnings. It should be noted that no allowance is made for costs of working. These depend very much on individual circumstances: according to the Department of Social Security (1993*a*: 10) up to one in three employees may have no travel-to-work costs, but others may have substantial commuting costs. There may also be other costs, notably those of child care.

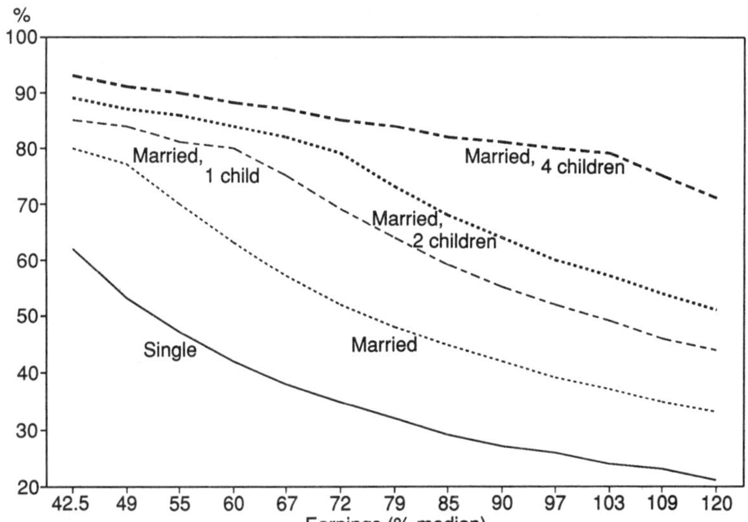

FIG 5.4. Replacement Rates, Great Britain

Notes: (1) See notes 1–7 to Fig. 5.3. (2) The replacement rate is calculated as the net income after rent and poll tax when unemployed and in receipt of income support, expressed as a % of that received when in work. (3) In the 1-child family, the age of the child is assumed to be 4; in the 2-child family the children are assumed to be aged 4 and 6; in the 4-child family the children are assumed to be aged 3, 8, 11, and 16.

Source: Dept of Social Security (1991).

The calculated replacement rates tend to rise with the number of children. For couples without children the replacement rate is less than 60% once earnings pass two-thirds of the median, and for a single person they are 50% or less once earnings pass half the median. It is for families with children that replacement rates are potentially high, being 80% or more for the two-child family earning less than 70% of the median (it would be higher if the children were teenagers). For the four-child family the rate exceeds 80% at all earnings levels below the median.

The importance of high replacement rates in reality depends again on the joint distribution of earnings and family composition. The Department of Social Security (1993*a*: 10) makes calculations of the replacement rates *of those in work*, using sample survey data. What these figures show is the net income people would receive if they became unemployed, relative to their actual net income. The projection for 1992–3 shows 160,000 families to have replacement rates of 80% or more, and 445,000 to have rates of 70% or more. These figures are only a small percentage of the total number of families in work.

It is in the nature of the calculation of a replacement rate that it involves assumptions about the alternative position. In the case of those currently employed, we have to make assumptions about the benefits they would receive. These depend on individual circumstances, and a hypothetical set of figures may be misleading. The entitlement to benefit depends on such matters as the past contribution record and the circumstances of entry into unemployment, and account has to be taken of the disqualification and other provisions. An unemployed person may not in fact receive income support. The problem of incomplete take-up, while less serious than for family credit, applies to income support. (The estimates cited in the previous paragraph assume 100% take-up.) The Department of Social Security (1993*b*: 20–1) estimates for 1989 show a take-up rate of 81% for non-pensioner families, or 88% on a spending basis, although these figures may understate take-up on account of the misreporting of benefit type.

Estimates of the replacement rates for those currently unemployed similarly raise questions regarding the calculation of the replacement rate. It is evident that a measure concerned with incentives has to be forward-looking, rather than backward-looking to past earnings, as would be appropriate if our concern were with the adequacy of benefit. But a forward-looking measure involves assumptions about the job to which the person would potentially exit and the wage that it would pay. The prospective job would not necessarily pay the same wage as the previous employment. The description of the job may involve more than simply a wage rate; jobs differ in their security. The 'pay-off' from accepting a job offer depends on its likely duration, and this may mean that the worker has to consider the implications of a future return to unemployment. In this context, the existence of flat-rate unemployment benefit may *encourage* a person to take the current offer of an insecure job, with the entitlement which it provides to future benefit on termination, rather than wait for a job with longer expected tenure. (Alternatively, it may mean that the insecure job can pay lower wages and still attract applicants.)

The exit from unemployment may also be to a labour market state other than employment, such as to a government training scheme or out of the labour force.In theory one might expect unemployment benefit to deter all forms of exit. The relevant ratio is now not that between benefit and income in employment, but that between benefit and income in training or out of the labour force. If, for example, the benefit level falls relative to student grants, this may make full-time education more attractive. The same may apply if the benefit falls relative to payments made to trainees on government schemes.

Unemployment has, like hours of work, a family dimension, and we need to consider the interrelation of the decisions of husbands and wives, and the impact of the system of unemployment benefit. If benefits are paid on a wholly individual basis, then there is purely an income effect on the decisions of others. The national insurance system in the United Kingdom is largely on an individual basis, but there remains the adult dependant's allowance of £*x* (approximately 60% of the benefit level) payable where the spouse's earnings do not exceed £*x*. Once the wife's earnings (where the husband is unemployed) pass £*x*, all of the additional allowance is lost. There is therefore a 'notch' in the budget constraint at this point, an extra £1 of wife's earnings causing a £*x* loss of benefit, but once past this level of earnings there is no further impact on the husband's benefit.

In contrast to the situation with NI benefit, receipt of IS by the unemployed person means that the earnings of the partner are (after a small disregard) subject to a 100% rate of withdrawal of benefit. For as long as the spouse works insufficient hours to qualify for family credit, there is no gain in family income from extra earnings until the IS is reduced to zero. As summarized by Dilnot and Kell, 'we would expect to find a smaller proportion of women married to unemployed men in work than we find in the population at large, since the financial return from work is much lower for this group' (1987: 6).

The issue of high replacement rates and the unemployment trap has received most attention in Britain, but it is possible that the disincentive effects of unemployment benefit are more marked among the partners of the unemployed in receipt of income support.

Position of Single-Parent Families

There are a number of special provisions for single-parent families. First, one-parent benefit is an additional flat-rate cash benefit, similar to child benefit, paid to single persons with the care of one or more children. The amount is the same regardless of the number of qualifying children, and is (in 1993) equal to around three-quarters of the rate of child benefit for second and subsequent children. There is also an additional personal allowance to single parents under the income tax, which in effect raises the tax threshold to the same as that for a married couple.

Secondly, a single parent may qualify for income support, there being no requirement that single parents be available for work in order to receive IS. To encourage single parents to take part-time work, the first £15 of earnings are disregarded. Part-time work is now defined to be for 15 hours a week or fewer. This figure was changed from 23 hours in April 1992, in line with the reduction in qualifying hours for family credit. If the single parent works more than 15 hours a week, he or she becomes eligible for family credit, which operates in the way described above. There are special provisions allowing the first £15 of maintenance to be disregarded when calculating FC.

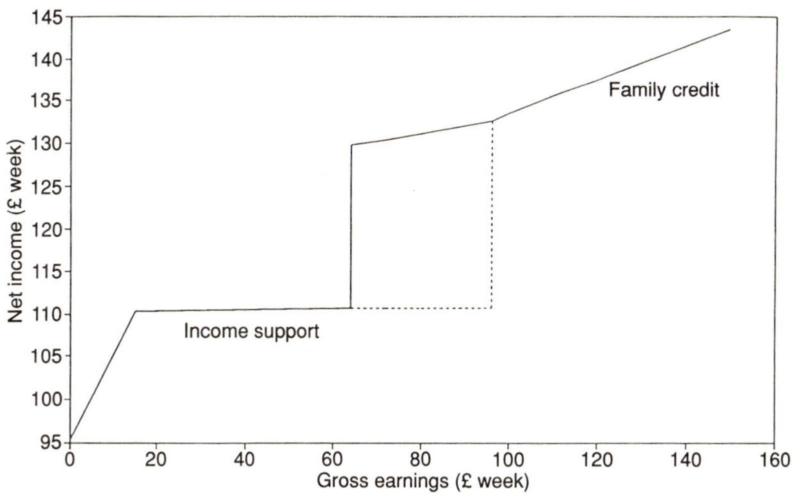

FIG 5.5. Budget Constraint, Single Parent, Great Britain
Notes: (1) See notes 1–7 to Fig. 5.3. (2) The child is assumed to be aged 3. (3) The hourly wage is assumed to be £4.
Source: Dept of Social Security (1991).

These provisions mean that single parents considering whether or not to work face a complicated budget constraint. It depends both on total gross earnings and on the hours worked, and a three-dimensional representation is really necessary (see e.g. Duclos 1992). In Fig. 5.5, an hourly wage rate of £4 an hour has been assumed (again the calculations relate to 1991, but, in contrast to the previous figures, earnings are shown in cash amounts). A single parent, with one child aged 3, faced a zero composite marginal tax rate for the first £15 a week, but after that the net income remained at the IS level plus £15, any additional earnings being deducted pound for pound from the income support. At 24 hours a week, with earnings £64, the person qualified for family credit, which leads to a discrete jump in net income (from D to A). The person is, however, subject to a high rate of withdrawal, on account of family credit, housing benefit, and council tax benefit.

We should therefore expect to find single parents clustering at the points A and B in Fig. 5.5. For comparison, the dashed lines show the situation if the hours condition were 16 hours a week, as after April 1992. The effect of this change may have been expected to be that some people shifted from B to C, increasing their hours, but that others moved from A to C, reducing their hours.

TABLE 5.2 Composite Marginal Tax Rates Faced by Working Single Parents in Britain, 1984

Composite marginal tax rate	% of single parents
0	6
9	6
10–38	5
39	32
40–49	4
50[a]	20
51–69	7
70–9	9
80–99	3
100 +	9

[a] Includes all those on SB subject to reduction of benefit; the marginal rate may be either 50% or 100%.

Source: Calculated from Dilnot and Duncan (1992: table 1), based on FES data 1981–6 (pooling years to obtain a sufficiently large sample).

Such hypothetical calculations serve to demonstrate how disincentives may arise; their quantitative importance depends on how many single parents are to be found in particular circumstances. As before, we may look at evidence about the distribution of composite marginal rates, but again with the important qualification that it is the full budget constraint that determines people's behaviour, not just the marginal rate at the observed level of income. In Fig. 5.5 we may observe a person at A, but this choice may have been affected by the location of the segment BD. Table 5.2 draws on the estimates made by Dilnot and Duncan (1992: table 1) of the composite marginal tax rates faced by working single parents as a result of the 1984 tax and benefit system. At that time, the basic income tax plus NI contribution led to a marginal rate of 39%. Of working single parents, around a third faced this composite marginal rate, and a further 17% faced lower rates. A sizeable proportion were subject to the withdrawal of supplementary benefit, which had a tapered disregard of 50%, and at least a quarter faced composite marginal rates in excess of 50% as a result of the withdrawal of means-tested benefits. The calculations assume 100% take-up and to this extent may overstate the problem, but they suggest that among single parents there may be serious disincentives.

Policy towards single-parent families raises particular issues with regard to the liability to maintain and to the definition of single parenthood. The British government has recently reviewed the provisions for enforcing payment of maintenance by absent parents, and set up the Child Support Agency with responsibility for handling such payments. Single parents in receipt of income support, family credit, or disability working allowance are required to make a claim for maintenance via the agency, and if information (such as the name of the absent parent) is withheld without good cause, benefit may be reduced. Moreover, the definition of single parenthood for the purpose of benefit receipt excludes cohabitation, and the application of this condition has been controversial: Matthewman refers to 'the notorious question of . . . what is meant by "living together as husband and wife" ', (1992: 60).

Conclusion

The system of benefits in Britain is highly complex, and its potential impact on individual decision-making is not easily summarized. The budget constraint depends on a wide variety of parameters and conditions. The position is considerably complicated by the important role played by means-tested benefits. We have seen how they may generate situations where there is little financial gain from working or where there are high composite marginal tax rates. Of particular potential significance are the disincentives faced by the partners of the unemployed and by single parents.

5.4. BENEFITS AND INCENTIVES

This section reviews the evidence regarding the effect of social-security benefits on work decisions in Britain. Have there been serious leakages as a result of the transfer system? It discusses in turn delayed return to work by the unemployed; benefit-induced entry into unemployment; non-participation in the labour force of the wives of unemployed men;

increased sickness absence and disability; non-participation in the labour force of single parents; and early retirement.

The amount of space allocated to each topic reflects the extent to which it has been the subject of research; the dominance of unemployment benefit on the political agenda is no doubt the reason why it has received much of the attention. It should be noted that the impact of the poverty trap on the hours of work of two-parent families is not covered, this subject having been illuminated by the studies discussed in Chapter 4.

As described in Chapter 2, there are several different types of empirical evidence: aggregate time-series analyses, cross-section studies based on sample surveys or panel data on individuals, and experimental evidence. These different sources are sometimes seen in adversarial terms, but they are in fact complementary. No one source is ideal, and each has its relative strengths. From one source of evidence, we may be able to illuminate aspects which are not captured in another source. And some kinds of evidence, such as that from experiments, are simply not available in Britain.

The Impact of Unemployment Benefit on Return to Work

The aspect of unemployment compensation that has received most attention is the impact of benefit levels on the transitions out of unemployment. One reason for the focus on outflows from unemployment may be their relative importance in explaining changes in overall unemployment levels. Rises in unemployment in Europe have been associated particularly with falls in outflows and lengthening durations of unemployment (Burda 1988). The first approach used historically to examine the impact of unemployment benefit on unemployment duration made use of aggregate time-series evidence. This approach promises to provide a direct answer as to the effect of temporal variation in parameters of benefit systems on aggregate unemployment flows or totals, and this is of obvious interest to policy-makers. For example, people have attempted to link the introduction of earnings-related benefit in the UK in 1966 to the sharp rise in unemployment which occurred at this time. In order to establish such a link it is, of course, necessary to estimate the contribution of other contemporaneous changes. The introduction of the earnings-related supplement was not a pure experiment, since other policies were not held constant, and since the external environment was changing.

The time-series approach, whether as a 'reduced form' with no explicit model of the labour market (e.g. Maki and Spindler 1975) or whether as a set of fully specified equations (as in Layard and Nickell 1986), has the advantage of capturing effects on both sides of the market. Unemployment benefit may affect wage-setting behaviour of firms, with no apparent direct effect on the duration of individual unemployment, and this would not be detected if we looked simply at the behaviour of workers. At the same time, a recent survey by Nickell concludes that 'here the evidence is much thinner and most estimated wage equations contain no such effect' (1990: 421), although he notes some significant responses found by Minford (1983) and in his own work (Layard and Nickell 1986).

The aggregate time-series approach cannot, however, allow for the diverse nature of the budget constraints which we have seen to face individuals. As far as research on the effects of benefit levels is concerned, the typical practice is to consider the benefits received by a 'representative' worker, or the average benefit payments actually received by the unemployed, and compare one of these measures with the average earnings of the employed. This fails to allow for the fact that the income while unemployed can vary enormously across the population, and in a manner that is not uniform across time. This results from, among other factors, the dual system of benefit through national insurance and income support, and the conditions governing entitlement to these benefits. It is difficult to pick a single series which will represent the changes over time in the generosity of a complex, two-tier unemployment compensation system.

It is primarily for this reason that research has tended to concentrate on microdata from sample surveys or administrative records, which allow the individual variation in benefit receipt and its relation to earnings to be modelled. This source of evidence has been extensively used in those studies motivated by search theory which have looked at the determinants of individuals' exit probabilities from unemployment, usually referred to as 'hazard' models, a terminology which derives from reliability theory, but which appears rather odd in the present context in view of the fact that the 'hazard' is that of exiting from unemployment, which is to be welcomed.

The use of microdata is not without problems. First, one should not underestimate the difficulties of accurately modelling the benefit system at the individual level. Allowance has to be made for the contribution conditions for national insurance, and for incomplete take-up of means-tested benefits. A single reported figure for the benefit in payment at one point of an unemployment spell may not provide enough information to calculate replacement histories (Atkinson and Micklewright 1985: ch. 6). Access to administrative data recording the sequence of actual benefit payments throughout a spell represents in this respect a substantial advantage.

A second problem is that differences in benefit do not represent a natural experiment. In particular, receipt of benefit is not independent of labour market behaviour. Eligibility for NI benefit may depend on having a good previous employment record, which in turn is associated with unobserved characteristics of the worker which mean that he or she is more likely to return to work anyway. In this context we may observe a negative correlation between benefit levels and unemployment duration. Conversely, the decision not to claim IS may reflect a sense of independence and an unwillingness to live off benefits and turn down job offers. In this case, the unobserved characteristic may lead to a positive correlation between recorded benefit receipt and duration. In neither case would there be a causal relation.

Thirdly, the modelling of individual probabilities of leaving unemployment has been based on the assumption that the individuals' experiences of unemployment are independent. While this may be true for the sample used in estimation, it may not be the case for the population from which the sample is drawn. Suppose that *ceteris paribus* we observe that persons with higher benefits exit unemployment more slowly. This does not necessarily mean that aggregate unemployment is higher, since the refusal of jobs by one group may lead to the work being offered to others. In other words, it is the *composition* of unemployment which is altered.

These qualifications need to be borne in mind when considering the evidence based on microdata. In fact, the estimated effects reported in these studies are rather modest. Lancaster and Nickell (1980) concluded from their two independent studies that the elasticity of unemployment duration with respect to benefits was about 0.6, which suggests that only quite large cuts in benefits could raise outflows sufficiently to reduce unemployment by a substantial amount. In broad terms, it implies that a reduction of 25% in benefit levels would reduce unemployment duration by about 15%. Atkinson *et al.* (1984) have drawn attention to the possible sensitivity of the findings to the assumptions made about the benefit system; their estimates showed that, when the benefit variable is based on the amounts reported as being received (rather than assumed benefits), its effect ceased to be significantly different from zero. The study by Narendranathan *et al.* (1985), using panel data supplemented with information from administrative records providing full benefit histories, found a well-defined benefit elasticity of duration, but the value of around 0.3 was even smaller than reported by Lancaster and Nickell.

The impact of benefits on the re-employment probability may vary with the length of time unemployed and with personal characteristics, notably age. Nickell (1979) allowed the coefficient on the replacement rate variable to vary with duration, and with his preferred version of the estimated equation found that after twenty weeks current benefits had no significant effect on the probability of returning to work. With a more detailed data set, Narendranathan *et al.* (1985) found a significant benefit effect persisting after six months only for teenagers. This evidence has important implications for policy suggesting that benefits for the long-term unemployed may be increased without concern for incentives, but it should be noted that the underlying model is one that treats individual decisions as 'myopic'. If people look ahead to future benefit entitlement, the impact may be different.

The bulk of work on the outflow from unemployment has modelled the total outflow to other labour market states, and not the flow which may be of most interest to policy-makers—that from unemployment to employment. We are interested in the effect of benefits on the outflow to employment, as opposed to increasing withdrawals from the labour force and increasing the rate of entry into government training schemes. The importance of distinguishing the exit state from unemployment is demonstrated by the work of Narendranathan and Stewart (1989). They find that a single-risk model, which does not distinguish the different transitions out of unemployment, understates by about a quarter the effect of unemployment benefits on transitions to employment. None the less, the estimated impact remains relatively small.

Entry into Unemployment and the Administration of Benefit

Unemployment benefit may affect entry into unemployment as well as exit. Evidence suggests that in the UK rather more persons quit their jobs voluntarily than in the USA but in neither country do such people form the majority of the unemployed (Johnson and Layard 1986).

Empirical evidence on the quantitative significance of the effect of unemployment compensation levels on the entry to unemployment is rather limited. A study using time-series data on flows by Nickell (1982) finds no strong evidence that benefits have much effect on inflows. Similarly, using micro-data Stern (1986) detects no effect of benefits on the probability that males in the UK re-enter unemployment within a given period of an earlier spell.

In considering voluntary quitting, as with the rejection of job offers, we have to consider the administration of unemployment compensation. A tightening of administration of benefits may be an easier step than cutting their level for policy-makers wishing to increase incentives. Besides passing a contribution or an income test, a person claiming unemployment benefit has typically to satisfy various conditions concerning the circumstances of entry to unemployment and to search for new work. Voluntary quitting without good cause, failure to be available for work, and the refusal of suitable job offers may all lead to a suspension or reduction of benefit payments or even complete disqualification.

Changes in the degree of severity of administration may affect transitions to and from unemployment with benefit levels held constant. Layard (1986) argued that the administration of unemployment compensation in the UK had become much less severe, and suggested this as a contributory factor in the rise in unemployment since the late 1960s. (He also cited the separation in the 1970s of benefit payment offices from the employment service and the ending in the 1980s of the requirement of the unemployed to register with the latter.) However, time-series on disqualifications are hard to interpret, a fall being entirely consistent with a decreased tendency to quit voluntarily as well as with the alternative of a more relaxed administration. There is the question of the direction of causation; increased leniency, particularly in the dealing with ongoing claims, could be a response to rising unemployment, rather than a cause of it.

In considering the implications of this kind of policy, the distinction between different types of exit is again important. The effect of claim-monitoring may be to increase the transition rate out of registered unemployment but not necessarily into employment. While some claimants may be stirred into increasing their search activity and hence their chances of re-employment, others may simply drop out of the labour force altogether.

Labour Force Participation of Wives of the Unemployed

The labour force participation rate of women married to unemployed men is substantially below that of women whose husband is in employment: in 1984 a woman married to an employed man was twice as likely to be in the labour force as a woman with an unemployed husband (Dilnot and Kell 1987: 8). Moreover, there is higher participation of wives where the husband is in receipt of unemployment insurance, where there is only the disincentive of the notch (loss of the adult dependant's allowance), than for those receiving the means-tested benefit, who face a 100% composite marginal tax rate. Dilnot and Kell compare the distribution of hours of women married to men with unemployment insurance benefit compared with those of women married to men in employment. The former group were less likely to work part-time, but more likely to be working full-time (1987: 10).

There are a number of possible explanations for these patterns, including the fact that spouses face similar labour market conditions. Using different data sets for the UK, Garcia (1989) and Kell and Wright (1990) attempt to isolate the disincentive effect by estimating microeconometric models of labour supply for wives of unemployed men, taking into account the effect of family means-testing on the budget constraint. Garcia concludes that a reform which extended unemployment insurance to unemployed men in receipt of means-tested income support would raise the overall participation rate of the wives in his sample of male unemployed by nearly 8 percentage points (1989: 179). This represents a substantial impact, although Garcia notes that it implies that the disincentive effect of means-testing accounts for only a quarter of the shortfall in the participation rate of such women compared to that for all married women. Kell and Wright treat separately the participation decision and the choice between full-time and part-time work. Their estimates of the former relation imply that a woman married to a man on means-tested benefits was 45 percentage points less likely to work, compared to a difference of 26 percentage points where the husband received unemployment insurance. The results for the full-time/part-time choice were less clear-cut.

These findings are important contributions in an area where little is known. At the same time, the models are essentially static, whereas the disincentive posed for a wife by her husband's receipt of income support is not permanent, lasting only as long as he stays unemployed and continues to receive assistance. In choosing her labour supply, a married women may need to form an expectation as to how long her husband is likely to remain unemployed; if the labour market is slack she may not be able easily to re-enter employment at a later date if she quits work. The disincentive effect on wives' work may therefore vary with the state of the labour market and, to the extent that duration dependence in re-employment probabilities exists, with the length of time her husband has been unemployed. (Moylan *et al.* (1984) provide descriptive evidence of labour-supply changes from panel data that is suggestive of the latter.)

Increased Sickness Absence

Sickness absence has been relatively less investigated in Britain than unemployment, a fact which is surprising in view of the large loss of working time that is involved. Doherty (1979) pointed out that the 300 million days lost a year due to certified incapacity for work were nearly 40 times those lost due to industrial stoppages, and at that time were of similar magnitude to those lost as a result of unemployment.

It might be held that sickness absence is determined entirely by considerations other than those of individual incentives and choice. Certainly the scope for individual choice should not be exaggerated, since sickness absence of any length requires medical certification. None the less, 'With many illnesses there is discretion regarding whether an individual absences his/herself from work. Similarly, there will be discretion regarding the timing of a return to work after a period of ill-health' (Holmes 1990: 21). Some of the same considerations may therefore apply.

Historically, there had been a rise over the 1960s in the average number of sickness spells per person at risk and in the average number of days per spell. Doherty (1979) estimated a time-series model which included the ratio of NI benefit to average net earnings. He found qualified evidence in favour of a positive relation between this benefit variable and the average number of spells of incapacity, although the coefficient was not well determined and the magnitude of the effect appears rather small. Moreover, the same qualifications apply to this approach as to the time-series analysis of unemployment. The rise in receipt of invalidity benefit, paid to the long-term sick, is similarly the starting-point of the analysis of Disney and Webb (1991), who note that the number of claimants doubled in the 1980s. They are interested in the role of benefit levels, but conclude that, since both the series for recipients and that for the value of benefits are heavily trended, 'time series specifications are not the best technique for answering the question posed here' (p. 254).

Microdata drawn from a survey of those reporting interruption in normal activity due to illness or injury have been used by Fenn (1981) to estimate a hazard model of sickness absence similar to that for unemployment. The elasticity of sickness duration with respect to the replacement rate was estimated to be about one tenth of that found in studies of unemployment duration: 'individuals appear to prolong sickness absence to a far lesser degree than unemployment in response to a given financial incentive' (Fenn 1981: 167). Fenn attributes this to, among other things, the greater degree of control exercised by the requirement to produce sickness certificates.

Microdata on individual male workers, including administrative information on benefit receipt, have been used by Molho (1989) to estimate the probability of receipt. He found that the benefit variable was significant only for the older age group (41–65), and concluded (p. 248):

> the general backcloth of 'non-economic' influences still dominated the results [age and proxies for medical history] and it is only at the margin . . . that some of the traditional demand and incentive effects appear to operate.

In considering the influence of state benefits, it is necessary to consider the effect of income taxation and the interrelation between state and occupational benefits. Occupational sick-pay schemes, and now the statutory sick-pay scheme, give rise to incentives for employers to minimize costs. One such scheme, which embodies experience-rating, is examined by Barmby *et al.* (1991), who find that the parameters of the scheme do appear to influence the duration but not the incidence of sickness absence.

Non-participation in the Labour Force of Single Parents

A further possible disincentive to work is that faced by single parents. A number of authors have drawn attention to the decline in labour force participation by single mothers in Britain over the 1980s, and the question has been asked as to how far this is related to the receipt of means-tested income support. At the same time, there have been other changes taking place. Dilnot and Duncan (1992) draw attention to the changing composition of single-parent families, with a marked increase in the proportion with preschool-age children. Since participation tends to be low for those with young children, the overall decline may in part be associated with this shift, and they do in fact show that the participation rates are relatively stable when disaggregated by the age of the youngest child.

The disentangling of the different effects has been attempted by studies using microdata. Several of these use cross-section data pooled over a number of years. Such pooling not only allows the sample to reach a reasonable size (single parents accounting for only a small proportion of the total population) but also introduces variation in the benefit parameters. Walker (1990) uses FES data 1979–1984 to estimate a discrete-choice model of the participation decision. He finds that the level of entitlement to supplementary benefit has a significantly negative effect on the participation decision of single mothers. A significant effect of SB is also found by Ermisch and Wright (1991) using General Household Survey data 1973–1982. On the other hand, the results of Walker (1990) show the estimated coefficient of the entitlement to family income supplement plus housing benefit (the means-tested benefits available to those in work) to be small and barely significant. The differential effects of different types of income maintenance clearly need to be further investigated.

In the analysis of the labour market choices of single parents, an important role is played by the availability of child care facilities. Dilnot and Duncan (1992) make use of information on the availability of child care places on a regional basis, combined with microdata from the FES 1981–8, and argue that there is a strong positive effect on participation (although the coefficient has a large standard error). To the participation equation they couple an equation to explain the choice of hours of work, of the type described in Chapter 4. From this they predict that the change from twenty-four to sixteen hours as the criterion for receipt of family credit would have led some 4% of the sample to move from a low level of participation to working between sixteen and twenty-four hours a week. (In terms of Fig. 5.5 this means a move from B to a point on CA. About the same number would reduce their labour supply below twenty-four hours, but the amount of the change would be smaller.)

The 1989 Lone Parents Survey contained much more detailed information on child care and work costs, and this has been used by Jenkins (1992) and Bradshaw and Millar (1991). Jenkins examines the probability both of working and of working full-time. The effect of income support is measured via the variation in housing benefit calculated as if the person were on income support. He finds that this variable has no significant influence on the probability of employment, and a significant negative impact on the probability of working full-time. The latter effect is, however, small: 'it would require very substantial reductions in benefit before there was a noticeable impact on the full-time employment rates of lone mothers' (Bradshaw and Millar 1991: 41).

Early Retirement

As with the impact of unemployment benefit, there have been both aggregate time-series and cross-section studies of early retirement, although the volume of evidence is much smaller.

The rate of labour force participation by men at older ages has been declining in the United Kingdom (although it is still at a higher level than in West Germany and France). In 1951, 87.8% of men aged 60–4 were in the labour force, and the percentage in 1970 was little different, but by 1989 this had fallen to 53.5% (Johnson and Falkingham 1992: table 4.1). For those aged 55–9, the figure was 95% (in both 1951 and 1970) but had fallen to 77% in 1989. The possible role of the state pension in this decline has been examined by Altmann (1981), who related the rate of labour force participation for different age groups to the ratio of benefits to average earnings, and other variables such as the unemployment rate over the period 1951–77. She found no significant effect for men aged 55–64, but also stressed the limitations of what could be learned from the time-series data.

Cross-section evidence about early retirement has been provided by the survey carried out by the Office of Population Censuses and Surveys (OPCS) in 1977 of older workers and retirement. The people interviewed were within ten years of the state pension age or older. The results were both qualitative and quantitative. When asked about the reasons for their retirement, the great majority of those retiring at the state pension age said that they retired of their own accord (32% for men, 44% for women) or that they had to retire (53% of men, 20% of women (Parker 1980: table

2.3.1). Those retiring before the state pension age were much more likely to attribute it to ill health (50% for men, 39% for women).

The quantitative analysis of the OPCS survey reported:

> The biggest single influence on retiring under pension age was found to be age . . . Another important factor is having done the same kind of work during one's working life . . . Not far behind in significance as predictors of early retirement are poor health . . . and an attitude of looking forward to retirement (Parker 1980: 13).

The role of financial variables was modelled by Zabalza *et al.* (1980), who examined the choice between three regimes: full-time work, part-time work, and retirement. For men aged under 65 they found that age and ill health were the largest determinants and that the role of the income differential between work and retirement was negligible (tables 5, 6). For women, on the other hand, the effect of the income differential is much more significant.

5.5. CONCLUSION

The title of this chapter posed the question as to whether social-security benefits have seriously damaged work incentives in Britain. It is not easy to give a firm answer on the basis of present knowledge. The social-security system in Britain is highly complex, and impinges in many different ways on the decisions of individuals. The impact depends on detailed institutional features and on the administration of benefits. There are many dimensions of behaviour which need to be considered. A great deal of progress has been made in different forms of research, notably in microeconometrics, but all types of evidence suffer from limitations. None corresponds to a pure experiment, and the observations of variation across time or across people can be interpreted in different ways.

Two broad conclusions seem to emerge. The first is that, despite the fears expressed about the potential disincentive effects, the adverse effects which have been identified are not large in magnitude. If there are major effects, they do not stand out from the empirical data. The second is that it is the work decision of women which appear to be most affected, whether as partners of the unemployed, as single mothers, or as early retirers.

6

Labour Responses to Taxes and Benefits in Germany

KLAUS F. ZIMMERMANN

6.1. INTRODUCTION

Since the Second World War, Germany has experienced major changes on its labour market. Directly after the war West Germany integrated a very large number of German refugees from East Europe into the economy. However, by the end of the 1950s labour shortages had already caused the creation of an active hiring policy of foreign workers, with recruitment treaties with Italy (1955), Spain and Greece (1960), Turkey (1961), Portugal (1964), and Yugoslavia (1968), which only stopped after the first oil crisis in 1973. Even after this time a considerable number of ethnic Germans migrated to West Germany. As in many other Western countries, German fertility declined substantially during the 1960s and 1970s. At the same time female work participation was rising, but it remained low in comparison with most other Western countries. As a consequence of the lower fertility rates, the population will rather age in the future: not only will there be a much larger share of pensioners in society, but the labour force will also be much older. Unification in 1990 caused further adjustment problems, especially on the labour market. All these problems add to the general crisis in Western economies, with low growth and high levels of unemployment, that is also affecting Germany.

A declining and ageing workforce may cause labour shortages and losses in productivity and mobility. Migrants may no longer move to seek work but to seek benefits. The welfare state and its regulations and transfers may create further disincentives for mobility, willingness to work, and labour motivation. In such an environment, it is important to consider policy measures to revitalize the driving forces of the economies. For several years there has been substantial interest in restructuring the tax and welfare system to create incentives. New developments in applied microeconomics and microeconometrics are providing useful tools to examine the chances for such a policy.

This chapter examines the conditions and evaluates the potentials in Germany. Section 6.2 outlines demographic trends and labour market changes, and reviews the consequences of unification for human resources. A brief description of the relevant tax and benefit system is contained in Section 6.3, where the analysis exclusively deals with income taxation and family and labour market policies. Differences in family and labour market policies between East and West Germany are also examined. Section 6.4 surveys the evidence on the conventional analysis of the income and wage effects on labour supply. In Section 6.5, empirical studies on the role of benefits and other work incentives are summarized. The final two sections are concerned with special issues: 6.6 deals with the West German shadow economy, 6.7 with the adjustments in the East German labour market. The adjustments in East Germany may provide an important insight into how large changes in the incentive structures affect economic behaviour. The advantage here is that one will be able to analyse actual behaviour instead of relying on simulations. Section 6.8 concludes.

6.2. SOME STYLIZED FACTS

6.2.1. General Trends in West Germany

This section will reveal some basic trends on demographic changes, labour force participation, and earnings in West Germany. Table 6.1 contains a first global picture between 1960 and 1990. Population size has increased by about 8 million since 1960. The net reproduction rate, the demographic measure that explains to what extent a woman will be replaced given current fertility behaviour, had its highest value in 1965, the year where the post-Second World War baby boom peaked. Since then it has drastically declined until it stabilized in the 1980s. This fertility decline is the major reason for the ageing of German society, especially its labour force. In 1990 the number of young workers, those in the age groups 20–39, was 19% larger than the number of older workers, those in the age groups 40–59. Under the current demographic structure, they will balance soon after the year 2000; in 2020, the group of young workers will be 18% smaller. The structure and consequences of European ageing is intensively discussed in Johnson and Zimmermann (1993*a*); an outline of the policy issues is given in Johnson and Zimmermann (1993*b*).

The population increase in post-war Germany was to a large extent driven by immigration (see further Schmidt and Zimmermann 1992). From 1950 to 1988, 4.8 million ethnic Germans came to West Germany, among them 3.2 million from the German Democratic Republic (GDR) and 1.6 million from East Europe. Until 1950, the gross inflow was 12 million. In the pre-unification period, immigration from this group was 774,000. (Note that German law treats ethnic Germans like natives, so that there is no statistic on foreign-born people as there are in the United

TABLE 6.1. Demographic and Labour Market Data for West Germany, 1960–1990

	1960	1965	1970	1975	1980	1985	1990
Population size (million)	55.4	58.6	60.7	61.8	61.6	61.0	63.3
Net reproduction rate	1.10	1.17	0.95	0.68	0.68	0.60	0.67[a]
Labour force participation rate	47.8	46.1	44.2	44.0	45.4	47.4	48.0
Share of foreign employment	1.1	4.2	6.8	7.9	7.5	5.9	6.2
Unemployment rate, total	1.3	0.7	0.7	4.6	3.6	8.9	6.9
Unemployment rate, males	1.3	0.7	0.7	4.3	3.0	8.6	6.3
Unemployment rate, females	1.3	0.7	0.7	5.4	5.2	10.4	8.4
Unemployment rate, foreigners	n.a.	n.a.	0.3	6.8	5.0	13.9	10.9

[a] 1989

Sources: Sachverständigenrat, Jahresgutachten 1992–3, Bundestagsdrucksache 12/3774, p. 296; Bundesanstalt für Arbeit, Amtliche Nachrichten, several vols.; Statistisches Bundesamt, Statistisches Jahrbuch für die Bundesrepublik Deutschland 1992, p. 74.

States.) From the early 1960s until 1989, a growing share of immigrants were foreigners. This development was only weakly moderated in 1973, when the Federal Government formally stopped the recruitment policy. Table 6.1 also shows that the share of foreign employment (remember that immigrating ethnic Germans are counted as Germans) was rising until the 1970s. It was highest in 1973, when the share was 10.8%.

As Table 6.1 shows, the overall labour force participation rate was close to 50% in the 1960s and at the end of the 1980s, but around 45% in the years between. The general unemployment rate was very low in the 1960s (below 1%) but increased in two steps, first in the 1970s and then in the 1980s (up to 9% in 1985) with considerable persistence. Only since the end of the 1970s have there been larger gender-specific differences in unemployment. Since the 1980s women have been substantially more unemployed than men, and the unemployment rates of foreigners are even higher.

A more differentiated picture of work participation is provided by Table 6.2. It shows that there is an overall decline in labour force participation for males and single females, but a dramatic increase in work participation of married women: the increase was about 4 percentage points only between 1960 and 1970, but 7 percentage points between 1970 and 1980, and 9 percentage points between 1980 and 1990. The bulk of these effects come from the age groups 20–50. The reduction in male labour force participation is due to a decline in the younger and older age groups, below 30 and above 55 years. Similar developments took place for single females, but there was an overall increase in all age groups between age 30 and age 55. It is clear from Table 6.3 that the increase in the labour force participation of married women did not take place in a

TABLE 6.2. Labour Force Participation in West Germany, 1960–1990[a]

	Male				Female							
					Single				Married			
Age	1960	1970	1980	1990	1960	1970	1980	1990	1960	1970	1980	1990
15–20	86.8	64.9	48.4	44.0	85.4	63.4	41.0	38.1	65.4	60.0	61.5	58.7
20–5	91.2	86.1	81.6	79.8	91.5	84.3	76.8	79.6	50.7	53.3	64.3	69.7
25–30	97.6	94.4	90.0	87.8	92.9	87.2	84.8	84.7	39.0	40.8	55.1	64.4
30–5	98.5	98.9	97.4	96.6	90.7	88.3	88.3	90.7	36.8	38.5	50.6	61.4
35–40	97.6	98.8	98.4	97.9	88.1	88.2	90.5	93.1	37.4	40.3	50.2	63.9
40–5	96.9	98.3	98.0	97.6	87.1	90.3	88.3	91.9	37.2	41.8	50.0	66.5
45–50	95.9	96.5	96.6	96.8	83.1	88.6	88.0	89.8	34.2	41.1	47.0	62.7
50–5	93.5	94.4	93.3	93.2	77.7	84.3	86.8	85.2	30.1	36.6	41.1	53.4
55–60	87.7	87.8	82.1	80.9	68.8	75.1	77.1	74.1	24.7	29.3	31.5	38.8
60–5	67.4	69.4	43.6	34.5	39.0	40.5	25.9	21.2	15.5	16.7	11.0	10.9
65 +	20.6	18.3	7.4	5.2	14.4	11.4	6.5	5.5	8.6	7.2	3.2	2.2
15–65	91.7	89.4	83.4	82.8	85.2	73.9	60.7	69.2	34.1	38.0	45.4	54.3

[a] Labour force as % of total population in the specific category. German Microcensus.

Source: Franz (1991); Statistisches Bundesamt, Fachserie 1, Reihe 4.1.1, 1990, p. 56.

TABLE 6.3. Labour Force Participation of Women Aged 15–65 with Young Children (%)

Year	Children ‹6	Children ‹15
1972	33.9	38.8
1973	35.2	40.2
1974	34.8	40.3
1975	34.0	39.9
1976	34.0	40.0
1977	34.5	40.6
1978	34.3	40.5
1979	34.7	41.1
1980	36.0	42.3
1981	36.4	42.6
1982	36.4	42.7
1985	35.0	40.6
1986	35.5	41.2
1987	35.6	41.7
1988	35.2	42.1
1989	36.3	43.0
1990	41.1	48.6

Source: Statistisches Bundesamt; Statistisches Jahrbuch für die Bundesrepublik Deutschland and Fachserie I, Reihe 3 (various issues).

similar way for women with small children (below 6) and with dependent children (below 15). As will be outlined in later sections, this can be explained by the inability of the German child care system to provide care that enables mothers to combine work with family formation.

Table 6.4 contains information about education and hours worked, and Table 6.5 measures the wife's contribution to family income. Both tables are based on microdata for West Germany, Sweden, and Holland and concentrate on married couples. All three countries exhibit a comparable size of welfare state, although they provide sometimes different incentive structures. These structures might be the cause for some marked differences in labour market behaviour. Table 6.4 compares first the educational degrees in the various countries and shows gender differences for three levels of education, 'compulsory', 'high school', and 'college', referring to low, middle, and high. Germans have the highest shares in the lowest educational category for both sexes, and the gender differences in percentage points is also highest, about 10 points in this group. Average working time of German women is between those of the two other countries, but this time is about the same for dual-earner couples in Sweden and Germany. Germany has the largest share of men working full-time (92%), and takes a middle position with respect to non-working women (48%). The majority of women with college education

TABLE 6.4. Education and Hours of Work

	Sweden		Germany		Netherlands	
	Wives	Husbands	Wives	Husbands	Wives	Husbands
% with education						
Compulsory	62.0	56.3	71.8	62.1	64.3	57.9
High school	29.3	31.5	22.0	23.3	24.2	23.1
College	8.7	12.2	6.2	14.6	11.5	19.0
Hours of work/week						
All couples	24.9	36.8	15.6	40.1	9.9	37.1
Duel-earner couples	30.8	40.9	30.2	42.6	23.9	41.4
% working weekly hours						
0	19.6	9.4	48.2	5.7	58.4	10.4
1–19	5.6	1.3	8.4	0.4	15.7	0.5
20–34	40.4	6.3	1.8	1.6	14.0	4.0
35 +	34.3	83.8	25.2	92.3	11.9	85.1
% with college education in labour force	78.6	96.2	61.2	91.2	66.4	90.4
of which full-time	48.2	84.6	28.9	82.8	20.9	83.9

Source: S. Gustafsson (1992*b*) based on microsurvey data from Sweden and Germany for 1984 and from Holland for 1988.

TABLE 6.5. Wife's Contribution to Earned Family Income as Percentage of Total Earned Family Income[a]

	Sweden	Germany	Netherlands
All	28.8	15.0	11.9
	(31.1)	(12.4)	(11.6)
Two-earner	37.6	32.2	30.2
	(40.6)	(31.0)	(29.5)
Without children under age 13	30.6	18.7	16.7
	(33.2)	(15.4)	(16.3)
With youngest child aged			
0–2	24.6	7.2	6.6
	(26.2)	(6.0)	(6.5)
3–6	27.6	10.3	8.7
	(29.7)	(8.5)	(8.4)
7–12	28.0	10.1	7.8
	(30.5)	(8.3)	(7.8)
According to education of wife			
Lower	27.0	14.2	9.2
	(29.0)	(11.7)	(9.0)
Higher	33.6	19.5	21.5
	(36.8)	(15.9)	(20.9)

[a] Before tax. After tax in parentheses.

Sources: Gustafsson (1992*b*) based on microsurvey data from Sweden and Germany for 1984 and from Holland for 1988.

work in all countries. Table 6.5 reveals that the contribution of females to earned family income is low, about 15% in Germany, 29% in Sweden, and 12% in Holland. It is even lower with small children.

6.2.2. Some Consequences of Unification

Monitoring the development of the German labour market since unification in 1990 is still difficult, as the data are still inaccurate and scarce. The following aspects are investigated. First, the process of transformation necessarily affects the level of employment negatively. The size of this process is only vaguely indicated by the officially published unemployment rates, owing to labour market policies, labour migration, and discouragement of workers. What does 'real' unemployment look like? Second, how is East Germany developing in comparison to the West in terms of key labour market statistics such as the level of gainful employment, short-time work, vacancies, and unemployment rates? Third, how different is the structure of employment in the East from that in the West, and how fast is it adjusting to Western standards?

The structure of unemployment in East Germany is evaluated in Table 6.6. Quarterly data are given for 1990–3. The aim is to explain the large differences between official and effective unemployment. The number of registered unemployed rose from 83,000 in the second quarter of 1990 to about 1.2 million in the first quarter of 1993. The official unemployment rate (based on the civil-employed labour force) reports about 1% in early 1990 and about 15% three years later. However, this is only the tip of the iceberg. At the end of 1990 and in early 1991, there were about 2 million short-time workers. Most of them became unemployed soon after. Therefore, the full-time equivalent of the short-time work was calculated using information on the distribution of actual hours worked within the periods. Row 2 in Table 6.6 demonstrates that the maximum of hidden unemployment from this source was 1.1 million full-time workers in the second quarter of 1991. In the first quarter of 1993, this measure was only 107,000 workers.

Public labour market policy measures have become more and more important since 1991. (They will be explained in Section 6.3.2 in more detail.) Basically, one has to differentiate between the employment creation programme (*Arbeitsbeschaffungsmaßnahmen, ABM*) and the measures on further education. Table 6.6 contains figures for both categories in rows 3 and 4. The problem with the latter is that it is based on estimates which differ between sources, and this is not necessarily full-time education. (Numbers used here follow the Deutsche Bundesbank,

TABLE 6.6. The Structure of Unemployment in East Germany (000)

	1990			1991				1992				1993
	II	III	IV	I	II	III	IV	I	II	III	IV	I
(1) Registered unemployment	83	309	556	756	835	1,023	1,037	1,254	1,172	1,158	1,097	1,165
(2) Full-time equivalent of short-time work	0	597	805	1,041	1,100	827	634	282	232	147	111	107
(3) Employment creation programme (ABM)	0	0	12	41	101	234	357	396	404	386	366	323
(4) Further education	0	0	60	127	223	316	395	458	507	499	493	432
(5) Sum of (1)–(4)	83	906	1,433	1,965	2,259	2,400	2,423	2,390	2,315	2,190	2,067	2,027
(6) Commuters to West, net	28	101	175	222	278	308	352	343	351	353	351	–
(7) *Übersiedler* (East–West labour migrants), cumulative	166	221	299	352	384	416	448	480	512	544	576	–
(8) Early pensioners, cumulative	190	310	410	430	516	563	661	776	792	844	835	–
(9) Official unemployment rate (%)	1.1	4.1	6.7	8.9	9.5	12	11.8	16.3	14.7	14.2	13.5	15.2
(10) Calculated unemployment rate (%)[a]	0.9	3.4	6.4	8.9	10.3	12.9	13.4	16.2	15.5	15.5	14.8	–
(11) Corrected unemployment rate (%)[b]	0.9	10.1	16.6	23.0	27.7	30.3	31.2	30.9	30.5	29.3	28.0	–
(12) Double corrected unemployment rate (%)[c]	4.9	16.0	24.3	31.1	36.8	40.0	42.1	42.7	42.9	42.6	41.8	–

[a] (1) divided by (1) + gainful employed persons.
[b] (5) divided by (1) + gainful employed persons.
[c] Sum of (5)–(8) divided by sum of (6)–(8) and denominator of (10).

Source: Deutsche Bundesbank, Monatsberichte, various issues, esp. Nos. 2/93 and 4/93; Amtliche Nachrichten der Bundesanstalt für Arbeit, various issues; DIW-Wochenbericht, 13/93.

as referenced in Table 6.6.) Summarizing the components registered unemployment, short-time work, employment creation programme, and further education more than doubles the size of measured unemployment, with a peak of 2.4 million workers in the third quarter of 1991, and more than 2 million in the first quarter of 1993.

This calculation ignores commuters, East–West migration, early pensioners, and discouraged workers. Rows 6–8 provide some data about the first three issues. The net number of commuters to the West is now about 350,000, whereas accumulated emigrated labour to West Germany from the end of 1989 numbered about 580,000 at the end of 1992. In the last quarter of 1992, some 835,000 former workers were paid early-retirement settlements. Of course, pensioners are out of the workforce, commuters actually work, and most labour emigrants work. However, it is very likely that the equivalent number of workers would have been unemployed additionally, had these people stayed in the East German labour market. Reliable numbers on discouraged workers are not available.

Based on these calculations, the East German unemployment rate can be re-evaluated. Whereas the 'official' unemployment rate in row 9 follows the monthly reports of the German Bundesbank, the numbers on which the re-evaluation is based are mostly from a joint research project of the Deutsches Institut für Wirtschaftsforschung (DIW) in Berlin, and the Institut für Weltwirtschaft in Kiel. As a consistent measure for comparisons, row 10 in Table 6.6 contains a recalculation of the unemployment rates using the numbers of registered unemployed of row 1 and the estimated total gainful employment from DIW-Wochenbericht 13/93. The resulting numbers are somewhat lower in 1990 and somewhat higher in 1991–2. Using the corrected size of unemployment from row 5, one obtains the corrected unemployment rate in row 11, which is typically more than twice as large than the 'standard' measure from row 10. Whereas unemployment was less than 1% in early 1990, it rose to about 16% or even 31% in 1992, depending on which measure one chooses. Taking into account commuters, early pensioners, and East–West labour migrants (*Übersiedler*), the unemployment figures have to be adjusted even further. The double corrected unemployment rate in row 12 was about 5% in early 1990, but about 42–3% (!) from the end of 1991.These numbers still ignore discouraged workers, and are at best optimistic.

A different way of evaluating the size of the unemployment problem is to compare the present size of effectively employed people to the size of employment at the end of 1989, the beginning of transformation. At the end of 1989, 9.89 million people were gainfully employed in the GDR. This was reduced to 6.297 million by the end of 1992. This number includes more than half a million self-employed. Subtracting the full-time equivalent of short-time work of 0.111 million, 0.366 million for ABM measures, and 0.493 for persons in further education results in 5.327 million effectively employed persons. This is only about 54% of the total employment at the end of 1989. Roughly speaking, nearly every second worker has lost employment in East Germany during the transformation.

Table 6.7 contains comparative numbers of the development of the East and West German labour markets. Whereas East German employment declined over the period, West German employment rose from about 28 to more than 29 million. Whereas the number of short-time workers in East Germany reached its maximum in early 1991 and is now declining, there is a general trend for rising numbers in West Germany over the whole period. In early 1993, short-time work was more than four times larger in West than in East Germany. By the end of 1992, vacancies in the East were only about 11% of vacancies in the West, although the size of employment in the East was about 21% of employment in the West. Official unemployment is much larger in the East than in the West, more than twice as high in early 1993.

The integration of East Germany absorbes a substantial amount of resources, mostly provided as benefits. It has also led to a general debate how the welfare state must be reorganized to be able to bear the burden and to revitalize the economy. However, the transformation process is also an important case study of how different systems of taxation and benefits affect economic behaviour. These important issues will be addressed again in Sections 6.3.5 on family policy and 6.7 on adjustments in the East German labour market.

6.3. THE TAX AND BENEFIT SYSTEM

6.3.1. The Income Tax System

German income taxation is characterized by a system of tax brackets with both proportional and progressive marginal tax rates. It is based on the sum of income a person or a married couple receives from self-employment, employment, capital, or rents. Married couples have the choice between being taxed separately and splitting income for tax purposes (*Ehegattensplitting*). In most cases the second alternative is chosen, where the income of the spouses is added and the appropriate tax rate for the family is found for 50% of this amount. The tax payment is then the proportion of income that is indicated by this tax rate. (In what follows, *Ehegattensplitting* will be called *split taxation*.) A detailed

TABLE 6.7. East–West Trends in the Labour Market[a]

	1990			1991				1992				1993
	II	III	IV	I	II	III	IV	I	II	III	IV	I
Gainful employment (m.)												
East	9.1	8.7	8.1	7.8	7.3	6.9	6.7	6.5	6.4	6.3	6.3	–
West	28.4	28.6	28.8	29.0	29.2	29.3	29.4	29.5	29.5	29.4	29.4	–
Short-time workers (000)												
East	–	1,295	1,736	1,926	1,962	1,464	1,113	511	440	292	237	232
West	49	30	46	121	140	136	183	243	241	164	485	987
Vacancies (000)												
East	–	–	–	22	26	42	37	36	31	32	32	34
West	312	316	317	325	334	338	328	340	338	324	290	261
Official unemployment rate (%)												
East: Total	1.1	4.1	6.7	8.9	9.5	12.0	11.8	16.3	14.7	14.2	13.5	15.2
Female	–	–	–	10.0	11.1	14.5	14.7	21.0	19.3	19.7	19.1	20.7
West: Total	7.1	6.9	6.6	6.8	6.0	6.2	6.2	6.7	6.3	6.0	6.3	6.7
Female	8.4	8.3	7.7	7.3	6.8	7.1	6.9	7.1	6.9	7.3	7.6	8.2

[a] Quarterly averages of monthly data. Civil employed work force.

Source: Deutsche Bundesbank, Monatsberichte, various issues, esp. Nos. 2/93 and 4/93; Amtliche Nachrichten der Bundesanstalt für Arbeit, various issues; DIW-Wochenbericht, 13/93.

technical presentation of the German tax system in 1984 is given in Wagenhals (1991). S. Gustafsson (1992*a*; 1992*b*) compares the German with the Swedish tax system, which relies on separate taxation. In what follows, taxation issues associated with children are ignored, since they are treated in Section 6.3.3.

The calculation of taxable income is complicated, as it has to be conducted in several stages. First of all, different rules apply to the calculation of gross income from the various sources. Whereas profit income (agriculture, self-employment) is derived according to enterprise tax laws, the bulk of income derived from employment and capital can be evaluated somewhat more easily. Basically, the gross amount of wage and interest payments is reduced by expenses necessary to obtain the relevant income (e.g. transportation costs between home and workplace). A number of special allowances further reduce the intermediate net income. Having aggregated income from all possible sources, a large set of possible tax deductions and exemptions may take effect. Most important are the following:

Committed expenditures comprise contributions to the national insurance system (pensions, health care, and unemployment insurance) and major private insurances (e.g. accident) as well as mortgage payments.

Extraordinary expenditures include costs necessary to maintain one's standard of living in cases of illness, physical handicap, or caring for the elderly.

Special expeditures are costs that are not connected with any sources of income and cannot be subsumed under the former headings. They may include subsistence contributions among divorced spouses, costs of education, and charitable donations.

Child care and household allowances are fixed amounts that can be deducted where there are dependent children in the household. The latter allowance, however, applies only to single parents with at least one child, whereas the former applies to every child in the household.

The expenditures which can be deducted from the net income are usually subject to upper limits. Married couples are granted twice the expenditures of single persons. Having subtracted those items from the net income, one obtains the taxable income, which serves as a basis for the computation of the tax debt of a person or couple.

The method of calculating taxable income has remained practically unchanged through the tax reforms implemented by various governments in recent years. The same applies to the basic structure of German income tax. First of all, a tax-free basic allowance is supposed to be necessary to finance the subsistence minimum. Any income beyond the basic allowance is taxed at a constant rate within the so-called 'lower proportional tax bracket'. Most persons, however, fall within the progressive tax bracket, which is characterized by rising marginal tax rates. High-income groups are, finally, taxed at the maximum rate, which remains constant within the 'upper proportional' bracket.

TABLE 6.8. Policy Measures on Taxation[a]

Date	Measure
1 Jan. 1975	Increase in maximum tax rate (56% of DM 130,000 and more), connected with a strong increase in marginal tax rates for incomes over DM 16,000 (progressive bracket). Increase in basic allowance to DM 3,000.
1 Jan. 1978	Marginal increase in basic and special allowances (e.g. committed expenditures).
1 Jan. 1979	Further increase in basic allowance to DM 3,690. Smoothing of transition from proportional into progressive tax bracket.
1 Jan. 1981	*Tax Relief Act* Increase in basic allowance to DM 4,212. Proportional bracket reduced to DM 18,000. Smaller progression in tax rate for low-income groups. Increase in special allowances.
1 Jan. 1986	*First Step of Tax Reform 1986–88* Increase in basic allowance to DM 4,536.
1 Jan. 1988	*Second Step of Tax Reform 1986–88* Large reduction of tax burden by flattening the tax progression rate. Basic allowance increases to DM 4,752.
1 Jan. 1990	*Tax Relief Package 1990* Increase in basic allowance to DM 5,616. Basic tax rate reduces to 19%. Proportional tax bracket decreases to DM 8,153. Tax progression is linearized, ranging to DM 120,000 (tax rate 53%). Further increase in other special allowances.
25 Oct. 1992	The Federal Constitutional Court declares the existing basic allowance incompatible with the basic law. The legislature has to make the subsistence level tax-free by 1 Jan. 1996

[a] Important measures related to family size are given in Tables 6.10 and 6.11.

Source: Sachverständigenrat, Jahresgutachten, various issues.

Major changes in tax rates and brackets are depicted in Table 6.8. During 1969–82, social-liberal governments have pursued a redistribution of income by means of an increasing progression, compared with a

TABLE 6.9. Social-Insurance Contributions (% of Gross Wages)

Year	Total	Sources		
		Pensions	Health	Unemployment
1970	26.5	17.0	8.2	1.3
1975	30.4	18.0	10.4	2.0
1980	32.4	18.0	11.4	3.0
1982	34.0	18.0	12.0	4.0
1983	34.9[a]	18.5[a]	11.8	4.6
1986	35.4	19.2	12.2	4.0
1989	35.9	18.7	12.9	4.3
1992	36.9	17.7	12.9	6.3

[a] From 1 Sept. 1983

Source: Sachverständigenrat, Jahresgutachten, various issues.

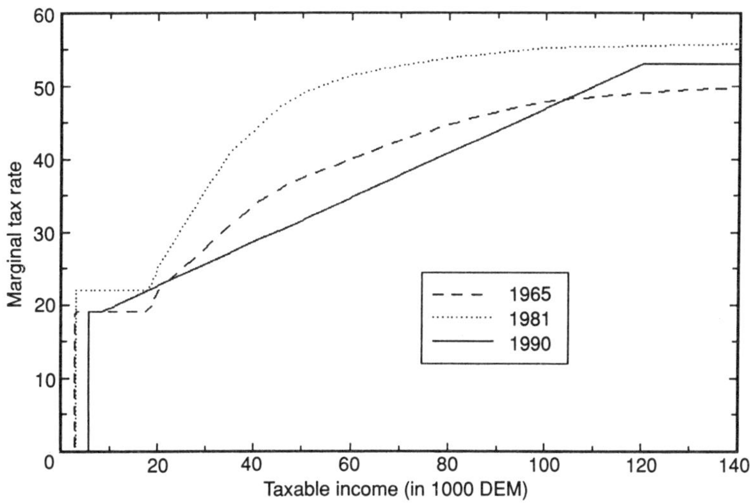

FIG 6.1. Marginal Tax Rates, 1965–1990

relatively moderate increase in the marginal tax rate in the 1965 tax scheme (see Fig. 6.1). This has been accompanied by a larger proportional tax bracket and allowances in favour of individuals with low incomes and with children. Especially after 1975, the average burden from taxes and social contributions of households dropped and remained lower for a few years. However, because of rising social insurance contributions (see Table 6.9), the average income deductions have not remained at a low level. In the course of the three-step tax reform of the conservative–liberal coalition after 1982, the steep progression has been reduced almost completely. As in 1965, the basic rate has been set at

19%, although the lower proportional bracket has nearly disappeared. The most striking feature of the post-1990 tax system is the linear increase of the marginal tax rate, going up to a maximum of 53%. Like the reforms in the 1970s, the conservative reform amounted to several billion DM reduction of the tax payments to create incentives for work and investment. However, as social-insurance contributions have risen to new record levels in 1992, the long-lasting effects of this reform are also in doubt, especially when the expected additional burden from the ageing population is taken into account.

6.3.2. Unemployment Compensation and Active Labour Market Policies

The definition of the unemployment status extends to individuals who are temporarily unemployed or who do not work for more than eighteen hours per week. Being part of the national insurance system, unemployment insurance is financed via compulsory payments of workers and employees as well as employers, each side contributing half of total contributions. As for every insurance, this means that receipt of benefits in the case of unemployment depends on having contributed to the system beforehand. Therefore, young people and women in particular are often not eligible for support. Eligibility for benefits requires, further, that a person is available for employment, i.e. being prepared and able to accept 'reasonable' job offers.

Payment of unemployment benefits is twofold. First, unemployed persons regulary receive unemployment insurance (*Arbeitslosengeld*) which is an equivalent to 68% of their last income for a period of more or less one year (depending on age and on the duration of previous employment). They receive only 63% if they have no children. If an employment relationship has been terminated by the unemployed person himself, payments are delayed for eight weeks. After one year, means-tested unemployment assistance (*Arbeitslosenhilfe*) is paid for an (in principle) unlimited time. The replacement ratio drops to 58% with children and 56% without children. Unemployment assistance has to be reapplied for yearly, and it is particularly checked that income from other sources, e.g. income of the spouse, does not exceed the official limits. Those who are not eligible for unemployment assistance will receive social assistance (see Lampert 1991).

The Federal Labour Office (*Bundesanstalt für Arbeit*) implements a substantial set of labour market policy measures. First, there are active measures like the employment creation programme (ABM) and support for further education and vocational training. Second, there are passive measures like unemployment benefits and unemployment aid, short-time working allowance, and old-age benefits supporting early retirements.

These programmes have been especially employed in the East. For instance, since October 1990 East Germans have been allowed to enter pre-retirement at age 57 as soon as they became unemployed. (The normal retirement ages are 65 for men and 60 for women in Germany.) In July 1991 eligibility was extended to workers as young as 55. The scheme remained valid until July 1992.

The more recent emphasis of labour market policy has been on employment creation and training. The measures were already created before unification, and the policies are now actively implemented in the East. Because the GDR labour force was seen to exhibit a high level of education, a retraining programme was expected to improve the speed of adjustment to the market system. Chambers of commerce or labour and private training companies are providing the education and training under the monitoring of the Federal Labour Office. Employment companies (*Beschäftigungsgesellschaften*), a measure that was introduced after unification, provide training and jobs. Unemployed persons are employed by specific firms to engage in public works that do not (or should not) compete with private enterprises. These firms pay union (or comparable) wages which are heavily subsidized by the Federal Labour Office. Employment companies are part of the employment creation programme (ABM) which enables the labour office directly to support firms that are willing to employ disabled, older, or long-term unemployed people.

6.3.3. Family Support and Family Policies

Germany has an extensive policy that aims to ensure the basic functions of the family, reproduction, socialization, and recreation, by balancing the financial burden of child-rearing. However, other objectives like population policy and labour market policies can be detected (see Zimmermann 1985). Over the last decades, important changes in family policy have taken place, especially concerning the protection of pregnant women (1952, 1965), the reform of family taxation and the introduction of income-splitting for tax purposes of married couples (*Ehegattensplitting*) in 1958, the legal position of illegitimate children (redefined in 1970), the reform of the law on the family, marriage, and divorce (1970), the reform of custody (1980), and the liberalization of abortion laws (1976, 1992). For a more detailed exposition see Oberhauser (1989), Münch (1990), and Willeke and Onken (1990). A review of the family policy in the former GDR is given in Obertreis (1986). (See also Section 6.3.5 below.) An East–West post-war comparison will be provided in Zimmermann (forthcoming). For the concept of family policy in the framework of the economics of the family, see also Zimmermann (1985).

The core of family policy is related to four types of measure: (i) income-splitting for tax purposes of married couples (*Ehegattensplitting*), (ii) child allowances (*Kindergeld*), (iii) child tax allowances (*Kinderfreibeträge*), and (iv) child-care subsidies (*Erziehungsgeld*). Since child allowances are transfers and child tax allowances affect the tax burden of the family, the combination of both measures is also called the dual system of family policy (*Duales System des Familienlastenausgleichs*). Split taxation of married couples, explained in Section 6.3.1, is not directly related to the presence of children. It was introduced in 1958 after the Federal Constitutional Court had considered separate taxation of married couples to be incompatible with the basic law, the German constitution. However, since split taxation encourages the second earner to specialize in home production as soon as there are differences in the earnings potential of both couples, this system is expected implicitly to support family formation. In practice, split taxation is seen as a major cause of the low female work participation in Germany.

TABLE 6.10. Child Tax Allowances

	No. of children		
Year	1	2	3 or more
1950–3	400	250	700
1954	600	600	840
1955–6	720	720	1,680
1957	720	1,440	1,680
1958–61	900	1,680	1,800
1962–74	1,200	1,680	1,800
1975–82	0	0	0
1983–5	432	432	432
1986	2,484	2,484	2,484
1990	3,024	3,024	3,024
1992	4,104	4,104	4,104

Source: Bundesregierung, Sozialbericht 1990, p. 76; Willeke and Onken (1990: 419).

Child tax allowances were introduced in Germany in 1920, and existed also in the Third Reich and during the government of the Allied Control Council after the Second World War. These types of tax deduction also existed at the beginning of the Federal Republic of Germany. The objective of this measure is to leave the subsistence level untaxed. In a system of progressive taxation, this results in larger reductions in tax payments at higher levels of gross income. Table 6.10 provides information about the structure of child tax allowances since the 1950s. In 1950 the tax allowance for the first child was DM 400, for the second DM 250, and for the third DM 700. From 1975 to 1982 child tax allowances were abolished, but they were reintroduced in 1983. Since 1992 tax allowances have been DM 4,104 for each child. In 1992 the Federal Constitutional Court decided that the current amount of the child tax allowance is too low to leave the subsistence level untaxed, and is therefore incompatible with the German constitution. It has to be adjusted by the government by the end of 1995.

Child allowances have a long tradition in Germany, going back to the Third Reich where, from 1941, financial support was given to families with children of third and higher birth order. To avoid any association with Nazi population policy, the German Federal Government took until 1954 to pass a law that allocated DM 25 to families for each child from the third. Originally only paid to working individuals, excluding civil servants, the money was raised from the employers and distributed by an independent body. Various revisions and modifications were undertaken in several steps, to include non-working people and civil servants, who were paid by the state. Since 1964 child allowances have been generally financed by the state and paid by the Federal Employment Office (*Bundesanstalt für Arbeit*).

The general development of child allowance payments, differentiated according to birth order, are given in Table 6.11. It shows that payments were extended to the second child in 1961 and to the first in 1975. For third and subsequent children the payments are about ten times higher in 1992 than in 1955. However, the numbers in Table 6.11 should be compared with care. For some periods the benefits were income-dependent, for others not. Child allowances were independent of income until 1 April 1961, and from 1 January 1975 to 31 December 1982. Between both periods, the DM 25 for the second child were not paid, if the yearly income crossed a certain threshold as listed in Table 6.11. Since January 1983, the given numbers in Table 6.11 are maximum values and are income-dependent. The system is rather complicated. On one hand, payments decline with income up to a minimum level, which is also given in Table 6.11. On the other hand, those families that do not receive sufficient benefits from the child tax allowances get an additional amount of child allowance (*Kindergeldzuschlag*), again depending on income with an upper bound. Civil servants receive additional child benefits.

A family measure aimed at encouraging female work participation was maternity leave, granted in 1979. It gave a working mother the opportunity of taking leave from a job until her child was six months old. The employer had to be notified only four weeks after the birth of the child, the job was guaranteed during the period of absence, and the mother received a monthly allowance up to DM 750, depending on previous income paid by the Federal Government. In 1984 this support was limited to DM 510. In 1986 the whole concept was replaced by a general child care subsidy (*Erziehungsgeld*) of DM 600 per month for a

TABLE 6.11. Monthly Child Allowances[a]

Valid since	Birth order of child 1	2	3	4	5
1 Jan. 1955	–	–	25	25	25
1 Sept. 1957	–	–	30	30	30
1 Mar. 1959	–	–	40	40	40
1 Apr. 1961	–	25	40	40	40
1 Apr. 1964	–	25	80	80	80
1 May 1964	–	25	50	50	50
1 July 1964	–	25	50	60	70
1 Sept. 1970	–	25	60	60	70
1 Jan. 1975	50	70	120	120	120
1 Jan. 1978	50	80	150	150	150
1 Jan. 1979	50	80	200	200	200
1 July 1979	50	100	200	200	200
1 Feb. 1981	50	120	240	240	240
1 Jan. 1982	50	100	220	240	240
1 July 1990	50	130	220	240	240
1 Jan. 1992	70	130	220	240	240

[a] Payments are partly income-dependent. The DM 25 for the 2nd child was only paid up to a maximum yearly income of DM 7,800 from 1 Apr. 1961, DM 13,200 from 1 Sept. 1970, DM 15,000 from 1 Jan. 1972, DM 16,800 from 1 Jan. 1973, and DM 18,760 from 1 Jan. 1974. Since 1 Jan. 1983 the payments for the 2nd and subsequent children have been income-dependent. Nos. in the table are maximum payments, and the minimum levels are 70 for the 2nd child and 140 for all subsequent children.

Source: Willecke and Onken (1980: 406).

ten-month period, extended to twelve months in 1988, to eighteen months in 1990, and to twenty-four months in 1992. This measure is now not only directed to working women but also at housewives and working men. The person taking the leave is only allowed to work part-time; a previous job is guaranteed under certain restrictions. The child care subsidy programme is complemented by some of the German states (*Länder*) with a conservative government. A basic condition for additional financial support is a withdrawal from the labour market.

In addition to those major instruments, many other measures are in use, among them housing programmes for families, tax allowances for child care or education, educational grants for students, and the inclusion of child-rearing in the pension system. Also, the German federal system allows for a larger differentiation of measures across the various states. The combination of measures often gives an unclear picture of the actual objectives of the policy-makers. An example is given in Fig. 6.2, where the dual system of family support is examined. Child allowances, child tax allowances, and total transfers are mapped against income. Since child allowances decrease with income in steps and child tax allowances do the reverse, the total effect is rather non-linear and exhibits a peculiar shape.

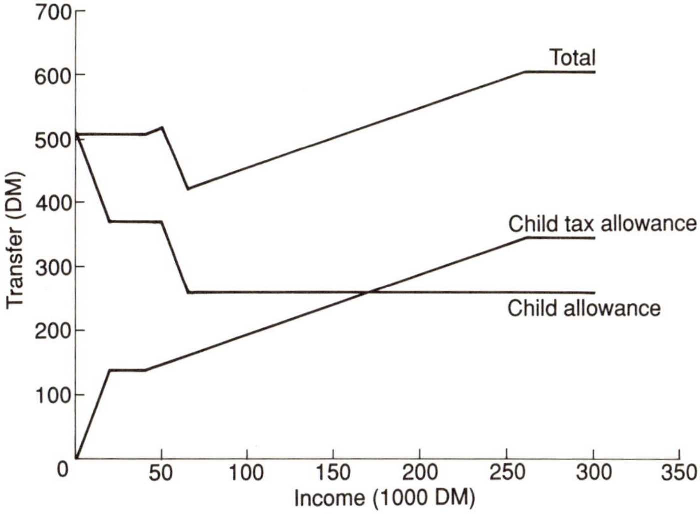

FIG 6.2. Monthly Marginal Transfers Due to *Kindergeld* and *Kinderfreibeträge* of Family with Three Children, 1988
Source: Oberhauser (1989: table 4); own calculations.

It clearly gives some low-income families a disincentive to work. There are other measures in the German benefit system that generate similar effects, for instance educational grants.

Table 6.12 summarizes federal expenditures on families between 1960 and 1990. Although the total social budget is more than ten times larger in 1990 (DM 703,058 million) than in 1960, the total spending on marriage and the family has only increased by a factor of 6. The share of the family budget has decreased from about 21% to about 13%, less than 4% of gross national product. Split taxation lost its central role in the family budget in 1960, when 46% of the expenditures came via this channel. In 1990, only 33% of the federal spending for marriage and family was due to this taxation rule. Therefore, more and more areas of expenditure were determined by the presence of children within the household. However, it should be noted that these child-related expenditures cover the whole dual system, including child allowances and child tax allowances. Most current family support operates through the tax system.

As explained above, there have been considerable changes in public expenditure on family affairs in Germany over the last decades. There were two determinants: (i) financial problems of the government to finance the budget, and in consequence the need to save money, and, more important, (ii) political changes in government, and hence the need

TABLE 6.12. Social Budget of West Germany, 1960–1990

	1960	1965	1970	1975	1980	1985	1990
Shares in % of total social budget							
Marriage and the family	20.5	20.4	17.1	13.8	14.2	12.4	12.8
Children	10.0	10.4	8.3	7.3	8.1	6.6	8.0
Split taxation	9.4	9.2	8.1	6.0	5.3	5.2	4.3
Motherhood	1.1	0.9	0.8	0.6	0.8	0.6	0.5
Million DM							
Total social budget	68,943	114,603	180,144	346,598	478,512	575,498	703,058
Marriage and the family	14,148	23,414	30,805	47,998	67,755	71,223	90,202
Children	6,903	11,867	14,901	25,143	38,920	37,831	56,441
Split taxation	6,500	10,549	14,528	20,696	25,128	29,788	30,008
Motherhood	744	998	1,376	2,159	3,707	3,604	3,753
Portion of gross national product (%)							
Total social budget	22.75	25.01	26.66	33.67	32.22	31.20	29.40
Marriage and the family	4.67	5.11	4.56	4.66	4.56	3.86	3.77
Children	2.28	2.59	2.21	2.44	2.62	2.05	2.36
Split taxation	2.15	2.30	2.15	2.01	1.69	1.62	1.25
Motherhood	0.25	0.22	0.20	0.21	0.25	0.20	0.16

Source: Bundesregierung, Sozialbericht 1986, p. 178; 1990, p. 205.

for major revisions in family policy. The different political objectives had quite different consequences for female work participation and also for redistribution policies.

In what follows, only labour market consequences are considered. It is possible to distinguish three phases in family policy since the end of the Second World War: the period of conservative governments (mostly including the liberals and other parties) in the 1950s and 1960s; the period of the social–liberal government (coalition between the social democrats and the liberals) from 1969 to 1982; and the conservative–liberal government from 1982. The primary goal in the first period was to strengthen the family as an institution. Public policy in the *laissez-faire* regime attempted not to interfere in the private decision-making of the family. The social–liberal government of the second phase was more engaged in redistribution issues, and abolished the dual system of family policy in 1975 by concentrating on child allowances. Child tax allowances were held to give unnecessary support for high-income families. The government also supported a more active involvement of females in the labour market by creating the maternity leave programme, which was thought to stabilize female work participation. A reform of the family law in 1976 made women an equal partner in family decision-making on financial issues. A married woman was now also legally entitled to decide alone on her labour force participation.

In the third phase, the conservative-led government re-introduced child tax allowances in 1983 and extended the system considerably. Child-dependent transfers to the family now work primarily through this channel. At the same time, child allowances were made income-dependent. As already explained above, the maternity leave programme was replaced by the child care subsidy programme, which supports the role of the non-working mother. An explicitly declared objective here is also to reduce female unemployment, which is considered to be a relief for the labour market in the face of the persistently high unemployment rates of the 1980s and 1990s.

6.3.4. The German Child Care System

A high labour force participation rate of women with small children requires a sufficient supply of child care facilities. Since mothers' decisions to enter the labour market depend on the availability, quality, and price of child care, subsidizing child care has important consequences for female labour supply. In the Federal Republic of Germany (and now in East and West Germany) institutional child care is mainly provided by local governments and by churches or other welfare organizations. There are relatively few commercial day care centres, less than 1% of all centres in 1986. The price of child care in a public centre charged to parents is on average quite low, so that the costs of the child care facility are in general much higher than its revenue. Since child care facilities run by welfare or non-profit-making organizations receive large subsidies from the local government if they satisfy certain conditions, they are in general able to supply high-quality care at a relatively low price. According to the German Socioeconomic Panel (SOEP), a representative sample of German households, the average monthly price of centre care was about DM 65 per child in 1987. Day care centres are more expensive than a normal kindergarten, and commercial facilities charge higher fees than others. In contrast to many European countries, child care expenses are not tax-deductible. There are also no subsidies for non-institutional child care.

Table 6.13 summarizes to what extent young children of kindergarten age (3–6 years) are covered by kindergarten child care. This coverage increased from 43.3% in 1975 to 64.6% in 1990, partly because of public efforts to improve the availability of kindergarten care but also because of declining fertility. It is also shown that the increase was similar in all age groups. In 1990, 37% of all 3-year-old children, 76% of all 4-year-old children, and 86% of all 5-year-olds were in kindergarten child care.

TABLE 6.13. Children in Kindergarten Care, 1975–1990

Year	% of all children in age group			
	3–6	3–4	4–5	5–6
1975	43.3	22.9	46.1	59.2
1980	58.5	34.0	64.7	76.3
1985	65.0	41.1	72.4	83.0
1990	64.6	36.7	75.9	86.1

Source: Merkle (1993), based on data from the German Statistical Office.

TABLE 6.14. Child Care Supply

Year	Government expenditure for child care centres (DM 000)[a]	No. of kindgergartens (total)[b]	No. of places in kindergartens (total)[c]	No. of places per 100 children age 3–6
1970	318,810	17,493	1,160,736	38.5
1975	1,009,935	23,130	1,478,856	65.5
1980	1,731,287	24,011	1,393,708	78.8
1986	2,488,489	25,890	1,472,819	81.2
1990	5,467,384	25,167	1,496,245	75.8

[a] Including expenditures for public child care centres and subsidies to child care centres run by welfare organizations or commercial centres.
[b] Public and commercial kindergartens and kindergartens run by welfare organizations.
[c] Spaces in public and commercial kindergartens and kindergartens run by welfare organizations.

Source: Merkle (1993), based on data from the German Statistical Office. No data available for 1985.

Within the last twenty years public interest in day care for children of age 3–6 (preschoolers) has increased considerably. Besides the growing labour force attachment of German women, the rising demand for additional, elementary education and socialization before school entry was a reason for this development. Between 1970 and 1990, total federal expenditure on child care (including subsidies to child care centres run by welfare or non-profit-making organizations, which account for approximately half the expenditure) increased from DM 3.2 billion to almost DM 55 billion. Within the same time-span, the number of kindergartens in Germany increased rapidly, as well as the number of available places in child care facilities for preschoolers (see Table 6.14). Whereas in 1970 only 38.5 kindergarten spaces were available for 100 children of age 3–6, in 1990 places were available for 75.8% of all children in the relevant age group. (This development was also reinforced by the decrease in the number of children.) The numbers of places in child care centres for 100 children of age 3–6 given in Table 6.14 overestimate the actual situation, because children who are older than 6 years and are not yet in school are often also in kindergarten care. For the analysis of the incentives of subsidized supply of child care for the labour force participation of mothers, it is important to notice that most child care centres accept children only for half a day. In 1984 only 9% of all places were full-time. There are also large regional differences in child care supply between rural and urban areas and between the different states.

Whereas the supply of child care for preschoolers has improved considerably in Germany within the last twenty years, there are still only very few day care centres in Germany which accept children under age 3. This fact is due to the conviction of many social groups that only the mother can provide adequate care for babies, and to the unwillingness of the government to provide institutional care for very young children. In 1990 there were only 1.4 places in child care centres (*Kinderkrippen*) available for 100 children under age 3, which were to a large extent reserved for children of lone and poor mothers. It was estimated that approximately the same number of places is available in family day care. The latter is in general more expensive than centre care because it is not subsidized by the government. Besides the insufficient day care for very young children, there is also a lack of child care facilities for school-age children. Since an average German schoolday is only about 5 hours, mothers who do not have informal child care available can only take up part-time work.

6.3.5. GDR/FRG Differences in Family Policy

As will be further investigated in Section 6.7, female work participation was much larger in East Germany than in the West, and male labour force participation was somewhat lower. This can be explained in part by differences in family policies. These differences will be addressed briefly in this section. A more detailed comparison is provided by Zimmermann (1993) and Koch (1991); for the East German family policy see also Obertreis (1986). First, an overview is given on the various phases of family policy in East Germany; and then the differences from the West are stressed.

During a first phase (1949–65) social norms concerning female labour force participation and the role of the family were established in the constitution of the GDR as the Mother and Child Care and Women's Rights Act of 1950. The aim was to establish the necessary environment for a working mother by creating a network of child care centres (*Kinderhorte*), kindergartens, and facilities for free school meals. Maternity leave of five weeks before and six weeks after delivery was established, during which period the mother was paid her net wage.

Women with children received a monthly day off, and support was given to single working mothers with sick children. This period ended with the establishment of a new family law (*Familiengesetzbuch*) that defined the role of the family in socialism (see Obertreis 1986: 232–59).

The second period (1966–71) was determined by the pressure of fertility decline. Hence, additional policy measures tried to enable women to combine work with family formation. Among them were cheap loans, childbirth subsidies, and easier access to housing. Female students with children were financially supported. Maternity leave was extended to eighteen weeks, during which the mother received her full net salary. For mothers with three or more children, working time was restricted to forty hours per week with full wage compensation (see Penrose 1990: 69).

The third phase (1972–89) began on 10 May 1972, when the most intensive pro-natalist population policy programme of the GDR was put into practice. Maternity leave was extended to twenty weeks. Starting with the second child, a 'baby year' was introduced to enable mothers to stay at home for one year after the birth. During this time they received financial support from health insurance. Young mothers who had to stay at home after the birth because of the unavailability of a child care centre nearby were paid a monthly allowance if they bore another child within the next three years. The working week of mothers with two children was restricted to forty hours, with full wage compensation. Efforts were made to provide child care services for all children. Whereas in 1970 only 64.5% of the children in kindergarten age had a place, it was already 92.2% in 1980. Child care centres covered only 29.1% of all infants in 1970, but the share increased to 61.2% in 1980 (see Obertreis 1986: 217–18).

To summarize: the East German government followed a more active policy to attract women to the labour force. In part, this was driven by communist ideology. However, there was also an economic need to do so, since there was a permanent loss of people to the West, even if these losses were significantly lower after the building of the Berlin Wall and the 'iron fence'. The GDR also never took the option of hiring a larger share of foreign workers to satisfy excess demand of labour. These conditions explain why the East German government took the drastic decline of fertility from the 1960s onwards more seriously than the Western side, and started active population policy measures. This included the provision of substantial financial support, with some stabilizing and increasing effects on fertility. But also very important was the creation of a better environment for the working mother, including a substantial increase in the provision of daily child care for infants and kindergarten children. Since the East German child care system was closed down soon after unification, it is important to examine how the East German fertility rate and the female labour force participation rate is now developing.

6.4. QUANTITY SUPPLY: THE EVIDENCE ON WAGE, INCOME, AND TAXATION

6.4.1. General Remarks

The bulk of the empirical literature on incentives has dealt with the proper estimation of a labour-supply model, and the evaluation of the income and compensated wage elasticities and their implications for income taxation. This section draws on this literature for West Germany. The first step will be to examine how flexible the quantity of supply of males and females is responding to changes in income and wages. Since male labour supply is rather inflexible anyway, most of the empirical applications deal with females. A further point of investigation is how explicitly they deal with the problems arising from progressive taxation. A final step in this section will be to examine how the estimates have been used to simulate tax reforms.

The international empirical literature on labour supply can be structured in three waves of contributions. The first generation related quantity of supply to measures of income and wages, without proper treatment of econometric issues and a strict theoretical basis of the estimates. The second generation attempted to address these issues. A third generation of investigations that has just begun considers further estimation problems of current research, as will be discussed below. Some parts of Section 6.4 deal with complicated econometric issues that can only be briefly explained. The interested reader is referred for further explanations and references to Killingsworth (1983).

Before the empirical findings for Germany are surveyed, some comments on the state of the art can be made (see also Zimmermann (1988) and Chapters 2–4). Despite many recent developments, mainstream labour-supply econometrics fails to account for the following problems:

1. Cross-sectional variation in actual hours worked usually has a very distinctive shape, with one or more extreme peaks. This is poorly explained by traditional models, which typically produce a smooth and unimodal distribution of predicted hours.
2. Work effort or labour quality should be central to the debate on incentives. It is not in practice, probably because data on work quality

are so difficult to obtain or to evaluate because of measurement errors. Labour supply-decisions should be analysed in a quantity-quality framework: demand for and supply of job characteristics have to be considered.

3. Institutional arrangements and other supply constraints, especially for hours worked, should not be ignored, especially in periods with high levels of unemployment.
4. Misspecification of the traditional labour-supply equations is likely caused by at least two exogeneity assumptions. First, the gross wage seems to be dependent on the number of hours worked. Second, one of the famous 'taste-shifters' in the female-supply equation, the number of children, is seen in the family economics literature to be jointly determined with labour supply. Both problems have severe consequences for the validity of the conventional labour-supply estimates.

Only some of these issues have actually found treatment in the literature. Mroz (1987) has examined the sensitivity of the results under alternative statistical and economic assumptions, and challenges the conventional wisdom that females respond more flexibly to wages and income than males. Dickens and Lundberg (1993) deal with hours restrictions. Their evidence suggests that traditional models failing to account for those constraints are likely to overestimate tax responses. Another issue of recent concern is that some of the more sophisticated econometric techniques may cause severe overestimations of wage and income elasticities and hence overstate the implied disincentive effects of taxes and transfers. For this literature see MaCurdy *et al.* (1990) and Flood and MaCurdy (1991). They suggest instrumental variable estimation, namely the replacement of endogenous regressors by an estimated function of truely exogenous variables, over the more conventional approaches to dealing with taxation, and also replace the gross wage and non-labour income by instruments. The resulting very low income elasticity and the negative uncompensated wage elasticity in Flood and MaCurdy (1991) have, however, a high price: the estimated compensated-wage elasticity is negative, which is inconsistent with economic theory. It is therefore not clear why the authors are so fully satisfied with these findings.

The outlined issues are important to keep in mind during the evaluation of the German findings in the next section, where first-generation studies are not investigated. Since the third-generation arguments are mostly not yet used in the German debate, there is a danger that the results reviewed overestimate the disincentive effects of taxes and benefits.

6.4.2. Supply of Quantity: Income and Substitution Effects

At the heart of the efficiency debate about incentives is the size of the income and wage elasticities which can be calculated on the basis of the labour-supply models. This section therefore reviews first those findings that fit straightforwardly in the conventional framework and analyse an hours equation. First, the chosen approaches and data sets are described in more detail. Second, the estimated elasticities are evaluated. The section closes with a review of more specialized papers that deal, for instance, with intertemporal or cross-section time-series approaches.

Franz and Kawasaki (1981) and Franz (1985) use data on 16,297 married women from the 1976 Microcensus of Baden-Württemberg, one of the larger states of the Federal Republic of Germany. Whereas the employed data sets and specifications of regressors are exactly the same, the earlier study applies the so-called Heckman two-stage probit/hours model and the 1985 paper uses the Tobit approach. Both approaches take care of the joint decision of an individual to work at all and to supply a certain quantity of labour. The Probit model examines the probability of work assuming a normal distribution, whereas the Tobit approach treats the participation decision and the supply of hours jointly.

The income effect in both papers is based on the inclusion of the variable 'net income of the husband', whereas the female wage rate is replaced by instruments using dummy variables for schooling and vocational training. A separate (net) wage regression on these determinants is also estimated, which provides the possibility of calculating an estimate for the wage elasticity. Franz (1985: S232 n.6) shows how this elasticity is derived on the basis of the estimates of the coefficients of the dummy variable 'vocational training' in the wage and Probit or Tobit hours equations. Note that vocational training is the only variable that appears to be significant in both equations so that there is clear identification, and this procedure has some justification. The elasticities provided by these studies are hours elasticities. The major deficiency in the context of this paper is that neither study deals with the taxation issue, which is a particular problem with the income variable. However, one should keep in mind that both papers are first and early applications of the second-generation approach and the available data is sometimes crude. For instance, income is given only in discrete intervals, which prevents a careful treatment of taxation.

All four other papers from West Germany that will be reviewed below use data from the German Socioeconomic Panel (SOEP), which is a random sample of West German households: Merz (1990), Stobernack (1991), Strøm and Wagenhals (1991), and Kaiser *et al.* (1992). Merz (1990) uses data from the 1984 first wave of the SOEP on 3,932 married women and 2,176 single (separated, divorced, widowed) women. The econometric technique is again the two-stage Heckman Probit/hours approach. For the calculation of the wage elasticity, an hours regression was used including an imputed wage from the previous step of estimating a wage function. (The paper, however, reports only explicitly on an hours regression, where the wage rate was substituted by its determinants as in the Franz and Kawasaki (1981) and Franz (1985) studies.) The estimates incorporated a large number of control variables, including various types of non-labour income of the household and net labour income of the husband. To evaluate the effects of 'total income', the income elasticity was calculated on the basis of the sums of the estimated coefficients of the income variables 'net earned income of husband last month' and of two types of household yearly property income. (Not included in this calculation were all types of personal and household transfer income which were included in the regression.) The wage rate used is probably the gross wage rate. The study provides participation and working-hours elasticities for wage and income of married women and single females. Although problems of estimating labour-supply functions incorporating benefits and taxes are mentioned, they are ignored in the estimation process. Hence, the major difference between Merz (1990) and the earlier German studies can be seen in the use of the imputed wage and of a data set that is representative for West Germany in total.

Stobernack (1991) explicitly deals with the problem of rationing, where the individual labour supply differs from the actual number of hours worked owing to labour market restrictions, using the method recently suggested by Ham (1982). The basic idea here is to create a specific sample selection variable for both cases of overemployment and underemployment, and estimate the labour-supply model for the subsample of unrestricted individuals using those selection variables as additional regressors. The study uses a sample of 1,585 males and 1,145 females (among them 326 singles) from the 1985 (second) wave of the SOEP. The individuals are 20–60 years old, German, and either employed, unemployed, or underemployed. The problem with this paper is first that the taxation issue is not addressed. Second, it concentrates on individuals who are at present in the labour market, which may result in a biased sample with the danger of achieving misleading results at least for females. Estimates are given and elasticities can be derived for men, women, single women, and the complete sample. The key variables for the elasticities are the gross hourly wage and the transfer income of the household in 1985 (excluding unemployment compensation). Note that the latter departs somewhat from the previous studies, where the estimate of the income effect was to some extent based on the labour income of the husband.

Strøm and Wagenhals (1991) is the first study that explicitly deals with taxes and social-security contributions, including the problem of family taxation. They ignore the problem of rationing that was approached by Stobernack (1991). Their analysis is based on a Box–Cox utility function, where the income elasticity is restricted to be negative. To ease the estimation problems, they use a stepwise maximum likelihood method on the basis of the Logit approach to identify the parameters of this utility function. (The Logit model is an alternative to the Probit approach based on a different distributional assumption.) The final analysis of hours worked relates to the marginal net wage rate and virtual income. After identifying the parameters of the utility function, compensated- and uncompensated-wage elasticities are calculated, and the difference between them is the total income elasticity. Strøm and Wagenhals (1991) use a sample of 1,629 married females from the 1984 wave of the SOEP. All women are between 25 and 65 years old and live in households that obtain wage income.

Similar to Strøm and Wagenhals (1991), the study by Kaiser *et al.* (1992) concentrates on the analysis of taxation. They apply the Hausman (1981) linear labour-supply model that specifies working hours as a linear function of the marginal net wage, virtual net non-labour income, and a vector of socioeconomic variables. This approach is simple but rather restrictive, since it imposes narrow constraints on the two key parameters, namely the wage and income coefficient, to fulfil the Slutzky conditions. However, the model is easy to estimate and the elasticities can be simply calculated. The chosen estimation procedure is similar to Merz (1990), in that the authors first estimate the Probit participation equation to correct for the sample selection bias in the OLS estimation of a wage function. This wage function then serves as a basis to obtain instrumental variable estimates for the final step of analysing the hours equation. In contrast to Merz (1990), they use a Tobit model for the hours equation, and the marginal net wage and the virtual net non-labour income as regressors. They instrument the former, which is certainly an improvement. Nevertheless, the marginal net wage rate is only poorly explained by the chosen regressors. Besides the constant, only a schooling variable appears to be significant, and this school education variable is just an index function with four different states. It should be possible to improve this specification, and one wonders why the imputed wage variable from this regression has performed rather well in the Tobit-hours equation. The data set is again from the first wave of the SOEP, using observations on 3,321 married men and 3,360 married women. Each group was analysed separately, although the family decison process could have been studied jointly. In contrast, it was assumed that males ignore the labour income of their wives whereas females treat their husbands' labour income as given and as part of their non-labour income.

The authors claim (p. 98) 'that the estimation for married men does not verify the neoclassical labour supply model'. This is misleading, since their negative wage coefficient is not sufficient to fail to satisfy the Slutzky condition for a large part of the sample due to the fact that most men work and the income coefficient is negative. (Only for males with an annual working time of less than 28.5 hours is the Slutzky condition not satisfied.) Of course, it is admitted that an overall negative linear wage coefficient is counter-intuitive. It is also worrying that the sample selection for men produced in 939 male individuals (28% of the sample) who were not fully employed. This size is in conflict with macro evidence and with my own experience with the SOEP. It seems that the authors have not excluded individuals in education, which certainly causes a problem.

TABLE 6.15. Estimated Elasticities for Hours Worked[a]

Study	Group	Wage elasticity		Total income elasticity
		Uncomp.	Comp.	
Franz and Kawasaki (1981)	Married women	1.08	1.28	-0.20*
Franz (1985)	Married women	1.37	1.66	-0.29*
Merz (1990)	Married women	-0.10*	-0.08	-0.02
	Single women	-0.08*	-0.08	-0.00
Stobernack (1991)	All	0.01	0.01	-0.00
	Men	0.03	0.03	0.00
	Women	0.01	0.01	0.00
	Single women	-0.00*	0.00	-0.00*
Strøm and Wagenhals (1991)	Married women	0.96*	1.02	-0.06*
Kaiser *et al.* (1992)	Married men	-0.00	0.22	-0.22*
	Married women	0.37*	0.38	-0.01*
Leu and Kugler (1986) (Switzerland)	Males	0.26*	0.33	-0.07*
	Married women	2.85*	3.03	-0.19*
	Single women	0.72*	1.11	-0.39*
Zweimüller (1987) (Austria)	Women	0.17*	0.19	-0.02

[a] Evaluated at sample means. The compensated-wage elasticities are calculated as the difference of the measured wage elasticities and the total income elasticities. * Indicates that underlying parameter estimates for the calculation of the uncompensated-wage and total income effects are significant at least at the 5% level. Note that the figures for Kaiser *et al.* (1992) are not those from their table 6, which are incorrect, but from my own calculations based on their estimates and sample means given in the paper.

The calculated uncompensated- and compensated-wage elasticities and the total income elasticity from all papers are collected in Table 6.15. Micro theory requests that the compensated-wage effect is positive, which is not satisfied for both equations in the Merz (1990) study. Therefore, one should also qualify his other findings, which indicate a rather unresponsive female labour supply. Most estimates in the international literature (see Killingsworth 1983; Pencavel 1986; Killingsworth and Heckman 1986) find negative income elasticities for both males and females, indicating that leisure is a normal good. The stylized fact is, further, that these estimates are likely to be more negative for males. Uncompensated-wage effects are often negative, or small if positive, for males, but mostly positive and often large for females. It is further true that second-generation estimates exhibit more responsiveness to incentives than first-generation estimates. However, the range of the estimates is still large: according to the studies listed in Pencavel (1986) between –0.08 and 0.17 for males, and according to Killingsworth and Heckman (1986) between –0.89 and 15.24. Compensated wage elasticities larger than 0.5 are seen to be indicative of substantial efficiency gains from lowering tax rates.

There are two West German studies that differ significantly from these findings. As already mentioned, the study by Merz (1990) fails to produce positive compensated-wage effects. Total income elasticities are practically zero. In contrast to most of the literature, the gross wage effects are negative. It is further surprising that married and single women exhibit practically identical patterns. The suspicion is that the very large number of control variables used in this study that are often correlated with the wage and income variables are partly responsible for this. The income variables were also probably split into too many pieces. The study is also not using marginal net wage rates and virtual income.

The second paper that gives strongly different findings is Stobernack (1991), who also fails to deal with the taxation issue properly, but approaches the rationing problem for the first time. Here, all estimates are close to zero and most of the underlying parameter estimates are insignificant. It is also noteworthy that men are more responsive to wage changes than women. Both results may well follow from the proper treatment of the rationing issue. Dickens and Lundberg (1993) also report that wage elasticities drop dramatically as restricted choice is added to some of their models, but fail to observe this for others.

The bulk of results in Table 6.15 are for females, mostly for married women. A natural way of looking at these findings is to differentiate between the early studies by Franz and Kawasaki (1981) and Franz (1985) on the one hand and the recent contributions by Strøm and Wagenhals (1991) and Kaiser *et al.* (1992) on the other. Only the latter group deals properly with the taxation issue and covers a representative sample for the whole of West Germany with more recent data. On the other hand, the data set of the first group is much bigger and is representative for one of the larger West German states. Franz and Kawasaki (1981) and Franz (1985) differ only in the chosen estimation method. The total income elasticities are negative and of relevant size; both wage elasticities are positive and rather high. These early estimates exhibit the most responsive findings obtained for West Germany.

Both later studies show substantially smaller (but still negative) estimates for the total income elasticity. Both wage elasticities are only marginally smaller in Strøm and Wagenhals (1991) but substantially closer to zero in Kaiser *et al.* (1992), which estimates them to be less than 40% of the Strøm and Wagenhals (1991) estimates. One way of explaining these differences is to refer to the proper treatment of the taxation issue in the later studies. The different sizes of the wage elasticities between the two recent papers is probably attributable to the instrumenting of the net marginal wage rate in the 1992 study. In regard to the stability of the findings in the German-speaking world, Table 6.15 also contains estimates for Switzerland by Leu and Kugler (1986) and for Austria by Zweimüller (1987). Whereas the Austrian findings demonstrate a low responsiveness, the Swiss estimates are rather high. We may conclude that taxation matters for German female work participation, but that the responsiveness is much lower than generally expected.

Given the substantially larger male work participation in Germany and the larger contribution of men to recorded national income, it seems that male responsiveness is the more important problem from a macroeconomic policy perspective. This is contrasted by the rather scarce available evidence for Germany. This ignorance is probably driven by the widely observed international experience that males are not very responsive.

There are only the two studies by Stobernack (1991) and Kaiser *et al.* (1992) that deal with men. The latter paper finds that the total income effect is substantially more negative for males than for females, whereas the former detects only zero elasticities. The gross wage effect of Kaiser *et al.* (1992) for men is negative but insignificant. They argue that this result is against economic theory, and disregard men in their further simulation of changes in the taxation system. Stobernack (1991) receives a reliable positive uncompensated-wage effect after dealing with rationing. But even in this case the elasticity is small, so that a decrease of tax rates might not change much. Note, however, that the Leu and Kugler (1986) estimates for Switzerland indicate a more substantial response there.

What can we learn from these findings? It is possible that there are some welfare gains from tax reforms for females. It is, however, unlikely that there would be relevant effects for males. All the findings need some qualifications. The proper treatment of rationing and the instrumenting of potentially endogenous regressors can substantially alter these results. There is the suspicion, which is based on some econometric work, that such treatment would result in much smaller elasticities, resulting in more doubts that taxation distorts incentives significantly. A further major caveat in all the studies surveyed (but also in the international literature) is the improper treatment of the number of children as exogenous regressor. Family size and female work participation are known to be jointly endogenous. If one believes that fertility should enter (instrumented) in the labour force participation equation, then there is a further channel for taxation, since fertility depends negatively on wages. (See Zimmermann (1985) for empirical support in the German context.) As a consequence, there is a potential for underestimating taxation effects.

All econometric parts of the studies reviewed above basically use a cross-section or static framework. This may be a further cause for biased estimates. There are a few exceptions. Kugler and Schwendener (1988) use cross-section Swiss data in a way that is consistent with a life-cycle framework. Wage effects are decomposed in movements along the expected life-cycle wage path and shifts of this curve, where the key variable used is the net marginal wage. They receive estimates for the intertemporal wage elasticities, the measure for movements along the curve, of about 1 for women and –0.2 (but insignificant) for men, and permanent wage elasticities for women of –0.2 and for men of –0.4, which were both statistically insignificant. The implication is that changes of the marginal tax rates cause only temporary changes in labour supply. Hujer and Schnabel (1991) examine the cross-section time-series approach using fixed-effect and random-effect Tobit models for the first four waves of the West German SOEP. This approach allows to deal with unobserved individual heterogeneity. However, they include no wage variable explicitly in their analysis, substituting schooling, experience, and experience-squared, the typical variables from the Mincerian earnings regression. Other variables used are non-labour income and number of children. Their finding is that cross-section studies overestimate the influence of non-labour income and underestimate the effect parameter of children, which is much more negative in the cross-section time-series framework.

6.4.3. Simulating Tax Reforms

Few studies simulate tax reforms on the basis of microeconometric models for Germany: Strøm and Wagenhals (1991), Wagenhals (1991), Kaiser *et al.* (1992) and S. Gustafsson (1992*a*). They all rely on estimates of female labour supply only. The first two studies are only different concerning the econometric framework in that they employ different assumptions about the correlation between the error terms in the wage equation and taste-shifting function. The next two studies investigate the full implications of the 1990 tax reform as it was outlined in Section 6.3.1. S. Gustafsson (1992*a*) imposes the Swedish separate-taxation system on German data and the German joint taxation-system on Swedish data to simulate possible effects on female work participation. This comparison is useful, since the Swedish and the German tax treatment of couples are polar cases. (See also Chapter 3 for the Swedish tax system.)

Split taxation is seen to exhibit strong disincentives to work for married women. Therefore, Strøm and Wagenhals (1991) analyse the potential effects that a removal of the system of split taxation would have on female labour force participation. In the separate taxation system, they keep the brackets and marginal tax rates unchanged from the split-taxation system and simply remove the husband from the tax schedule of the woman. This change of regimes induced an increase in female work participation from 44.5% to 52.8%. This is significant, but not substantial. In practice, male labour supply is expected to decline after such a reform, but this reaction was not modelled in the paper. However, since the male reaction is probably small, the overall benefits of the reform in terms of increased supply of work and of larger tax revenues remain.

S. Gustafsson (1992*a*) compares the effects of the different taxation systems in Sweden and Germany for female work participation. The paper uses 632 married women from the Swedish HUS data set and 1897 married women from the German SOEP. Data are from 1984, and only individuals aged 20–59 were included. The central econometric estimates are Logit regressions for the probability of working at all and for the probability of working more than thirty hours. Wage and income data are adjusted so that they cover average tax rates at ten hours' and at forty hours' work, and net family earnings (including husband's labour income) if the wife does not work. The regression equations also contain wife's age and wife's age squared, and a set of dummy variables on the ages of children present in the household.

The income effect is strongly negative in all estimates for both countries. Quite surprisingly, the average after-tax rate at forty hours work has no significant effect (at the 5% level) on the probability of working thirty hours and more in both samples. Whereas the estimate is positive for Sweden, it is negative for Germany. However, the average after-tax wage rate exhibits a positive and significant effect on the general probability of working in both countries. Gustafsson then uses the estimates to impose the Swedish tax system on German data and the reverse. From the Logit regressions for the general probability of working it follows that Swedish women would reduce participation from 80% in the sample to 60%, and that German women would increase participation from 50% to 60%. This indicates a quite responsive female labour supply in both countries.

Strøm and Wagenhals (1991) have also studied the effects of the first (1988) step of the last tax reform in Germany. During this reform the shape of the marginal tax rate became flatter. Because the change of the system was only minor, they find a decrease of female work participation which was close to zero.

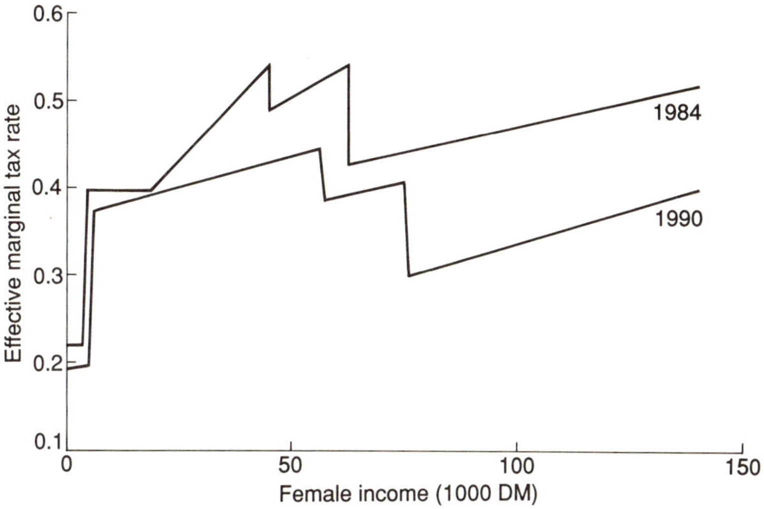

FIG 6.3. Composite Marginal Tax Rates
Note: The graph corresponds to a married mother with 2 children and a husband who earns DM 30,000.
Source: Wagenhals (1991).

Both Wagenhals (1991) and Kaiser *et al.* (1992) investigate the complete change in the tax system between 1984 and 1990, and also consider not only the changes in the marginal tax rates but also marginal social-security contributions. Fig. 6.3 draws from Wagenhals (1991) and shows the composite marginal tax rates in 1984 and 1990, including the marginal social-security contributions. The graph corresponds to a married mother with two children and a husband who earns DM 30,000. The analysis demonstrates that these marginal rates are very high for low- and medium-income groups, and that the schedule is rather complex.

Wagenhals (1991) finds that the per capita welfare gain of the reform is rather positive. The equivalent gain, the amount of money which the household would have accepted before the reform as equivalent to the reform, is about DM 3,300 per household per year. However, some poor households lose from the reform. Similarly, Kaiser *et al.* (1992) obtain welfare gains for married women based on their analysis and an explicit modelling of taxes and social-security contributions. They find an average increase in female labour supply per year of 3.6% or of about 98 hours. Their estimate for the equivalent gain is about DM 4,600 and the yearly cash gain about DM 2,600. The reduction in the excess burden, the difference between the welfare losses if taxes did not affect behaviour and actual losses of welfare due to taxation, is about DM 1,500. The results of both studies indicate that there is an efficiency increase due to the reform. Of course, the reliability of the findings depends heavily on the quality of the model estimates.

6.5. THE ROLE OF BENEFITS AND OTHER WORK INCENTIVES

6.5.1. Evidence on Labour Supply

Literature that covers the impact of benefits on labour supply directly is rather scarce. One way to look at the issue, however, is to treat benefits as part of non-labour income and to evaluate their potential effects by using the estimated total income elasticities. According to this procedure, we find on the basis of the estimates in Table 6.15 that the direction is negative. This implies that, in general, we expect a negative impact of transfers on labour supply. As noted in Section 6.4.2, the income elasticities vary considerably between various studies with a tendency to receive weaker effects the more recently the analysis was carried out. Most child care benefits also operate via the tax system, either because they are child tax allowances or because they are income-dependent like child allowances and child care subsidies. Other measures like the split-taxation system were created to support family formation. It is obvious from the analysis in the previous section that these institutional constraints will work effectively through the marginal tax rates and will have a negative impact on labour supply.

A direct approach to analysing the effects of benefits on labour supply was undertaken by Merz (1990), who differentiates between old age/widow's pension, private support, unemployment benefits in the previous year, housing benefits, and welfare benefits. When statistically significant (and most of them are), all effect parameters have a negative sign for both married and single females. However, contrary to this finding Stobernack (1991) obtains in his rationing approach a positive and significant effect parameter for all subsamples (male, female, single females, total sample), and the estimated parameters are all about the same size.

All econometric investigations of labour supply traditionally contain some regressors that measure the presence of small children, or include the number of children in the household in total. One way of justifying this is by arguing that these variables operate as taste-shifters. A different way to justify their presence is to acknowledge that they measure some opportunity costs of work. Both arguments allow us to explain why children exhibit a negative impact on female work participation, an effect which is actually found in all the studies listed in Table 6.15 for married women. In this context it is interesting to note that S. Gustafsson (1992*a*) finds that the child effects are strongly negative for German female labour supply, whereas they have no effects for Swedish women. This can be seen as a support of the hypothesis that the number of children in the German labour-supply equation operates as a proxy for the restrictions in the child care system which are not present in the Swedish kindergarten system.

However, the total number of children has no effect on the labour supply of males in Stobernack (1991), and a positive and significant effect on the hours supplied by married men in Kaiser *et al.* (1992). The positive effect can be explained by a larger work motivation of married men with children, as is suggested in the economics of the family literature (see e.g. Cramer 1980; Kenny 1983). Additionally, it is more efficient for the husband to specialize in market work. Of course, these effects are conditional on the child benefit and child care system within the environment in which the couple is working. Public interventions to subsidize home production and child care by the mother, or to provide alternatives to combine work in the labour market and at home, are potentially powerful instruments to influence family labour supply. It is also obvious from the analysis of family policy in Sections 6.3.3–.5 that the low female labour force participation is likely to be caused, at least in part, by the specific structure of German family policy. Direct evidence is lacking, but the comparatively small simulated effects of the abolition of split taxation on female labour supply in Strøm and Wagenhals (1991), already discussed in Section 6.4.3, points in this direction.

Empirical studies analysing the impact of child care subsidies, which in general lower the price of market child care and/or lead to a larger supply of care or quality improvements, are rare for Germany. Merkle (1993), which is the only study available, analyses the effect of changes in the price of child care and the availability of care on labour force participation of women with at least one preschooler, using data from the 1987 wave of the SOEP and from the German Statistical Office. The results of the estimation of a bivariate Probit model, which explains the probabilities of labour force participation and child care use simultaneously, show that lowering the price of child care or providing more kindergarten spaces has no significant effect on the labour force participation of a mother with at least one child of age 3–6, but would increase the use of kindergarten care in general. There exists also no significant relationship between the probability of using child care and the probability of participating in the labour market. In Germany, housewives use kindergarten care almost as often as employed women. Additionally, multinominal Logit estimates analysing the probabilities of various alternative states show that neither the price nor the availability of child care influences a mother's decision between part-time and full-time employment.

Considering the characteristics of the day care system in Germany and taking data limitations into account, these results are not surprising. The monthly price of day care in Germany is in general sufficiently low to represent no constraint on employment, and its variance is relatively small (in the data set as well as in reality). The variable which describes child care availability measures (owing to data limitations) the supply of kindergarten spaces within geographical regions without differentiating between full-time and part-time care. Most kindergartens offer, as indicated above, only part-time care (four hours in the morning or four hours in the afternoon), and a larger supply of day care means primarily a better availability of part-time places. Even if part-time child care is readily available, the time provided is very often far too short to allow a mother who has no further (informal) child care alternatives available to participate in the labour market. Therefore, child care subsidies which leave the structure of the day care system in Germany unchanged have no effect on mothers' labour supply.

The whole debate on work incentives may be a misallocation of resources if quantity of work is rather inflexible. It probably is. In this case, it would be more important to study the effects of incentives on work quality. However, this is difficult to evaluate empirically, since there are normally no good data available, if there are data at all. A possibility is to analyse subjective data given by the individuals themselves about the demanded job characteristics, work preferences, and motivation. Zimmermann and Schmidt (1986) have undertaken a Probit analysis of such data for West Germany. Their results suggest that the size of net income has no effect on work preferences, but a negative and statistically significant effect on the the self-evaluated importance of earning a high income. However, there is a positive and significant impact of the size of earned net income on the individual demand for independent work.

6.5.2. Unemployment and Labour Mobility

One way to mobilize the economy is to reduce disincentive effects caused by the tax and benefit system. This might be a particular problem in Germany, whose labour force will age considerably over the next thirty years. This may induce an increase in the frequency of unemployment, and a decrease in the job mobility which is so important in a market system. In such a framework, an immigration policy might be a way to induce competition and to create a flexibility reserve. The paper by Winkelmann and Zimmermann (1993) investigates this issue by studying the frequency of direct job changes and the frequency of unemployment spells for natives and foreigners in West Germany during the ten-year period 1974–84, using a count data approach and the SOEP. The estimates are then applied to evaluate the effects in several simulations: What is the age-mobility profile? How is it affected by migration? What are the potential effects of labour force ageing as it is predicted for Germany and Europe up to the beginning of the next century?

The empirical evidence shows that foreign labour is more ready to change jobs on average, but that these workers are also more frequently unemployed, especially in the older ages. Robust Poisson estimates that deal with the count data properly indicate that there is a U-shaped relationship between age and frequency of unemployment for both German and foreign workers, but that foreigners have lower unemployment risks in the early stages of their work career and higher risks in the later stages of their work career. Direct job changes for natives decline with age, and with duration of stay in Germany for foreigners. The share of foreign labour significantly affects only unemployment, whereas the likely increase can be substantial. Simulations with the predicted age structures for Germany and the European Community (EC) from 1995 to 2020 show that the age structure induces first a decrease and then an increase of both measures of labour mobility (unemployment, frequency of direct job changes), but the structure of the EC leads to a flatter development than that of Germany.

Unemployment variables may have an effect on individual labour supply. For instance, regional unemployment may just proxy the unobserved rationing of the individual. It is, therefore, interesting to note that in Stobernack (1991) regional unemployment remains relevant even within a framework that accounts for possible individual rationing. Whereas the estimate is insignificant for the male sample, the effect parameter is significantly positive for females and for the subsample of single females. Stobernack argues that this is caused by the fact that females are the second earners in the family; but this explanation is not consistent with the observation that the coefficient for even single women has a much larger size. (There is actually no evidence in the paper that shows that *married* women have a coefficient of the same size.) Perhaps women are just more risk-averse than men, and work harder if they observe unemployment around them.

As already mentioned in Section 6.5.1, the receipt of unemployment benefits in one year shows a negative impact on the labour supply of married women (and no effect for single women) in Merz (1990), but only positive effects for males, females, and single females in Stobernack (1991). Since unemployment risks are correlated across time, it seems that the negative association between labour supply and past unemployment benefit is driven by this correlation. Excluding cases where the individual is constrained in the period investigated may provide a basis on which to test the relevant hypothesis whether unemployment benefits are causing unemployment or a smaller work effort as it is postulated in search theory. Stobernack (1991) concludes that his estimates reject this hypothesis. A more detailed elaboration of this result can be found in Stobernack (1990), where a comparison is also made with the USA. Using the Panel Study of Income Dynamics data, Stobernack also receives a positive effect of unemployment compensation on labour supply.

A similar conclusion to Stobernack (1990; 1991) was reached by Hujer and Schneider (1989), who examined duration models to measure the transition of men from unemployment to employment. They find that the transition rate of persons eligible for unemployment insurance does not differ from that of other persons. Furthermore, the transition rate of persons receiving unemployment assistance is lower than that of other persons and statistically significant. These results were further confirmed for by H. Schneider (1990) in a more detailed analysis. Contradictory evidence was given by Franz (1991: 219), who showed that those unemployed who are entitled to receive unemployment benefits have a higher reservation wage. However, the estimated coefficient is small and only marginally significant. In sum, there is not much evidence that would confirm the hypothesis that the German system of unemployment compensation causes unemployment by creating disincentives to work.

6.6. TAX AVOIDANCE: THE SHADOW ECONOMY

Disincentives of taxes and benefits may also result in an increase of the shadow economy. Several studies in the last decade have estimated the size and the development of the shadow economy in West Germany, including Frey *et al.* (1982), Kirchgässner (1983; 1984), and Langfeldt (1984). The approaches summarized here operate mainly in a macroeconomic framework. This seems useful, since one wants to study the evolution of the shadow economy over time.

By its very nature, the shadow economy is a 'latent' variable for the researcher. A measure of the shadow economy is considered to inform about 'that part of economic activity which contributes to value added and which should be included in national income according to national accounting conventions, but which is presently not registered by the societal measurement agencies' (Frey *et al.* 1982: 499). This excludes various unmeasured activities such as home production (see further Kirchgassner 1983; 1984 and Frey *et al.* 1982). Whether the definition mentioned above is useful is debatable. Mogensen (1992: 177) for instance, 'concentrated on the informal markets for goods and services, excluding illegal activities. The basic subject of the studies therefore are productive activities that should be included in the Gross National Product (GNP) but are usually left out because the activities are not statistically tracked or available to the tax or customs authorities.'

The basic attempt is to find a framework in which the size of the shadow economy can be measured. A direct method consists of voluntary surveys of individuals (see e.g. Mogensen 1992). However, it is rather difficult to evaluate to what extent illegal activities are covered. It is also difficult to provide estimates about the development of the hidden activities over time. Therefore, estimates are often based on macro-economic indicators such as (i) the discrepancy between income and expenditure, (ii) the development of labour force participation rates, (iii) the size of currency demand, and (iv) the relation between the volume of transactions and the national income.

Kirchgässner (1984) provides a complete set of estimates for West Germany for 1960–80 on a yearly basis, using four types of approach: (i) the Tanzi method of estimating a money demand function using the ratio between the currency and the quantity of money M2 as a dependent variable, and using the marginal tax rate of the average earner, income, and interest rates among others as regressors, (ii) the Klovland method, using real currency demand as a dependent variable instead of the currency/money ratio in (i), (iii) the transaction cost approach of Feige, which elaborates around the size of the transactions in the economy following the quantity theory of money, and (iv) the model approach, where the size of the shadow economy is an explicit function of its determining variables. Methods (i)–(iii) then derive the size of the shadow economy by assuming that the income velocity of money is the same in the official economy as in the shadow sector.

Kirchgässner (1984) argues that the transaction approach, although theoretically appealing, suffers from measurement problems. Similarly, the model approach requires the availablity of a data set for all relevant determinants. The estimates provide the following picture for the size of the shadow economy as a percentage of the official GNP, measured in 1970 prices:

1960: (i) 2.0, (ii) 2.1, (iii) 1.0, (iv) 1.6;
1970: (i) 3.1, (ii) 2.7, (iii) 16.0, (iv) 5.8;

1980: (i) 10.3, (ii) 11.2, (iii) 27.3, (iv) 8.0.

The dramatic increase of measure (iii), which was also observed in other countries, supports the doubts about the reliability of this approach. The model approach predicts a more conservative increase, perhaps because not all relevant variables were actually included. Kirchgässner concludes that, in 1980, the size of the shadow economy was about 8–12% in West Germany. It is interesting to note that the substantial increase according to methods (i) and (ii) took place in the 1970s when marginal tax rates were increased substantially by the social–liberal government. It would be of much interest to know whether the increase of the shadow economy came to a halt or even a decline in recent years, when the conservative–liberal government reduced marginal tax rates in the 1980s. However, it is still too early to carry out this analysis, since most measures of tax reforms are only in effect for a short period. Also, social-security contributions are rising. Further, there is evidence that more German currency has been hoarded outside the country since the political changes in East Europe. This suggests that the currency approach to measuring the shadow economy has become more problematic.

The sizes of the shadow economy discussed here are similar to the findings in other countries around 1980: 5–10% in Austria and about 5% in Switzerland (see Weck-Hannemann *et al.* 1989) and 8–13% in Denmark, 6–16% in Norway, and about 7–17% in Sweden (see F. Schneider 1986). The survey approach to the measurement of the shadow economy has resulted in much smaller numbers. For instance, Mogensen (1992) estimates the size of shadow economy in Denmark in 1986 at about 3.9% and the total non-declared sector at about 5.5%. (A more detailed analysis of the Danish shadow economy is given in Chapter 7.) The survey approach may suffer from a tendency towards under-reporting. More 'objective' approaches based on measures of money demand are, however, not superior since even monetary economists hardly have a clear and stable view what money is and how it can be measured.

6.7. ADJUSTMENTS IN THE EAST GERMAN LABOUR MARKET

6.7.1. Monitoring Change

Transformation in East Germany can be seen as a case study of how the exposure to a completely new incentive structure affects behaviour. Here it is of particular interest how female labour supply responds to the changes in the child care system and the tax and benefit structure. Table

6.7 demonstrates that in both parts of the country, female unemployment is higher than the male counterpart. However, the gender difference is rising for the East. Lately, female unemployment rate was about 20%, twice as much as male unemployment. Why?

TABLE 6.16. Age-Specific Labour Force Participation Rates, GDR and FRG, 1988 (%)[a]

Age group	GDR			FRG		
	Male	Female	Total	Male	Female	Total
15–25	62.2	62.9	62.5	65.8	59.7	62.8
25–35	81.5	84.7	83.1	91.4	65.2	78.6
35–45	88.8	90.8	89.8	97.4	63.9	81.0
45–55	88.0	84.4	86.2	94.9	57.4	76.4
55–60	87.6	74.9	81.0	79.8	41.1	60.4
60–5	80.0	28.7	49.6	34.5	11.1	21.4
15–65	80.4	75.7	78.1	82.5	55.0	68.8

[a] GDR: employment shares; FRG: participation rates.

Source: Lippe (1992).

One of the few marked differences on the labour market between the former GDR and the FRG has been the labour force participation rates of males and females. Although increasing over time, female participation was substantially lower in the West than male participation, whereas the gender differences were marginal in the former GDR. As Table 6.16 shows, male labour force participation in the GDR was 80.4% for age groups 15–65 in 1988 and 75.7% for females. The same numbers for the former FRG were 82.5% and 55.0% respectively. Whereas the age-specific pattern of female participation in the FRG follows the family life-cycle and male participation is substantially declining after age 45, female participation in the East was even higher than for males in younger age groups, but lower in higher age cohorts. This indicates a substantial need for adjustment during unification. It is unlikely that these differences will have a chance of persisting in the labour market. If adjustments are indeed in order, female participation has to decline and male participation has to rise in the East.

Table 6.16 also indicates that the overall participation in the East was much higher (78.1%) than in the West (68.8%). The communist system had created a large amount of hidden unemployment, and a reduction of the employment level in the East to Western standards seems unavoidable. Unemployment or a loss of jobs due to this adjustment process have to be evaluated differently than losses of employment below the Western standard. From a political point of view, it seems 'fair' to stabilize the Eastern employment level only around these standards. How is Germany doing here? Is unemployment really as severe as outlined above, and really as unexpected? Some simple calculations provide us with a quite surprising answer: the overall employment ratio in the East is still above the Western standard.

How can this be? For this analysis, the current relative size of gainfully employed persons in the East is compared with the levels that must be achieved if one is to reach the Western standards. To avoid confusion, measures of the gainfully employed persons are used and not the labour force statistic, which also includes the unemployed. Actually, it is only of interest to what extent potential labour is needed. The *Arbeitsmarkt-Monitor für die neuen Bundesländer* (Bielenski *et al.* 1992: 97), an important micro-survey of labour market adjustments in East Germany, reports that in November 1991 population size in the working age group (15–65) was 10.527 million and gainful employment was 7.271 million, 3.204 million of them females. (Note that the 7.2 million are consistent with Table 6.7, if one adds 0.5 million commuters.)

Applying a female share of population size in East Germany of 50.1%, the 'effective' employment rates were 60.8% for females, 77.1% for males, and 69.1% for both groups combined. Referring to Table 6.16, this is substantially smaller only for females than in 1988, where the rate was 75.7%. The current male rate is not much below the 80.4% reported there. The corresponding employment rates in April 1990 for West Germany were 53.8% for females and 78.5% for males (my calculations on the basis of microcensus data reported in the *Statistisches Jahrbuch 1992 für die Bundesrepublik Deutschland*). An application of these numbers results in an overall 'normal' employment rate for East Germany in November 1991 of 66.1%. This rate is still 3 percentage points lower than the effective current rate, though the effective male rate (77.1%) is slightly lower than the normal (78.1%). The reason is that the effective female rate (60.8%) is still somewhat higher than the normal rate (53.8%). Nevertheless, a considerable adjustment process has already taken place. Even more, a further reduction of employment has to be expected.

As we know from Table 6.6, a substantial part of employment in the East is caused by active labour market policy. What remains if one makes this comparable to the West? To analyse this, domestic employment levels given in Table 6.7 are studied. Among the 6.3 million employed persons in the East at the end of 1992, the full-time equivalent of short-time work was 110,000, employment creation programme (ABM) 366,000, and further education 493,000. This roughly amounts to 0.97 million. About 300,000 jobs will have to be lost to adjust to the West German employment structure. Adjusting for this buffer leaves 670,000, or about 11% of East German employment. A corresponding number for West German employment can be derived (*Amtliche Nachrichten der Bundesanstalt für Arbeit, 4/1993*): At the end of 1992, in West Germany, the full-time equivalent of short-time work was about 243,000, 68,000 were in ABM, and 397,000 in further education. This results in 708,000, or about 2.4% of West German gainful employment of 29.6 million. 8% or about 0.5 million workers are currently not effectively employed in the East if one accounts for the need for structural adjustment to the current standards in the West.

TABLE 6.17. Domestic Employment Shares (%) in Sectors, East/West[a]

	1990		1991		1992	
	East	West	East	West	East	West
Agriculture, forestry and fishing	9.1	3.5	6.7	3.3	5.0	3.1
Producing sector	44.9	39.7	42.8	39.3	36.6	38.4
Trade and transportation	16.9	18.7	18.1	19.0	20.7	19.2
Services and public sector	29.1	38.1	32.4	38.4	37.7	39.2

[a] Gainfully employed persons. East: excluding employment creation programme (ABM).

Source: Statistisches Bundesamt, Fachserie 18, Reihe 1.2, 1992.

Table 6.17 investigates how the employment structure across sectors in the economy is developing between East and West. In 1990, there were some marked differences between the large aggregates (i) agriculture, forestry and fishing, (ii) the producing sector, (iii) trade and transportation, and (iv) services and the public sector. The first two were larger, the other two smaller in East Germany than in the West. Table 6.17 indicates that this adjustment process has already largely taken place. Of course, this refers to the employment structure, not to the modernization of the enterprises behind it.

The analysis above indicates that women in East Germany withdraw from the labour force; in that they adjust to West German standards. However, this is not associated with an increase in fertility. In contrast, fertility declines sharply. Fig. 6.4 shows the development of total fertility in East and West Germany since 1950. (The numbers are estimated for West Germany in 1991–2 and in 1990–2 for East Germany.) The picture clearly demonstrates that fertility was largely moving in parallel until the early 1970s. Then the East German government began active population policy measures to stabilize fertility, with some success. The uncertain economic future in East Germany together with the change in the child care system, as well as newly developed consumption preferences, are likely to be responsible for the rapid decline in fertility after unification, although female work participation has also declined.

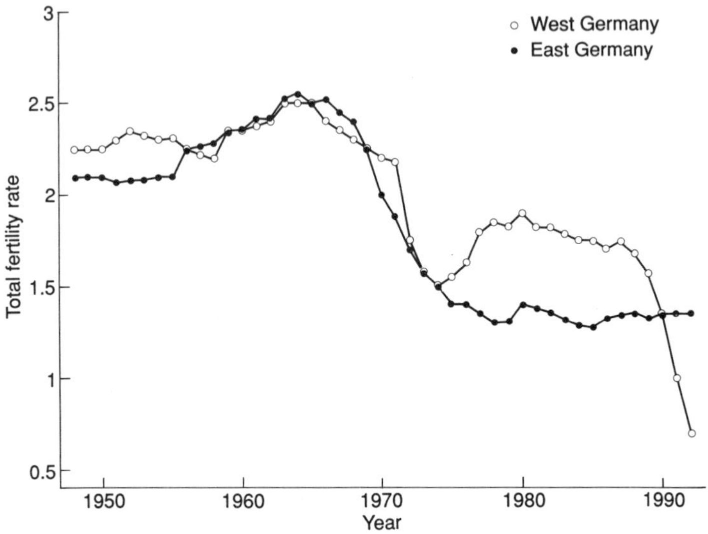

FIG 6.4. East/West Total Fertility Rates
Source: BIB-aktuell, 1/93.

6.7.2. Empirical Studies

Since only a brief period has passed since unification, there are only a few empirical studies available that examine the adjustment process in the East German labour market. However, the transformation process is of great interest, because East Germans now operate under a completely different set of incentives. The problem is that these effects are interacting with the disequilibrium evidenced by the large effective unemployment rates which were calculated in Section 6.2.2.

All studies available use the SOEP. Lechner and Pfeiffer (1992) examine the plans for self-employment at the beginning of the market economy, using data of the first wave of the SOEP in East Germany in 1990. 8.3% of the workers in the sample planned self-employment within the next two years in 1990, just before unification. Young, highly educated males were more ready to engage in entrepreneurship. Professional degrees were found not to be important, with the exception of the master's degree. In the view of the authors this confirms that the 'Craft Regulation Act' exhibits already an institutional entry barrier in the crafts sector, because individuals without this qualification are not allowed to become self-employed in this sector. They conclude that there are welfare losses due to the existence of this government regulation. They also find that the threat of unemployment is not a relevant cause of self-employment plans. Preliminary investigations with the second wave of the SOEP from 1991 indicate that plans are actually put into practice to some extent.

Krueger and Pischke (1992) find the wage distribution much more compressed in East than in West Germany. They use data from the 1988 survey of blue- and white-collar households in East Germany and from the SOEP East and SOEP West. Like Schwarze (1992) and Geib *et al.* (1992), who also used SOEP data, they find similar earnings–human capital patterns in the East as in the West before unification. Schwarze (1992) found a somewhat steeper earnings profile depending on years of work experience in the West than in the East. If normalized by average earnings in the respective part of Germany, the time-paths of earnings cross at seventeen years of work experience. However, all findings also show that human capital was largely devaluated after unification. Those individuals who migrated to the West are shown to earn returns on their educational degrees comparable to native Westerners. Most authors conclude that the wage structure imposed by the unions and government policies to stabilize employment of low-qualified workers have hindered the necessary adjustment processes in the East.

6.8. CONCLUSIONS

Do taxes and incentives matter in Germany? Only partly so. Estimates of labour-supply functions show that male labour supply is not very responsive to wage and income changes. This is important, since the German labour market is still dominated by male labour force participation. Female labour supply is more flexible, but less than expected by the proponents of the second-generation labour-supply approach. Female labour supply reacts positively to changes of wages, and both genders exhibit a negative income effect. Simulation studies that removed the system of split taxation demonstrate that female work participation would be significantly higher within a system of separate taxation. This confirms the view of many analysts that the German tax system is designed to encourage females to engage in home production and family formation. Some studies of recent tax reforms have concluded that the reduction of marginal tax rates actually has significant welfare gains.

This negative effect of the split-taxation system is reinforced by the provision of child tax allowances, which play an important role in today's German family policy. Family benefits in general have a disincentive potential for lower-income groups. It is also shown that benefits in general exhibit a negative effect on work participation. However, no convincing evidence was found for the proposition that unemployment compensation increases further unemployment.

It has further been argued that lack of data makes it difficult to analyse the effects of incentives on work effort, motivation, and labour mobility, although these issues are probably more important than the supply of work quantity. Some analyses of subjective measures, however, exhibit no relevant influence of income variables. A different way of studying disincentive effects is to measure the size and development of the shadow economy. It has been shown that the underground economy grew considerably between 1970 and 1980, a period in which the marginal tax rates were increased significantly. German unification offers a case study of how fast individuals are adjusting to significant changes in the incentive structure. Preliminary evidence shows that the adjustment process is significant, although not as strong as one would expect from traditional theories.

In sum, incentives matter. However, the disincentive effects of benefits and taxation are not strong enough to justify large revisions of the welfare state. The equity–efficiency trade-off has to be carefully examined.

7

The Welfare State and Taxation in Denmark

PEDER J. PEDERSEN

7.1. INTRODUCTION

One of the spectacular facts in relation to the development of the welfare state in Denmark is the extraordinary speed of the transformation that has taken place in Danish society during the latest decades. In 1950, Denmark next to Switzerland was the OECD country with the smallest share of the labour force employed in the public sector. Thirty years later, around 1980, the public-sector employment share in Denmark was surpassed only in Sweden, by a small margin. During the same period cash transfer programmes expanded greatly. The speed of the transformation process is even more spectacular as the major part of the expansion of the welfare state took place in only about fifteen years from the beginning of the 1960s to the second half of the 1970s. At the beginning of the 1960s, total taxes relative to GNP stood at about 25%. By the second half of the 1970s the relative level of taxation had risen to about 45%. The increase continued, but much more slowly, until a maximum of 52% in 1988. Since then, taxes relative to GNP have decreased slightly, to a level currently just below 50%.

A profound change in society raises many questions in relation both to the driving forces behind the change and to the impact of a transformation of this kind. In the present context the main interest lies in the derived effects on the incentives to work from the big changes in the level and structure of taxes and benefits.

In the field of both taxes and benefits, the structures developed in Denmark differ from those found in most other OECD countries. The level of taxes does not differ significantly from a number of other OECD countries. The structure of taxes, on the other hand, differs very much, by the great emphasis on the personal income tax and the near-absence of labour market contributions. The lowest marginal income tax rate in 1991 was 52% and the top level was 68%. Indirect taxes, both the VAT at 25% and specific taxes, are also high by international standards. The benefit system, too, has a number of characteristics different from most other OECD countries. As in Sweden, but different from most other countries, unemployment insurance is run by unions, with the residual financial burden carried by the state. Benefits are not means-tested and the maximum duration of benefits is very long by international standards.

The other programmes for income transfers cover a broad field, to be discussed in more detail below. Benefits from some of the programmes are means-tested against individual or family income, while others are extended independently of income from other sources. The same applies in relation to taxation, where benefits from some of the programmes are taxable income, while others are exempt from taxation.

Two main features of the Danish benefit system should be emphasized here. One is the universal principle already adopted at the turn of the century. Except for unemployment insurance, the dominant part of the benefit system is independent of individual labour market status and experience, with eligibility being dependent on citizenship and the specific criteria for a given programme. The other main feature is related to the combination for some of the programmes of the consequences of means-testing and the very high marginal rates of income tax mentioned above. The result of this interaction is that high composite tax rates, creating poverty or unemployment traps, become an important problem.

Section 7.2 gives a short summary of Danish macroeconomic performance. The major problem in this area has been to establish acceptable levels at the same time for unemployment and for the current account of the balance of payments. Priorities in economic policy have shifted during recent decades, but the trade-off does not seem to have improved in a significant way. Section 7.3 supplements the comparative presentation in Section 1.3 of some main trends in the labour market. A main feature of the Danish labour market is a high labour force participation rate, for both women and men, at the same level as in the other Nordic countries, and a rate of unemployment comparable to the level in the other EC countries. Along with Sweden, Denmark has one of the highest participation rates for married women (cf. Chapter 1). Part of the strong public-sector expansion is a reflection of this fact.

Sections 7.4 and 7.5 present some of the main characteristics respectively of the tax and the benefit systems. In relation to taxes, special emphasis will be given to the personal income tax being the major source of revenues. Also, the very high rates of taxation, relative to other countries and effective already from a rather low level of income, makes the personal income tax especially relevant to the incentive issue considered here. Besides the description of the current structure and working of personal income tax, Section 7.4 contains a short description of major changes in the income tax through time and a short description of the other elements in the Danish tax structure. Section 7.5 describes the specific benefit programmes directed to people below the normal retirement age. Emphasis is given to unemployment insurance and to means-tested public-transfer programmes, such as welfare benefits, some of the benefit programmes for families with dependent children, housing benefits, early-retirement programmes, and subsidized day care for children with means-tested payment from parents.

7.2. ECONOMIC BACKGROUND

Around 1960 the Danish economy experienced a short spell of overall macroeconomic balance: the rate of inflation was low, rapidly expanding employment had reduced unemployment to a low level, and the current account was in balance. The following thirty years have been characterized by an overall macroeconomic imbalance, consisting of either a deficit on the current account, fairly high unemployment, or both of these problems at the same time. It is obviously difficult to assess the magnitude of the combined macroeconomic problem of imbalance. In recent reports, the Danish Council of Economic Advisers concludes that the combined disequilibrium problem has not been reduced in spite of a high balance-of-payments surplus and a very low rate of inflation in the most recent years. The costs of these achievements have been an increase in unemployment to the highest level in the post-war period, during six years of low or no economic growth from 1987 to 1993.

During the fifteen years from around 1960 to the first oil price shock in 1974, unemployment in Denmark was low and the current account showed persistent deficits. Public-sector employment grew rapidly, as did employment in non-traded industries like building and construction. As a consequence, inflation accelerated throughout this period. The first oil price shock had severe impacts on the Danish economy, at that time nearly fully dependent on imported fuels. Unemployment rose dramatically, which was due not only to the negative supply shock but also to the way in which the shock was absorbed in the domestic economy. The growing imbalances throughout the preceding years restricted policy options. Besides, the parliamentary situation was in some turmoil after a general election in 1973, resulting in a major break-up of established patterns in Parliament. One third of the seats went to completely new parties, of which the biggest was a tax protest party. The immediate impact of the increase in oil prices was reinforced by an automatic indexation of wages, with a short lag and a high coverage. This came on top of the lagged effects from excess demand in the labour market in 1973. Overall, the result was an increase in hourly wages of nearly 40% from 1973 to 1975. At the same time, Danish currency alignment with the German mark in the years 1972–7 during the so-called 'Currency Snake Arrangement' resulted in an 8% appreciation. The combined effect of these negative factors, on top of a gradual weakening of the competitive position of the Danish economy in the preceding fifteen years, was an exceptionally strong increase in unemployment in 1974–5.

Unemployment kept on rising slowly in the years between the two oil price shocks. Public-sector employment continued to expand while private-sector employment contracted. At the same time the years from the mid-1970s to the beginning of the 1980s saw the highest rate of increase in the labour force ever recorded in the Danish labour market, as female participation in the labour force increased rapidly. Fiscal policy was designed to 'twist' demand from employment-extensive, import-intensive components to employment-intensive and import-extensive components. Eventually, this 'twist' strategy broke down, and the second negative supply shock in 1979–80 resulted in a new strong increase in unemployment.

In 1982 a conservative–liberal government came into office announcing a major change in economic policy. A fixed exchange rate policy in relation to the German mark and an end to public-sector expansion were among the main priorities. The first has until now succeeded, while the other was modified to a significantly slower public-sector growth compared to the preceding years.

From 1982 to the beginning of the 1990s the Danish economy has moved countercyclically in relation to the other EC countries. From 1982 to 1987 private-sector employment expanded more strongly than ever before recorded in the Danish labour market and unemployment fell fairly rapidly. But, as the expansion took place primarily in the sheltered sectors of the economy, the balance of payments deteriorated to the point of a record deficit of about 4% of GNP in 1986. The years 1986–7 became a cyclical turning-point, from which time unemployment has been increasing again in contrast to the falling trend in EC unemployment, at least until 1991. This new strong increase in unemployment was once again the result of different factors reinforcing each other. First, fiscal policy was tightened through a reform of the personal income tax, described in more detail in Section 7.4. Second, the extremely strong growth in employment up to 1986 induced wage increases in the collective agreements of 1987 that were completely out of line with the fixed exchange rate policy. The combined impact was a sequel of years with low or no economic growth, stagnating employment, and rapidly increasing unemployment.

Throughout the period of rising unemployment, two main topics in the debate on economic policy have been the importance of the international competitive position and the inadequate adaptation to shocks in the labour market. The importance of the first of these topics in a small open economy is illustrated in Figs. 7.1 and 7.2. Years with Danish inflation above the OECD average correlate nearly perfectly with years with Danish unemployment below the OECD average and vice versa.

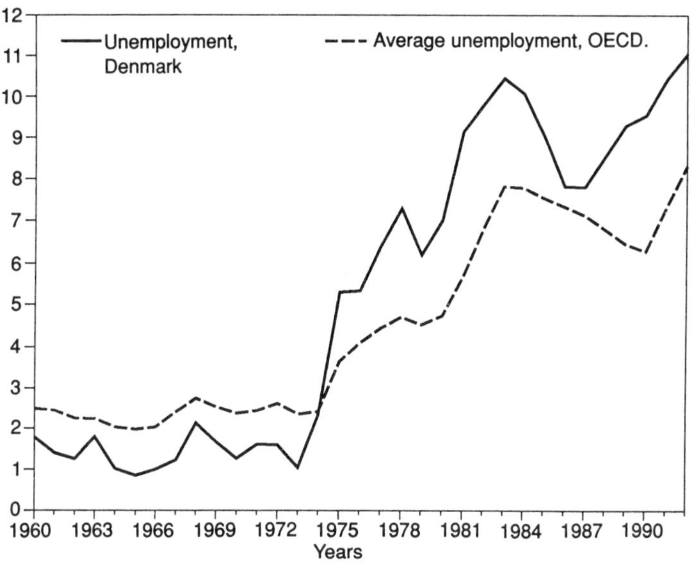

FIG 7.1. Rate of Unemployment in Denmark and Average Rate of Unemployment in the OECD Countries, 1960–1992
Source: OECD (1992).

The second point, concerning the functioning of the labour market, is related to the first. A more flexible labour market would reduce the need of high unemployment as an instrument for disinflation relative to other countries. At the same time the functioning of the labour market is influenced by incentives in relation to both taxes and benefits, being the main topic in the present context. The specific topics in the Danish debate have been the same as in other OECD countries, i.e. the impact of high tax rates and a comprehensive benefit system on the decision to enter or leave the labour market, on hours supplied dependent on participation, and on the incentives to supply labour in the 'shadow' economy. The specific characteristics of the Danish situation are the combination of high tax rates even at low levels of income, a high degree of compensation in the benefit systems for people with low potential incomes from a job, and long maximum duration of benefits. High tax rates create a dilemma in relation to means-tested benefits. If benefits are reduced quickly when income exceeds a given level, the result inevitably is very high composite tax rates over certain intervals, with corresponding negative incentive effects. If, to avoid this problem, benefit reduction is stretched out over a wide range of income, total expenditure on the

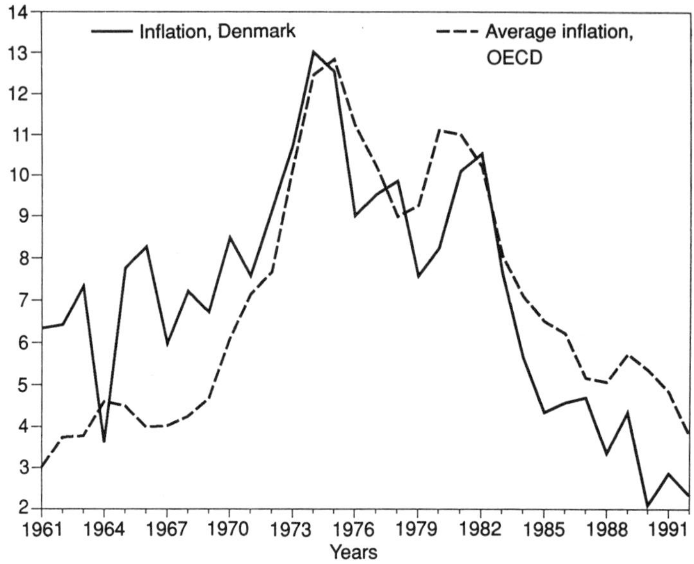

FIG 7.2. Rate of Inflation in Denmark and Average Rate of Inflation in the OECD Countries, 1961–1992
Source: OECD (1992).

programme goes up, taxes must be increased, and negative incentives become stronger in relation to taxes.

Against the background of persistent economic imbalance and with potentially strong negative incentives from the tax and benefit system, research on the effects of incentives to work in the Danish economy is an important topic. Regrettably, few microeconometric studies are available with Danish data. Besides, a number of analyses apply alternative tax and benefit rules to representative samples in order to study changes in potential incentives to work. As behavioural responses are not introduced in these analyses, their main purpose is to identify areas where incentive problems are especially important, to determine the number of households affected by high composite tax rates, etc. Finally, a number of empirical studies are available on the extent and development of the shadow economy. The available Danish empirical evidence is surveyed in Section 7.6.

7.3. TRENDS IN THE LABOUR MARKET

The unemployment profile in Denmark was introduced in the previous section as an important element in the general economic background.

Table 1.1 in the introductory chapter showed some key factors of the Danish labour market compared to the other countries in the present survey. In this section we present a somewhat broader picture of some main trends in the Danish labour market. The impact from tax and benefit incentives is expected to differ quite significantly for different aspects of labour supply, i.e. the decision to enter or leave the labour market and the supply of hours given participation. Institutional restrictions on the number of weekly hours could imply that incentives are especially important in relation to the choice of part-time or full-time employment. The entry or exit decision is especially relevant in relation to tax and benefit incentives for married women and for older men. Further, incentives are relevant in relation to working overtime or having extra jobs, both of which have increased during the 1980s.

Fig. 7.3. shows the employment frequency along with the overall participation rate for the population between 15 and 64 years of age. The employment rate is untrended, while participation goes up strongly from the mid-1970s to the mid-1980s. The untrended employment rate is the net outcome of a decreasing share of employment in the private sector and a strong increase in the public sector. The increase in the overall participation rate is a reflection of the strongly increasing participation by women shown in Fig. 7.4. During the period reviewed in Figs. 7.3 and 7.4, female participation increased to nearly the same level as for men. At the same time, the overall participation rate for men has been affected by a steady decline for men in the age group 55–64 shown in Fig. 7.5. The participation among men 60 years and older was especially affected by a labour-market-related early-retirement scheme, introduced in 1979, to which we return below. The increased female participation initially led to an increase in the frequency of part-time jobs shown in Fig. 7.6. From around 1980 the frequency has decreased as cohorts of young women increasingly enter the labour market in full-time jobs which are kept also after childbirth. Finally, Fig. 7.7 shows average annual working hours from 1960 to 1991. It is interesting to note that the major decrease occurs in the full employment years before 1974. The overall decrease is so big that it more than outweighs the increase in employment throughout the period. The net effect is a decrease in the total number of hours worked of about 10% from 1960 to 1991.

One could conclude from the trends illustrated in this section, compared with the unemployment profile in Fig. 7.1, that rationing has become such a dominant situation in the labour market that the discussion below of negative incentives in relation to taxes and benefits is less relevant in the present situation of high and increasing unemployment. But the main importance of potentially negative incentives from taxes and

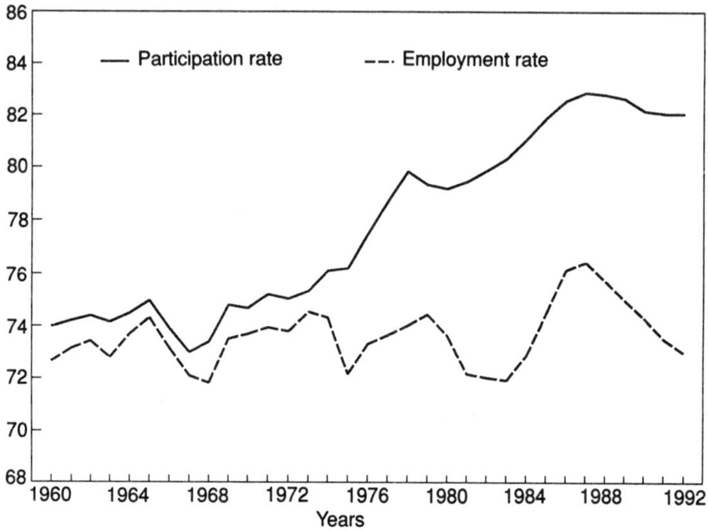

FIG 7.3. Participation and Employment Rate, Denmark, Population Aged 15–64, 1960–1992
Source: OECD (1992).

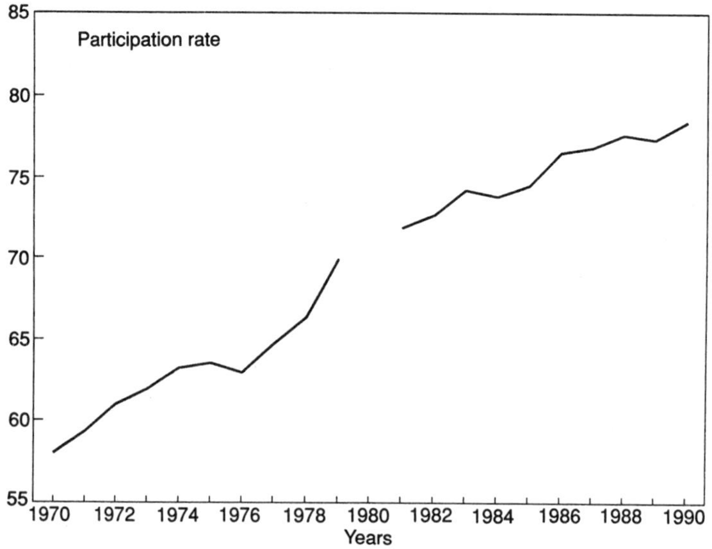

FIG 7.4. Participation Rate for Women Aged 15–64, 1970–1990
Source: OECD (1992).

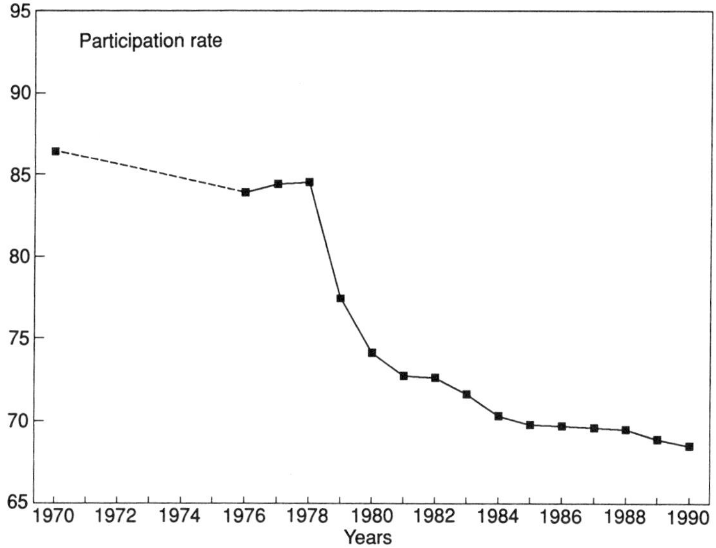

FIG 7.5. Participation Rate for Men Aged 55–64, 1970–1990
Source: Census data 1970; survey data 1976–9; register data 1980–90.

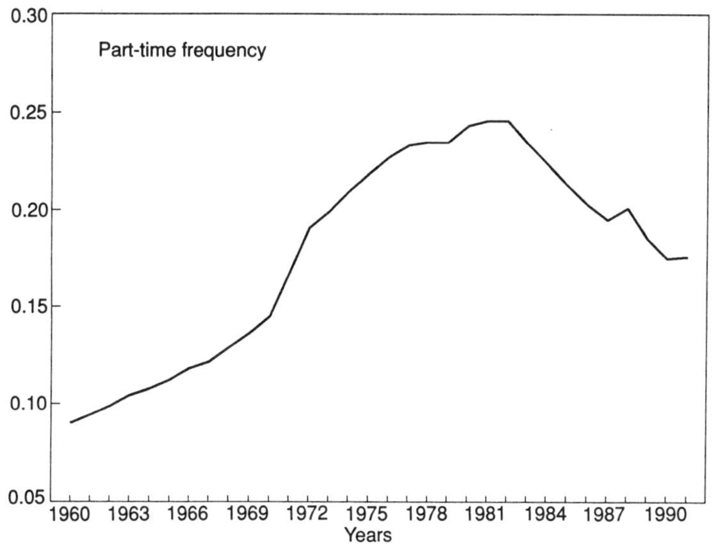

FIG 7.6. Part-Time Frequency, 1960–1991
Source: ADAM Databank.

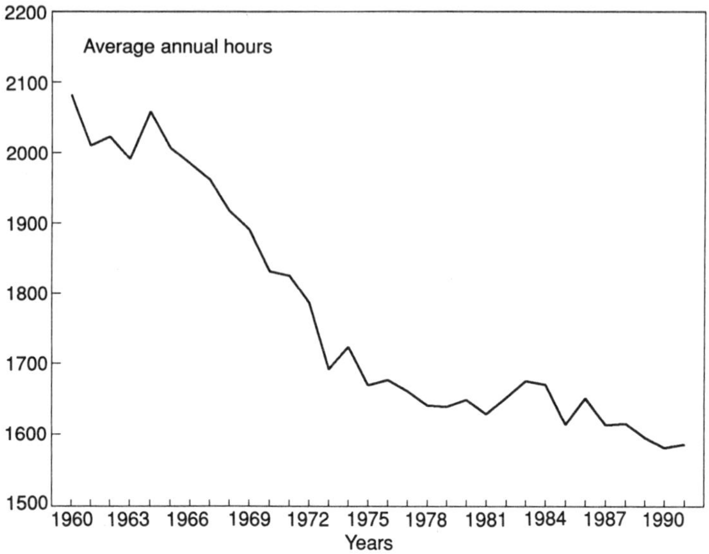

FIG 7.7. Average Annual Hours, 1960–1991
Source: ADAM Databank.

benefits is related to the impact on effective labour supply. If effective labour supply is reduced, without a reduction in NAIRU, the non-accelerating inflation rate of unemployment, the consequence is a fall in equilibrium employment. So the possible job-rationing for many groups in the labour market is not in conflict with the need to minimize negative incentives relative to the supply of labour originating in the system of taxes and benefits.

7.4. THE STRUCTURE OF THE DANISH TAX SYSTEM

The strong increase in total taxes relative to GNP since the Second World War was pointed out in Section 7.1. The development is shown in more detail in Fig. 7.8. It was further mentioned in Section 7.1 that income taxes were of greater importance in relation to revenue than in any other OECD country; see Table 7.1. The major shift during the last forty years has been a still greater emphasis on direct taxes, a corresponding decrease in the relative importance of indirect taxes, and an even stronger relative decrease in the importance of social-security contributions. Among the direct taxes, the personal income tax is completely dominating, in 1991 providing 90% of the total revenue from direct taxes. The first topic in this section is the structure and incidence of this predominant part of the overall tax structure in Denmark.

FIG 7.8. Total Taxes Relative to GNP, 1947–1991
Source: Taxes and duties, Statistics Denmark, various years.

TABLE 7.1. Relative Composition of Total Tax Revenue, Selected Years

	1950	1960	1970	1980	1991
Direct taxes	45.2	47.2	53.0	56.6	60.3
Indirect taxes	46.3	47.0	42.4	40.8	35.9
Capital taxes	0.8	0.6	0.4	0.7	0.5
Social-security contributions	5.3	4.5	3.9	1.8	3.0
Compulsory fees, fines and penalties	2.4	0.7	0.3	0.2	0.3

Source: Taxes and duties, Statstics Denmark, various years.

The major part of the revenue from personal income tax, 82%, was paid by wage- and salary-earners in 1989, the most recent year for which detailed data are available on the distribution of taxes on different groups. Pensioners paid 10% and a further 8% was paid by self-employed persons. In the following we describe that part of the personal income tax which is relevant for wage and salary earners. First, this is most relevant in the present discussion of incentives to work, where, for instance, labour supply is difficult to measure for self-employed persons. Second, rules governing income assessment, etc., for self-employed persons are much more difficult to present briefly. Finally, specific rules in the tax laws in relation to pensioners are mostly excluded in the present context, where the topic is incentives for people below the normal retirement age.

The most recent Danish tax reform with effect from 1984 has, of course, not yet been the subject of empirical research, and it has, therefore, not been included in the present analysis. The latest major changes of the personal income tax relevant to the present analysis were those, enacted with the tax reform, which became effective from 1987. Until 1987 a basic concept in the income tax law was taxable income calculated as gross income minus net capital income and other deductions. Taxes due were then calculated by applying a progressive scale to the taxable income. As a consequence of this principle, the 'tax value' of a given amount in deductions depended on the level of the taxable income. The major innovation in the 1987 reform was a break with this principle, so that the tax reduction from a given amount of negative net capital income and most other deductions became independent of the level of taxable income. The tax reduction is calculated by applying the lowest income tax rate on deductions. With given tax rates this would result in increased taxation for people with negative net capital income and a decrease in taxation if net capital income was positive. To reduce the distributional impact from this and to create incentives for higher private saving, an asymmetry was introduced by taxing positive capital income with a higher rate than the tax-reduction rate applied to negative capital income. Further, the distributional impact was affected by the introduction of an income-independent allowance paid to all families with children below the age of 18, depending on the number of children.

TABLE 7.2. Income Concepts in Relation to Personal Income Tax

Gross factor income		A
Interest income + Imputed surplus from owner-occupied dwelling		B
Returns from stocks		C
Transport to work expenditures + Contributions to unemployment insurance and unions		D
Contributions to pension schemes		E
Interest expenditures		F
Gross income	A + B + C	
Personal income	A - E	
Capital income	B - F	
Taxable income	A + B - (D + E + F)	
Stock-return income	C	

Technically, the reform introduced a number of new concepts of income in relation to taxation. Where taxes before 1987 were calculated on the basis of taxable income, they have since the reform been calculated on the basis of three different income concepts: taxable income, personal income, and capital income. The definitions underlying these income concepts are summarized in Table 7.2. The new concept 'personal income' differs from gross factor income by the contributions to a number of pension schemes. Contributions to these pension schemes are treated like all deductions before the reform: their 'tax value' is the full marginal tax rate depending on income. If they had been treated like other deductions, taxes could be calculated from gross income, and the tax reduction could be calculated with the same percentage for all applied to net deductions, i.e. D + E + F–B, conditional on (F–B) being positive.

Next, we shall describe the principles for the actual calculation of the income tax in relation to wage- and salary-earners. A progressive tax scale is applied to personal income (A–E) to calculate a gross tax amount. This gross tax is then reduced, with the tax value of deductions calculated as the product of the base rate of the tax scale and deductions consisting of net capital income, if interest expenditures are greater than interest income, different deductible expenditures (D) and a base deduction, common for all taxpayers. For 1991 the basic income tax rate was 51.9% in an average municipality. On top of this, 6% is paid on the part of personal income that exceeds 155,100 DKK and a further 12% on the part of personal income that exceeds 227,200 DKK.

A number of modifications apply to these basic principles. First, if a taxpayer has a positive net capital income this is added to personal income, and the part of the sum of these two incomes that exceeds 155,100 DKK is taxed with the basic tax rate + 6%. Another modification follows from the rule that the marginal income tax rate is maximized at 68%. Income tax is paid to the state, to counties and to municipalities. The basic tax rate to the state is 22%. With the 6% and 12% surtaxes mentioned above, the maximum marginal tax rate to the state becomes 40%. Tax rates vary between counties, and more so between municipalities. In cases where the sum of the 40% tax to the state and the tax rates to counties and municipalities exceeds the maximum of 68%, taxes due to the state are reduced by the difference between the actual combined marginal rate and 68%. The range of variation in the municipal tax rate is 10 percentage points, but the variance is fairly low. In the average municipality the 68% restriction becomes binding, as the unrestricted maximum rate is 69.9 (51.9 + 6 + 12). As a consequence of the variation in local taxes, the top marginal income tax rate lies in an interval between 63% and 68%, close to 68% in most municipalities.

The main principles in the Danish income tax system, therefore, are a progressive tax to the state and proportional taxes to counties and municipalities. The base deduction is fairly low, and the combined tax begins around 50%, rising to around 56% at a level about the average income for unskilled workers and to 68% at a level about the average income of skilled workers. With the few modifications mentioned above, deductions have a tax value of 51.9% in an average municipality, and in contrast to e.g. the UK, there is no upper limit on deductible interest expenditures. The marginal tax rates of 50, 56, and 68% are thus combined with average tax rates varying according to income and the amount of deductions. The difference between marginal tax rates and the actual average personal income tax relative to average personal incomes is illustrated in Fig. 7.9 over a range of personal incomes, which covers the major part of full-time wage- and salary-earners.

Fig. 7.9 also shows average deductions, i.e. the sum of average negative net capital income and income deductions as a ratio of personal income. It is evident that the widening gap between the marginal tax rate and the actual average income tax rate depends on average deductions rising faster than average personal income. It should be emphasized, however, that the variation in average taxes is fairly wide within each income interval, reflecting large variations in deductions. The same relationship as in Fig. 7.9 is shown in Fig. 7.10 between average personal income tax and average personal income for different socioeconomic groups.

Personal income tax, representing 52.9% of total tax revenue in 1991, is a very dominant part of total taxes in Denmark. In relation to incentives to work it is also the most relevant to study. Other parts of the tax structure are, therefore, only described briefly. Other income taxes, corresponding to 6.1% of tax revenue in 1991, are corporation tax (3.7% of revenue) and a number of capital-gains taxes (2.4%).

Taxes on wealth and real property correspond to 4.0% of revenue in 1991, composed of 0.2% from tax on wealth, 0.5% from estate duty and gift tax, 1.1% from motor vehicle weight duty, and 2.2% from taxes on real estate. The tax on wealth was 1% of taxable wealth above 1,482,100 DKK for single persons and 2,964,200 DKK for married couples in 1991. The 5% of taxpayers with the highest personal income (above 300,000 DKK in 1989) paid about 50% of the total revenue from the wealth tax. For persons with high wealth relative to income, this could create situations where total taxes, including the wealth tax, would exceed current income. To avoid this possibility there is—besides the 68% maximum rate for income tax—a 78% overall maximum including the wealth tax. If the total of income and wealth taxes exceeds 78% of taxable income, the wealth tax and after that—if necessary—the income tax to the state is reduced until the 78% limit is reached.

Indirect taxes constitute in total about one-third of the total tax revenue. As shown in Table 7.1, this share has decreased significantly during recent decades. Two-thirds of the revenue from indirect taxes are

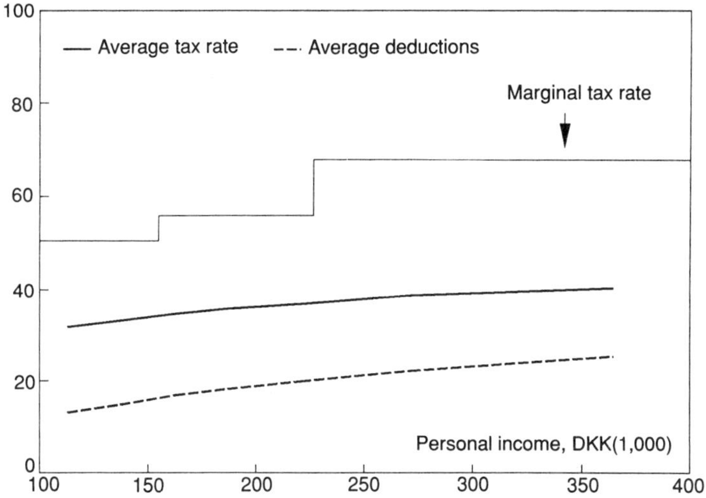

FIG 7.9. Marginal Tax Rate, Actual Average Tax, and Actual Average Deductions, 1989
Source: Calculated from taxes and duties, Statistics Denmark, 1992.

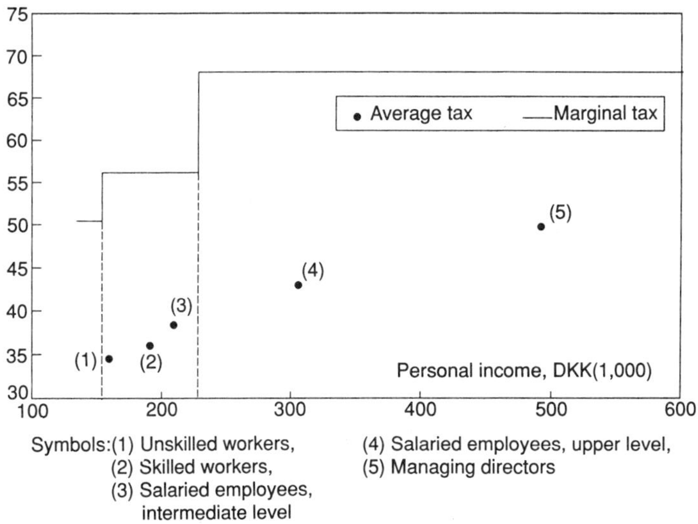

FIG 7.10. Actual Average Tax and Marginal Tax Rates, 1989
Notes: (1) Unskilled workers; (2) skilled workers; (3) salaried employees, intermediate level; (4) salaried employees, upper level; (5) managing directors.

Source: Taxes and duties, Statistics Denmark, 1992.

from VAT, currently applied at a uniform level of 25%. The rest of the revenue comes from a multitude of specific taxes, of which the most important are levied on cars, tobacco, and on alcoholic beverages. Both the VAT rate and a number of the specific tax rates are among the highest in the EC. Recently a number of the specific taxes have been abolished or reduced, in preparation for the single European market.

Finally, as already mentioned, labour market contributions have, up till now, hardly played any role in the Danish tax structure. This point is of major importance in relation to the very high level of personal income tax. The importance in relation to international comparisons can be illustrated by a recent study from the (Danish) Economic Council (1989). For Denmark, the Netherlands, and West Germany, a detailed study was made of how, on average and on the margin, the sum of personal income tax and compulsory labour market contributions from both employer and employee varied with different levels of the wage cost for the firm. The results are shown in Figs. 7.11 and 7.12.

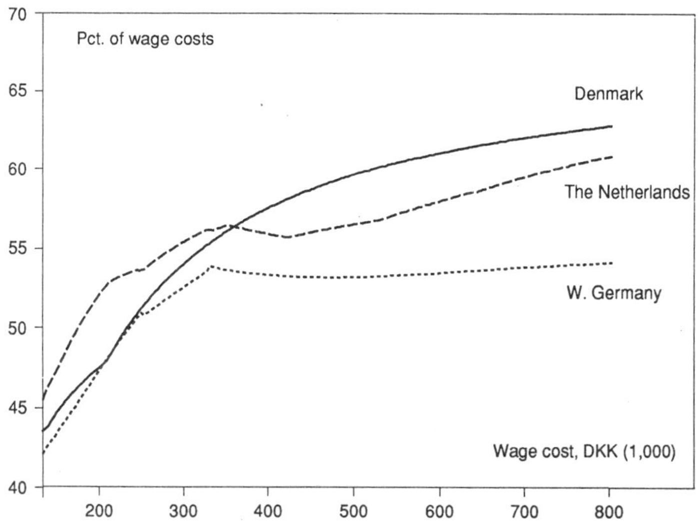

FIG 7.11. Sum of Income Tax and Compulsory Labour Market Contributions in Relation to Wage Costs in the Interval up to 800,000 DKK, 1989, Denmark, West Germany, and the Netherlands
Source: Economic Council (1989).

It can be seen from Fig. 7.11 that average income tax + compulsory contributions in Denmark are lower than in the Netherlands and on the same level as in West Germany, up to an annual wage cost about 300,000 DKK, i.e. up to a level comprising the great majority of wage- and salary-earners in the three countries. Fig. 7.11 can be interpreted as showing the average total taxation at different levels of wage cost. Correspondingly, Fig. 7.12 shows the marginal rate of income tax and compulsory contributions at different wage costs. The marginal rate is calculated by relating the marginal change in the sum of the income tax and compulsory contributions to the marginal change in wage costs.

Somewhat surprisingly, the marginal rate is lower in Denmark up to a level corresponding to the average wage costs for skilled workers. Over the next range of wage costs, of 100,000–150,000 DKK, the marginal rate in Denmark is slightly higher than in the two other countries. Only for a small group in top-level management jobs is the marginal rate in Denmark significantly higher. The big fall in the marginal rates in the Netherlands and West Germany at a fairly high income level reflects the fact that compulsory contributions are subject to a ceiling. Since 1989 tax reforms have been enacted in Germany and the Netherlands. The main points from Figs. 7.11 and 7.12 are, however, still valid. In the long run the composition of the wedge between the real product wage and the real consumption wage on direct taxes and labour market contributions should be of less or no importance. Labour costs of firms are related to productivity, and both income tax and compulsory contributions will be shifted fully to wage- and salary-earners. In relation to the discussion of EC tax harmonization, the conclusion from the comparison of labour-related taxes was that the relatively larger public sector in Denmark is reflected first of all in a relatively higher level of indirect taxation. For income tax alone, incentives to supply labour in one of the other two countries exist only for a small high-wage group. This aspect of tax-related international migration is taken up below. Also in relation to the discussion of tax harmonization in the single market, the main problem in the Danish context seems to be with indirect taxation.

7.5. THE BENEFIT AND TRANSFER SYSTEM

The total amount of cash transfers to private households in 1991 was nearly 158 billion DKK, close to 20% of GNP. The distribution on a number of main categories is shown in Table 7.3. Part of the programmes shown in this table are not relevant in the present context, with a focus on the incentives to work. This is the case for national old-age pension (*Folkepension*), where people are eligible only from the age of 67.

A part of the other pension programmes is also directed to people who are permanently outside the labour market. A precise distribution of transfer incomes by age group and relative to labour force attachment is

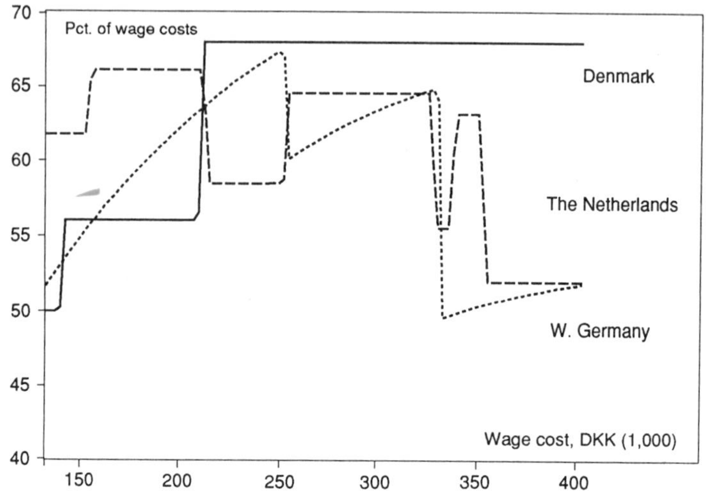

FIG 7.12. Marginal Income Tax and Compulsory Labour Market Contributions, 1989, Denmark, West Germany, and the Netherlands
Source: Economic Council (1989).

TABLE 7.3. Main Categories of Cash Transfers to Households, 1991 (million DKK)

Pensions		80,909
National old-age pension	37,547	
Pensions to public servants	9,605	
Early-retirement pension	20,260	
Labour market pension	1,702	
Post-employment wage	10,301	
Other pensions	1,494	
Unemployment insurance benefit		28,872
Cash welfare benefits		11,409
Rehabilitation benefits		1,292
Illness and maternity benefits		9,264
Families with dependent children		10,986
Housing benefits		6,170
Education benefits		4,945
Other benefits		3,991
TOTAL		157,838

Source: Public-sector finances 1987–91. Series: National Account, Public Finances, and Balance of Payments, 1992: 21. Statistics Denmark.

difficult, but in 1991 an estimated amount of 100 billion DKK was spent on programmes directed to people in the age groups below the formal pension age of 67. For 1989 the Danish Social Commission (1992) found, in a study based on representative data drawn from administrative registers, that 80.2 billion DKK of income transfers, out of a total of 140.4 billion DKK went to people between 18 and 66 years old. Unemployment has gone up since 1989, so the share of transfer incomes going to people younger than 67 will be higher in 1991 than it was in 1989.

Transfer incomes can be classified by different criteria. One important classification comprises programmes compensating a loss of income relative to income-supporting programmes. Among the programmes in Table 7.3, unemployment benefits, cash welfare benefits (*kontanthjælp*), early-retirement pension (*førtidspension*), and post-employment wage (*efterløn*) are classified as income-compensating programmes in the study from the Danish Social Commission (1992). Such classifications will, of course, always be somewhat arbitrary. For instance, some of those receiving early-retirement pension are people with such serious mental or physical handicaps that they have always been unable to earn an ordinary income from labour, while some of those who receive illness benefits have lost their labour income due to illness. Anyway, accepting this crude classification it is possible from the individual 1989 data to gain an impression of how the transfer incomes are distributed across age groups and how the share of the income-compensating programmes varies over the ages below 67 years. This is shown in Fig. 7.13. It is evident that age and labour market position are important factors. Among the income compensating transfers, the relative importance of unemployment benefits and cash welfare transfers decrease with age, while that of early-retirement pension increases. For the group between 60 and 66 years the so-called post-employment wage programme (described more fully below) plays a major role, as it is restricted to this age group.

Unemployment Insurance

After this introduction to the structure of the Danish benefit system, the major individual programmes are described in more detail. Outside the area of pensions, unemployment insurance (UI) is the most important programme of compensation for loss of income. Unemployment insurance is administered through insurance funds closely related to the unions. Along with Belgium, Finland, Iceland, and Sweden, Denmark has thus retained the so-called Ghent system, where insurance is voluntary, in contrast to the compulsory state-run insurance systems found in most OECD countries. Neumann *et al.* (1991) argue that this fact is an important factor in the explanation of high and rising unionization in these countries in recent years, in contrast to other OECD countries. Rising

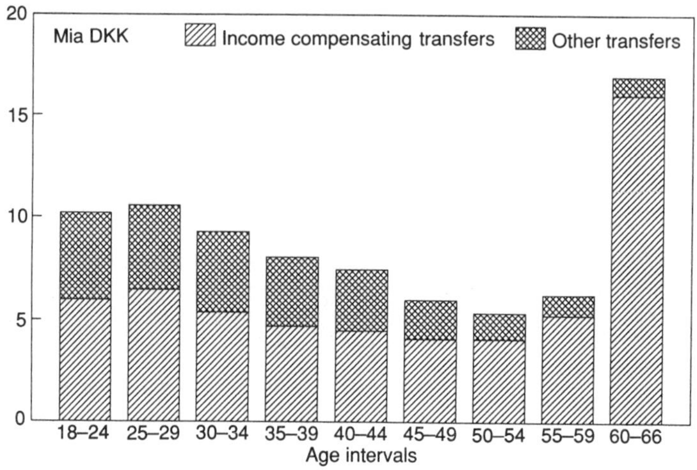

FIG 7.13. Absolute Distribution by Age and Type of Transfer Income, 1989
Source: Danish Social Commission (1992).

unemployment creates an incentive to insure, and in a union-administrated system the insurance decision is closely related to joining the union. Over time the pure insurance element has been very much reduced. There is no experience rating of contributions to UI, and members' contributions are the same to all funds and thus independent of the great variations in unemployment between funds in the range between nearly full employment of all members (nurses) and about 25% (unskilled women). Since 1989 the system has contained a certain element of experience rating, as firms must pay benefits for the first day of all spells of unemployment. In 1993 this was increased to two days. To become insured, workers must fulfil either an employment condition of more than 300 hours of work in the preceding 10 weeks or they must have completed a vocational or theoretical education lasting at least 18 months. Eligibility for benefits is obtained after one year of membership, and is further conditional on at least 26 weeks of employment during the previous 3 years. For new graduates from vocational and theoretical educations there is no prior-employment obligation, but insurance benefit is paid at a reduced level.

UI benefits are calculated as 90% of the previous labour income. This is supplemented with an absolute benefit maximum at a rather low level. The result is 90% or close to 90%, compensation for groups with low wages, a fairly low compensation for skilled workers, and still lower for salaried employers with higher pre-unemployment wages. The average degree of compensation for manual workers is currently about 65%. Since

1960 the level has shifted considerably, as shown in Fig. 7.14. The big increase from around 40% to nearly 80% took place before the dramatic increase in unemployment in 1974–5.

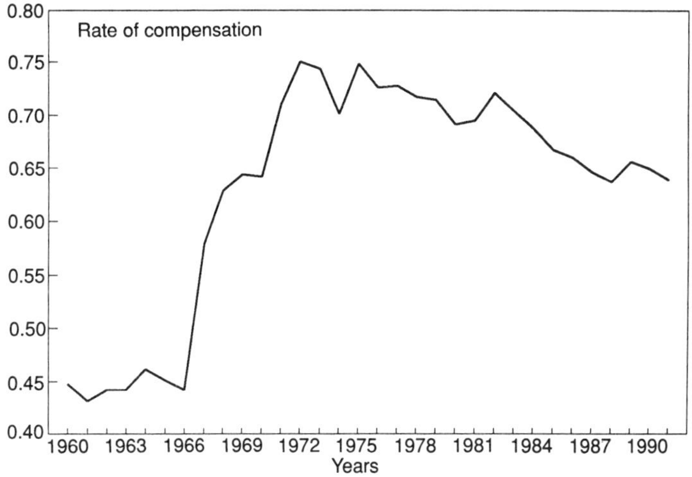

FIG 7.14. Average Benefit/Wage Ratio, 1960–1991
Source: ADAM Databank.

Since the mid-1980s compensation has been stationary around 65%. Part-time insurance is an option for those working 15–30 hours per week. Another option in the UI system is supplementary benefits for full-time insured people who take a part-time job. Benefits are paid for the number of hours between full-time and the specific part-time job. A number of restrictions exists for receiving supplementary benefits. First, a full-time insured person receiving supplementary benefits must be available for a full-time job at immediate notice, i.e. the part-time employer must accept a quit without notice. Second, the maximum duration of supplementary benefits is fairly short, 12 months, compared with a much longer period under ordinary insurance conditions.

There is no waiting period for UI benefits. (The only exception is that benefits are not paid for under 9 hours of unemployment in a week.) The combination of absence of experience rating and very liberal rules for laying off workers results in a widespread use of temporary lay-off unemployment (cf. the discussion of results in this area in Section 7.6).

The formal maximum duration of UI benefits is 2.5 years. Since the late 1970s effective duration has been much longer, as unemployed workers before benefit expiration are entitled to a job or education offer through which benefit eligibility is re-established for a new maximum duration of

2.5 years. If a worker is still unemployed at the end of this new period of benefits, he or she is entitled to a second job offer, once again re-establishing eligibility for a maximum of another 2.5 years. Considering all available activation and benefit programmes, effective maximum duration goes up to 7–8 years. (The structure of the effective maximum period of UI benefits is described in detail in OECD 1990.) Benefits are only stopped if an unemployed worker rejects a job or education offer. If no job is secured after he or she has passed through the different phases in the benefit and activation programmes, the financial consequence depends on the marital status of the worker. If the person is legally married and the spouse has an income, the provision of support is carried over to the spouse. If the person is single he or she is eligible for cash welfare benefits.

Welfare Benefits

The unemployed whose benefit eligibility has expired constitute just one group among potential recipients of cash welfare benefits. Another consists of the non-insured unemployed, i.e. people who are registered at labour offices (*Arbejdsformidlingen*) as seeking and being available for a job. Cash welfare benefits for these two groups of unemployed are regulated by a broad law about social welfare (*bistandsloven*) first enacted in 1976. The general principle governing this law is to provide for everyone who is unable to provide for himself. In contrast to UI benefits, cash welfare benefits are means-tested against a person's own income and against the income of a spouse. The means-testing implies in principle a 100% marginal tax on eventual income from work. (After 3 months on welfare benefits, up to 1,000 DKK per month in labour income is accepted for a maximum period of 6 months without deduction from welfare benefits.) Welfare benefits consist of three parts. First is a so-called base amount which is reduced after 9 months on benefits; second is a fixed amount for each child in the household; and finally rents are paid fully. Welfare benefits are tax-free, but the base deduction of the income tax is reduced by the amount paid out in benefits during a year. For a person having wage income during part of the year and receiving welfare benefits for the rest of the year, this means that only the part of income from benefits that exceeds the base deduction for the income tax is tax-free.

The dependence on the number of children and on the actual rent paid makes total income from welfare benefits a fairly variable amount. This is reinforced by a further option under this law to apply for support to cover specific non-regular expenditures. The number of people receiving welfare benefits doubled from the beginning to the end of the 1970s, mainly as a result of the dramatic change in the employment situation. During the 1980s a fairly constant number of people received welfare benefits. The constant level, in spite of much higher unemployment compared with the 1970s, is explained by a very strong increase in the propensity to enter UI funds which, as mentioned above, is a voluntary decision in Denmark. The increase from the 1970s to the beginning of the 1990s in expenditure in real terms has been much higher than the annual increase in the number of recipients of benefits. Part of this is due to legal changes, but the major reason is assumed to be increasing duration of welfare spells. Duration data in this area is, however, not available before 1989.

Early-Retirement Programmes

Next to unemployment benefits, early-retirement pension is the most expensive income-compensating programme for those below 67 years. The current rules in relation to early-retirement pension were enacted in 1984, through a reform of the more strictly health-related system of disability pensions. Early-retirement pension is available at three different levels or classes:

Highest early-retirement pension (*højeste førtidspension*). Eligibility is conditional on being younger than 60 years and possessing only an insignificant ability to work.

Intermediate-level early-retirement pension (*mellemste førtidspension*). Available in the age group 18–59 if ability to work is reduced by about two-thirds. Available for people between 60 and 66 years who fulfil conditions for highest early-retirement pension.

Ordinary early-retirement pension (*almindelig førtidspension*). Available for people between 18 and 66 years whose ability to work is reduced by at least 50% for health reasons, or for health reasons in conjunction with other problems. In addition, pension at the ordinary level is available for people between 50 and 66 years in cases where social and health-related factors create a need for permanent provision. People younger than 60 years receive a compensating extra amount, as their expenditure typically is higher than for the 60–6 age group.

The early-retirement pension structure is fairly complicated, as a number of different components enter at the different levels of the pension described above. Some of these components are means-tested against income from other sources, while others are independent of income. Further, some components are taxed, while others are tax-free. The structure is illustrated in Table 7.4. In addition to the standard elements in the pension system shown in Table 7.4, persons in early retirement are entitled to additional individual benefits depending on specific circumstances in relation to health and other conditions. In relation to incentives to work the structure is complex. It is also quite difficult to compare the disposable income for people in early retirement with the disposable income from work. The only combination in relation to tax treatment and income dependence not found in Table 7.4 is the one of tax exemption and means-testing.

TABLE 7.4. Components in Early Retirement Pension

Component	Base amount[a]	Additional pension[b]	Disability amount[c]	Work inability amount[d]	Compen sating amount[e]
Tax treatment	Taxed	Taxed	Tax-free	Taxed	Tax-free
Means-testing	Means-tested	Means-tested			
Highest level	Included	Included	Included	Included	
Intermediate level	Included	Included	Included		
Ordinary level	Included	Included			
Ordinary level, 18–59 years	Included	Included			Included

Notes: [a] Base amount (grundbeløb). [b] Additional pension (pensionstil-læg). [c] Disability amount (invaliditetsbeløb). [d] Work inability amount (erhversudygtigheds-beløb) is only granted to those with the highest level of pension as a condition for eligibility at this level is an insignificant remaining ability to work. [e] Compensating amount (førtidsbeløb).

Source: Pedersen and Smith (1993*a*); Danish Social Commision (1992).

In relation to the labour market and incentives to work, the original idea behind the three classes of early-retirement pension is that the remaining ability to work in the two lower classes should be supplied to the labour market. In reality this has not been the case. For 1989, register-based data shows that only 13% of the group with early-retirement pension had a wage income and 4% had income from independent business (Danish Social Commission 1992). For the small group with a supplementary income from work, the same data shows that the average labour income is very low, about 25% of the average annual income for an unskilled worker. Two points should be added. First, there exist wage subsidy arrangements which make the employment costs for a person in early retirement very low. Second, means-testing of the base amount and the additional pension is not done before the income from work exceeds an amount higher than the average labour income for the small proportion of people in early retirement who actually work. In a survey of people in early retirement published in 1992 (Juul 1992) nearly half of those with an early-retirement pension who did not work indicated a wish to work. The majority of the other half of the respondents consisted mainly of people who were unable to work for health-related reasons. A major obstacle to higher employment among those in early retirement thus seems to be rationing in a labour market with high unemployment.

While the history of early-retirement pensions goes back to the first systems for disability pensions at the beginning of the century, the post-employment wage programme is fairly new. It was enacted in 1979 and it is—as indicated by the name—intended to be a labour market policy programme and not an integrated part of social policy. It is possible to enter the programme both from unemployment and from a job. Since 1979 the number of people in early retirement under this programme has stabilized around 100,000. To be eligible, an individual must be between 60 and 66 years, have been a member of a UI fund for 20 out of the previous 25 years, and be eligible for unemployment benefits. Benefits under the programme depend on individual labour market status at the time of entry. If an entrant to the programme comes directly from employment, benefits equal the UI benefits to which the person would be entitled, i.e. either 90% of the previous wage or the maximum UI benefits, for the maximum duration of UI benefits of 2.5 years. Benefits are reduced to 80% of this level for the rest of the period until the person reaches the age of 67. From that age, both people with an early-retirement pension and people in the post-employment wage programme are transferred to the national old-age pension system. The only difference regarding benefits for a person who enters from unemployment is a reduction of the maximum period with full UI benefits by the length of the spell of unemployment interrupted by entry into the programme.

As a reflection of the original idea in the programme of creating job openings for unemployed younger than 60 years, participants are only allowed to work a maximum of 200 hours per year. Benefits are not reduced for persons having an income from work respecting this limitation and—like UI benefits—they are not means-tested against the income of other family members. Payments from pension schemes from previous employers are deducted from the post-employment wage benefits.

Sickness and Maternity Benefits

The last of the major income-compensating programmes is sickness and maternity benefits, relevant for workers without income from their employer during spells of sickness and for unemployed people who become sick. The rules for sickness benefits are close to those for UI benefits. The main differences are a shorter qualification period, shorter maximum duration (one year), and a degree of compensation of 100% up to the same maximum as for UI benefits. For a fairly small group of workers with low wages, sickness benefits are thus financially more attractive than UI benefits. The majority of workers will, however, receive the same amount, i.e. maximum benefits, in case of both sickness and unemployment. For spells of sickness lasting two weeks or less, benefits are paid by the employer. After two weeks, the financial responsibility is shifted to the municipality.

Maternity benefits follow the same main rules as sickness benefits. The exceptions are that benefits are paid fully by the municipality, to reduce discrimination against young women in relation to the employment decision, and that up to two of the eighteen weeks of leave can be transferred to the father. The major part of the benefits goes to mothers, in spite of the option open for fathers.

Benefits to Families with Dependent Children

Among the income-supporting programmes the biggest group comprises benefits to families with dependent children. There are two major programmes in this area. The first is benefits to families with children (*børnefamilieydelsen*); the second is child-benefit (*børnetilskud*). A purpose of the first programme is to compensate for the lack of any child-related deductions in the tax law (cf. the description in Section 7.4). The programme consists of payments of fixed annual amounts to all families with children younger than 18 years. Benefits depend on the age of the child, and are tax-free and independent of income. The income support under the child-benefit programme is paid on top of the benefits to families with children amount. They are tax-free and independent of income. The target group for the programme are families with only a single adult present and children who are orphans.

Rent Support

In relation to incentives to work, income-supporting programmes for families with children have a pure income effect. No substitution effects exist, as all programmes in this area are independent of other income in the family and, furthermore, are tax-free. Benefits under the other major income support programme, rent support (*boligsikring*), are also tax-free but are means-tested, in contrast to benefits related directly to children. Rules in the area of rent support are extremely complex (a recent book with explanatory comments in relation to the law for the rent support programme is 140 pages long). The amount of support due to a household is a function of family status, income, number of children, expenditure on rent, and size of apartment. For married couples without children rent support cannot exceed 15% of the rent. Furthermore, means-testing implies that married—and other cohabitating—couples where both have an income are usually excluded from rent support. The main target group is thus households consisting of a single adult with children.

The means-testing of the rent support is supplemented by a number of other restrictions. There is an implicit minimum rent in relation to the programme, as the net rent paid, i.e. gross rent reduced with rent support, must be above a minimum amount (7,200 DKK in 1992). There is also a maximum rent, dependent on the number of children in the family; finally, there is an absolute maximum to the amount paid in rent support. The resulting rent support is shown in Fig. 7.15, dependent on personal income for a single adult with 0, 1, or 2 children. For the same three family types, Fig. 7.15 shows the dependence on the gross rent. The three graphs in the upper part of the figure are for a case where the gross rent is at the maximum. The lower three graphs illustrate the situation where gross rent is at 50% of the allowed maximum level.

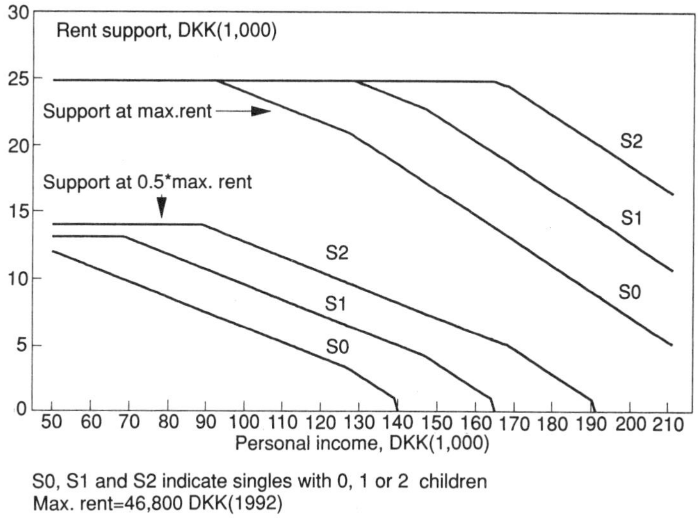

FIG 7.15. Rent Support

Notes: S0, S1, and S2 indicate single parents with 0, 1, or 2 children. Max. rent = 46,800 DKK. (1992).

Source: ADAM Databank.

There are two steps in the calculation of rent support. First a so-called limit amount is calculated as 15% of personal income up to a threshold level and 25% of personal income above this level. Personal income is reduced by a given amount for each child in the family. Rent support is calculated as 75% of the difference between the gross rent and the limit amount, subject to the absolute restrictions mentioned above, i.e. the maximum values for the gross rent and rent support and the minimum value for the family's own part of the rent. The means-testing formula implies an addition to the marginal tax rate of 11.25 or 18.5 percentage points over part of the range of personal income. The specific income intervals at which this high composite marginal taxation takes place very much depend—as shown in Fig. 7.15—on circumstances relating to the number of children and the gross rent. In relation to the average full-time wage income, reduction of rent support takes place at a level corresponding to fairly low wages. In many cases people receiving a low wage are thus exposed to composite marginal tax rates at the same level, or higher, as people with very high incomes.

Subsidies for Day Care

Most public transfers in kind are extended free of charge, i.e. services from doctors and hospitals and the major part of education. An interesting exception is parents' payments for day care of children. Municipalities, who run most of the day care institutions, can charge up to 30% of these costs. Parents with low incomes can apply for a reduced charge. The reduction is means-tested in relation to the total taxable income of the parents, independently of whether they are married or cohabitating. The place is free of charge if taxable income is below 45,000 DKK. Between 45,000 and 46,000 DKK parents are charged 5% of the normal price, and the price goes up by 1% of the full price for every increase of 1,000 DKK in the interval between 46,000 and 140,000 DKK annual taxable income. Families with both parents in the labour force will normally have taxable incomes well above this level. For single-parent families, the means-testing rule implies a significant addition to the composite marginal tax over the relevant range of taxable income. For instance, the presence of one child younger than 4 years and an average annual price for day care of 24,000 DKK means an implicit addition to the marginal tax of 24 percentage points over the range between 46,000 and 140,000 DKK in annual taxable income. A rebate on day care charge is given in cases where more than one child younger than 7 years is in day care. The consequence is that the addition to the marginal tax for a single parent with two children will be in the interval between 15–20 percentage points and 25–30 percentage points over the relevant range of taxable income. The specific outcome depends on the age of the children, and is affected by variation in the prices charged by different municipalities. The last of these factors may be of less consequence, as municipalities charging high prices tend to have fairly low municipal taxes and vice versa. As rent support in many cases is reduced over the same range of income, the result is very high composite marginal tax rates for a number of single parents with low wages. The extent of this problem is described more fully in Section 7.6.

Educational Benefits

The last major income-supporting programme is educational benefits (*Statens Uddannelsesstt*ø*te*). Those eligible for these benefits include everybody 18 years and older who follows a recognized education of at least 3 months' duration without pay during the educational period. For people 18 years old, benefits are means-tested relative to parents' income. For people 19 years and older, benefits are means-tested relative to the student's own income and taxable, but independent of parents' income.

A number of smaller benefit programmes, referred to in Table 7.3, are not described in the present context. Two facts should be emphasized here. The first is the strong increase in the coverage of income transfers for the group between 18 and 66 years of age. Income transfers under one or more of the programmes are extended to 68% of this age group. Income transfers are the sole source of income for about 20% of the age group. Secondly, total cash transfers relative to GNP are fairly low in Denmark compared to a number of other countries in north-western Europe. In a European context, the large public sector in Denmark is due more to collective consumption than to an especially high share of GNP going to cash benefits and transfers.

7.6. EMPIRICAL EVIDENCE ON INCENTIVES TO WORK FROM TAXES AND BENEFITS

Incentives to work arising from the system of taxes and benefits can follow a number of different channels. There is a potential impact on the decision to enter the labour force, and on the supply of hours conditional on entry. For people in the labour force there are further possible impacts on transitions between employment and unemployment, and on mobility. Finally, tax and benefit structures have a potential impact on the decision to retire early.

The Danish Debate

The tax and benefit structure is superimposed on a labour market which—according to Freeman (1988)—next to Sweden has the lowest variance in wage distribution among a number of OECD countries. In the absence of more adequate data, Freeman uses the dispersion of wages between industries; his conclusions are supported, however, by cross-country comparisons of rates of return to education, which are low in Denmark and Sweden compared to most other countries. The minimum wage is high relative to average wages and the income tax is high, also at moderate incomes (cf. Section 7.4). Benefits from income-compensating programmes are very high for people with low potential wages, and duration is long. This is a rough sketch of the background for the political debate in Denmark on incentive effects in relation to work. For low-income groups, discussions and analyses have centred on the potential effects of a high composite marginal tax creating 'traps' where the net gain of moving from living on benefits to a low-wage job is very small or even negative. In the same way, incentives for accepting temporary overtime or for mobility with only a small gross wage gain could be very small or nonexistent (cf. Chapter 2). The majority of wage- and salary-earners are outside the range of income where means-tested benefits imply additions to the marginal rate of income taxation. For this majority, the debate has centred on the labour-supply effects of a high marginal tax, and on the effects on saving and capital accumulation.

Further important topics in the debate have been the influence of UI benefits on transitions between employment and unemployment through an impact on search intensity, and on employers' choice between temporary lay-offs and alternative ways of adjusting to temporary shifts in demand or inflow of raw materials. Besides the potential impact on the extent and structure of unemployment, there has also been fairly intense discussion of the potential impact of UI benefits on wages, influencing unemployment in a more indirect way by affecting international competitiveness. Parallel to this, a potential impact could run from taxes to wages. Finally, a much-debated issue is the impact of taxes, both income tax and the VAT, on the supply of labour to the shadow economy. A legal counterpart to this is the devotion of time to do-it-yourself activities. As long as the individual efficiency is above one-third of the level of a professional in a specific activity, the return from doing it yourself is positive.

Taxes and Labour Supply

Considering the high level of taxes, the extensive benefit programmes, and the central role of the labour market in a small open economy, the amount of solid empirical evidence in relation to work incentives is disappointingly small. Starting with the impact of income tax, only one econometric study is available, Smith (1991). The data in this study come from a representative longitudinal sample of nearly 3,000 married couples, with annual observations covering 1980–6. Only people between 25 and 59 years of age are included in the sample. Cohabitating and single individuals are not included. Cohabitation is a widespread alternative to marriage, especially among younger people. The database from which the sample used by Smith is drawn does not identify cohabitating couples. Two versions of a labour-supply model are estimated. In the first version, unemployment is interpreted as voluntary, with the result that UI benefits are treated as a choice variable—or (in technical terms) maximum UI benefits are treated as part of virtual income. In the second version, unemployment is treated as fully involuntary, and UI benefits are not included in the budget restriction. In most labour-supply studies, supply is defined by the number of hours in employment, as in version 1 of Smith's (1991) model. This has been a necessary method in many studies, where reliable evidence on the number of hours spent in unemployment is not available. With progressive taxes the budget restriction becomes kinked, reflecting the five steps of the function describing income tax before 1987. The actual marginal tax is in this case an endogenous variable, the size of which depends on the supply of labour. Another problem that can be solved using longitudinal data is the impact from unobserved individual heterogeneity, which will bias the estimated coefficients unless corrected for. Unobserved heterogeneity reflects the fact that any conceivable data set is insufficient with respect to important individual characteristics, which are difficult or impossible to quantify. The first problem is handled by use of an iterative least-squares method, accommodating the non-linear nature of the budget restriction. The second is handled by use of the so-called fixed-effect method, where the influence from unobserved individual factors is eliminated by replacing the absolute values of individual variables by the deviation from their mean value for each individual in the sample during the years 1980–6. With respect to estimation results, the supply elasticities, defined as the relative change in labour supply following a 1% change in the wage, differ very little between the two versions of the model. For women, the uncompensated supply elasticity with respect to the wage evaluated at mean sample values is found to be between 0.06 and 0.09. The corresponding estimates for men are between .10 and .11. The finding of higher elasticities for men is surprising, and stands in contrast to the typical finding of higher elasticities for women than for men in most studies. Overall, the estimated elasticities are fairly small compared with many studies on labour supply.

The estimates are used to simulate the labour-supply impact of tax reforms. The strongest effects are found in a simulation eliminating the progression in the tax schedule. In that case the model predicts an increase of 4.8% in male labour supply and an increase of 1.4% for married women. Considering the extent of a reform like this, the estimates are quite small. It should be emphasized, however, that single and cohabitating people are not included in the estimations, which could mean that the overall effect is somewhat higher.

The estimated elasticities from Smith (1991) have been used in a simulation study by the Ministry of Economics (1993). The calculations are based on a representative sample, with data on all types of income, wealth, and taxes paid. A subsample like that in Smith (1991) is selected, i.e. a sample consisting of married people between 25 and 59 years. The dynamic effects, i.e. the part of the initial revenue loss covered by new revenue generated by the increase in supply, are calculated for two tax reforms. For the first of these, a reduction of the base-level income tax to the state from 22% to 20%, the dynamic effect is found to be 21% of the initial loss of tax revenue. The latter reform, an abolition of the 6% and 12% surtaxes to the state, is accompanied by a dynamic effect of 47%. The much higher dynamic effect in the latter case is due to the fact that the relative change in the net wage for the affected groups is very large in this case. A full model should—besides these partial effects on labour supply—include the derived effects from the increase in aggregate demand and the effects on wages from the increase in effective labour supply.

In another econometric study, Smith *et al.* (1993) analyse the impact of the combined tax and benefit system on the labour market behaviour of lone mothers. In the mid-1980s there was one adult only in about 15% of the households with children. The great majority of these were lone mothers. About 40% of the lone-parent households received cash welfare benefits, and average transfer incomes accounted for up to one-third of the disposable household income. In comparison, only 4% of disposable income came (on average) from transfers for households where both parents were present and were labour market participants.

The data used in the analysis was a cross-section subsample for 1985 from a 5% representative longitudinal database. The subsample consisted of lone mothers with at least one child younger than 17. Compared to other mothers, the full-time and non-participation frequencies were higher for lone mothers. Among the group of lone mothers it was—surprisingly—found that mothers with young children (younger than 7) worked more full-time and had a lower non-participation rate than mothers with older children.

The modelling strategy was to estimate a discrete three-state model, i.e. being a non-participant, part-time, or full-time participant. Each individual in the sample was assigned an income net of taxes and benefits in each of the three states. UI benefits were treated as non-wage income, i.e. not as a choice variable. Treating UI benefits as a choice variable would imply that unemployment was treated as being voluntary and the absence of any work test in the UI system. It would further imply very flat or negative budget restrictions for many lone mothers, which would conflict with their actual labour supply. A statistical model (Probit) was estimated for the choice between part- and full-time work conditional on participation. In relation to economic variables, results were broadly in accordance with theoretical expectations. Net income as non-participant had a significantly negative impact on the probability of participation, while the impact from full-time net income was significantly positive. Conditional on participation, net income as part-time worker had a significantly negative impact on the probability of full-time participation, while full-time net income had a significantly positive impact.

The estimation results were used in two simulations. The first simulated an actual change, where the child subsidy was made independent of income in 1987. This was combined with a lump-sum benefit to lone mothers, resulting in a fall in the composite marginal tax in the range of earlier means-testing. The model prediction of an increase in non-participation and a decrease in full-time participation could—owing to the panel nature of the data—be confronted with the actual change from 1987 to 1988. The model prediction turned out to be correct regarding the direction of the change, but the extent of the effect of the change was biased upwards. The second simulation was a calculation of the effects of removing means-testing of all benefits in relation to rent and children and introducing a lump-sum, tax-free subsidy per child. The resulting decrease in the composite marginal tax leads to a dramatic fall in non-participation. By itself, i.e. without regard to the impact on labour supply, a reform along these lines would result in an increased income inequality for lone mothers. The induced supply reactions change the outcome to a more equal income distribution. This impact on the income distribution depends on an assumption of no restrictions from the demand side of the labour market.

Two main points from this analysis should be emphasized. The first concerns the actual labour supply of lone mothers. In light of the very high composite marginal tax rates, lone mothers are working 'too much'. Consequently, the labour market behaviour must not only be interpreted as dependent on static optimization but must be viewed in a life-cycle perspective in which non-financial aspects of attachment to the labour force should be included. The second is the finding of significant reactions on the margin to changes in economic incentives in relation to labour supply.

Interaction between Taxes and Benefits

The main discussion of problems in relation to the interaction between taxes and means-tested benefits has not been based on the results from econometric analyses, but on casual evidence based on comparison of disposable income for specific family types. As mentioned, means-testing is effective only at fairly low incomes. The purpose in the construction of typical cases has, therefore, mainly been to compare disposable incomes for the household with cash welfare benefits relative to UI benefits and the income from a low-wage job. As UI is voluntary, it is of interest also to compare incentives between cash welfare benefits and UI benefits in case of unemployment for specific family types. This type of casual analysis is of interest mainly for single-adult households and for couples where only one person is in the labour force. For couples where both are participants, full-time work will almost always result in higher disposable income than UI benefits, which in turn will result in higher disposable income than cash welfare benefits.

Figures showing the situation in 1992 for some typical cases are shown in Table 7.5. For single adults with children, the financial gains from a low-wage job compared to being on welfare benefits are very small or even negative. The disposable income for a person with maximum UI benefits is not strictly comparable with the income from a job at the minimum wage. For people on the minimum wage, UI benefits will be 90% of the minimum wage and thus somewhat lower than the maximum UI benefits shown in Table 7.5. It should be emphasized in relation to this table that a static picture like this neglects both dynamic financial considerations in labour force attachment and non-financial benefits from working. In a life-cycle perspective, present labour market behaviour will influence future employment and wage prospects.

For couples, situations like those shown in Table 7.5 will usually not occur. Exceptions are couples where both are close to the minimum wage, and couples where only one is in the labour force. If the participant becomes unemployed without being insured, disposable income for the family will increase if the pre-unemployment wage is below the average wage of a skilled worker. The reason is that both become eligible for welfare benefits in that case. As a general rule, however, disposable income increases significantly if an unemployed spouse finds a job. Calculations in Ministry of Economics (1992: 21) show an increase of 36% in disposable family income from a situation with one spouse fully unemployed and the other in full-time employment to a situation where both spouses are full-time employed.

Calculations like those in Table 7.5 point to the existence of a problem, but contain no direct evidence on the extent or incidence of the problem. This can be illustrated a little more fully based on data from the Ministry of Economics (1989*a*). The elements in the composite marginal tax for a single person with two children are illustrated in Fig. 7.16, for the situation as it was in 1989. The maximum marginal tax of around 100% is

TABLE 7.5. Monthly Disposable Income After Taxes, Benefits, Rent, and Payment for Day Care: Different Family Types, 1992 (DKK)

Family type	Cash welfare benefits	Max. UI benefits	Minimum wage[a]	Unskilled wage[b]	Skilled wage[c]
Single, no children	2,900	3,300	3,100	5,200	6,200
Single, one child	4,900	4,700	4,600	5,600	6,600
Single, two children	6,900	6,500	6,500	7,300	8,200

Notes: Same apartment (70 m^2) assumed for all family types. 1st child assumed to be 4–6 yrs., 2nd child > 3 yrs. Recipients of cash welfare benefits assumed not to contribute to UI. Children of recipients of cash welfare benefits and UI benefits assumed to remain in day care institutions.

[a] Full-time income on minimum wage. [b] Full-time income with average wage for unskilled female workers. [c] Full-time income with average wage for skilled workers.

Source: Danish Social Commission (1992: fig. iv.4 (p. 99); table iv.1 (p. 106).

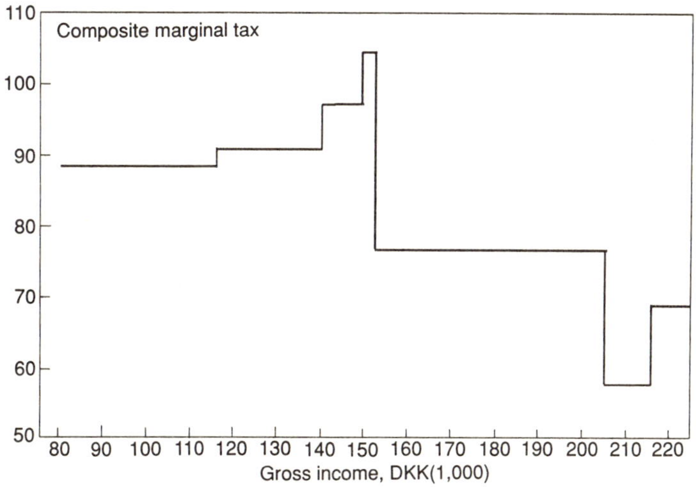

FIG 7.16. Composite Marginal Tax Rate: Single Parent with Two Children
Source: Calculated from Social ABC (1992).

found in the gross income interval that would be relevant for most single unskilled female workers.

Another approach is to examine the incidence of a composite marginal tax rate above the maximum for the income tax alone for different family types; see Fig. 7.17. For single persons without children and for couples, the shares with a composite marginal tax above 70% is negligible. For single persons with children, 20–25% of the households have a marginal

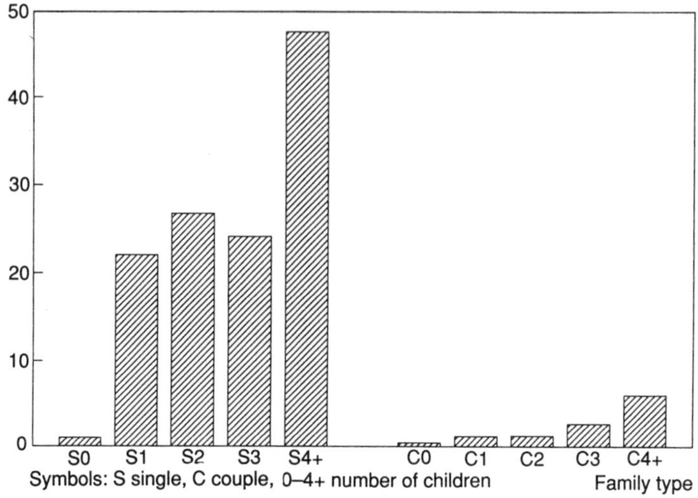

FIG 7.17. Share with Composite Marginal Tax Above 70% for Different Family Types

Notes: S = single; C = couple; 0–4+ = no. of children.

Source: Ministry of Economics (1989*a*).

tax rate above 70%. In case of four or more children, the share is nearly 50%, but extremely few singles have so many children.

The incidence of a composite marginal tax rate above 70% for singles is shown against disposable income in Fig. 7.18. Between 12% and 16% had a marginal tax above 70% in the disposable-income intervals between 100,000 and 175,000 DKK in 1989.

In relation to the size of the total labour force, this interaction problem may seem to be of minor importance. Furthermore, many people in the affected groups actually work in spite of weak financial incentives. This may reflect dynamic considerations or non-financial benefits from work, or it may reflect ignorance to some extent about the highly complex rules in the field of taxes and benefits. It seems difficult to defend the existence of situations where a person moving from living on benefits to providing for herself or himself either gains very little in financial terms from the change or even—in extreme cases—has to pay for going to work. The problem is, however, difficult to reduce for two reasons. The former is the high marginal rate of income tax at even a low level of income. The latter is due to the mechanism stressed by Moffitt (1992). Reducing income-dependent benefits over a longer range of income may increase labour supply at the lower end of the income range; but the increase in the maximum income at which benefits are paid may create counteracting

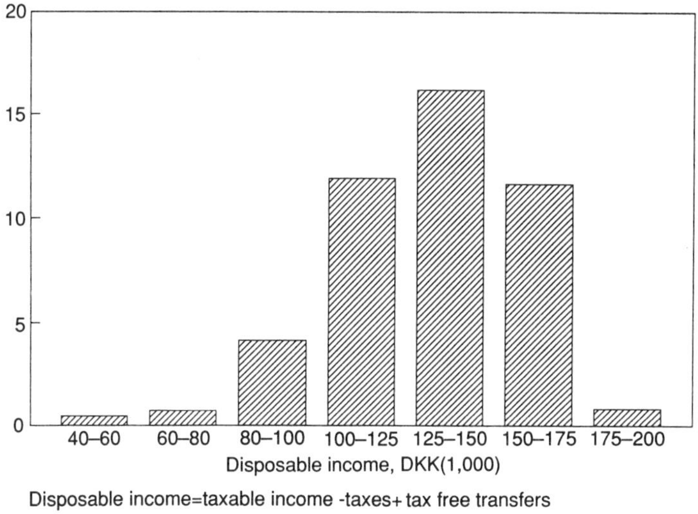

FIG 7.18. Share of Single Households with Composite Marginal Tax Above 70%, Dependent on Income Level.

Notes: Disposable income = taxable income – taxes + tax-free transfers. Family type: single.

Source: Ministry of Economics (1989*a*).

negative incentives at the upper end of the income range, over which benefits are now reduced (see also Section 7.2). Interaction problems also exist for pensioners. This is not treated in the present context, where the focus is on incentives to work. An indirect impact will, however, exist through the impact on saving behaviour in the labour-market-active part of the life-cycle.

Early Retirement and Incentives

Early retirement is another area where interaction between taxes and benefits in combination with fairly complex rules has a potential or actual impact on the incentives for either complete or partial withdrawal from the labour force. It should be emphasized that persistently high unemployment at the same time creates a situation where an increased labour supply from older workers and from people with a reduced capacity to work will probably be restricted by job-rationing, at least in the short run. (The reminder mentioned earlier is, however, also necessary here: i.e. high unemployment is not *per se* an argument for accepting negative incentives to work.) The most recent programme in this area is the labour-market-related Post-Employment Wage (PEW) introduced in 1979 (see Section 7.5). In relation to incentives to work, the PEW was designed to redistribute jobs to younger workers. People in the programme are not allowed to work more than 200 hours per year. The benefit structure in the programme—UI benefits for up to 2.5 years and 80% of maximum benefits thereafter—creates an incentive structure which renders the programme financially most attractive to workers with fairly low wages. The number of programme participants stabilized rather quickly around 100,000 people, corresponding to about 4% of the labour force. For the target group of unskilled workers aged 60–66, the programme has probably resulted in a welfare gain for the majority of the participants. (Recently, an addition to the programme has been introduced in the form of a so-called transition benefit programme. People who will be eligible for PEW at the age of 60 are eligible between the ages of 55 and 59 for a pre-PEW benefit of 80% of maximum UI benefits). The efficiency of the programme as an instrument to reduce unemployment is much more dubious; see the discussion in Layard *et al.* (1992) of experiences in a number of countries with this type of early-retirement programme.

The normal pension age in Denmark is 67 years. The actual average age at retirement has fallen to 63 during recent years. The introduction of the PEW programme discussed above is one factor behind this development. Another is the increasing number of people drawing early-retirement pension for health or combined health and social reasons (see Section 7.5).

Individual factors behind exit from the labour force, either with early-retirement pension or through other routes, are analysed by Pedersen and Smith (1993*b*), estimating a duration model for the time to early-retirement. The length of the spell to be explained by the model is the time from the age of 55 years—and being in the labour force—to either early-retirement or the age of 67, being still in the labour force until then. The data for the analysis comes from a longitudinal register-based sample covering the years 1976–86. Based on indirect evidence, different routes are identified into early retirement, i.e. early-retirement pension, the PEW programme, other pensions, and retirement without pension. Based on income variables, individual degrees of compensation are calculated for the different early retirement routes being chosen. The degree of compensation is calculated as the ratio between income in the first year of retirement and income in the last year in the labour force. The degree of compensation is used in combination with other individual background factors as explanatory variables in a competing-risks model with a so-called Weibull baseline hazard function. With a Weibull hazard the escape rate from the labour force into early retirement is a monotonics function of time spent in the labour force. The expectation here is of an increasing escape rate. This is very significantly confirmed by the estimations. The degree of compensation is found to have a significantly positive impact on the transition to PEW and to exit with another non-health related pension, while it is insignificant in relation to early-retirement pension. Lagged individual unemployment is likewise found to have a significantly positive impact on the transition to PEW and to 'other pension'. In conclusion, economic factors are found to have a significant impact on that part of early retirement that does not depend on health factors.

Finally, as mentioned above, rules in the area of early retirement are so complex that they may be perceived incompletely by potential recipients. This makes it difficult to compare disposable incomes between early retirement and continuation in the labour force and disposable incomes between different routes to early retirement. An example of the latter problem can be found in Pedersen and Smith (1993*a*), comparing the ordinary-level early-retirement pension with the PEW programme for a single person. Looking at the ratio between the two gross income amounts, the early-retirement income is only about half the level of the PEW. Looking instead at the ratio between disposable incomes, the picture is completely reversed. The shift is due to the person in early retirement having twice the base amount in deductions for income tax and further being eligible for a much higher amount of rent support. Problems in relation to a clear perception of often very complex rules are relevant—not only for decisions about early retirement, but for all areas where interaction occurs between taxes and benefits.

Wages and Taxation

Taxes can influence the labour market outcome through their impact on labour supply, as discussed above and in Chapter 2. Another, indirect impact could occur if wages were affected by taxation. In the long run wages are usually assumed to be independent of taxes, i.e. taxes are shifted fully to the after-tax consumption real wage. If this were not the case, the long-run rate of unemployment would depend on the level of taxation (see the discussion in Layard *et al.* 1992). In the short to medium term, on the other hand, taxes may have an impact on wages. Theoretical models of wage bargaining conclude that the structure of income tax may affect wages; see e.g. Hersoug (1984) and Hoel (1989). It is found in these models that increases in the marginal income tax rate lowers the pre-tax real wage while increases in the average rate of income tax results in an increase in the pre-tax real wage. Tax variables have been entered in a number of empirical Danish wage equations. The quite dominant result is insignificance for the tax variable. This is the case in the multi-country study by Alogoskoufis and Manning (1988), in the Danish macroeconometric models ADAM and SMEC, in Andersen and Risager (1990), Andersen and Overgaard (1990), and in P. S. Andersen (1992). The exceptions are Bean *et al.* (1986), who find an elasticity for wage relative to income tax of 0.2 and Hansen (1990), who finds an elasticity of 0.3.

Overall, theoretical predictions are unclear in this area. Bargaining models point, as mentioned, to the possibility that a tax increase could lower or increase the pre-tax wage depending on the specific change of the tax function. In a competitive labour market a tax increase may reduce supply and thus result in an increase in the pre-tax wage. Empirical evidence so far does not indicate any significant impact from the income tax on the pre-tax wage. Somewhat surprisingly, both Andersen and Risager (1990) and P. S. Andersen (1992) find an elasticity of 1 for the wage relative to the rate of indirect taxes, i.e. changes in indirect taxes are found to have a full impact on the gross wage.

Emigration and Taxation

It has been claimed in the Danish debate that taxation - especially the high rate of marginal income taxation—could induce migration abroad, especially among highly educated people. This question has been analysed by the Ministry of Economics (1989*b*). Using register data covering 1973–88 for all emigrants, it was found that average income and wealth for emigrants above 30 years of age to EC countries was higher than the average for the whole population in this age group. The analysis showed at the same time the opposite pattern for emigrants to other Nordic countries. It showed further that the number of emigrants is rather small, is cyclically sensitive—but without a trend—and, finally, showed a high rate of return migration. The conclusion seems to be that tax-induced emigration is a minor problem.

UI Benefits, Transitions in the Labour Market and Wages

The recent survey by Atkinson and Micklewright (1991) concluded that effects from UI benefits on labour market transitions in US and UK studies typically were significant and in the direction predicted by search theory—but fairly small. It was also concluded that no significant effects were found in many studies using data for Continental European countries. This is confirmed in the broad survey of results from panel data studies by Pedersen and Westergård-Nielsen (1993).

The main findings in the rather few Danish studies of labour market transitions are either insignificant or significant but fairly small effects from UI benefits. A first round of studies used panel data for the years 1979–80. Pedersen and Westergård-Nielsen (1984) found a significantly positive effect from the replacement rate on the number of unemployment spells, while no significant effect was found with respect to the average duration of spells. In estimations using the annual individual degree of unemployment (defined in Danish unemployment statistics as the part of the year spent in unemployment) as dependent variable, Pedersen and Westergård-Nielsen (1986) found no significant effect from the replacement rate. Finally, Jensen (1987) used the same panel data set in estimation of a duration model explaining transitions between employment and unemployment. For the transition from employment to unemployment it was—surprisingly—found that the hourly wage rate had a significantly positive impact, i.e. an implicitly negative impact from the replacement rate, as there exists an inverse relationship between the wage level and the replacement rate. For the transition from unemployment to employment, the finding of predominantly negative and significant effects from the replacement rate was more in line with standard search theory.

The longitudinal sample used in the studies reviewed above has later been refined to include data on employers. It thus became possible to distinguish between temporary lay-off unemployment ending in re-employment with the former employer and unemployment spells ending with employment in a new job. Data for 1979–84 was used by Jensen and Westergård-Nielsen (1990) in estimation of single-risk and competing-risks duration models, respectively with and without a distinction between the two types of unemployment spell. (Duration models explain the time spent in a given state. In a single-risk model, transitions can occur only to one other state, while there are more possible destinations in competing-risks models.) The results in relation to the replacement rate were mixed, but all significant coefficients were negative. Further, this study found a significantly negative effect from the replacement rate on the probability of being hit by a spell of temporary lay-off unemployment. This could be interpreted as an indication of the existence of compensating-wage differences, a higher unemployment risk being compensated by a higher wage when employed, and could at the same time partly explain the mixed results from studies where no distinction was made between different types of unemployment.

Considering the facts that the replacement rate—especially for people with low wages—is high and maximum benefit duration is long, it seems to be a robust conclusion that effects on labour market transitions from UI benefits are fairly small.

UI benefits can have another—indirect—effect on labour market outcomes through an impact on wages. In most multi-country studies no significant effect is found from the replacement rate on wages (cf. the survey in Sørensen 1992). Indirect evidence is found in the multi-country unemployment analysis in Layard *et al.* (1992). It is found here that the replacement rate is significant in the explanation of cross-country differences in the sensitivity of real wages to unemployment. The results from Danish empirical studies are mixed. Andersen and Risager (1990) and Andersen and Overgaard (1990), estimating union models for the level of the real wage, find no significant effects from the replacement rate in line with the typical result in multi-country studies. The typical result in other Danish studies is the finding of significantly positive effects, also in the long run. This is the case for the official macroeconometric models ADAM and SMEC, and in Hansen (1990), all three being models of the so-called error-correction type. Finally, casual evidence from the Danish Social Commission (1992: 96–7) indicates an impact from the maximum UI benefits on the structure of wages. For the period 1970–90 the profile of the ratios between maximum benefits and average skilled wages, and between the 10% fractile of the wage distribution and the average skilled wage, follow each other quite well. The effect from the indirect UI impact on wages would in this case consist of mainly higher unemployment among workers with low wages.

Overall, there seems to be empirical consensus—with the Andersen and Risager (1990) and Andersen and Overgaard (1990) as exceptions—on an impact, also in the long run, from the replacement rate on wages.

Incentives, Do-It-Yourself Activities, and the Shadow Economy

A high level of income tax and VAT means a high taxation on the division of labour. A marginal income tax rate of up to 68% and a VAT rate of 25% implies that do-it-yourself (DIY) activities are economically attractive as long as the individual efficiency is above 25–30% of the level for a professional in the specific activity, assuming the same pre-tax wage for the involved persons. Some DIY activities also convey an—at least intramarginal—utility, which means that the 'reservation efficiency' will be even lower compared with a professional. At the same time, taxation at this level makes un-taxed activities, work in the shadow economy, financially attractive. Those who demand and those who supply shadow activities have a very big wedge between pre- and post-tax wages and prices to split between them.

In the nature of things, precise estimates of the level and trend of DIY and shadow activities are difficult to produce. Pedersen (1990) and Mogensen (1990) present results concerning DIY activities based on a survey covering activities in 1988 and on a retrospective survey. According to the retrospective survey, the share of people undertaking DIY activities has grown rapidly. Concerning individual background factors, age has a negative effect on DIY activities, while the impact from income is positive but at a decreasing rate. A tax variable is entered in statistical analyses of DIY activities and is found significantly positive in relation to DIY done at weekends. The degree of explanation, however, is low in analyses with individual survey data.

Difficulties in producing precise estimates of the importance of taxes for DIY activities reflect the fact—among others—that DIY activities are expected to grow even in a society with a constant and/or low relative level of taxes. Economic growth with productivity evolving more slowly—or not at all—in many service activities results in changes in relative prices, making service-oriented DIY activities more attractive even without the further incentive from taxes.

Mogensen (1990) reports results on the extent of shadow activities based on a survey from 1988. Under-reporting with respect to shadow activities means that the estimates are interpreted as minimum values. It is found that 12% of the population between 20 and 69 years took part in shadow activities in the year preceding the survey. On average, participants in the shadow economy supplied 53 minutes of labour per day. Applying these estimates to the population at large, the shadow sector of the Danish economy corresponded to 3.7% of GNP in 1988. Including individual background factors in the analysis, it was found that age, sex, place of living, and occupation were significant.

The trend over time of the shadow economy is estimated in two ways by Mogensen (1990). Earlier surveys give information for 1980, 1984, and 1986 about the share of the population between 20 and 69 years who participate in shadow activities. For those three years, the shares were 7.3%, 12.8%, and 13%. Compared with the 12.2% found in the 1988 survey, the shadow economy seems to stabilize from the mid-1980s. One earlier survey, carried out by the Ministry of Labour in 1982, contains information also on the time spent in shadow activities. Comparing the 1982 and 1988 surveys in this respect, time supplied in shadow activities went up by 36% overall, somewhat stronger, with 62%, for women and somewhat lower, with 26%, for men.

Finally, looking at the occupational composition of shadow labour, it was found that the stagnating share of the population in shadow activities from the mid-1980s masked some strong shifts. For skilled workers participation went up strongly, while it decreased for people without a vocational education.

Somewhat greater estimates of the size of the shadow economy are found by Lundager and Schneider (1986) and by Schneider (1986) using a different approach, the so-called currency demand approach. The idea in this method is that a measure of the marginal income tax rate is entered as a supplement to conventional explanatory variables in a money demand function. If the tax variable is found significant, an estimate of the size of the shadow economy is found from the difference between actual money demand and money demand calculated from the estimated function with the lowest value for the tax variable inserted for all years in the period. Using this method, the size of the shadow economy is estimated at 7% of GNP at the beginning of the 1980s, having risen from an estimated level of 4–5% in the 1960s.

As mentioned, precise quantitative analyses have a hard time in the field of DIY and shadow market activities. It seems, however, to be a robust conclusion that a non-trivial amount of labour is spent in—legal and illegal—untaxed activities. More importantly, the studies surveyed indicate a significant increase in recent years in these activities. Available empirical evidence does not make it possible to relate trends in this area in a precise way to the development in taxes.

Trends in the Labour Market, Taxes and Benefits

Few econometric studies are available on the interaction between the Danish labour market and the structure and level of taxes and benefits. Therefore, we shall try in a more casual way to relate some major trends in the labour market during the last thirty years to the broad development in taxes and benefits.

Total employment has risen by about 20% from 1960 to 1991. At the same time, the average annual number of hours has fallen, the net effect being a decrease of 9.1% in the total number of hours. The major decrease in the average number of hours took place in the years with full employment from 1960 to 1973 (cf. Fig. 7.7). Back in these years, in spite of increasing taxation, the real consumption wage increased quickly, and a dominating income effect is the most obvious interpretation of the strong decrease in working hours. The broad picture from the late 1970s is a stagnating real consumption wage, reflecting the combined effect from stagnation, or only slow growth, in productivity and increasing taxation. A constant real consumption wage should not by itself, by conventional labour-supply theory, induce any change in working hours. This prediction is born out by Fig. 7.7, where the decrease in working hours from 1987 to 1991 was a result, not of collective bargaining, but of government intervention as part of a labour market package. An increasing trend in the number of people with extra jobs indicates that agreed working hours have been felt as rationing by a growing number of people.

The profile over time of the part-time frequency shown in Fig. 7.6 is difficult to relate in any causal way to the trend in taxes and benefits. A possible interpretation of the decrease in part-time frequency through the 1980s is a mixture of an added worker effect—women shifting from part-time to full-time - reacting on the higher risk of unemployment for married men and a cohort effect for women. The first round of increase in female participation was a broad move into part-time jobs. This was followed by new generations of women beginning their labour market career in full-time jobs in which they typically stay on, including after childbirth.

The next stylized fact is the strong increase in participation, being stronger in the years with high and increasing unemployment than in the preceding period of full employment. It has been claimed that part of this increase was induced by easy access to UI benefits with very long duration and with few job openings available. No doubt, induced labour supply of this type exists. But very little hard evidence is available to suggest that this is a factor of any major importance in explaining the development in labour force participation. International studies point to the very long benefit duration in Denmark as a factor that could explain the high level of unemployment compared to the other Nordic countries (Layard *et al.* 1992; Burda 1989; Jackman *et al.* 1990; Jackman 1990). The consequence of a *de facto* indefinite period with benefits is the lack of any incentive to drop out of the labour force. Larsen (1992) has estimated the cyclical sensitivity of the participation rate in twenty-two OECD countries for the period 1970–89. For Denmark, no sensitivity at all is found in the participation rate. In contrast to this, a strong cyclical sensitivity is found for Japan, Norway, and Sweden. Smaller but also significant cyclical sensitivity is found for most other OECD countries.

A final stylized fact is the increasing concentration of the labour supply in the middle-aged group. Forty years ago, the typical middle-aged family consisted of a housewife and a husband working 48 hours per week for 49 weeks per year. In the same typical family today both work full-time 37 hours per week for 46 weeks per year. Their annual labour supply has consequently risen by 40–50%. Average age at entry to the labour market has gone up and average age at retirement has gone down. During recent years, part of the explanation of this is a combination of low economic growth and a relatively high minimum wage. Over the longer run this development is related to benefits. Free education and fairly generous income support to students delay entry to the labour market. Early-retirement programmes, especially the Post-Employment Wage, have created strong incentives to early retirement for groups with fairly low wages. In relation to the creation of a more flexible labour market, the educational part is of great importance. The early retirement programmes, on the other hand, are hardly effective instruments for bringing down unemployment.

7.7. CONCLUDING COMMENTS

In Sections 7.2–5 the background was described for the Danish debate, and for empirical analyses of the impact on labour market behaviour from incentives in the tax and benefit structure. In macroeconomic terms, the Danish economy has followed a fairly unbalanced course. In recent years unemployment has increased rapidly, at the same time as the balance of payments has shown a big surplus and the rate of inflation has been very low. In the labour market the overall participation rate has been increasing, while the employment frequency has been untrended. The increasing rate of participation is the net outcome of increasing participation for women, a decreasing part-time frequency, and a decreasing participation among older men. The total number of hours supplied to the labour market has gone down by nearly 10% since 1960. This has been the net effect from an increase in employment dominated by a decrease in average working hours.

The Danish tax structure deviates considerably from the structure found in other OECD countries. This is most evident in the facts that personal income tax raises a very large share of tax revenue and that compulsory labour market contributions are close to negligible in Denmark. On the benefit side, a characteristic feature of the Danish system is the widespread use of a 'universality' principle: eligibility is usually not dependent on labour market experience and contributions. Another characteristic feature—related to the dominance of personal income tax on the revenue side—is the interaction between means-tested benefits and high rates of income taxation, resulting in some cases in extremely high composite marginal tax rates for people with fairly low incomes.

The political debate in Denmark on the issue of incentives in relation to the labour market has centred on much the same topics as in other OECD countries. The poverty or unemployment trap mentioned above has been a major issue. Other topics have been the impact from unemployment insurance on transitions in the labour market, the impact from taxes on labour supply, and the extent and development of DIY activities and labour supply in the shadow economy.

While the topics studied have been the same as in other OECD countries, empirical evidence based on econometric studies and other quantitative analyses has been sparse in Denmark until now. In relation to taxes, significant but fairly small effects have been found from income tax. For people exposed to very high marginal tax rates, the tax and benefit structure is found to have a significant impact on the margin. There are, however, non-financial or dynamic factors in relation to work having an intramarginal impact on the supply of labour by those affected by the interaction between taxes and means-tested benefits. Early retirement among older workers for non-health reasons is found to be significantly affected by economic incentives, measured by the degree of income compensation attached to the different routes to early retirement. Finally, in relation to taxes, the typical result in wage equations has been that no significant effects are found from income tax on wages.

The impact from unemployment benefits on labour market transitions has been analysed in a number of studies, using panel data. Results are mixed, but when significant effects are found they have typically been fairly small. The rate of income compensation from unemployment insurance has been entered among the explanatory variables in a number of wage equations. The evidence is mixed, but the major part of the results points to a significant impact, also in the long run.

Finally, survey-based studies of DIY activities and labour supply in untaxed activities point to both an increasing incidence of such activities and an increasing intensity for those who are involved.

As econometric evidence is sparse, reference has been made also to more casual evidence of trends probably related to the long-term development of benefits and taxes. The share of people in labour-market-active ages who are provided for on a full year basis by benefits has increased from about 5% around 1950 to about 20% today. Part of this development is related to the high level of unemployment, but more long-run structural factors may also be important. Other pieces of casual evidence—difficult to substantiate by econometric analyses—are the decreasing total number of hours supplied to the ordinary labour market, the increasing supply in untaxed activities, and the decreasing trend in the rate of private saving.

The discussion in this chapter has mainly concerned the disincentive effects of the major build-up of taxes and benefits that followed the expansion of the Danish welfare state. It should be emphazised that this build-up has also resulted in welfare gains for many people and most probably has resulted also in a more equal distribution of disposable incomes. This, however, does not obviate the need to design taxes and benefits in such a way that negative incentives are kept at a minimum level, conditional on the political choice of the relative size of the public sector.

8

Conclusions

A. B. ATKINSON

THE POLICY ISSUE

Many people hold strong views about the effect of the welfare state on economic performance. These views are highly influential in policy-making, yet they are all too often based on a superficial analysis of economic behaviour and unsupported by rigorous empirical evidence as to how work incentives have in fact been affected. The aim of this book has been to try and bridge the gap between the assumptions of public debate and the findings of scientific research, with particular reference to the often cited issue of work incentives.

To this end, it has set out a framework for analysing the impact of the welfare state on work incentives (Chapters 1 and 2) and reviewed the empirical evidence regarding work incentives: Chapters 3–7 have concentrated on evidence from Denmark, Sweden, West Germany and the UK, providing a European perspective. Not only are these European welfare states distinctly different from welfare provisions in, say, the United States or Canada or Australia or Japan, but there are reasons to expect their impact on work incentives to be different.

The four countries studied are both similar and dissimilar. They are all drawn from Northern Europe and all have sizeable welfare states. At the same time, there are important differences, including the demographic situation, family structure, patterns of child care, the role of trade unions in the payment of transfers, and the extent of employer-provided benefits. On reading the country chapters, one is struck by the differences across countries in the issues which have generated concern. An aspect of incentives which has received a great deal of attention in one country may have been scarcely discussed in another.

The economic impact of the welfare state depends first on the taxes necessary to finance transfers, income maintenance representing a major part of the government budget. As reviewed in Chapter 2, there are a number of dimensions of labour supply which may be affected by taxation, whether income, payroll, or indirect taxes, all of which create a 'wedge' between the cost of labour to the employer and the value of the goods which the worker can buy with his or her wages. In most cases the impact of taxation is in theory ambiguous, with both a 'substitution effect' reducing the marginal return to working, and hence discouraging work, and an 'income effect', causing people to be worse off and hence typically wanting to restore some of their lost income by working harder. While both affect the overall decision, it is the latter which determines the extent of distortion of individual decisions. The balance between these depends in part on the structure of the tax system. An income tax with graduated marginal rates, for example, may adversely affect decisions to invest in education, but a progressive flat-rate tax may leave this decision unaffected.

There is ambiguity in much of the policy discussion as to whether we should be concerned with the total effect (both income and substitution effects) or just with the substitution effect. Much of the American literature has tended to focus on the latter, on the grounds that it is the distortion of individual choice that imposes the cost (the income effect being a necessary concomitant of raising revenue). However, there are reasons to believe that politicians, at least in Europe, are concerned with the level of marketed output, or its rate of growth, so that the total impact is of importance. They appear to attach less value to leisure than do individual workers. Since the empirical findings are rather clearer with regard to the total effect, this receives most attention in the summary.

The second impact of the welfare state is via the benefits paid. Here it is the negative effect which has tended to be emphasized, notably the 'moral hazard' whereby social insurance, like private insurance, may cause people who are insured to make less effort to avoid the contingency against which they are covered. Examples include the possibility that unemployment benefits delay return to work by the unemployed, that sickness benefit means that people take more time off work, and that pensions mean that people retire earlier. All of these reduce effective labour supply, and hence may reduce output or its rate of growth. (Again, this refers to the total effect and takes no account of the value of the extra leisure.)

The analogy has been used of a 'leaky bucket'. Transferring income may involve costs, either through disincentives or administrative expenses, and these 'leaks' from the bucket have to be balanced against the social benefits from the redistribution of income. This analogy is a vivid one, but there are respects in which it is misleading. The welfare state may have a positive, and not just a negative, effect on economic performance. The existence of social insurance may bring people into the labour force, in order to qualify for future benefits; the link between benefits and contributions may reduce the incentive to enter the shadow economy; the safeguard provided by unemployment insurance may encourage people to make riskier career choices.

The central issue regarding the welfare state is therefore an empirical one. Both taxes and benefits in theory have effects which are either positive or negative with regard to the level of labour supply, and evidence is needed to determine the direction of the effect. Moreover, to the extent that the balance is adverse, it is the *magnitude* of the adverse effect which ultimately determines the appropriate policy stance with regard to the scale of the welfare state. The question is not whether the welfare state affects economic behaviour, but the size of any such effect. The mere existence of a discouragement to work is not in itself a sufficient argument against taxes or transfers; the question is whether it is large enough to call into question the balance of advantage and disadvantage. If the bucket leaks only a moderate amount, then this may be quite acceptable.

THE FINDINGS

What does the evidence show? In brief, we have seen that in all four countries there are reductions in labour supply which have been attributed to the existence of cash transfers, and the taxes necessary to finance them. Even if most European countries are currently characterized by serious levels of unemployment, in the medium and long term there may be adverse consequences for economic performance. However, the predominant impressions are (*a*) the small size of many (but not all) of these effects, (*b*) that it is the labour supply of women, particularly married women and lone mothers, which is more likely to be reduced, and (*c*) the lack of consensus about many aspects, and qualifications which surround many estimates of the magnitude of disincentives.

A more detailed summary follows, drawing attention to the differences between different elements of the welfare state and between the four countries studied.

TAXATION

It is in the field of taxation that disincentives have been most commonly discussed, and concern has particularly been expressed about the marginal rates of tax and social-security contribution. In Sweden, for example, at the beginning of the 1980s the marginal tax rate faced by an average blue-collar worker was around 60% and that for an average white-collar worker was around 70%. In the UK the top income tax rate was then 60% (now 40%), and that in West Germany is in excess of 50%. In Denmark, the top marginal income tax rate is close to 68% in most municipalities. The possibility that these high marginal rates discourage work effort was one of the main considerations behind the reforms of income taxation in countries such as the UK and Sweden, where the marginal rates of income tax have been reduced.

The existence of high marginal tax rates, however, does not in itself mean that a serious disincentive exists. It is to learn about this that empirical studies of labour supply are necessary. As is explained in Chapter 3, before the tax reform in Sweden there was already a high level of labour force participation by both men and women, so that a positive effect from tax cuts on labour supply would have to take the form of increased hours or of improved 'quality'. The empirical evidence mostly relates to the former. In the case of Sweden there are a variety of results, with disagreement both about the direction and about the size of the response of hours of work to net wage rate changes (the elasticity of labour supply). A positive elasticity means that labour supply increases with the net wage, and hence falls with rises in the tax deducted. In the case of prime-aged men, the estimated elasticities are typically positive, but small, and for women they are larger, with values up to around 1.0 (which means that a 10% rise in the net wage leads to a 10% rise in hours worked). On the other hand, alternative methods yield elasticities which are negative, indicating that the overall response to a tax increase would be an increase in labour supply. The conclusion reached is that research on the incentive effects of labour supply has a long way to go.

The evidence for the UK in Chapter 4 concentrates on the labour supply of married women, on the grounds that the participation of prime-age married men is relatively fixed, and that for the majority hours of work is a collective, rather than individual, decision. In the case of married women, the average effect is in the direction of reduced hours of work as a result of a decrease in the net wage, but for more than a quarter the response is in the opposite direction (the response varies across the population). In West Germany (Chapter 6) male labour supply is not very responsive to changes in net wages; female labour supply reacts positively, but there is a range of estimates of the elasticity from negative to greater than 1.0. The evidence in Denmark (Chapter 7) is limited. The estimated elasticities are fairly small and, interestingly, appear to be around 0.1 for both men and women. This means that a 10% rise in the net wage is associated with only a 1% rise in labour supplied. (Of course, a small elasticity may lead to a large change in labour supply if there is a very large change in the net wage, as is illustrated by the Danish simulation for married persons showing a sizeable behavioural effect from the abolition of the two top tax rates.)

The overall impression is that, apart from Denmark, there is evidence of a larger negative response to taxation by married women, but little clear evidence that overall taxation has reduced the hours of work of prime-age male workers. It may be that there are adverse effects, but in most cases they do not stand out distinctly from the empirical observations of labour-supply behaviour. This is consistent with the fact that tax reforms in countries such as the UK do not appear to have led to dramatic increases in labour supply. (The analysis by Dilnot and Kell (1988), for example, of the reduction in income tax rates between 1978–8 and 1985–6 concluded that the evidence was consistent with a positive behaviourial response by the top 1%, but that this was modest in size and could be explained equally by changes on the demand side.) The absence of a marked response may represent the cancelling out of different effects. The evidence for the United States suggests that the substitution effect may indeed be more significant than the overall change, but the European studies reviewed here do not in general reach the same conclusions, at least for prime-aged males.

The absence of clear findings of major disincentive effects or distortion of decisions does not mean that tax reform is without value. This is particularly true when we go beyond taxation as an aggregate to an examination of its 'fine' structure. This is well illustrated by the issue of the tax treatment of married couples. There is a major difference between the Swedish separate taxation and the regime of income-splitting in West Germany. Simulation of the effects of changing the tax treatment of married couples in West Germany (Chapter 6) suggests that the adoption of the Swedish system of separate taxation could increase the labour force participation rate of married women by some 8–10 percentage points, a finding of especial interest in view of the lower rate of participation among married women in West Germany than in the other countries studied.

CASH BENEFITS

When we turn to the benefit side of the equation, the need to consider the fine structure is immediately apparent, since it makes little sense to talk about cash transfers in general. There may be quite different effects from cash transfers to families, from child care provisions, from sickness benefit, from unemployment benefit, or from active labour market measures. While we may be able to say little about welfare benefits in general, studies of more narrowly defined aspects may indicate more definite conclusions.

In seeking to summarize the evidence, one is also struck by the differences in welfare-state institutions across the countries studied. In Denmark and Sweden the trade unions play an important role in unemployment compensation, unlike the government systems in Germany and the UK. In Sweden, cash transfers for unemployment have been traditionally less prominent than retraining and active labour market measures. In the UK there has been particular concern with transfers to lone parents and the impact on their work incentives. In Germany there is an interesting contrast in family policy between West and East, notably the pro-natalist and pro-employment stance adopted in East Germany.

The disincentive effects of transfers may be studied at two levels. First, there is the impact on the opportunities open to an individual or a family (the individual budget constraint); secondly, there are the decisions made in the light of these opportunities. The individual budget constraint has been studied in several chapters, and has shown how each country makes use of income-testing to seek to concentrate benefits on those with low incomes. In the UK a substantial proportion of the population are in receipt of income support, family credit (with a marginal withdrawal rate of 70%), housing benefit, or other means-tested benefits. In Sweden there is, in addition to social assistance, municipal housing benefit and income-related amortization of student loans, and the fees for public child care may be income-related. Germany has social assistance and unemployment assistance, and child allowances are income-limited. Denmark has means-tested social assistance; it applies means-testing to elements of the early-retirement pension; there is means-tested rent support and educational benefit; and the charges for public day care involve an implicit marginal tax rate of up to 24%.

As a result of income-testing, people may face a high rate of withdrawal of transfers as income rises, which means that a 10% increase in gross income (for example, by working additional hours) may generate a much smaller proportionate increase in net income. The effect of income-testing is exacerbated by the complexity of the interaction between different transfer programmes and between transfers and the tax system. It is this which leads to the 'poverty trap', where the composite marginal rate of tax, combining both the withdrawal of transfers and the taxation of income, may be higher on those receiving benefits than on top taxpayers. In Denmark, a significant number of lone mothers are found to have composite marginal rates above 70%; in the UK at least a quarter of lone parents faced a composite rate in excess of 50%. In Sweden the composite rates for couples with children using public day care are 50% or more over a considerable range of incomes.

The poverty trap appears in all of the countries studied, but what is striking is the extent of difference between countries in the programmes which give rise to high rates of withdrawal and in the income groups affected. The role of charges for day care in Sweden and Denmark contrasts with the income-testing of family benefits in the UK. In the UK the withdrawal of family credit happens at a relatively low level of family income, and hence the poverty trap directly affects relatively few people, whereas in Germany the limits on receipt apply at relatively higher incomes. The high composite marginal rates appear to arise more in the middle of the distribution in Denmark and Sweden.

The existence of high marginal rates is one reason why benefits may have led to reduced labour supply, but disincentives may also arise from the categorical benefits which represent the greater part of welfare state expenditure. The impact of categorical benefits may be measured in terms of the extent to which they replace incomes in work (the replacement rate). The findings reviewed here present a mixed picture. In some cases, such as unemployment benefit in the UK (Chapter 5) and West Germany (Chapter 6), there is little clear evidence that benefits represent a major discouragement to returning to work. The estimated elasticity of duration with respect to the replacement rate is small. In the case of sickness absence, the estimated elasticity is typically even smaller. On the other hand, in Sweden (Chapter 3), there appears to be evidence that for sickness cash benefits a higher replacement rate is associated with higher absence rate, and there seems to be an effect via partial retirement, although this may reflect re-arrangement of work effort over the life-cycle. In Denmark, there is estimated to be significant, but fairly small, effects. Early retirement is found to be significantly affected by the replacement rate, at least for those not retiring on health grounds. There are signs that unemployment insurance in Sweden results in longer periods of unemployment, but also in a higher propensity to stay in the labour market. This is an example of the fact that benefits may have positive as well as negative effects (those without benefits exiting from the labour force).

Positive effects from transfers are illustrated by parental cash benefits in Sweden, which provide an incentive for women to participate in the labour force, although at the same time they lead to increased amounts of time off work. Benefits paid to those in work, or subject to minimum hours of work conditions, may act as an inducement, and evidence for the UK (Chapter 5) and Denmark (Chapter 7) suggests that lone parents may be particularly sensitive to changes in this element of the budget constraint.

QUALIFICATIONS

Conclusions drawn from the studies reviewed here must be qualified in several respects, as will have been clear from the discussion in each chapter. Here, three points only will be reiterated.

First, given that the effects we are seeking to measure do not stand out in any dramatic way from the empirical observations, it is not surprising that economists have had to devise more and more subtle instruments of research. These refinements are not an elaborate piece of academic ritual but are necessary to understand complex and changing phenomena. Labour supply cannot be treated as a purely static decision; the life-cycle has an important influence. Nor can decisions be treated as a purely individual matter without regard to the family context.

Research in this area has followed a pattern of evolution. It began with relatively simple statistical information, often used to draw strong conclusions; these conclusions in turn were criticized by researchers, who pointed to problems in interpretation, to the need for more sophisticated techniques, and to the potential of other sources of data. The picture almost invariably becomes less sharp as we become more aware of the limitations, and the reader should be aware that the different studies reviewed here can be placed at different points along this spectrum.

Secondly, the studies have tended to concentrate on certain dimensions of labour supply to the exclusion of others. Certain areas are distinctly under-researched. Reference was made above to the 'quality' of labour supply. More research is needed on the effects of taxation and transfers on decisions regarding effort and motivation, and the related issues of job choice, search for promotion, and career planning. Human capital-formation features more in the theoretical literature and policy debate than in applied econometric studies. The interrelation with family-formation, migration, and other decisions may be of central importance.

Thirdly, the labour-supply decision has to be seen within a wider economic context. Changes in individual decisions may affect the labour market and the level of wages; their impact depends on the operation of the labour market and its current state. Disincentives associated with welfare benefits may be irrelevant at times of high unemployment. Adjustments in labour supply may affect the allocation between sectors of the economy, such as the balance between the formal and shadow economies. There may be repercussions on the supply and demand for goods. We have focused on part of the picture—an important part, but only part.

FINAL REMARK

To sum up, there are undoubtedly ways in which the welfare state, and the taxes necessary to finance it, cause people to work less than they would otherwise have done. In the medium and long term there may be adverse consequences for economic performance. In this sense there are leakages from the bucket in carrying out redistribution. However, the extent of such disincentives should not be exaggerated. Our review of the evidence suggests that a number of the effects which have been identified are relatively small in size. Perhaps more importantly, there are relatively few situations in which a disincentive effect has been clearly established: there are many areas where we have a great deal still to learn. To dismantle the welfare state on the grounds that it causes disincentives would risk losing its very definite redistributive advantages for the sake of an uncertain pay-off in terms of improved economic performance.

Our findings may be seen as negative, in that we have emphasized the limits to the conclusions, rather than definite findings. As such, our conclusions are in sharp contrast to the widely held popular opinion that the welfare state has seriously damaged economic incentives. It may, however, be that the value of economic research lies not so much in leading us to clear policy prescriptions as in teaching about the limits of our knowledge.

REFERENCES

AABERGE, R., STRØM, S., and WENNEMO, T. (1989), 'Skatt, arbeidstilbud og intektsfordelning i Sverige' (Tax, Labour Supply and Income Distribution in Sweden), in RINK IV.

ABEL-SMITH, B., and TOWNSEND, P. (1965), *The Poor and the Poorest*. London: Bell.

ACKUM, S. (1991), 'Youth Unemployment, Labour Market Programs and Subsequent Earnings', *Scandinavian Journal of Economics*, 93: 531–43.

AGELL, J. (1990), 'Skattereformen och kapitalbeskattningen: Halvmesyr eller förståndig kompromiss?' (Tax Reform and Taxation of Capital: Half-measures or Reasonable Compromise?), in J. Agell, K.-G. Mäler, and J. Södersten (eds.), *Ekonomiska perspektiv på skattereformen*, 25–52, Ekonomiska Rådet, Konjunkturinstitutet, Nordstedts Tryckeri, Stockholm.

AGUILAR, R., and GUSTAFSSON, B. (1992), 'Social Assistance and Public Expenditures', Dept. of Economics, Univ. of Göteborg.

ALOGOSKOUFIS, G., and MANNING, A. (1988), 'On the Persistence of Unemployment', *Economic Policy*, 7.

ALTMANN, R. (1981), 'The Incomes of Elderly Men in Britain', Ph.D. thesis, Univ. of London.

ALTONJI, J. G. (1986), 'Intertemporal Substitution in Labour Supply: Evidence from Micro-Data', *Journal of Political Economy*, 94: S176–215.

ANDERSEN, P.S. (1992), 'Taxes and Labour Market Developments', in Bilag til Finansredegørelse 92, *Forskning om arbejdsmarkedet* (Addendum to Fiscal Report 92, Research on the Labour Market), 7–96. Copenhagen: Ministry of Finance.

ANDERSEN, T. M., and OVERGAARD, P. B. (1990), 'Demand and Capacity Constraints on Danish Employment', in J. H. Drèze and C. Bean (eds.), *Europe's Unemployment Problems*. Mass.: MIT Press.

—— and RISAGER, O. (1990), 'Wage Formation in Denmark', in L. Calmfors (ed.), *Wage Formation and Macroeconomic Policy in the Nordic Countries*. Oxford: Oxford Univ. Press.

ANDERSSON, I., and GUSTAFSSON, B. (1992*a*), 'Fattigdomsfällor' (Poverty Traps), Rapport till ESO, Finansdepartementet, Stockholm.

—— —— (1992*b*), 'Modelling Poverty Traps and Marginal Effects in Sweden', Dept. of Economics, Univ. of Gothenburg.

ANDERSSON, I. A.-K. (1989), *Familjebeskattning, konsumtion och arbetsutbud* (Taxation of the Family, Consumption and Labour Supply). Nationalekonomiska institutionen, Univ. of Gothenburg.

—— and DAGSVIK, J. K., STRØM, S., and WENNEMO, T. (1988), 'Nonconvex Budget Sets, Hours Restriction and Labour Supply in Sweden', Central Bureau of Statistics, Oslo.

ARONSSON, T., and WIKSTRÖM, M. (1991), *Nonlinear Taxes in a Life-Cycle Consistent Model of Family Labour Supply*. Umeå Economic Studies 249, Umeå.

ARRUFAT, J. L., and ZABALZA, A. (1986), 'Female Labor Supply with Taxation, Random Preferences, and Optimization Errors', *Econometrica*, 54: 47–63.

Ashworth, J. A., and Ulph, D. T. (1981), 'Household Models', in C. V. Brown (ed.), *Taxation and Labour Supply*. London: Allen and Unwin.

Atkinson, A. B. (1983), *The Economics of Inequality*, 2nd edn. Oxford: Oxford Univ. Press.

—— (1991), 'The Development of State Pensions in the United Kingdom', in W. Schmähl (ed.), *The Future of Basic and Supplementary Pension Schemes in the European Community*. Baden-Baden: Nomos.

—— and Champion, B. (1989), 'Family Income Supplement and Two Parent Families', in A. B. Atkinson, *Poverty and Social Security*. Hemel Hempstead: Harvester Wheatsheaf.

—— Gomulka, J., Micklewright, J., and Rau, N. (1984), 'Unemployment Benefit, Duration and Incentives in Britain: How Robust is the Evidence?', *Journal of Public Economics*, 23: 3–26.

—— and Micklewright, J. (1985), *Unemployment Benefits and Unemployment Duration*. London School of Economics.

—— —— (1989), 'Turning the Screw: Benefits for the Unemployed 1979–88', in A. Dilnot and I. Walker (eds.), *The Economics of Social Security*. Oxford: Oxford Univ. Press.

—— —— (1991), 'Unemployment Compensation and Labor Market Transions: A Critical Review', *Journal of Economic Literature*, 29: 1679–1727.

—— and Stern, N. H. (1979), 'A Note on the Allocation of Time', *Economics Letters*, 3: 119–23.

—— —— (1980), 'On the Switch from Direct to Indirect Taxation', *Journal of Public Economics*, 14: 195–224.

—— —— (1981), 'On Labour Supply and Commodity Demands', in A. Deaton (ed.), *Essays in the Theory and Measurement of Consumer Behaviour in Honour of Richard Stone*, 265–96. Cambridge: Cambridge Univ. Press.

Auerbach, A. J., and Kotlikoff, L. J. (1987), *Dynamic Fiscal Policy*. Cambridge: Cambridge Univ. Press.

Axelsson, R. (1989), *Svensk arbetsmarknadsutbildning* (Swedish Labour Market Training). Umeå Economic Studies 197, Umeå.

Bäckman, D. (1992), 'Sjukfrånvaro och arbetslöshet—samband eller skensamband?' (Sickness Absence and Unemployment: Relation or Pseudo-relation?), *Sociologisk Forskning*, 29: 38–49.

Barmby, T. A., Orme, C. D., and Treble, J. G. (1991), 'Worker Absenteeism: An Analysis using Microdata', *Economic Journal*, 101: 214–29.

Bean, C. R., Layard, R., and Nickell, S. (1986), 'The Rise in Unemployment: A Multi-Country Study', *Economica*, 53, supplement, 1–22.

Becker, G. S. (1965), 'A Theory of the Allocation of Time', *Economic Journal*, 75: 493–517.

Berglind, H. (1977), 'Förtidspension eller arbete?' (Disability Pension or Work?), in *Förtidspensionering*, SOU 1977: 88.

Beveridge, Sir W. (1942), *Social Insurance and Allied Services*. London: HMSO.

Bielenski, H., Enderle, J., and von Rosenbladt, B. (1992), *Arbeitsmarktmonitor für die neuen Bundesländer* (Labour Market Monitor for the New Länder). Bayreuth: Druckhaus Bayreuth.

Bingley, P., Symons, E., and Walker, I. (1992), 'The Labour Supply of UK Lone Mothers: The Effects of Maintenance, and the Welfare System', paper presented at the Fiscal Incentives and Labour Supply Conference, IFS, London, June.

Björklund, A. (1978), 'On the Duration of Unemployment in Sweden, 1965–1976', *Scandinavian Journal of Economics*, 80: 421-39.

—— (1981), *Studies in the Dynamics of Unemployment*. Stockholm: EFI.

—— (1990), 'Evaluations of Swedish Labour Market Policy', *Finnish Economic Papers*, 3: 3–13.

—— (1991), 'Vem får sjukpenning? En empirisk analys av sjukfrånvarons bestämningsfaktorer' (Who Receives Sickness Pay? An Empirical Analysis of Determinants on Sickness Absence), in SOU 1991: 82, *Arbetskraft, arbetsmarknad och produktivitet*.

—— and Holmlund, B. (1989), 'Effects of Extended Unemployment Compensation in Sweden', in B. Gustafsson and A. Klevmarken (eds.), *The Political Economy of Social Security*. Amsterdam: North Holland.

—— —— (1991), 'The Economics of Unemployment Insurance: The Case of Sweden', in A. Björklund *et al.*, *Labour Market Policy and Unemployment Insurance*. Oxford: Clarendon Press.

Blomquist, N. S. (1983), 'The Effect of Income Taxation on the Labour Supply of Married Men in Sweden', *Journal of Public Economics*, 22: 169–97.

—— (1985), 'Skatter och arbetsutbud' (Taxes and Labour Supply), *Ds Fi* 1985: 10, Stockholm.

—— (1989), 'Beskattningens effekt på arbetsutbudet' (The Effects of Taxes on Labour Supply), in *Reformerad inkomstbeskattning*, Del IV, Bilaga 7, Betänkande av utredningen om reformerad inkomstbeskattning, SOU 1989: 33.

—— (1992), *Estimation Methods for Male Labour Supply Functions: How to Take Account of Taxes*, paper presented at the Fiscal Incentives and Labour Supply Conference, Uppsala, June.

—— and Hansson-Brusewitz, U. (1990), 'The Effects of Taxes on Male and Female Labour Supply in Sweden', *Journal of Human Resources*, 25: 317–57.

Blundell, R. (1987), 'Econometric Approaches to the Specification of Life-Cycle Labour Supply and Commodity Demand Behaviour', *Econometric Reviews*, 6/1: 103–65.

—— Duncan, A., and Meghir, C. (1992), 'Taxation and Empirical Labour Supply Models: Lone Parents in the UK', *Economic Journal*, 102: 265–78.

—— —— —— (1993), 'Robust Estimation of Labour Supply Responses in the Presence of Taxes', paper presented at the Fiscal Incentives and Labour Supply Conference, IFS, London, June.

—— Fry, V., and Walker, I. (1988), 'Modelling the Take-Up of Means-Tested Benefits: The Case of Housing Benefit in the UK', *Economic Journal*, 98: 58–74.

—— Ham, J., and Meghir, C. (1987), Unemployment and Female Labour Supply', *Economic Journal*, 97: 44–64.

—— Meghir, C., Symons, E., and Walker, I. (1988), 'Labour Supply Specification and the Empirical Evaluation of Tax Reforms', *Journal of Public Economics*, 36: 23–52.

—— and WALKER, I. (1982), 'Modelling the Joint Determination of Household Labour Supplies and Commodity Demands', *Economic Journal*, 92: 351–64.

—— —— (1986), 'A Life-Cycle Consistent Empirical Model of Labour Supply Using Cross Section Data', *Review of Economic Studies*, 53: 539–58.

BOSWORTH, B., and BURTLESS, G. (1992), 'Effects of Tax Reform on Labor Supply, Investment and Survey', *Journal of Economic Perspectives*, 6: 3–26.

BOUND, J., BROWN, C., DUNCAN, G. J., and RODGERS, W. L. (1990), 'Measurement Errors in Cross-Sectional and Longitudinal Labour Market Surveys: Validation Study Evidence', in J. Hartog *et al.* (eds.), *Panel Data and Labour Market Studies*. Amsterdam: North Holland.

BOURGUIGNON, F., and MAGNAC, T. (1990), 'Labour Supply and Taxation in France', *Journal of Human Resources*, 25: 358–89.

BOVER, O. (1989), 'Estimating Intertemporal Labour Supply Elasticities Using Structural Models', *Economic Journal*, 99: 1026–39.

BRADSHAW, J., and MILLAR, J. (1991), *Lone Parent Families in the UK*. London: HMSO.

BROSE, P. (1992), *En studie av sjukfrånvaron inom HUS* (A Study of Sickness Absence within HUS). Dept. of Economics, Univ. of Göteborg.

BROWN, C. V. (1983), *Taxation and the Incentive to Work*. Oxford: Oxford Univ. Press.

—— and LEVIN, E. (1974), 'The Effects of Income Taxation on Overtime', *Economic Journal*, 84: 833–48.

—— —— ROSA, P. J., RUFFELL, R. J., and, ULPH, D. T. (1986), 'Payment Systems, Demand Constraints and Their Implications for Research into Labour Supply, in R. W. Blundell and I. Walker, (eds.), *Unemployment, Search and Labour Supply*. Cambridge: Cambridge Univ. Press.

BROWNING, M. J., DEATON, A., and IRISH, M. (1985), 'A Profitable Approach to Labour Supply and Commodity Demands over the Life-Cycle', *Econometrica*, 53: 503–43.

BURDA, M. (1988), 'Wait Unemployment in Europe', *Economic Policy*, 7: 393–425.

BURTLESS, G., and HAUSMAN, J. (1978), 'The Effect of Taxes on Labour Supply', *Journal of Political Economy*, 86: 1103–30.

CALMFORS, L., and FORSLUND, A. (1991), 'Real-Wage Determination and Labour Market Policies: The Swedish Experience', *Economic Journal*, 101: 1130–48.

—— and NYMOEN, R. (1990), 'Real Wage Adjustment and Employment Policies in the Nordic Countries', *Economic Policy*, 11: 397–448.

CARD, D. (1990), 'Intertemporal Labour Supply: An Assessment', paper presented at the 6th World Congress of the Econometric Society, Barcelona, August.

CENTRAL STATISTICAL OFFICE (1952), *Annual Abstract of Statistics 1938–1950*, No. 88. London: HMSO.

—— (1961), *Annual Abstract of Statistics*, No. 98. London: HMSO.

—— (1992), *Annual Abstract of Statistics*, No. 128. London: HMSO.

—— (1993), 'The Effects of Taxes and Benefits on Household Incomes 1990', *Economic Trends*. (Jan.). London: HMSO.

COGAN, J. F. (1981), 'Fixed Costs and Labor Supply', *Econometrica*, 49: 945–64.

COWELL, F. A. (1990), *Cheating the Government*. Cambridge Mass.: MIT Press.

CRAMER, J. C. (1980), 'The Effects of Fertility on Husband's Economic Activity: Evidence from Static, Dynamic, and Nonrecursive Models, in J. L. Simon and J. DaVazo (eds.), *Research in Population Economics*, 2: 151–182.

DAGSVIK, J. K. (1988), *The Continuous Generalized Extreme Value Model with Special Reference to Static Models of Labour Supply*. Oslo: Central Bureau of Statistics.

—— and STRØM, S. (1988), *A Labour Supply Model for Married Couples with Non-Convex Budget Sets and Latent Rationing*. Oslo: Central Bureau of Statistics.

Danish Social Commission (1992), *Uden arbejde. Overførselsindkomst til midtergruppen* (Out of Work: Transfer Incomes to the Middle-Aged Group). Copenhagen.

Dept. of Health and Social Security (1980), *Social Security Statistics 1980*. London: HMSO.

—— (1985), *Reform of Social Security*. London: HMSO.

—— (1989), *Social Security Statistics 1989*. London: HMSO.

—— (1991), *Tax/Benefit Model Tables*. London: DSS.

—— (1993*a*), *Social Security: The Government's Expenditure Plans 1993–94 to 1995–96*. London: HMSO.

—— (1993*b*), *Income Related Benefits: Estimates of Take-Up in 1989*. London: DSS.

DICKENS, W. T., and LUNDBERG, S. J. (1993), 'Hours Restrictions and Labor Supply', *International Economic Review*, 34: 169–92.

DILNOT, A., and DUNCAN, A. (1992), 'Lone Mothers, Family Credit and Paid Work', *Fiscal Studies*, 13: 1–21.

—— and KELL, M. (1987), 'Male Unemployment and Women's Work', *Fiscal Studies*, 8: 1–16.

—— —— (1988), 'Top-Rate Tax Cuts and Incentives: Some Empirical Evidence', *Fiscal Studies*, 9: 70–92.

DISNEY, R., and WEBB, S. (1991), 'Why Are There So Many Long-Term Sick in Britain?', *Economic Journal*, 101: 252–62.

DOHERTY, N. (1979), 'National Insurance and Absence from Work', *Economic Journal*, 89: 50–65.

DORSET, R., and HEADY, C. (1991), 'The Take-Up of Means-Tested Benefits by Working Families with Children', *Fiscal Studies*, 12(4): 22–32.

DUCLOS, J.-Y. (1992), *Progressivity, Redistribution and Equity, with Application to 1985 Britain*. London School of Economics.

DUNCAN, A. S., and JONES, A. M. (1991), *WP-REG*. London: IFS.

DUNCAN, G. J., and HILL, D. H. (1985), An Investigation of the Extent and Consequences of Measurement Errors in Labour Economic Survey Data, *Journal of Labour Economics*, 3: 508–22.

ECKSTEIN, Z., and WOLPIN, K. (1989), 'Dynamic Labour Force Participation of Married Women and Endogenous Work Experience', *Review of Economic Studies*, 56: 375–90.

ECONOMIC COUNCIL (1989), *Dansk Økonomi, maj 1989* (Danish Economy, May 1989). Copenhagen.

EDELBALK, P.-G. (1975), *Arbetslöshetsdebatten. En studie i Svenska socialpolitik 1892–1934* (The Debate on Unemployment: A Study in Swedish Social Policy, 1892–1934). Skrifter utgivna av Ekonomiska-Historiska föreningen i Lund, Lund.

—— (1988), 'Från motstånd till genombrott: Den svenska arbetslöshetsförsäkringen 1935–54' (From Resistance to Breakthrough: Swedish Unemployment Insurance, 1935–54), *Meddelanden från Socialhögskolan*, 1988:3.

—— and WADENSJÖ, E. (1978), 'Unemployment and Seasonal Unemployment, *Economy and History*, 21: 3–12.

—— —— (1988), Contractually Determined Insurance Schemes for Manual Workers, in B. Gustafsson and A. Klevmarken (eds.), *The Political Economy of Social Security*. Amsterdam: North Holland.

—— —— (1989), 'Contractually Determined Insurance Schemes for Manual Workers', in B. Gustafsson and A. Klevmarken (eds.), *The Political Economy of Social Insurance*. Amsterdam: Elsevier-North Holland.

EDIN, P.-A. (1988), 'Individual Consequences of Plant Closure'. Ph.D. thesis, Univ. of Uppsala.

—— and HOLMLUND, B. (1991), 'Unemployment, Vacancies and Labour Market Programmes: Swedish Evidence', in F. P. Schioppa (ed.), *Mismatch and Labour Market Mobility*. Cambridge: Cambridge Univ. Press.

—— —— (1992), *The Swedish Wage Structure: The Rise and Fall of Solidarity Wage Policy?* Dept. of Economics, Univ. of Uppsala.

—— and ÖSTROS, T. (1993), *Wage Behaviour and Labour Market Programs in Sweden: Evidence from Micro Data*. Dept. of Economics, Univ. of Uppsala.

ERMISCH, J. F., and WRIGHT, R. E. (1991), 'Welfare Benefits and Lone Parents' Employment in the UK', *Journal of Human Resources*, 26: 424–56.

FELDSTEIN, M. S. (1982), 'Inflation, Tax Rules and Investment: Some Econometric Evidence', *Econometrica*, 50: 825–62.

FENN, P. (1981), 'Sickness Duration, Residual Disability, and Income Replacement: An Empirical Analysis', *Economic Journal*, 91: 158–73.

FLOOD, L. (1988), *Measurement and Estimation of Male Labour Supply*. Dept. of Economics, Univ. of Gothenburg.

—— (1990), 'Att mäta och estimera utbudet av arbetskraft' (Measuring and Estimating Labour Supply), in A. Klevmarken (ed.), *Tid och Råd*. Stockholm: Almqvist and Wicksell.

—— and KLEVMARKEN, N. A. (1990), 'Tidsanvändningen i Sverige 1984' (Time Use in Sweden), in *Kvinnors roll i ekonomin*, Bilaga 23 till LU90. Finansdepartementet, Stockholm. (A shorter version in English is available as *Market Work, Household Work and Leisure: An Analysis of Time-Use in Sweden*). Dept. of Economics, Univ. of Gothenburg (1992).

—— and MACURDY, T. (1991), *Work Disincentive Effects of Taxes: An Empirical Analysis of Swedish Men*. Dept of Economics, Univ. of Gothenburg.

—— —— (1992), 'Work Disincentive Effects of Taxes: An Empirical Analysis of Swedish Men', paper presented at the Fiscal Incentives and Labour Supply Conference, IFS, London, June.

FORSLUND, A. (1992), 'Arbetslöshet och arbetsmarknadspolitik' (Unemployment and Labour Market Policy), *Bilaga 7 till Långtidsutredningen 1992*. Stockholm: Allmänna Förlaget.

Fraker, T., and Moffitt, R. (1988), 'The Effect of Food Stamps on Labour Supply', *Journal of Public Economics*, 35: 25–56.

Franz, W. (1985), 'An Economic Analysis of Female Work Participation, Education and Fertility: Theory and Empirical Evidence for the Federal Republic of Germany', *Journal of Labor Economics*, supplement, 3: 218–34.

—— (1991), *Arbeitsmarktökonomie* (Labour Market Economics). Berlin: Springer.

—— and Kawasaki, S. (1981), 'Labour Supply of Married Women in the Federal Republic of Germany: Theory and Empirical Results from a New Estimation Procedure', *Empirical Economics*, 6: 129–43.

Freeman, R. (1988), 'Labor Market Institutions and Economic Performance', *Economic Policy*, 6: 63–80.

Frey, B., Weck, H., and Pommerehne, W. W. (1982), 'Has the Shadow Economy Grown in Germany? An Exploratory Study', *Weltwirtschaftliches Archiv*, 118: 499–524.

Garcia, J. (1989), Incentive and Welfare Effects of Reforming the British Benefit System, in S. Nickell *et al.*, *The Nature of Unemployment in Britain*, Oxford: Oxford Univ. Press.

Geib, T., Lechner, M., Pfeiffer, F., and Salomon, S. (1992), *Die Struktur der Einkommensunterschiede in Ost- und Westdeutschland ein Jahr nach der Vereinigung* (The Income Structure in East and West Germany One Year after Unification). Mannheim: ZEW.

Government Actuary (1991), *Occupational Pension Schemes 1987*. London: HMSO.

Gustafsson, B. (1984), 'Macroeconomic Performance, Old Age Security and the Rate of Social Assistance in Sweden', *European Economic Review*, 26: 319–38.

—— Hyden, L., and Salonen, T. (forthcoming), 'Decision-Making on Social Assistance in Major Swedish Cities', *Scandinavian Journal of Social Welfare*.

—— and Kjulin, U. (1993), *Public Expenditures on Day Care and the Distribution of Economic Well-Being: The Case of Sweden*. Dept. of Economics, Univ. of Gothenburg.

Gustafsson, S. (1992*a*), 'Separate Taxation and Married Women's Labor Supply: A Comparison of West Germany and Sweden', *Journal of Population Economics*, 5: 61–85.

—— (1992*b*), *Public Policies and Women's Labor Force Participation: A Comparison between Sweden, the Netherlands and Germany*. Univ. of Amsterdam.

—— and Stafford, F. (1992), 'Daycare Subsidies and Labour Supply in Sweden', *Journal of Human Resources*, 27: 204–30.

Haas, L. (1992), *Equal Parenthood and Social Policy: A Study of Parental Leave in Sweden*. Albany, NY: State Univ. of New York Press.

Hall, R. E. (1975), 'Effects of the Experimental Negative Income Tax on Labor Supply', in J. A. Pechman and P. M. Timpane (eds.), *Work Incentives and Income Guarantees*. Washington DC: Brookings Institution.

Ham, J. C. (1982), 'Estimation of a Labor Supply Model with Censoring Due to Unemployment and Underemployment', *Review of Economic Studies*, 49/2: 335–54.

—— (1986*a*), 'Testing Whether Unemployment Represents Life-Cycle Labor Supply Behaviour', *Review of Economic Studies*, 53: 559–78.

—— (1986*b*), 'On the Interpretation of Unemployment in Empirical Labour Supply Analysis', in R. W. Blundell and I. Walker (eds.), *Unemployment, Search and Labour Supply*. Cambridge: Cambridge Univ. Press.

HANSEN, V. S. (1990), 'Løn og fagforeninger: Estimation af makro-lønrelationer' (Wages and Unions: Estimation of Macro Wage Functions), *Nationaløkonomisk Tidsskrift*, 128: 309–24.

HANSSON, I. (1984), 'Marginal Cost of Public Funds for Different Tax Instruments and Government Expenditures', *Scandinavian Journal of Economics*, 86: 115–30.

HANSSON-BRUSEWITZ, U. (1992), 'Labour Supply of Elderly Men. Do Taxes and Pension Systems Matter?'. Diss., Dept. of Economics, Univ. of Uppsala.

HAUSMAN, J. A. (1979), 'The Econometrics of Labour Supply on Convex Budget Sets', *Economic Letters*, 3: 171–74.

—— (1980), 'The Effect of Wages, Taxes and Fixed Costs on Women's Labor Force Participation', *Journal of Public Economics*, 14: 161–94.

—— (1981), 'Labour Supply', in H. J. Aaron and J. A. Pechman (eds.), *How Taxes Affect Economic Behaviour*. Washington DC: Brookings Institution.

—— (1985), 'The Econometrics of Nonlinear Budget Sets', *Econometrica*, 53: 1255–82.

—— and POTERBA, J. M. (1987), 'Household Behaviour and the Tax Reform Act of 1986', *Journal of Economic Perspectives*, 1: 101–19.

—— and RUUD, P. (1984), 'Family Labour with Taxes', *American Economic Review*, (May).

HECKMAN, J. J. (1974*a*), 'Shadow Prices, Market Wages and Labor Supply', *Econometrica*, 42: 679–94.

—— (1974*b*), 'Life-Cycle Consumption and Labour Supply: An Explanation of the Relationship between Income and Consumption over the Life-Cycle', *American Economic Review*, 64: 188–94.

—— (1974*c*), 'Effects of Child-Care Programs on Women's Work Effort', *Journal of Political Economy*, 82: S136–63.

—— (1976), 'A Life-Cycle Model of Earnings, Learning, and Consumption', *Journal of Political Economy*, 84: S11–44.

—— and MACURDY, T. E. (1980), 'A Life-Cycle Model of Female Labour Supply', *Review of Economic Studies*, 47: 47–74.

—— and WALKER, J. R. (1990*a*), 'The Relationship Between Wages and Income and the Timing and Spacing of Births: Evidence from Swedish Longitudinal Data', *Econometrica*, 58: 1411–41.

—— —— (1990*b*), 'The Third Birth in Sweden', *Journal of Population Economics*, 3: 235–75.

HEDSTRÖM, P. (1980), *Förtidspensionering: Välfärd eller ofärd?* (Disability Retirement: Welfare or Misfortune?). Stockholm: Instituttet för Social forskning.

—— (1987), 'Disability Pension: Welfare or Misfortune?', in R. Erikson *et al.* (eds.), *The Scandinavian Model: Welfare States and Welfare Research*. New York: M.E. Sharp.

HEIKENSTEN, L. (1984), *Studies in Structural Change and Labour Market Adjustment*. Stockholm: EFI.

HERSOUG, T. (1984), 'Union Response to Tax Changes', *Oxford Economic Papers*, 36: 37–58.

HILL, R. C., and STAFFORD, F. P. (1985), Lifetime Fertility, Child Care and Labour Supply, in F. T. Juster and F. P. Stafford (eds.), *Time, Goods and Well-Being*. Ann Arbor: Univ. of Michigan.

HILLS, J. (ed.) (1990), *The State of Welfare*. Oxford: Oxford Univ. Press.

HM Treasury (1990), *The Government's Expenditure Plans 1990–91 to 1992–93: Department of Social Security*. London: HMSO

—— (1993), *Public Expenditure Analyses to 1995–96*. London: HMSO.

HOEL, M. (1989), *Income Taxes and Non-market Clearing Wages*. Univ. of Oslo.

HOEM, J. (1991), 'To Marry, Just in Case . . . : The Swedish Widow's-Pension Reform and the Peak in Marriages in December 1989', *Acta Sociologica*, 34: 127–35.

—— (1992), *Public Policy as the Fuel of Fertility: Effects of a Policy Reform on the Pace of Child Bearing in Sweden in the 1980s*. Univ. of Stockholm.

HOLLAND, D. M. (1969), 'The Effect of Taxation on Effort: Some Results for Business Executives', in *Proceedings of the 62nd Annual Conference of the National Tax Association*.

HOLMES, P. (1990), 'The Provision, Role and Economic Impact of State Sickness Insurance: A Review', *British Review of Economic Issues*, 12: 17–39.

HOLMLUND, B. (1986), *Vägar ut ur Arbetslöshet: Stockholmsungdomars erfarenheter 1981–1982* (Roads out of Unemployment: Experiences of Stockholm Youth 1981–1982). Stockholm: Fackföreningsrörelsens Institut för Ekonomisk Forskning.

—— (1990), *Svensklönebildning: Teori, emperi, politik; Bilaga 24 till LU 90* (Swedish Wage-Setting: Theory, Practice, Policy; Addendum to the Medium-Term Plan 1990). Stockholm: Allmänna Förlaget.

HUJER, R., and SCHNABEL, R. (1991), 'Spezifikation und Schätzung eines Lebenszyklusmodells des Arbeitsangebots' (Specification and Estimation of a Life-Cycle Labour Supply Model), *Ifo-Studien*, 37: 271–96.

—— and SCHNEIDER, H. (1989), 'The Analysis of Labor Market Mobility Using Panel Data', *European Economic Review*, 33: 530–36.

ILO (International Labour Office) (1985), *The Cost of Social Security: Eleventh International Inquiry, 1978–1980*. Geneva: ILO.

—— (1992), *The Cost of Social Security: Thirteenth International Inquiry, 1984–1986*. Geneva: ILO.

JACKMAN, R. (1990), 'Wage Formation in the Nordic Countries Viewed from an International Perspective', in L. Calmfors (ed.), *Wage Formation and Macroeconomic Policy in the Nordic Countries*. Oxford: Oxford Univ. Press.

—— Pissarides, C., and Savouri, S. (1990), 'Labour Market Policies and Unemployment in the OECD', *Economic Policy*, 11: 449–90.

JAKOBSSON, R. (1982), *Three Papers on Estimation of Labour Supply Responses on Swedish Data*. Dept. of Economics, Univ. of Umeå.

JAKOBSSON, U., and NORMANN, G. (1974), *Inkomstbeskattningen i den ekonomiska politiken* (Personal Income Taxation and Economic Policy). Uppsala: Almqvist and Wiksell.

JENKINS, S. P. (1992), Lone Mothers, Employment and Full-Time Work Probabilities, *Economic Journal*, 102: 310–20.

JENSEN, P. (1987), 'Arbejdsløshed og beskæftigelse: en empirisk analyse af individuel arbejdsmarkedsadfærd', (Unemployment and Employment: An Empirical Analysis of Individual Labour Market Behaviour), *Nationaløkonomisk Tidsskrift*, 125: 337–54.

—— and WESTERGÅRD-NIELSEN, N. (1990), 'Temporary Layoffs', in J. Hartog *et al.* (eds.), *Panel Data and Labour Market Studies*. Amsterdam: North-Holland.

JOHNSON, G., and LAYARD, R. (1986), 'The Natural Rate of Unemployment', in O. Ashenfelter and R. Layard (eds.), *Handbook of Labour Economics*. Amsterdam: North-Holland.

JOHNSON, P., and FALKINGHAM, J. (1992), *Ageing and Economic Welfare*. London: Sage.

—— and STARK, G. (1989), 'Taxation and Social Security 1979–1989: The Impact on Household Incomes', Institute for Fiscal Studies, *Commentary*, (May).

—— and WEBB, S. (1992), 'Recent Trends in UK Income Inequality: Causes and Policy Responses', paper presented at the Royal Economic Society Conference, City Univ., London, Mar.

—— and ZIMMERMANN, K. F. (eds.) (1993*a*), *Labour Markets in an Ageing Europe*. Cambridge: Cambridge Univ. Press.

—— —— (1993*b*), 'Ageing and the European Labour Market: Public Policy Issues', in Johnson and Zimmermann (1993*a*).

JUUL, S. (1992), *Yngre førtidspensionister* (Younger People with Early-Retirement Pensions). Copenhagen: Danish National Institute of Social Research.

KAISER, H., VAN ESSEN, U., and SPAHN, P. B. (1992), 'Income Taxation and the Supply of Labour in West Germany', *Jahrbücher für Nationalökonomie und Statistik*, 209/1–2: 87–105.

KANGAS, O. (1991), *The Politics of Social Rights*. Stockholm: Swedish Institute for Social Research.

KELL, M., and WRIGHT, J. (1990), 'Benefits and the Labour Supply of Women Married to Unemployed Men', *Economic Journal*, 100: 119–26.

KENNY, L. W. (1983), 'The Accumulation of Human Capital During Marriage by Males', *Economic Inquiry*, 11: 223–31.

KILLINGSWORTH, M. R. (1983), *Labour Supply*, Cambridge: Cambridge Univ. Press.

—— and HECKMAN, J. J. (1986), 'Female Labour Supply: A Survey', in O. Ashenfelter and R. Layard (eds.), *Handbook of Labour Economics*. Amsterdam: Elsevier.

KIRCHGÄSSNER, G. (1983), 'Size and Development of the West German Shadow Economy, 1955–1980', *Zeitschrift für die gesamte Staatswirtschaft*, 139: 197–214.

—— (1984), 'Verfahren zur Erfassung des in der Schattenwirtschaft erarbeiteten Sozialprodukts' (Measuring the Shadow Economy), *Allgemeines Statistisches Archiv*, 68: 378–405.

KLEVMARKEN, N. A. (1990), *Household Market and Nonmarket Activities (HUS) Design, Field Work and Nonresponse*. Dept. of Economics, Univ. of Gothenburg.

Klevmarken, N. A. and Tasiran, A. (1991), *A Duration Analysis of Fertility in Sweden*. Dept. of Economics, Univ. of Gothenburg.

Koch, A. (1991), 'Familienpolitik und Arbeitsmarkt 1945–1990' (Family Policy and Labour Market 1945–1990), in M. Assenmacher (ed.), *Probleme der Einheit, Frauen am Arbeitsmarkt* (Problems of Unification, Women on the Labour Market). Marburg: Metropolis.

Korpi, T. (1991), *Labour Market Policy, Employment Alternatives, and the Probability of Leaving Unemployment in Sweden*. Stockholm: Univ. of Stockholm.

—— (1992), *Employment Stability Following Unemployment and Manpower Programs*. Stockholm: Univ. of Stockholm.

Korpi, W. (1992), *Halkar Sverige efter?* (Is Sweden Lagging Behind?). Stockholm: Carlssons.

Krueger, A. B., and Pischke, J. (1992), *A Comparative Analysis of East and West German Labor Markets Before and After Unification*. Mannheim: ZEW.

Kruse, A., and Söderström, L. (1989), 'Early Retirement in Sweden', in W. Schmähl (ed.), *Redefining the Process of Retirement: An International Perspective*. Heidelberg: Springer.

Kugler, P., and Schwendener, P. (1988), 'Arbeitsangebot, Grenzsteuerbelastung und der permanente Lohnsatz: Empirische Ergebnisse für die Schweiz' (Labour Supply, Marginal Tax Burden and Permanent Wage: Empirical Results for Switzerland), *Schweizerische Zeitschrift für Volkswirtschaft und Statistik,* 124: 243–56.

Lampert, H. (1991), *Lehrbuch der Sozialpolitik* (Social Policy). Berlin: Springer.

Lancaster, T., and Nickell, S. J. (1980), 'The Analysis of Re-Employment Probabilities for the Unemployed', *Journal of the Royal Statistical Society*, Ser. A, 47: 1–12.

Langfeldt, E. (1984), *Die Schattenwirtschaft in der Bundesrepublik Deutschland* (The Shadow Economy in the Federal Republic of Germany). Tübingen: Mohr.

Lantto, K., and Lindblom, E. (1987), 'Är arbetslösheten hälsosam?' (Is Unemployment Healthy?), *Ekonomisk Debatt*, 15: 333–6.

Larsen, K. A. (1992), 'Arbejdsstyrkens konjunkturfølsomhed' (Cyclical Sensitivity of the Labour Force), *Søkelys på arbeidsmarkedet*, 93–8.

Layard, R. (1986), *How to Beat Unemployment*. Oxford: Oxford Univ. Press.

—— Barton, M., and Zabalza, A. (1980), 'Married Women's Participation and Hours', *Economica*, 47: 51–72.

—— and Nickell, S. (1986), 'Unemployment in Britain', *Economica*, 87: S121–70.

—— —— and Jackman, R. (1991), *Unemployment*. Oxford: Oxford Univ. Press.

—— —— —— (1992), *Unemployment: Macroeconomic Performance and the Labour Market*. Oxford: Oxford Univ. Press.

Lazear, E. P. (1983), 'A Competitive Theory of Monopoly Unionism', *American Economic Review*, 73: 631–43.

Lechner, M., and Pfeiffer, F. (1992), *Planning for Self-Employment at the Beginning of a Market Economy: Evidence from Individual Data of East German Workers*. Mannheim: ZEW.

LEU, R. E., and KUGLER, P. (1986), 'Angebotsorientierte Ökonomie: ein Rezept für die schweizerische Wirtschaftspolitik?' (Supply-Side Economics: An Alternative for Swiss Economic Policy?), *Geld und Währung*, 2: 16–35.

LINDER, B. S. (1970), *The Harried Leisure Class*. New York: Columbia Univ. Press.

LINDQVIST, R. (1990), *Från folkrörelse till välfärdsbyråkrati* (From Popular Movement to Welfare Bureaucracy). Arkivs avhandlingsserie 33, Lund.

LIPPE, L. (1992), 'Die Umwälzungen auf dem Arbeitsmarkt der früheren DDR und ihre Folgen für die Lebensverhältnisse von Jugendlichen' (Labour Market Changes in the Former GDR and the Consequences for the Living Conditions of Young People), in G. Engelbrech *et al.* (eds.), *Bedingungen der Frauenerwerbsarbeit im deutsch-deutschen Einigungsprozeß, Beiträge zur Arbeitsmarkt- und Berufsforschung* (Conditions of Female Labour Force Participation During Unification). Nürnberg: BfA.

LJONES, O., and STRØM, S. (1987), *Tilbud av arbeid i Sverige* (Labour Supply in Sweden). Stockholm: Allmänna Förlaget.

LOCKWOOD, B., and MANNING, A. (1993), *Wage-Setting and the Tax System: Theory and Evidence from the UK*. London: LSE, Centre for Economic Performance.

LÖFGREN, K. G., and WIKSTRÖM, M. (1991), *Lönebildning och arbetsmarknadspolitik* (Wage-setting and Labour Market Policy). Stockholm: Arbetsmarknadsdepartementet.

LUNDAGER, J., and SCHNEIDER, F. (1986), 'En sammenligning af udviklingen i den sorte økonomi for Danmark, Norge og Sverige' (A Comparison of the Development of the Shadow Economy in Denmark, Norway and Sweden), *Nationaløkonomisk Tidsskrift*, 124: 369–79.

LUNDBORG, P. (1991), 'Determinants of Migration in the Nordic Labour Market', *Scandinavian Journal of Economics*, 93, 363–75.

MCCLOSKEY, D. (1986), *The Rhetoric of Economics*. Brighton: Harvester Wheatsheaf.

MACURDY, T. E. (1981), 'An Empirical Model of Labour Supply in a Life-Cycle Setting', *Journal of Political Economy*, 89: 1059–85.

—— (1983), 'A Simple Scheme for Estimating an Intertemporal Model of Labour Supply and Consumption in the Presence of Taxes and Uncertainty', *International Economic Review*, 24: 265–89.

—— (1985), 'Interpreting Empirical Models of Labour Supply in an Intertemporal Framework with Uncertainty', in J. J. Heckman and B. Singer (eds.), *Longitudinal Analysis of Labour Market Data*. Cambridge: Cambridge University Press.

—— GREEN, D., and PAARSCH, H. (1990), 'Assessing Empirical Approaches for Analyzing Taxes and Labour Supply', *Journal of Human Resources*, 25: 415–90.

MAKI, D., and SPINDLER, Z. A. (1975), 'The Effect of Unemployment Compensation on the Rate of Unemployment in Great Britain', *Oxford Economic Papers*, 29: 128–40.

MATTHEWMAN, J. (1992), *Social Security and State Benefits 1992–93*. London: Tolley.

MATTHIESEN, L. (1973), 'Marginaleffekterna, indexregleringen och regeringens skatteförslag' (Marginal Effects, Indexation and Government Tax Proposal), *Ekonomisk Debatt*, 1: 275–89.

MERKLE, L. (1993), 'Die Nachfrage nach Kinderhilfen und Frauenerwerbstätigkeit' (Child Care Demand and Female Labour Force Participation). Mimeo., Munchen.

MERZ, J. (1990), 'Female Labour Supply: Labour Force Participation, Market Wage Rate and Working Hours of Married and Unmarried Women in the F.R.G.', *Jahrbücher für Nationalökonomie und Statistik*, 207: 240–70.

MICKLEWRIGHT, J. (1990), *Why Do Less Than a Quarter of the Unemployed in Britain Receive Unemployment Insurance? Discussion Paper 147*, London School of Economics.

MINFORD, P. (1983), 'Labour Market Equilibrium in an Open Economy', *Oxford Economic Papers*, 35: 207–44.

MINISTRY OF ECONOMICS (1989*a*), *Lov Model, maj 1989* (Law Model, May 1989). Copenhagen.

—— (1989*b*), *Økonomisk Oversigt* (Economic Survey). Copenhagen.

—— (1992), *Lovmodel, juni 1992* (Law Model, June 1992). Copenhagen.

—— (1993), *Arbejdsudbudseffekten i lovmodelkontorets skattemodel* (Labour Supply Effects in the Tax Model of the Office of the Law Model). Copenhagen.

MITCHELL, D. (1990), *Comparing Income Transfer Systems*. Luxembourg: LIS.

MOFFITT, R. (1986*a*), 'Work Incentives in the AFDC System: An Analysis of the 1981 Reforms', *American Economic Review*, 76: 219–23.

—— (1986*b*), 'The Econometrics of Piecewise-Linear Budget Constraints: A Survey and Exposition of the Maximum Likelihood Method', *Journal of Business and Economic Statistics*, 4: 317–27.

—— (1990), 'The Econometrics of Kinked Budget Constraints', *Journal of Economic Perspectives*, 4: 119–39.

—— (1992), 'Incentive Effects of the US Welfare System: A Review', *Journal of Economic Literature*, 30: 1–61.

MOGENSEN, G. V. (1990*a*), 'Time Used on Paid but Untaxed Activities', in G. V. Mogensen (ed.), *Time and Consumption*. Copenhagen: Statistics Denmark.

—— (1990*b*), 'Do-it-yourself', in G. V. Mogensen (ed.), *Time and Consumption*. Copenhagen: Statistics Denmark.

—— (1992), 'Black Markets and Welfare in Scandinavia: Some Methodological and Empirical Issues', in United Nations (ed.), *Guide-Book to Statistics on the Hidden Economy*. New York: UN.

MOLHO, I. (1989), 'A Disaggregate Model of Flows onto Invalidity Benefit, *Applied Economics*, 21: 237–50.

MOYLAN, S., MILLAR, J., and DAVIES, R. (1984), *For Richer, For Poorer?* London: HMSO.

MROZ, T. (1987), 'The Sensitivity of an Empirical Model of Married Women's Hours of Work to Economic and Statistical Assumptions', *Econometrica*, 55: 765–800.

MÜNCH, U. (1990), *Familienpolitik in der Bundesrepublik Deutschland* (Family Policy in the Federal Republic of Germany). Freiburg: Lainbertus.

MYRDAL, G. (1978), 'Dags för ett bättre skattesystem?' (Time for a Better Taxation System?), *Ekonomisk Debatt*, 6: 493–506.

NAKAMURA, A., and NAKAMURA, M. (1981), 'A Comparison of the Labor Force Behavior of Married Women in the United States and Canada, with Special Attention to the Impact of Income Taxes', *Econometrica*, 49: 451–90.

NARENDRANATHAN, W., NICKELL, S. and STERN, J. (1985), Unemployment Benefits Revisited, *Economic Journal*, 95: 307–29.

—— and STEWART, M. (1989), *Modelling the Probability of Leaving Unemployment*. Univ. of Warwick.

NATIONAL ASSISTANCE BOARD (1966), *Report for the Year Ended 31st December 1965*. London: HMSO.

NEUMANN, G., PEDERSEN, P. J., and WESTERGÅRD-NIELSEN, N. (1991), 'Long-Run International Trends in Aggregate Unionization', *European Journal of Political Economy*, 7: 249–74.

NICKELL, S. J. (1979), 'The Effect of Unemployment and Related Benefits on the Duration of Unemployment', *Economic Journal*, 89: 34–49.

—— (1982), 'The Determinants of Equilibrium Unemployment in Britain', *Economic Journal*, 92: 555–75.

—— (1990), 'Unemployment: A Survey', *Economic Journal*, 100: 391–419.

NILSSON, A. (1984), *Studiefinansiering och social rekrytering till högre utbildning 1920–1974* (Student Loans and Social Recruitment to Higher Education, 1920–1974). Skrifter utgivna av ekonomisk-historiska föreningen i Lund 41, Lund.

NORDIC SOCIAL-STATISTICAL COMMITTEE (1993), *Social Security in the Nordic Countries 1990*. Copenhagen.

NORDLING, D. (1991), *Skattetryck och skattepolitik* (Tax Pressure and Tax Policy). Stockholm: Skattebetalarnas forening.

OBERHAUSER, A. (1989), *Familie und Haushalt als Transferempfänger* (Family, Household, and Transfers), Frankfurt: Campus.

OBERTREIS, G. (1986), *Familienpolitik in der DDR 1945–1980* (Family Policy in the GDR 1945–1980). Opladen: Leske.

OECD (Organisation for Economic Co-operation and Development) (1985), *Social Expenditure 1960–1990*. Paris: OECD.

—— (1988), *The Future of Social Protection*. Paris: OECD.

—— (1990), *Economic Survey: Denmark*. Paris: OECD.

—— (1991), *Economic Outlook*. Paris: OECD.

—— (1992*a*), *Historical Statistics 1960–1990*. Paris: OECD.

—— (1992*b*), *OECD Economic Outlook*. (Dec.). Paris: OECD.

OKUN, A. M. (1975), *Equality and Efficiency: The Big Trade-Off*. Washington DC: Brookings Institution.

OLOFSSON, G., and PETERSSON, J. (1993), 'Sweden: The Older Workforce in a Changing "Work Society" ', in F. Naschold and B. de Vroom (eds.), *Between VUT and Shukko: Firm-Level Practices of Early Exit and Lifelong Work in Industrialized Countries*. Berlin: de Gruyter.

OLOFSSON, T., and SÖDERLIND, P. (1990), 'Samhällsekonomiska effekter i ett intertemporalt perspektiv' (Economic Effects in an Intertemporal Perspective), in J. Agell *et al.* (eds.), *Ekonomiska perspektiv på skattereformen*. Stockholm: Ekonomiska Rådet, Konjunkturinstitutet, Nordstedts Tryckeri.

OLSON, M. (1990), *How Bright Are the Northern Lights? Some Questions about Sweden*. Lund: Lund Univ. Press.

PARKER, S. (1980), *Older Workers and Retirement*. London: HMSO.

PECHMAN, J. A., and TIMPANE, P. M. (1975), *Work Incentives and Income Guarantees*. Washington DC: Brookings Institution.

PEDERSEN, L. (1990), 'Determinants for Time Use Patterns for Men and Women in the Work Force', in G. Viby Mogensen (ed.), *Time and Consumption*. Copenhagen: Statistics Denmark.

PEDERSEN, P. J., and SMITH, N. (1993*a*), 'Early Exit in the Danish Labour Market: The Development in Recent Years', in E. Wadensjö (ed.), *Leaving the Labour Market Early in the Welfare State: Comparison of the Nordic Countries*. Forthcoming. Amsterdam: North-Holland.

—— —— (1993*b*), 'A Duration Analysis of the Decision to Retire Early', in E. Wadensjö (ed.), *Leaving the Labour Market Early in the Welfare State: Comparison of the Nordic Countries*. Forthcoming. Amsterdam: North-Holland.

—— and WESTERGÅRD-NIELSEN, N. (1984), 'Varighed og frekvens af ledighedsperioder på det danske arbejdsmarked' (Duration and Frequency of Unemployment Spells on the Danish Labour Market), *Nationaløkonomisk Tidsskrift*, 122: 401–11.

—— —— (1986), 'A Longitudinal Study of Unemployment: History Dependence and Insurance Effects', in R. Blundell and I. Walker (eds.) *Unemployment, Search and Labour Supply*. Cambridge: Cambridge Univ. Press.

—— —— (1993), 'Unemployment: A Review of the Evidence from Panel Data', forthcoming *OECD Economic Studies*.

PENCAVEL, J. (1986), 'Labour Supply of Men: A Survey', in O. Ashenfelter and R. Layard (eds.), *Handbook of Labour Economics*. Amsterdam: Elsevier.

PENROSE, V. (1990), 'Vierzig Jahre SED-Frauenpolitik' (Fourty Years of Communist Women's Policy)'. Institut Frau und Gesellschaft, *Frauenforschung*, 4: 60–77.

PERSSON, M. (1989), 'Effekterna på bostadsmarknaden av en ändring av kapitalinkomstbeskattningen' (The Effects of Changes in Taxation of Capital on the Housing Market), in *Reformerad inkomstbeskattning*, Del IV, Bilaga 15, Betankande av utredningen om reformerad inkomstbeskattning, SOU 1989: 33. Stockholm: Allmänna Forlaget.

REUTERBERG, S.-E., and SVENSSON, A. (1987*a*), 'Students' Financial Aid and Participation in Swedish Higher Education: I', *Scandinavian Journal of Educational Research*, 31: 139–50.

—— —— (1987*b*), 'Students' Financial Aid and Participation in Swedish Higher Education: II', *Scandinavian Journal of Educational Research*, 31: 151–61.

—— —— (1992), 'Social bakgrund: Studiestöd och üvergang til högre studier' (Social Background: Study Support and Transition to Higher Education), SOU 1992:122.

RINK, I, *Reformerad inkomstbeskattning: Skattereformens huvudlinjer* (Reformed Income Taxation: The Tax Reform's Main Principles), Betänkande av utredningen om reformerad inkomstbeskattning, SOU 1989: 33.

RINK, IV, *Reformerad inkomstbeskattning: Bilagor Expertrapporter* (Reformed Income Taxation: Appendices), Betänkande av utredningen om reformerad inkomstbeskattning, SOU 1989:33.

RODGERS, W. L., DUNCAN, G. J., and BROWN, C. (1991), *Error in Survey Reports of Earnings, Hours Worked and Hourly Wages*. Ann Arbor: Univ. of Michigan.

ROSEN, H. (1976*a*), 'Taxes in a Labour Supply Model with Joint Wage-Hours Determination', *Econometrica*, 44: 485–507.

—— (1976*b*), 'Tax Illusion and the Labour Supply of Married Women', *Review of Economics and Statistics*, 58: 167–72.

ROSEN, H. S. (1980), 'What is Labor Supply and Do Taxes Affect It?', *American Economic Review*, 70: 171–76.

ROWNTREE, B. S. (1901), *Poverty: A Study of Town Life*. London: Macmillan.

SANDMO, A. (1991), 'Economists and the Welfare State', *European Economic Review*, 35: 213–39.

SCHMIDT, C. M., and ZIMMERMANN, K. F. (1992), 'Migration Pressure in Germany: Past and Future', in K. F. Zimmermann (ed.), *Migration and Economic Development*. Berlin: Springer.

SCHNEIDER, F. (1986), 'Estimating the Size of the Danish Shadow Economy using the Currency Demand Approach: An Attempt', *Scandinavian Journal of Economics*, 88: 643–68.

SCHNEIDER, H. (1990), *Determinanten der Arbeitslosigkeitsdauer* (Determinants of the Length of Unemployment). Frankfurt: Campus.

SCHWARZ, B., and GUSTAFSSON, B. (1991), 'Income Redistribution Effects of Tax Reforms in Sweden', *Journal of Policy Modelling*, 13: 551–70.

SCHWARZE, J. (1992), *Qualifikation, Überqualifikation und Phasen des Transformationsprozesses: Die Entwicklung der Lohnstruktur in den neuen Bundesländern* (Qualification, Overqualification and Phases of Transformation: The Development of Wage Structures in the New Länder). Technical University of Berlin.

SEHLSTEDT, K., and SCHRODER, L. (1989), *Språngbräda till arbete?* (Springboard to Work?). Stockholm: EFA.

SHAW, K. (1989), 'Life Cycle Labour Supply with Human Capital Accumulation', *International Economic Review*, 30: 431–57.

SKEDINGER, P. (1990), *Real Wages, Unemployment and Labour Market Programmes: A Disaggregative Analysis*. Dept. of Economics, Univ. of Uppsala.

SMEEDING, T. M., O'HIGGINS, M., and RAINWATER, L. (1990), *Poverty, Inequality, and the Distribution of Income in an International Context*. Brighton: Wheatsheaf.

SMITH, N. (1991), *Labour Supply, Unemployment and Taxes in Denmark*. Institute of Economics, Univ. of Aarhus.

—— WALKER, I., and WESTERGÅRD-NIELSEN, N. (1993), *The Labour Market Behaviour of Danish Lone Mothers*. Univ. of Aarhus, Keele Univ., Aarhus School of Business.

Social ABC 1992–3. Copenhagen: Forlaget Aktuelle Bøger.

Social trygghet i de nordiske land: Omfang, utgifter og finansiering 1990 (Social Security in the Nordic Countries: Dimensions, Costs and Financing) (1992). Nordisk statistisk skriftserie no. 58. Copenhagen.

SOCIALDEPARTEMENTET (1992), *Ensamförälderstöd* (Support to Single Parents). Stockholm.

SØRENSEN, T. Ø. (1992), 'Arbejdsløshedsdagpenge, løndannelse og ledighed' (Unemployment Benefits, Wage Formation and Unemployment), in *Bilag til*

Finansredegørelse 92. Forskning om arbejdsmarkedet (Addendum to Fiscal Report 92. Research on the Labour Market). Copenhagen: Ministry of Finance.

SOU: Statens Offentliga Utredningar (Public Investigations of the State). Cited by year and no. of publication. Stockholm: Allmänna Förlaget.

SOU 1989:101, *Förtidspensionering och rörlig pensionsålder* (Early Retirement and Flexible Retirement Age).

SOU 1992:21, *Bostadsstöd til pensionärer* (Housing support to Retirees).

SOU 1992:89, *Bostadsbidrag: enklare, rättvisare, billigare* (Housing Assistance: Simpler, Fairer, Cheaper).

STÅHL, I. (1978), 'Unemployment Insurance: The Swedish Case', in *Unemployment Insurance: Global Evidence of its Effects on Unemployment*. Fraser Institute.

STÅHLBERG, A.-C. (1990), 'Life Cycle Income Redistribution in the Public Sector: Inter- and Intragenerational Effects', in I. Person (ed.), *Generating Equality in the Welfare State: The Swedish Experience*. Oslo: Norwegian Univ. Press.

STATISTICS SWEDEN (1986), *Den framtidiga befolkningen: Prognos för åren 1986–2025* (The Future Population: Forecast 1986–2025). Stockholm.

STERN, J. (1986), 'Repeat Unemployment Spells', in R. Blundell and I. Walker (eds.), *Unemployment, Search and Labour Supply*. Cambridge: Cambridge Univ. Press.

STERN, N. (1986), 'On the Specification of Labour Supply Functions', in R. Blundell and I. Walker (eds.), *Unemployment, Search and Labour Supply*. Cambridge: Cambridge Univ. Press.

STIGLITZ, J. E. (1988), *Economics of the Public Sector*, 2nd edn. New York: Norton.

STOBERNACK, M. (1990), 'Die Bedeutung der Arbeitslosenversicherung für Erwerbslosigkeit und Arbeitsangebot' (The Consequences of Unemployment Insurance for Unemployment and Labour Supply). Frankfurt: Campus.

—— (1991), 'Das Arbeitsangebot in der Bundesrepublik Deutschland: Eine Schätzung auf der Basis des Sozio-Ökonomischen Panels' (Labour Supply in the Federal Republic of Germany: An Estimation on the Basis of the Socio-Economic Panel), *Jahrbücher für Nationalökonomie und Statistik*, 208: 625–41.

STORRIE, D. (1993), *The Anatomy of a Large Swedish Plant Closure*. Univ. of Gothenburg.

STRÖM, S. and WAGENHALS, G. (1991), 'Female Labour Supply in the Federal Republic', *Jahrbücher für Nationalökonomie und Statistik,* 208: 575–95.

STUART, C. (1981), 'Swedish Tax Rates, Labour Supply, and Tax Revenue', *Journal of Political Economy*, 89: 1020–38.

SUNDSTRØM, M. (1987), *A Study of the Growth of Part-Time Work in Sweden*. Stockholm: Arbetslivscentrum.

—— (1991*a*), 'Sweden: Supporting Work, Family and Gender Equality', in S. B. Kamerman and A. J. Kahn (eds.), *Child Care, Parental Leave and the Under 3s*. Westport, Conn.: Policy Innovation in Europe.

—— (1991*b*), 'Hur påverkar föräldreledighet lönerna?' (How Does Parental Leave Affect Salaries?), *Ekonomisk Debatt*, 19: 230–37.

—— and STAFFORD, F. (1992), 'Female Labour Force Participation, Fertility and Public Policy', *European Journal of Population*, 8: 199–215.

SVENSKA KOMMUNFÖRBUNDET (1990), *Barnfamiljernas och kommunernas taxor* (Families with Children and Local Tax Rates). Stockholm.

TASIRAN, A. (1993), *Wage and Income Effects on the Timing and Spacing of Births in Sweden and the United States*. Dept. of Economics, Univ. of Gothenburg.

TEGLE, S. (1983), 'Den ordinarie veckoarbetstiden i Sverige, 1860–1980: En översikt' (Regular Weekly Working Hours in Sweden 1860–1980. A Review). Dept. of Economics, Univ. of Lund.

TITMUSS, R. M. (1955), 'Pensions Systems and Population Change', *Political Quarterly*, 26: 152–66.

WADENSJÖ, E. (1975), 'Disability Pensioning of Older Workers in Sweden: A Comparison of Studies Based on Time-Series and Cross-Section Data'. Stockholm: Institute of Social Research.

—— (1991), 'Sweden: Partial Exit', in M. Kohli *et al.* (eds.), *Time for Retirement: Comparative Studies of Early Exit from the Labour Force*. Cambridge: Cambridge Univ. Press.

WAGENHALS, G. (1991), *Income Tax Reform in Germany: A Welfare Analysis*. Univ. of Paderborn.

WAHLUND, R. (1987), 'Does Lowering of the Marginal Tax Rates Matter?', in *Understanding Economic Behavior*, i. Aarhus School of Business.

WALES, T. J., and WOODLAND, A. D. (1977), 'Estimation of the Allocation of Time for Work, Leisure and Housework', *Econometrica*, 45: 115–32.

WALKER, I. (1990), 'The Effects of Income Support Measures on the Labour Market Behaviour of Lone Mothers', *Fiscal Studies*, 11: 55–75.

WEBSTER, L., WOOD, P., SIMMONS, D., VAUX, G., and HANNAM, J. (1993), *National Welfare Benefits Handbook*, 23rd edn. London: Child Poverty Action Group.

WECK-HANNEMANN, H., POMMEREHNE, W. W., and KIRCHGÄSSNER, G. (1989), 'Abgabenpolitische Ideen zur Eindämmung der Schattenwirtschaft' (How to Reduce the Shadow Economy), in H. Scherf (ed.) *Beschäftigungsprobleme hochentwickelter Volkswirtschaften (Employment Problems of Developed Economies)*. Berlin: Duncker and Humblot.

WILLEKE, F.-U., and ONKEN, R. (1990), *Allgemeiner Familienlastenausgleich in der Bundesrepublik Deutschland* (Family Policy in the Federal Republic of Germany). Frankfurt: Campus.

WILLIAMS, A., (1966), *Tax Policy: Can Surveys Help?*. London: PEP.

WINKELMANN, R., and ZIMMERMANN, K.F. (1993), 'Ageing, Migration and Labour Mobility', in P. Johnson and K. F. Zimmermann (eds.), *Labour Markets in an Ageing Europe*. Cambridge: Cambridge Univ. Press.

ZABALZA, A., PISSARIDES, C., and BARTON, M. (1980), 'Social Security and the Choice Between Full-Time Work, Part-Time Work and Retirement', *Journal of Public Economics*, 14: 245–76.

ZIMMERMANN, K. F. (1985), *Familienökonomie* (Family Economics), Berlin: Springer.

—— (1988), 'Labor Supply and a Shorter Workday: Comment', in R. A. Hart (ed.), *Employment, Unemployment and Labor Utilization*. Boston: Unwin Hyman.

ZIMMERMAN, K. F. (ed.) (forthcoming), 'Family Policies in Post-War Germany: East–West Differences and the Pressure of Transformation'.

—— and SCHMIDT, C. M. (1986), 'Quellen des Wachstums: Leistungsbereitschaft der Erwerbstätigen oder Nachfrage kinderreicher Familien?' (Incentives to Growth: Work Motivation or Demand of Large Families?), in K. F. Zimmermann (ed.), *Demographische Probleme der Haushaltsökonomie* (Demographic Problems of Household Economics). Bochum: Brockmeyer.

ZWEIMÜLLER, J. (1987), 'Bestimmungsgründe der Frauen-Erwerbsbeteiligung' (Determinants of Female Work Participation): Schätzergebnisse aus dem Mikrozensus', in K. W. Rothschild and G. Tichy (eds.), *Arbeitslosigkeit und Arbeitsangebot in Össterreich*. Vienna: Springer.

INDEX